HANS KELSEN'S PURE THEORY OF LAW

Hans Kelsen's Pure Theory of Law

Legality and Legitimacy

LARS VINX

OXFORD
UNIVERSITY PRESS

OXFORD
UNIVERSITY PRESS

Great Clarendon Street, Oxford OX2 6DP

Oxford University Press is a department of the University of Oxford.
It furthers the University's objective of excellence in research, scholarship,
and education by publishing worldwide in

Oxford New York

Auckland Cape Town Dar es Salaam Hong Kong Karachi
Kuala Lumpur Madrid Melbourne Mexico City Nairobi
New Delhi Shanghai Taipei Toronto

With offices in

Argentina Austria Brazil Chile Czech Republic France Greece
Guatemala Hungary Italy Japan Poland Portugal Singapore
South Korea Switzerland Thailand Turkey Ukraine Vietnam

Oxford is a registered trade mark of Oxford University Press
in the UK and in certain other countries

Published in the United States
by Oxford University Press Inc., New York

© Lars Vinx, 2007

The moral rights of the author have been asserted

Crown copyright material is reproduced under Class Licence
Number C01P0000148 with the permission of OPSI
and the Queen's Printer for Scotland

Database right Oxford University Press (maker)

First published 2007

British Library Cataloguing in Publication Data

Data available

Library of Congress Cataloging in Publication Data

Vinx, Lars.
  Hans Kelsen's pure theory of law: legality and legitimacy / Lars Vinx.
    p. cm.
  Includes bibliographical references and index.
  ISBN 978–0–19–922795–2
  1. Kelsen, Hans, 1881–1973. Reine Rechtslehre. 2. Law—Philosophy.
  3. State, The. 4. Rule of law. 5. Legal positivism. I. Title.
  II. Title: Pure theory of law.
    K339.V558 2007
    340'.1—dc22   2007024142

Typeset by Newgen Imaging Systems (P) Ltd., Chennai, India
Printed in Great Britain
on acid-free paper by
Biddles Ltd., King's Lynn

ISBN 978–0–19–922795–2

1 3 5 7 9 10 8 6 4 2

To my Father

Acknowledgements

I would like to thank David Dyzenhaus for his unfailing encouragement and unwavering support. The completion of this work would not have been possible without the rich intellectual stimulation David generously provided in numerous discussions, about legal philosophy in general and Kelsen in particular. The ideas presented here are deeply indebted to David's philosophical outlook as well as to his many insightful comments on my drafts.

Gopal Sreenivasan commented on the entire manuscript with exceptional care. His probing questions and valuable suggestions were extremely helpful in clarifying many central issues and concepts. I am very thankful to have been able to benefit from a reader this keen and diligent. I am indebted, moreover, to Robert Gibbs for providing me with many valuable ideas and insights and for encouraging me to engage with a thesis project that straddled the divide between continental and analytical approaches.

Frederick Schauer, Arthur Ripstein, as well as three anonymous reviewers for OUP made many important suggestions for further improvement. I was very fortunate to receive their comments on my work. Finally, I would like to thank Gwen Booth at OUP for her help and support.

The book benefited greatly from the financial support I received as a Connaught Fellow at the University of Toronto from 2001 to 2005 and as a Max Weber fellow at the European University Institute in 2006–2007. It is dedicated to my father who, I hope, will accept it as a token of my gratitude for all he has done for us.

Contents

1

Introduction

Eine der Idee des Rechtsstaates adäquate Rechtssystematik steht heute noch aus. Die Rechtsstaatsidee aber ist noch nicht überwunden, ihre allseitige rechtslogische Entwicklung bleibt Aufgabe der Zukunft.

(Hans Kelsen, 1913)[1]

This book offers an analysis of Hans Kelsen's pure theory of law. It will proceed from a somewhat unorthodox starting point. Instead of reading Kelsen's work as a contribution to the tradition of positivist analytical jurisprudence, I will treat it as an attempt to develop a legal theory committed to the full realization of an ideal of the rule of law. In other words, I will explore the question whether it makes sense to regard the full-fledged edifice of the pure theory of law as the performance of the legal theoretical task that the young Kelsen, in 1913, as we can see from the epigraph, regarded as desirable: to develop a conceptual framework for legal thought adequate to the idea of the '*Rechtsstaat*'.[2]

I hope that this approach will allow us to understand the way in which two key themes in Kelsen's work relate to each other, his well-known attempt to establish an autonomous science of jurisprudence, separate from both empirical social science as well as moral theory, on the one hand, and his less well-known attempt to employ the pure theory in the defense of liberal democracy and individual freedom, on the other. The relationship between these two aspects of Kelsen's work is little understood and has not attracted much attention.[3] Those who read Kelsen as part of the analytical jurisprudential tradition usually take little notice of his political works or treat

---

[1] Hans Kelsen, 'Rechtsstaat und Staatsrecht' in Hans Klecatsky, René Marcič and Herbert Schambeck (eds), *Die Wiener rechtstheoretische Schule. Ausgewählte Schriften von Hans Kelsen, Adolf Julius Merkl und Alfred Verdross*, 2 vols (Wien, 1968) II, 1532: 'A legal systematics adequate to the idea of the rule of law state has not yet been developed. The idea of the rule of law state, however, has not therefore become obsolete. Its comprehensive legal-logical development remains the task of the future.' [my translation]

[2] The claim that the pure theory is committed to an ideal of the rule of law is not wholly without precedent. See Norberto Bobbio, 'Kelsen e il problema del potere' in Norberto Bobbio, *Diritto e potere. Saggi su Kelsen* (Napoli, 1992) 103–22, at 121–2.

[3] Two notable exceptions are David Dyzenhaus, *Legality and Legitimacy. Carl Schmitt, Hans Kelsen and Hermann Heller in Weimar* (Oxford, 1997) 102–60 and Horst Dreier, *Rechtslehre, Staatssoziologie und Demokratietheorie bei Hans Kelsen* (Baden-Baden, 1986).

them as unrelated to the pure theory of law.[4] Those who have commented on
Kelsen's political works from a political-theoretical perspective, on the other hand,
typically find them woefully deficient precisely in virtue of their reliance on the
pure theory of law.[5] I believe, by contrast, that both aspects of Kelsen's work can be
given an interpretation under which they mutually support each other. The full
strength of Kelsen's legal theoretical as well as his political theoretical views, I will
argue, cannot be adequately understood unless their relationship is made explicit.

Of course, the claim that the pure theory of law is best understood in the light of
its relation to Kelsen's political works, and ultimately in the light of the aim to
develop a legal theory adequate to the ideal of the rule of law, appears to fly in the
face of Kelsen's own description of the nature of his legal-theoretical project. This
description emphasizes both that the pure theory is a positivist and that it is a scientific theory of law. It will therefore be necessary to explain the interpretive strategy I
have chosen in a little more detail and to convey at least a rough impression of why
it might turn out to be worth pursuing.

A successful attempt to understand how the political and the legal-theoretical
Kelsen relate to each other would, I believe, be of more than purely exegetical
significance. The tension between Kelsen's political-theoretical and his scientific
ambitions is a tension that characterizes legal positivism in general. Is legal positivism
to be understood as a mere effort at value-neutral description of the law? Or is it to
be understood, in addition to and perhaps in competition with the descriptive project, as a form of social criticism? The way in which Kelsen relates his theory of law to
a political theory, I will argue, shows that he understands legal positivism primarily
as a form of social criticism. What is more, Kelsen's understanding of legal positivism as social criticism leads to a legal theory that, even while being concerned
with the practical importance of the positivity of law, is not positivist in the contemporary sense of the term. The pure theory of law tries to create the conceptual
space for the view that acts of state necessarily draw at least some legitimacy from
their conformity with positive law, even if they are not considered as perfectly just.
This legitimacy will in many cases be insufficient to ground conclusive duties to
obey the law. But Kelsen believes that the legitimating force of positive law can be
strengthened, through the introduction of constitutional structures of the right
kind, to the point where it can function as a bridge between the different groups in
a modern pluralist society characterized by deep moral disagreement. Kelsen's

---

    [4] The two most important collections of articles on Kelsen's pure theory contain little or no mater-
ial on Kelsen's theory of the state, his theory of democracy, or his constitutional theory. See Stanley
Paulson and Bonnie Litschewski-Paulson (eds), *Normativity and Norms. Critical Perspectives on
Kelsenian Themes* (Oxford, 1998) and Richard Tur and William Twining (eds), *Essays on Kelsen*
(Oxford, 1986).
    [5] See for critical perspectives on Kelsen's political theory Dyzenhaus, *Legality and Legitimacy* (n 3
above); Wolfgang Schluchter, *Entscheidung für den sozialen Rechtsstaat. Hermann Heller und die staat-
stheoretische Diskussion in der Weimarer Republik* (Köln/Berlin, 1968) 26–52; Weyma Lübbe,
Legitimität kraft Legalität. Sinnverstehen und Institutionenanalyse bei Max Weber und seinen Kritikern
(Tübingen, 1991) 25–66.

emphasis on the autonomy or purity of legal normativity is meant to clear the way for an attempt to realize constitutional conditions capable of achieving this aim.

I will defend this interpretation by arguing that the pure theory of law carries normative commitments that, according to the view of most contemporary positivists, should not figure in the choice of a concept of law. The fundamental assumptions about the nature of legal normativity that underpin the pure theory as a legal theory, I will try to show, only make sense if we read them as part of the political-theoretical project to develop an account of legal legitimacy. If we did not value the normative ambitions expressed in Kelsen's conception of legal legitimacy or if we did not think that the hope for a political order that realizes the conditions of legal legitimacy is a reasonable hope there would be no reason to prefer Kelsen's peculiar account of legal normativity over normatively less-committed positivist accounts. But if the pure theory as a legal theory can make good on its claim to descriptive generality, despite its relation to a political ideal, and if Kelsen's conception of the relation between his legal and political theory is coherent, positivist conceptions of legal normativity that reject the view that legality can be an autonomous ground of legitimacy will no longer be justifiable on purely methodological grounds.

In order to provisionally substantiate these claims and to provide a framework for further discussion, I will give a short overview of recent debates about the methodological status of legal positivism and explain how these contemporary debates relate to Kelsen's understanding of the legal-theoretical project. I will then go on to provide a thumbnail sketch of the cornerstone of Kelsen's attempt to develop a theory of legal legitimacy, his thesis of the identity of law and state, and try to present an outline of the defense of the coherence of the identity thesis I intend to undertake.

Three paradigms of legal positivism

Contemporary legal positivists do not just disagree, on a substantive level, over the precise nature of a positivist conception of law.[6] They also disagree over the methodological status of legal positivism as a jurisprudential theory.[7] In what follows, I want to outline three different contemporary paradigms of positivism; methodological positivism, political positivism, and Razian positivism, in order to establish a background for my attempt to classify Kelsen's jurisprudential position.

---

[6] I am thinking here of the debate between inclusive and exclusive positivism. See Wilfrid J Waluchow, *Inclusive Legal Positivism* (Oxford, 1994); Jules Coleman, *The Practice of Principle. In Defence of a Pragmatist Approach to Legal Theory* (Oxford, 2001) 103–48; Joseph Raz, 'Authority, Law, and Morality' in Joseph Raz, *Ethics in the Public Domain. Essays in the Morality of Law and Politics* (Oxford, 1995) 210–37, at 226–30.

[7] See Joseph Raz, 'Can There be a Theory of Law?', in Martin Golding and William Edmundson (eds), *Blackwell Guide to the Philosophy of Law and Legal Theory* (Oxford, 2005) 324–42; Julie Dickson, *Evaluation and Legal Theory* (Oxford, 2001); Wilfrid J Waluchow, *Inclusive Legal Positivism*, 9–30 (n 6 above); John Finnis, *Natural Law and Natural Rights* (Oxford, 1980) 3–22; Stephen Perry, 'Hart's Methodological Positivism' in Jules Coleman (ed), *Hart's Postscript. Essays on the Postscript to 'The Concept of Law'* (Oxford, 2001) 311–54.

Methodological positivism[8] assimilates legal theory to descriptive social science and treats the existence of law as a matter of social fact. The thesis that there is no necessary connection between law and morality is seen as a consequence of the conventionality of the social rules that govern the identification of valid law. There at least could be legal systems that exist as a matter of social fact but which do not incorporate any moral standards into their standards of legality.[9] Political positivists, on the other hand, claim that our understanding of legal practices shapes the nature of our law. Choices between different concepts of law that meet basic standards of descriptive adequacy are not perfectly determined by objective matters of fact beyond our control. Hence, such choices should reflect our ideal of good law. The separation of law and morality, the political positivist goes on to argue, can be defended on the ground that adopting a positivist standard of legality will have morally beneficial consequences for a society.[10] Razian positivists, finally, claim that positivism is required to explain how the law can function as an independent and distinctive standard for the guidance of human action. This position is descriptive-explanatory in that it rejects the political positivist idea that our conception of law should be responsive to our ideal of good law. But at the same time, it openly rejects the assimilation of legal theory to empirical social science that characterizes methodological positivism.

The work of H L A Hart is a source for both methodological and political positivism. Hart famously described his jurisprudential approach in *The Concept of Law* as an 'enterprise in descriptive sociology'.[11] In the postscript to *The Concept of Law*, he further explained his methodology by claiming that the positivist project aims to give a general theory of law that is descriptive and not evaluative.[12] Positivists, then, do not just argue that standards of legality either do not or at least need not include or make reference to standards of morality. They make the further meta-theoretical claim that legal theory is a descriptive-explanatory project that 'can and should offer a normatively neutral description of a particular social phenomenon, namely law'.[13] According to the view Hart presents in the *Postscript*, substantive and methodological

---

[8] I borrow the term from Stephen Perry, 'The Varieties of Legal Positivism' in *Canadian Journal of Law and Jurisprudence* 9 (1996) 361–81. See also Perry, 'Hart's Methodological Positivism' (n 7 above).

[9] See for a recent defense of this view Jules Coleman, *The Practice of Principle* (n 6 above) 74–102.

[10] Variants of this argument for positivism are defended by Frederick Schauer, 'Positivism as Pariah' in Robert P George (ed), *The Autonomy of Law. Essays on Legal Positivism* (Oxford, 1996) 31–55; Neil MacCormick, 'A Moralistic Case for A-Moralistic Law?' in *Valparaiso University Law Review* 20 (1985) 1–41; Liam Murphy, 'The Political Question of the Concept of Law', in Coleman (ed), *Hart's Postscript* (n 7 above) 371–409.

[11] H L A Hart, *The Concept of Law*, edited by Penelope Bulloch and Joseph Raz (2nd ed Oxford, 1994) vi.

[12] See ibid 239–40: 'My aim in this book was to provide a theory of what law is that is both general and descriptive. It is general in the sense that it is not tied to any particular legal system or legal culture... My account is descriptive in that it is morally neutral and has no justificatory aims: it does not seek to justify or commend on moral or other grounds the forms and structures which appear in my general account of law, though a clear understanding of these is, I think, an important preliminary to any useful moral criticism of the law.'

[13] Perry, 'Hart's Methodological Positivism' (n 7 above) 311. See also Perry, 'The Varieties of Legal Positivism' (n 8 above) 361: 'Methodological positivists maintain that legal theory is a purely

positivism are intimately related. The substantive thesis that there is no necessary connection between law and morality, Hart suggests, will be defensible if and only if it is possible to offer a non-evaluative description of the essential features of legal order.[14]

As many interpreters have noted, however, in his earlier work Hart appears to present a normative argument for positivism as a substantive theory of legality.[15] Like Bentham, Hart thought that natural law theories carry a social danger, the danger of favoring 'obsequious quietism' in the face of unreasonable or unjust legal directives.[16] Hart's worry arises from the following line of thought: natural law theory claims that there is at least a prima facie general moral duty to obey the law. It also claims that formally valid laws, laws duly enacted by official authorities, lack genuine legal validity if they are too unjust.[17] But despite this proviso, natural law theory will at least establish a presumption to the effect that duly enacted laws merit obedience. Few laws, after all, will turn out to be so intolerably unjust that they obviously fail whatever proviso the natural lawyer introduces. Hart argues that a dissenter, in denying a duty to obey the law, will thus no longer be able to rely on a simple appeal to the immorality of the law. Rather, he will have to 'present the moral criticism of institutions as propositions of a disputable philosophy' which can only weaken his case against the duty to obey morally defective law.[18] A positivist conception of legality, in Hart's view, is the best antidote to the presumption in favor of authority engendered by natural law since it explicitly denies that a legal demand must, unless we are faced with extraordinary circumstances, in some sense be morally justified. Of course, this second argument for a separation of law and morality sits uneasily with the claim that legal positivism is an exercise in descriptive sociology. It appears to rely on an ideal of good social order and to advocate adoption of the separation thesis on the ground that doing so will be instrumental to the realization of that ideal.

Pragmatic modes of argument for a positivist standard of the identification of law are, of course, deeply rooted in the legal positivist tradition,[19] though they are sometimes motivated by practical aims that differ from Hart's. The most salient

---

descriptive, non-normative enterprise that sets out, *in the manner of ordinary science*, to tell us what one particular corner of the world we inhabit is like.' [my emphasis] This latter description suggests that the mere value neutrality of a legal theory is not sufficient to characterize it as methodological positivism. The commitment to value neutrality must result from the view that jurisprudence is part and parcel of ordinary science. In what follows, I will employ the term 'methodological positivism' in this narrow understanding only.

[14] See Hart, *The Concept of Law* (n 11 above) 268–72.

[15] This argument is more prominent in Hart's early work than in his later efforts. See H L A Hart, 'Positivism and the Separation of Law and Morality' in H L A Hart, *Essays in Jurisprudence and Philosophy* (Oxford, 1983) 49–87; Hart, *The Concept of Law* (n 11 above) 205–12.

[16] Jeremy Bentham, *A Fragment on Government* (Cambridge, 1988) 111.

[17] The idea of a moral proviso was first introduced by Gustav Radbruch, 'Gesetzliches Unrecht und übergesetzliches Recht' in Gustav Radbruch, *Rechtsphilosophie*, edited by Ralf Dreier and Stanley L Paulson (Heidelberg, 1999) 211–19. For a recent defense see Robert Alexy, *Begriff und Geltung des Rechts* (Freiburg, 1994) 70–108.

[18] Hart, 'Positivism and the Separation of Law and Morals' (n 15 above) 77–8. See also Hart, *The Concept of Law* (n 11 above) 205–6.

[19] See Gerald Postema, *Bentham and the Common Law Tradition* (Oxford, 1986).

6 *Introduction*

concern that drives political positivists is to defend the practice of rule-based decision-making against views that endow judges and administrators with the power
to depart from legal rules in order to optimize the substantive moral quality of
particular decisions. In Jeremy Waldron's version of political positivism, decision-
making in accordance with democratically enacted rules is mandated by the 'circumstances of politics', by the fact that political decisions need to be taken in the face of
pervasive and reasonable disagreement about the good. Democratic legislation is the
only form of collective decision-taking, Waldron argues, that adequately respects the
moral views of all members of society, even while unavoidably disappointing some.[20]
Judges in a democratic society, therefore, ought to accept formally valid legislation as
binding and to avoid treating their own moral opinions as standards of legality.

Frederick Schauer's development of political positivism emphasizes the 'silent
virtues' of rule-based decision-making.[21] Decision-makers in official contexts ought
to adopt the default stance of sticking with applicable legal rules, Schauer argues, even
in particular cases where there seem to be sound substantive reasons for a departure
from a rule. Adopting a policy of sticking with the rules, at least unless the costs of
doing so become clearly unbearable in a particular instance, allows for a much needed
simplification of decision-making. More importantly, rules do not merely guide official decision-making. They also constrain and limit it since an official bound to a
rule is excluded from considering a number of factors that might, from a substantive
point of view, seem to bear on the question at hand. Rules continue to serve this
function of constraining official power even where their application may seem to
lead to substantively suboptimal results. If we have an independent interest in such
constraint, Schauer concludes, we cannot allow officials to abandon rule-based decision-making whenever doing so holds the prospect of improving the substantive
quality of particular official decisions.

The fact that Hart defends methodological positivism while being drawn, at the
same time, towards a pragmatic justification for legal positivism raises the question
whether both commitments are compatible. Stephen Perry has given a negative
answer to this question and argued that the substance of Hart's views conflicts with
methodological positivism. The way in which Hart solves the 'persistent puzzles' of
jurisprudence,[22] is interesting, Perry claims, only because his approach fails to exhibit
fidelity to methodological positivism.[23] Any identification of the central puzzles of
legal theory presupposes a view as to why we should be interested in solving them and
as to what would constitute a solution. Any answer to these questions will be value-
dependent, shaped by human interest. And an account of the central features of law[24]

[20] See Jeremy Waldron, *Law and Disagreement* (Oxford, 1999).
    [21] Frederick Schauer, *Playing by the Rules. A Philosophical Examination of Rule-Based Decision-Making in Law and Life* (Oxford, 1991) 135–66 and 229–33.
    [22] See Hart, *The Concept of Law* (n 11 above) 1–17.
    [23] See Perry, 'Hart's Methodological Positivism' (n 7 above) 353–4.
    [24] For the idea of central features see John Finnis, *Natural Law and Natural Rights* (Oxford, 1980) 3–22.

would be empty and meaningless if it answered the questions: 'What are the central features of law?' and 'What does it mean to account for them?' by claiming, explicitly or implicitly, that the central features of law are those that can be explained from the point of view of methodological positivism.

It is unclear, however, whether acceptance of this point forces us to abandon all attempts to offer a non-evaluative legal theory, to admit that Dworkin is right to claim that all viable conceptions of law have to attribute some normative purpose to the law.[25] The most influential recent defense of descriptive-explanatory positivism against normative or political positivism—offered by Joseph Raz and Julie Dickson—does not constitute a form of methodological positivism in Perry's narrow sense and it can certainly make a plausible claim to have taken the problem of value-dependence into account.

Raz and Dickson admit that a general theory of the nature of law will inevitably be value-dependent in the sense that any theoretical description of the law presupposes an answer to the question which of its observable features are most important for an adequate understanding of legal institutions. Giving an answer to this question of importance requires that we determine *whose* perspective and interests should guide our judgment. Raz rejects the view that the standard of importance can be derived from considerations of 'theoretical sociological fruitfulness'. Legal theory, rather, has to be sensitive to the fact that 'the law' 'is a concept used by people to understand themselves'.[26] A theory of law, therefore, will have to rely on conceptual resources that reflect how people who use the concept see themselves and their actions in its light.[27] In keeping with this general idea, Raz's account of the central features of law rests on a view of what makes the law qua positive law a distinctive element in the practical deliberations of those subject to it. The law, Raz argues, necessarily claims, but it does not necessarily possess, legitimate authority.

The authority thesis, as an answer to the central features-question, is evaluative insofar as it privileges the practical point of view of participants in legal practice who are confronted by the law's claims over the theoretical interests of an external sociological observer. But while the thesis is evaluative, it is only indirectly so since it does not entail that any legal system's claims to authority are justified and since it does not commit the legal theorist to any view as to whether it is a good (or a bad) thing that legal systems should claim authority. To say that something is a central and important feature of some social institution, Dickson argues, is simply not the same thing as to offer a moral evaluation of that feature.[28] The indirect value-dependence of legal theory, therefore, does not threaten the project of a descriptive theory of law.

---

[25] See Ronald Dworkin, *Law's Empire* (London, 1986) 87–101.
[26] See Joseph Raz, 'Authority, Law, and Morality', in Joseph Raz, *Ethics in the Public Domain. Essays in the Morality of Law and Politics* (Oxford, 1994) 210–37, at 237.
[27] See Julie Dickson, *Evaluation and Legal Theory* (Oxford, 2001) 41–3.
[28] See ibid, 51–69.

Dickson argues that political positivists who want to make the concept of law directly dependent on a conception of good social order are no longer engaged in analytical jurisprudence.[29] Analytical jurisprudence has the task of 'attempting to identify and explain the nature of law' as an 'actually existing social institution'.[30] But this enterprise is incompatible with the idea that 'value judgments concerning the beneficial moral consequences of espousing a certain theory of law may legitimately feature in the criteria of success of legal theories'.[31] Political positivists do not talk about the nature of law, they are engaged in the project of describing ideal law, a project that is best left to 'novelists and utopian schemers'.[32]

But there is more to Raz's position, it seems to me, than Dickson's argument lets on. In order to defend the claim that the authority thesis is only indirectly evaluative, one has to show that we can understand what it means for some person or institution to claim authority without having to evaluate the claim. This requirement cannot be fulfilled, in a Razian framework, in the way in which a methodological positivist would attempt to fulfill it, namely by describing the empirical social conditions under which de facto authority can be said to exist.[33] Raz insists that 'authority is a practical concept'. The task of explaining authority, therefore, falls to the formal part of practical philosophy which 'concerns the logical features of concepts like value, reason for action or norm' and not to an empirical social science.[34] In order to understand claims to authority, we must therefore understand the way in which exercises of authority purport to impact on our practical reasoning, how norms enacted by authority are 'capable of figuring in practical inferences'.[35] The required explanation is provided by the idea that the law claims that those to whom it addresses itself have reason to treat its directives as exclusionary reasons, as second-order reasons for action that exclude or replace their own assessment of the balance of first-order reasons.[36]

The formal-practical idea that legal norms purport to be exclusionary reasons allows us to characterize their logical role in practical reasoning without evaluating the substantive soundness of any claim to legal authority. The view also leads to an elegant defense of substantive positivism that is neither dependent on the idea that jurisprudence is a species of descriptive sociology nor on a political argument that relies on positivism's allegedly beneficial moral consequences. Legal norms can guide behavior in the way in which exclusionary reasons presume to guide

---

[29] See ibid, 83–93. Dickson targets Frederick Schauer, 'Positivism as Pariah' (n 10 above). For Schauer's response see Frederick Schauer, 'The Social Construction of the Concept of Law: A Reply to Julie Dickson' in *Oxford Journal of Legal Studies* 25 (2005) 493–501.   [30] See ibid, 89.
[31] Ibid, 9.   [32] Ibid, 90.
[33] See Joseph Raz, 'Legitimate Authority' in Joseph Raz, *The Authority of Law. Essays on Law and Morality* (Oxford, 1979) 3–27 and Joseph Raz, *The Morality of Freedom* (Oxford, 1986) 62–9 where Raz classifies his account of authority as 'normative-explanatory'.
[34] Joseph Raz, *Practical Reason and Norms* (Princeton, 1990) 10.
[35] Raz, 'Legitimate Authority' (n 33 above) 10.
[36] See Raz, *Practical Reason and Norms* (n 34 above) 35–48; Joseph Raz, 'The Claims of Law', in Raz, *The Authority of Law* (n 33 above) 28–33.

behavior only if they can replace the individual practical judgment of those who are to be guided by the law. But legal norms can replace the judgment of the subjects of the law only if they are identifiable on the basis of social facts and without any resort to moral or political judgment on the basis of the excluded first-order reasons.[37]

However, the view that authority is a practical concept also entails that it is not possible fully to understand the structure of claims to authority without understanding what *would* justify them. According to Raz's *normal justification thesis*, agents can reasonably treat authoritative legal directives as exclusionary reasons only if doing so will enhance the overall conformity of their actions with reason, ie with the first-order reasons that apply independently of the authoritative directive. In order for the view that law necessarily claims authority to remain compatible with positivism, Raz must argue that all relations between claimed legal authority and justified legal authority are contingent, that there are no structural features of legal order that suffice for a wholesale attribution of justified authority to the law.[38] The normal justification thesis indeed carries the implication that the law's claim to authority can never be generally justified. Whether we will enhance our overall conformity with reason by deferring to legal directives will depend on whether those who enact them either possess expertise that we lack or have the ability to bring about forms of coordination that could not be achieved in any other way than by submission to their directives. Whether either of these conditions is satisfied depends on contingent facts about us and the persons or institutions that enact legal directives. The justification of authority is therefore limited to a 'piecemeal approach'.[39]

The question whether Raz's account of the nature of law is defensible on descriptive-explanatory grounds depends to a considerable degree on whether the law's alleged claim to authority can really be separated from the question of justification as sharply as Raz suggests. There are reasons to believe that the normal justification thesis fails to take account of some intuitively appealing justifications of legal authority whose availability would make it much harder to drive a wedge between claims to authority and their justification.[40] Raz accepts that an adequate

[37] One interesting feature of this argument is that it rejects certain forms of legal positivism while it has room, at least in principle, for some forms of natural law theory. The argument from authority rules out all legal theories that claim that the identification of law must or may involve moral judgment. But as Raz himself points out, this does not entail that there can be no necessary connection between law and morality. See Joseph Raz, *Practical Reason and Norms* (n 34 above) 162–70. Raz, 'Authority, Law, and Morality' (n 26 above) 227 claims that 'it is very likely that there is some necessary connection between law and morality, that every legal system in force has some moral merit or does some moral good even if it is also the cause of a great deal of moral evil'. Raz goes on to argue that the connection, though necessary, is too weak to establish a general prima facie obligation to obey the law. I will argue that Kelsen can be read as claiming that the relationship is at least potentially much stronger than Raz believes.   [38] See Raz, *The Morality of Freedom* (n 33 above) 53–7.
[39] See ibid, 80.
[40] In particular, it has been argued that Raz's conception fails to make room for the claim that democracy enhances a political system's authority. See Thomas Christiano, 'The Authority of

understanding of the nature of law has an important practical function, namely to enable subjects of the law to act as reasonably as possible. Raz's position, then, must respond to challenges that try to show that its understanding of the grounds of justification of legal authority is incomplete. If such challenges could be mounted, Razian legal positivism would require a normative defense. Kelsen's legal theory, I will argue, might contain one such challenge.

Kelsen's legal science

Let us now turn to the question how Kelsen's position relates to the three paradigms just outlined. The first and most obvious proposal for a classification of Kelsen's positions would seem to be the claim that the pure theory is a form of methodological positivism. No other jurisprudent, after all, put as much rhetorical emphasis on the claim that jurisprudence must strive to be scientific. Kelsen goes so far as to argue that the pure theory is preferable to other legal theories in virtue of the fact that it is the only theory of law capable of lifting jurisprudence to the status of a genuine science.[41] But Kelsen's understanding of what it would mean for jurisprudence to be scientific has proven to be rather elusive.

Many of Kelsen's declared ambitions and convictions appear to fit well into the methodological positivist paradigm. The pure theory aims to give a general theory of law that points out the essential features shared by all legal systems; it is not an interpretation of any particular legal order. The pure theory, moreover, is concerned to describe the law as it is, not to prescribe how it ought to be. It aims to be mere cognition and to stay clear of legal politics.[42] What is more, Kelsen famously claimed that 'any content whatever can be law' and that law is nothing but a technique of social control.[43] It seems, then, that Kelsen's pure theory of law must be a form of methodological positivism that tries to understand the law as a kind of social fact.

This classification of the pure theory, however, clearly contradicts a central aspect of Kelsen's understanding of legal science, namely his emphasis on the irreducibility of legal normativity to social fact. This irreducibility entails that legal theory cannot be an enterprise in descriptive sociology. According to Kelsen, the pure theory is a *normative science*.[44]

Legal science tells us what people's rights and obligations are according to the law. And in doing so it uses normative language. Examples of such language are statements like 'Peter ought to pay 1000 dollars to Max' or 'He who steals goods worth more than 1000 dollars is to be punished with a prison sentence of two years'. Like

'Democracy' in *The Journal of Political Philosophy* 13 (2004) 266–90 and Scott Hershovitz, 'Legitimacy, Democracy, and Razian Authority' in *Legal Theory* 9 (2003) 201–20.

[41] See for example Hans Kelsen, *Introduction to the Problems of Legal Theory. A Translation of the First Edition of the Reine Rechtslehre or Pure Theory of Law*, translated and edited by Stanley L Paulson and Bonnie Litschewski-Paulson (Oxford, 1992) 1–5.   [42] Ibid, 7–8.
[43] Ibid, 56.   [44] Ibid, 7–14.

Hart, Kelsen rejected the view that the meaning of such statements is explicable in terms of habitual obedience of subjects to sovereigns, in terms of expectations about how courts will decide certain cases, or on the basis of the likelihood that someone will suffer harm as a result of certain acts.[45]

Kelsen's arguments against such reductionism, however, are not based on the kinds of considerations that Hart invokes against Austin. Hart's arguments against Austin emphasize that reductionist theories lead to an impoverished account of the structure of positive legal order that fails to explain certain of its key features: the structural variety of legal rules, the continuity of legal system, the relative independence of legal validity from effectiveness, and so on.[46] But Hart claimed that he was able to put forward these criticisms within the framework of a jurisprudential approach that allows us to continue to conceive of the existence of law as a complex social fact and thus to hold on to the separation of law and morality.

Kelsen, by contrast, believes that the rejection of reductionism must go along with a rejection of the attempt to explain the existence of law as a kind of social fact. He frequently engaged in polemics against legal sociology and some of the authors he attacked held views that are in certain respects not too dissimilar from Hart's.[47] Kelsen argues that legal sociology is parasitical upon normative jurisprudence. A conception of law as social fact is meaningful to us only because we already understand the concepts it uses from a normative jurisprudential point of view. But legal sociology cannot explain the normative meaning of the law as it is understood by those who use legal statements to make claims upon each other.[48] Jurisprudence must therefore be a normative science even though it can and ought to be kept separate from morality or, as Kelsen frequently puts it, from the theory of justice.

The pure theory's concept of legal validity expresses this demand by relating legal validity to an idea of justification.[49] To show that a law is valid, according to Kelsen, is to show that it was enacted in accordance with the procedures authorized by a basic norm. This, of course, is standard positivist fare. But a Kelsenian basic norm, unlike a Hartian rule of recognition, does not merely serve the function to allow us to identify valid law. It also confers normative force on all norms that have membership in a legal system. Someone who makes a normative legal statement, according to Kelsen, presupposes that the fact that the norm to which the statement refers was enacted in accordance with the basic norm justifies or confers binding force on the demand raised by the norm and expressed by the

---

[45] Ibid, 32–6.   [46] See Hart, *The Concept of Law* (n 11 above) 18–78.

[47] See the attack on Max Weber's legal sociology in Hans Kelsen, *Der soziologische und der juristische Staatsbegriff. Kritische Untersuchung des Verhältnisses von Staat und Recht* (Tübingen, 1928) 156–70.

[48] See ibid, 114–204.

[49] This has been emphasized by Joseph Raz, 'Kelsen's Theory of the Basic Norm' in Raz, *The Authority of Law* (n 33 above) 122–45, at 134 and Carlos Santiago Nino, 'Some Confusions Surrounding Kelsen's Concept of Validity' in Paulson and Litschewski, *Normativity and Norms* (n 4 above) 253–61. Stanley Paulson, 'The Weak Reading of Authority in Hans Kelsen's Pure Theory of Law', in *Law and Philosophy* 19 (2000) 131–71 contains a very clear exposition of different indications of a normative concept of validity in Kelsen at 155–68.

statement. Without this assumption, Kelsen believes, legal discourse would be meaningless. To show that a legal norm is valid by showing that it was enacted in accordance with a basic norm, then, is to offer at least a conditional justification for the practical demand raised by that legal norm.[50]

It is not perfectly clear whether Kelsen thought it possible to presuppose a basic norm without having to endorse the normative claims raised by that basic norm, without considering the law authorized by it to be genuinely justified at least to some extent. Much, though not all, of what Kelsen says certainly suggests that he aspired to keep the pure theory free of any genuine normative commitment.[51] But even if we accept that Kelsen intended the presupposition of a basic norm to be morally non-committal, we will still be left with the question whether the intention is compatible with the theory of the basic norm and with the general idea that legal science is a normative science. How can legal science, despite the fact that it is a normative science and not an exercise in descriptive sociology, avoid being prescriptive or evaluative?

Many positivist commentators, for example Alf Ross and Eugenio Bulygin, have argued that Kelsen's account of legal normativity is incompatible with his positivist commitments and ought to be abandoned in favor of a more austerely positivist approach that does not rest on a normative conception of validity.[52] Kelsen's normative conception of validity, according to this view, is a regrettable leftover of Kantian influences on his early work that should be dropped in order to turn the pure theory into a genuinely descriptive and value-free positivist legal science.

Not all scholars, however, have given such short shrift to Kelsen's theory of legal normativity. Kelsen's attack on legal sociology has found a contemporary echo in Joseph Raz's criticism of Hart. Raz's claim that any satisfactory account of legal normativity must be based on a conception of justified authority and not on attempts to specify the conditions under which norms can be said to exist in a sociological sense is inspired by the pure theory of law.[53] The second classificatory suggestion, then, would be to treat Kelsen's pure theory as an anticipation of the Razian paradigm.

In adapting Kelsen's conception of legal normativity, Raz develops a sophisticated reconciliation of the idea that jurisprudence is a practical science with the positivist commitment to value-neutrality: the conception of a 'legal point of view'.[54]

---

[50] See Kelsen, *Introduction to the Problems of Legal Theory* (n 41 above) 58.

[51] For a striking counterexample see Hans Kelsen, *Allgemeine Staatslehre* (Berlin, 1925) 99, quoted in Paulson, 'The Weak Reading of Authority' (n 49 above) at 166.

[52] See Alf Ross, 'Validity and the Conflict between Positivism and Natural Law' in Paulson and Litschewski, *Normativity and Norms* (n 4 above) 147–63; Eugenio Bulygin, 'An Antinomy in Kelsen's Pure Theory of Law' ibid, 297–315. See also Deryck Beyleveld and Roger Brownsword, 'Methodological Syncretism in Kelsen's Pure Theory of Law' ibid, 113–45.

[53] See Raz, 'Kelsen's Theory of the Basic Norm' (n 49 above); Joseph Raz, 'The Purity of the Pure Theory', in Paulson and Litschewski, *Normativity and Norms* (n 4 above) 237–52.

[54] See Raz, *Practical Reason and Norms* (n 34 above) 170–7.

Normative legal statements, Raz argues, are neither a species of practical judgments about what ought to be done, all things considered, nor are they descriptions of complex social facts. In using normative statements that report what ought to be done according to the law the lawyer therefore has to adopt and to speak from the point of view of the law, from the point of view according to which the legal norms belonging to some legal system possess justified normativity. But this does not entail that the lawyer is committed to an evaluation or endorsement of the normative claims of the legal system whose point of view he is adopting. All he does is state 'what one has reason to do from the legal point of view, namely, what ought to be done if legal norms are valid norms'. Normative legal language, if used in this detached manner, is comparable to 'statements made on the assumption that something is the case, for example, that a certain scientific theory is valid'.[55]

A normative legal statement is true, according to Raz, if the legal system in fact contains a norm making the practical demand reported in the statement. It also expresses, even while it does not necessarily endorse, the law's claim to authority. If the legal norm in virtue of which the statement is true happens to be a valid exclusionary reason for some addressee, in addition to being legally valid, it will be the case that the action demanded by the norm ought to be performed by that addressee because it is demanded by the law. But what is a valid exclusionary reason for some need not be such a reason for all subjects of the law. The legal scientist can make true or false normative legal statements without committing himself to a view on this further justificatory issue.

Normative legal statements, Raz readily acknowledges, are typically employed in a more committed way. People commonly use them to make demands on each other and the state or its representatives use them to make demands on us. Judges are professionally required to act on the assumption that the laws they apply ought to be obeyed by the subjects of the law. The detached uses are in a sense parasitical, hence, even if they are constitutive of the possibility of a legal science that is not directly evaluative. They are parasitical since there would be no use for a detached employment of legal statements on the part of legal scientists if people did not tend to make genuinely committed use of legal language and to treat the law as a justified standard of behavior. What is more, the detached use is parasitical in the stronger sense that it must at least potentially be reasonable for some people to treat some laws as authoritative standards of behavior in order for legal discourse to be non-ideological. But despite being parasitical, the class of detached normative statements has a central importance for legal theory. It identifies the minimum commitments a legal scientist has to make in order to be able to take the legal point of view, ie to describe the law as an institution that necessarily claims, but that does not necessarily possess, legitimate authority.

This analysis departs from Kelsen's own view in one central respect. Kelsen's basic norm clearly makes a general attribution of normativity to the law. By presupposing

---

[55] Ibid, 175.

the basic norm, the Kelsenian legal scientist assumes that all norms that have membership in the legal system, insofar as they are justified, are equally justified, that they are all justified for the same reason, and that this reason equally binds all subjects of the law. In other words, Kelsen implicitly rejects the piecemeal approach to the justification of authority. This rejection, in turn, makes it difficult to hold on to the view that the detached and non-evaluative use of normative legal statements, even while being parasitical on committed uses, has paradigmatic importance in explaining legal-scientific discourse. If the law's normative claims are essentially general, legal-scientific discourse will be meaningful only if we can offer a general endorsement of the law's claim to authority. And such a general endorsement of the law's claim to authority would lead us into a form of natural law.

If Kelsen's view fails to fit either the methodological positivist paradigm or the Razian conception of a non-evaluative jurisprudence, what remains of his claim to have offered a legal science? According to an answer that frequently appears in Kelsen's writings, the pure theory is a science because or insofar as it is not an ideology.[56] Somewhat surprisingly, this defense of the scientific status of the pure theory puts Kelsen into the close neighborhood of the political understanding of legal positivism.

This closeness to political positivism is somewhat surprising insofar as Kelsen's distinction between science and ideology emphasizes that a theory of the nature of law must not be defended by an appeal to the theory's alleged beneficial moral consequences. In Kelsen's view, it is the mark of an ideology, as opposed to a science, that it is adopted because its advocates consciously or unconsciously desire its practical effects as furthering their subjective interests.[57]

An ideology, according to the classical understanding, is more than just a mistaken system of belief. It is a system of belief that stabilizes relationships of authority which are structurally illegitimate, by preventing those who are subject to authority from making autonomous use of their own understanding in deciding how to act. The pure theory, Kelsen argues, is not guilty of this charge, while all other, 'impure' legal theories are. The pure theory, then, serves our interest in ridding ourselves of ideological accounts of the law that will tend to stabilize autonomy-denying institutional structures. As a form of social criticism, it is not just attempting to pave the way for frank moral criticism of bad legal content. It helps undermine authoritarian political structures by withdrawing the ideological support

[56] See Kelsen, *Introduction to the Problems of Legal Theory* (n 41 above) 18–19; Kelsen, *Der soziologische und der juristische Staatsbegriff* (n 47 above) 205–53.

[57] See for example Hans Kelsen, *The Pure Theory of Law. Translation from the Second German Edition*, translated by Max Knight (Berkeley 1970) 106: 'Precisely this anti-ideological tendency shows that the Pure Theory of Law is a true science of law. For science as cognition has the immanent tendency of revealing its subject. Ideology, however, veils reality either by glorifying it with the intent to conserve and to defend it, or by misrepresenting it with the intent to attack, destroy, and to replace it by another. Such ideology is rooted in wishing, not in knowing; it springs from certain interests or, more correctly, from interests other than the interest in truth—which, of course, is not intended to say anything about the dignity of those other interests.'

they receive from conservative natural law theory. The pure theory, to quote Bernard Williams, serves the 'enlightenment ideal of finding a stable and decent form of human community that was (to put it moderately) minimally dependent on myths'.[58]

Despite undoubted Kelsen's allegiance to this aspiration, his official defense of the claim that the pure theory is scientific in the sense of being non-ideological is meant to be normatively uncommitted. What disqualifies all competitors of the pure theory, even apart from their ideological function, Kelsen argues, is the fact that they lead to irresolvable antinomies or involve crudely reductionist accounts of legal normativity. The pure theory is the only legal theory that is even coherent. Acceptance of the pure theory, Kelsen argues, is therefore required solely on the basis of a purely theoretical interest in truth. As we will see, this argument expresses a piece of wishful thinking on Kelsen's part. The claim that the pure theory is non-ideological can only be defended, I will argue, once the normative aspiration to create a decent and stable society minimally dependent on myth is openly acknowledged as the motivation for the pure theory of law and once that aspiration, even though practical, is recognized as something other than the expression of a subjective will to power. The resources for such a defense of the pure theory are available in Kelsen's political works. It is to these that we now have to turn.

Kelsen's legal politics and the thesis of the identity of law and state

Kelsen's political works show him as a passionate defender of parliamentary democracy and of liberal constitutionalism.[59] His attempts to defend democracy and liberal constitutionalism, moreover, were not restricted to the writing of theoretical treatises. Kelsen also took an active part in efforts to build democratic and constitutionalist institutions. He drafted the Austrian constitution of 1920 and served for a while on the Austrian constitutional court.[60] He intervened, moreover, in the crisis of the late Weimar Republic, trying to defend the parliamentary system against the drive towards authoritarianism, before he had to leave Germany for Switzerland and later the US after the Nazi takeover of power.[61] Throughout his career, finally, Kelsen

---

[58] Bernard Williams 'Relativism, History, and the Existence of Values' in Joseph Raz, *The Practice of Value. The Berkeley Tanner Lectures 2001* (Oxford, 2003) 106–18, at 117.

[59] The main works to be analyzed here are the following: Hans Kelsen, 'Über Staatsunrecht' in Klecatsky et al, *Die Wiener rechtstheoretische Schule* (n 1 above), vol I, 957–1057; Hans Kelsen, *Vom Wesen und Wert der Demokratie* (Tübingen, 1929); Hans Kelsen, 'Wesen und Entwicklung der Staatsgerichtsbarkeit' in *Die Wiener rechtstheoretische Schule* (n 1 above), vol II, 1813–72; Hans Kelsen, 'Wer soll der Hüter der Verfassung sein?' in ibid, 1873–912; Hans Kelsen, 'Foundations of Democracy' in *Ethics* 66 (1955) 1–101.

[60] See Stanley Paulson, 'Constitutional Review in the United States and Austria: Notes on the Beginnings' in *Ratio Juris* 16 (2003) 223–39, at 228–33.

[61] See Dyzenhaus, *Legality and Legitimacy* (n 3 above) 102–60. The only biography of Kelsen is Rudolf Aladar Metall, *Hans Kelsen. Leben und Werk* (Wien, 1969).

actively supported the ideal of an international legal order that would provide for binding mechanisms of peaceful conflict resolution amongst states.[62]

That an author who is commonly considered a legal positivist should have intervened in political debates is, of course, not in itself surprising. However, in contrast to Hart's political interventions, Kelsen's political-theoretical works, in keeping with the ambition to offer a critique of ideology, rather openly employ the pure theory as a tool of attack on political positions he rejected. Kelsen, in other words, is not wearing two different hats when speaking as legal theorist and when speaking as political philosopher. Rather, he tends to present his political-theoretical criticisms as corollaries to the pure theory of law. Hence, he must clearly have assumed that there is some kind of relationship between the pure theory of law and the political values that he attempted to defend.

The exact nature of that relationship, however, is difficult to pin down. In the epigraph to this introduction Kelsen at least gives us a clue. He expresses the ambition to develop a theory of law 'adequate to the idea of the rule of law'. We have to ask, therefore, what exactly it could mean for a positivist to claim that his theory of law is adequate to the idea of the rule of law.

According to Kelsen's official answer to this question, a theory of law is adequate to the idea of the rule of law if it does not artificially or unnecessarily restrict the possibility of a full realization of the ideal of the rule of law. By contrast, a theory can turn out to be inadequate to the ideal of the rule of law if it puts artificial or unnecessary obstacles in the way of its realization. The prime example, in Kelsen's view, are dualist theories of the law-state relationship. Such theories hold that the political authority of the state is prior to the law and that a capacity to act without legal authorization or even in disregard of the law is an essential element of statehood. The laws, according to the dualist, are general commands of the sovereign representative of the state. The sovereign will, for the most part, govern on the basis of general commands. But he can (and sometimes ought) to choose to work around or to disregard his own commands and exercise legitimate political authority in other ways than through mechanisms of legality. Any state, the dualist claims, possesses the power to act in legally unauthorized ways, regardless of the restrictions positive law may purport to put on the exercise of public power.

Kelsen argues that jurisprudence is forced to reject dualist views of the relation between law and state since a state above the law, a state capable of illegal or legally unauthorized action, is jurisprudentially inconceivable.[63] If this is indeed the case, Kelsen is certainly justified to claim as well that dualist views put scientifically unjustifiable ideological obstacles in the path of the full realization of the rule of law. According to the pure theory, the question of the extent of the state's powers

---

[62] See Hans Kelsen, *Das Problem der Souveränität und die Theorie des Völkerrechts. Beitrag zu einer reinen Rechtslehre* (Tübingen, 1920); Hans Kelsen, *Law and Peace in International Relations. The Oliver Wendell Holmes Lectures, 1940–1941* (Cambridge/Mass, 1942).

[63] Kelsen, *Der soziologische und der juristische Staatsbegriff* (n 47 above) 86–91; Kelsen, *Über Staaksurecht* (n 59 above) 986.

depends solely on the content of the positive law, which is open to change. One cannot draw any inferences about a state's legitimate powers from a general theory of the state as a political entity prior to law. The pure theory, Kelsen claims, is not itself normatively committed to any particular conception of the scope of the state's legitimate powers. But its rejection of the dualist view of the law-state relationship at least forces those who prefer a relatively unrestrained state to defend their preference openly on normative grounds, as a view about the best content of positive law and not as an alleged insight into the nature of the state.[64]

This official reading of the adequacy thesis can be distinguished from a second, more openly political reading according to which the pure theory's dismissal of dualist theories of the law-state relationship is inseparable from a normative endorsement of the aim to subject the exercise of state power to stringent legal restraints. There would be no reason to adopt the pure theory's account of the law-state relationship, according to this second reading, for someone who did not also support the ideal, on the level of political theory, of subjecting the state as fully as possible to constraints against uncontrollable exercises of power. Under this reading of the adequacy thesis, the pure theory does not purport to establish that dualist views of the law-state relationship can simply be dismissed as incoherent. Rather, it makes the more modest claim that a dualist understanding of the law-state relationship cannot be defended on purely jurisprudential grounds since it embeds contestable normative assumptions about the proper function of the rule of law and about its relation to political power. Moreover, the pure theory of law establishes an attractive legal-theoretical alternative to a dualist understanding of the law-state relationship.

The alternative offered by the pure theory is attractive mainly because it is much more congenial to our intuitive understanding of the point and purpose of the ideal of the rule of law, of democracy, and of the principles of constitutionalism than dualism. The pure theory, then, is adequate to the ideal of the rule of law, understood broadly so as to include democratic procedures of legislation and a commitment to constitutional protections against the tyranny of a majority, insofar as it develops a conception of legal normativity that aligns with the normative aim to subject organs of state as fully as possible to legal constraints against arbitrary exercises of power. This second reading, it should be admitted, fails to preserve the ideological neutrality of the pure theory's concept of law. But it is alone capable, or so I will argue, to make sense of Kelsen's conception of legal normativity and the attack on dualist understandings of the law-state relationship that goes along with it.

It will be helpful to take a short look at the legal theories Kelsen argued against. As I already intimated, Kelsen developed the pure theory as a theory of law *and*

---

[64] See for example Kelsen, 'Wer soll der Hüter der Verfassung sein' (n 59 above) 1918–1922. The claim that the pure theory keeps open a morally important choice—here the choice between national sovereignty and lawful international order—is prominent as well in Kelsen's work on international law. See Kelsen, *Das Problem der Souveränität* (n 62 above) 314–20.

state. Questions about the law-state relationship were of constant concern to German legal scholars in the last decades of the 19th and the first decades of the 20th century, due to the fact that Wilhelmine Germany had not fully grown out of an absolutist constitutional framework. To be sure, questions of the law-state relationship are bound to arise in any political order. But the constitutional situation of late 19th and early 20th century Germany put them into especially stark relief. The Wilhelmine Emperors, despite the fact that Germany was officially a constitutional state, still successfully claimed, in effect, to be sovereign representatives of the state. It was commonly recognized amongst jurisprudents that the monarch possessed the power to govern by decree and thus to bypass the constitutional requirement of parliamentary assent to legislation if he deemed such action to be necessary.[65]

Kelsen viewed this situation as a case of arrested development towards a truly constitutional order that had merely postponed an unavoidable choice between autocracy and democracy. But this view was not shared by all German authors of the time. Georg Jellinek, arguably the most influential German legal and constitutional theorist of the *Kaiserreich*, abstracted a general theory of the relation between law and state from the German constitutional situation.[66] According to Jellinek, the state cannot be fully comprehended from one particular scientific perspective. It is unavoidably both a fact of power that can only be understood sociologically and a normative order bound to the rule of law. Dogmatic jurisprudence conceives of the state as a normative order, but in so doing it does not provide us with a fully sufficient theory of the state. The normative order of the law is dependent, for its creation and protection, on the state as a fact of power. While the state as a fact of power has the primary function of creating and maintaining normative order, it cannot reasonably assume an unconditional commitment to act in accordance with the rule of law since this would defeat its ability to effectively protect normative order. For Jellinek, the state's commitment to normative order, to what Lon Fuller calls the congruence of official act and declared law,[67] is therefore the result of a voluntary obligation (*Selbstverpflichtung*)[68] that is subject to exceptions of which the state as a fact of power must be the judge.

This thesis, according to Jellinek, expresses a general truth about the law-state relationship in all its instances that is unaffected by the particular content of a political system's constitutional law. The high level of abstraction reached in Jellinek's theory ensured that dualist accounts of the law-state relationship remained influential in Germany, and were even radicalized, after the democratic

---

[65] See Peter Caldwell, *Popular Sovereignty and the Crisis of German Constitutional Law: The Theory and Practice of Weimar Constitutionalism* (Durham/NC, 1997) 13–39.

[66] Georg Jellinek, *Allgemeine Staatslehre* (Darmstadt, 1960, first published 1900). See Michael Stolleis, *Geschichte des öffentlichen Rechts in Deutschland, vol. 2: Staatsrechtslehre und Verwaltungswissenschaft 1800–1914* (München, 1992) 450–5.

[67] See Lon L Fuller, *The Morality of Law. Revised Edition* (New Haven, 1964) 81–91.

[68] See Jellinek, *Allgemeine Staatslehre* (n 66 above) 367–75. Kelsen criticized this view repeatedly. See Kelsen, *Der soziologische und der juristische Staatsbegriff* (n 47 above) 114–40; Kelsen, *Introduction to the Problems of Legal Theory* (n 41 above) 97–106.

revolution of 1918. The views of Kelsen's main theoretical opponent during the Weimar Republic, Carl Schmitt, which came close to identifying authentic democracy with the sovereign dictatorship of a charismatic leader, are a famous case in point. Kelsen's pure theory is motivated, in large part, by the attempt to offer a principled response to dualist theories of the law-state relationship. The lynchpin of this response is the thesis of the identity of law and state.[69]

The state, Kelsen claims, does not exist in the manner of an individual human being that has a biological and psychological existence independent of the law. When we say, for example, that the state acts in a certain way we must be saying, in effect, that certain acts performed by human beings are to be attributed to the state as a legal person. Such attribution is possible only on the basis of legal norms that empower certain human beings to act in the name of the state. And in order for a human being so empowered successfully to act in the name of the state, that human being's actions must comply with the authorizing norm that opens up the possibility of interpreting some of its actions as acts of state or exercises of public power. If the actions in question fail to conform to the authorizing norms that allow us to interpret the actions of some human being as acts of state, they will fail to be attributable to the state, even if they are carried out, by the human being in question, with the subjective intention of performing an act of state. A violation of the law or an act that has no legal authorization therefore cannot be attributed to the state. As a result, it is impossible to conceive of illegal acts of state.

Kelsen argues that dualist theories mistakenly conceive of the state as a 'real' person behind the nexus of authorizing norms whose actual power forms the ultimate basis of all legal order.[70] The state, as a transcendent source of all positive law, is then taken to have the power to exempt itself from the observance of the positive law whenever it sees fit.[71] This claim, in Kelsen's view, enables those who control government not to respect existing positive law, if doing so does not suit their interest, without having to pay the political price for openly denying its validity.[72] But if the identity thesis holds true, Kelsen argues, the dualist claim that the state or its alleged representatives can suspend the positive law, and still continue to act in a public capacity, must turn out to be meaningless. According to the identity thesis, an act performed by some human being will qualify as an act of state only if it conforms to the legal norms that purport to govern the relevant category of acts of state. This principle will either entail that acts not in conformity with a legal norm that purports to govern the relevant category of acts of state are illegal and

---

[69] See Kelsen, *Introduction to the Problems of Legal Theory* (n 41 above) 97–106; Hans Kelsen, *Allgemeine Staatslehre* (Berlin, 1925) 16–21, 71–6; Kelsen, *Der soziologische und der juristische Staatsbegriff* (n 47 above) 114–204. For a recent analysis and qualified defense see Alexander Somek, 'Stateless Law: Kelsen's Conception and its Limits' in *Oxford Journal of Legal Studies* 26 (2006) 753–74.   [70] See Kelsen, *Introduction to the Problems of Legal Theory* (n 41 above) 97–106.

[71] See Schmitt, *Politische Theologie. Vier Kapitel zur Lehre von der Souveränität* (Berlin, 1922) 19: 'The exceptional case reveals the nature of the state's authority most clearly. The decision separates itself from the legal norm and (to formulate paradoxically) the authority proves that it does not have to act lawfully in order to create law.' (my translation)

[72] See Kelsen, *Der soziologische und der juristische Staatsbegriff* (n 47 above) 136–40.

therefore fail to qualify as exercises of public power or else that the norm in question is lacking in legal force, since conformity with it is not, in fact, necessary for an act to qualify as an exercise of public power.

In the light of the identity thesis, a constitutional situation such as that of the German *Kaiserreich*, must be interpreted as an essentially unstable hybrid between constitutional democracy and autocracy. If the government is considered to have the power to override constitutional requirements on the basis of an appeal to its sovereign authority, then these requirements should be regarded as lacking in legal force. If, on the other hand, the constitutional norms are to be taken seriously, one must be willing to embrace the principle that governmental acts in violation of those norms do not qualify as exercises of public power. Dualist legal theories serve to postpone this inevitable choice between an affirmation and a denial of the validity of the law that can allegedly be suspended by the state. In effect, they postpone the transition, in constitutional reality, from an autocratic legal order that leaves wide discretion to the rulers to a constitutional order that makes constraints of legality effectively binding on those who exercise political power. Of course, the ruling elite of an autocratic regime may well have an interest in such postponement. But legal theory, Kelsen argues, should not lend a helping hand to such efforts.

The question we need to ask about this line of argument is whether Kelsen's critical intention finds sufficient ground in the first reading of the thesis of the adequacy of the pure theory to the idea of the rule of law or whether it is implicitly committed to the second, more openly political reading of that thesis.

The pure theory, Kelsen officially claims, remains scientific and non-evaluative since it is not committed to the view that we ought to choose constitutionalism over autocracy.[73] Neither is it to be preferred over dualism because it is adequate to the idea of the rule of law. Dualism, rather, in addition to being inadequate to the idea of the rule of law, must be rejected by legal science on the independent ground that illegal or legally unauthorized acts of state are jurisprudentially inconceivable. The claim that the pure theory is adequate to the idea of the rule of law is therefore perfectly compatible, Kelsen argues, with the view that there is sufficient reason to adopt the pure theory on scientific grounds that have nothing to do with its alleged adequacy to the idea of the rule of law.

However, there are good reasons to suspect that Kelsen's criticism of dualism, or at least its intended normative import, cannot be sustained on the basis of the first reading of the adequacy thesis. It appears undeniable that legal norms are needed to characterize human acts as acts of state. However, it appears equally undeniable that it is perfectly possible for human beings to act in an official capacity and yet to violate the law. Particular organs of state often act in ways that fail fully to conform to all legal norms that purport to govern and direct their activities but that are nevertheless recognized as acts of state. The claim that the state is incapable of

<hr/>

[73] See Kelsen, 'Wer soll der Hüter der Verfassung sein?' (n 59 above) 1921–2; Kelsen, *Pure Theory of Law* (n 57 above) 106.

acting illegally, it seems, is defensible only if we interpret the term 'legal' in a trivial sense according to which any final decision taken by a formally authorized organ of state is to be considered legal, even if it violates some material legal standard.[74]

But this trivial interpretation of the identity thesis creates a dilemma for Kelsen. If the identity thesis is defended on the basis of a trivial standard of legality, it is alone insufficient to ground the critical implications Kelsen is interested in. According to the trivial identity thesis, governmental organs that choose to act without material legal authorization or to work around material legal and constitutional standards will usually be identifiable as governmental organs easily enough, on grounds of formal rules of competence. The claim that the state is a creature of law will then pose no obstacle to an understanding of the relation between law and state that is dualist in effect, if not in name. To make the claim that acts performed by persons or institutions who are identifiable as organs of the state on formal grounds may nevertheless lack public quality, and here we come to the second horn of the dilemma, will require that we adopt a stricter standard of legality in interpreting the identity thesis. We will have to claim, it would appear, that no act can constitute a valid exercise of public power unless it *fully* complies with *all* formal and material norms that purport to govern the relevant category of exercises of public power. But such a strong principle of legality can hardly be defended on the ground that it is inconceivable for a state, or those who act on its behalf, to violate it. It very much looks like a contestable substantive principle of legitimate governance that needs to be defended on normative grounds.

This point has been much emphasized in recent legal theory. Raz, for example, goes along with the gist of the identity thesis as a conceptual claim: 'Actions not authorized by law cannot be the actions of government as a government. They would be without legal effect and often unlawful.'[75] But this acknowledgment, according to Raz, fails to put any interesting normative constraints on actions that are attributable to the person of the state on the basis of formal rules of competence. When we invoke the rule of law as a political ideal, Raz observes, we clearly have in mind more substantive restrictions on the state's actions that go some way towards protecting citizens from arbitrary exercises of state power.

Raz argues that insofar as descriptions of the normative aims of the rule of law are not mere platitudes which stand in for one's preferred policies they will refer to certain virtues of legality. These virtues—publicity, clarity, generality, stability of laws, access to independent courts, respect for principles of natural justice—play a double role. They constitute a moral ideal of legality that can be realized to a larger

---

[74] The claim that the identity thesis is normatively empty is frequently voiced in the literature. See for example Neil MacCormick, 'The Interest of the State and the Rule of Law' in Neil MacCormick, *Questioning Sovereignty* (Oxford, 1999) 27–48, at 40–4; and Lon L Fuller, 'A Reply to Critics' in Lon L Fuller, *The Morality of Law. Revised Edition* (New Haven, 1964) 187–242, at 236; Michel Troper, 'Réflexions autour de la théorie kelsenienne de l'Etat' in Michel Troper, *Pour une théorie juridique de l'état* (Paris, 1994) 143–60.

[75] Joseph Raz, 'The Rule of Law and its Virtue' in Raz, *The Authority of Law* (n 33 above) 210–29, at 212.

or lesser extent, but they also form conditions of the successful pursuit of social goals through legal means by making the law into a good instrument of policy that is able to guide the behavior of the individuals subject to it. Any use of the law for political purposes will have to exhibit the virtues to some degree in order to be effective. But the degree of observance of the principles of the rule of law that is necessary to make the law effective as a means of guidance may fall short of a full realization of the moral ideal of the rule of law. What is more, it is not clear whether we should always want the state to comply with that ideal to the fullest possible extent. If maximum fidelity to the virtues of the rule of law should conflict with the realization of valuable substantive purposes it would be a practical mistake, Raz suggests, to give unthinking priority to the principles of the rule of law. Finally, even perfect conformity of law with the virtues of the rule of law, though usually desirable, will not necessarily protect subjects of the law from substantively arbitrary or morally obnoxious rule. The conclusion to be drawn, it seems, is that the ideal of the rule of law can only play a rather limited role in justifying exercises of political power.[76] Kelsen's identity thesis, therefore, even if it does not altogether trivialize the idea of the rule of law, is likely to be guilty of inflating its normative scope in irresponsible ways.

Throughout this book, I will challenge the view that the identity thesis, as developed by Kelsen, is either trivial or normatively unsustainable and defend the claim that the pure theory is a legal theory adequate to the ideal of the rule of law. As should be clear by now, I believe that such a defense will have to embrace a strong principle of legality as well as the second reading of the adequacy thesis. In other words, I will argue that Kelsen's understanding of the identity thesis is based on an endorsement of the normative aim to subject the state's power, as far as possible, to legal restraints that will protect subjects of the law from arbitrary exercises of official power.

This endorsement expresses a rejection of the view that positive legality is deserving of respect only insofar as it perfectly expresses or realizes some meta-legal ideal of social justice. Kelsen characterizes natural law theory as a family of views that claim that one should refuse to grant the title 'law' to legal systems the content of which falls short of some absolute conception of good or just social order. In other words, natural law theory, as Kelsen defines it, is committed to a denial of the autonomous value of the rule of law and by implication the autonomy of jurisprudence as an intellectual endeavor that can contribute to the creation and maintenance of a reasonable society. There is a way of interpreting positivism according to which positivism is essentially a mirror image of this view. Positivism, so interpreted, denies that we should withhold the title of law from systems of social rules that fail to live up to a substantive standard of justice. But it agrees with the natural lawyer, as Kelsen describes him, that the practical authority

---

[76] See for a recent defense of this view Timothy Endicott, 'The Reason of the Law' in *American Journal of Jurisprudence* 48 (2003) 83–106.

of such systems exclusively depends on whether they conform in content to some standard of moral evaluation that is external to the positive law.

Moreover, both positivism and natural law theory as Kelsen understands it, taken as mirror images, have a certain affinity to the distinction of law and state, or a tendency to emphasize the discontinuity between the 'law and order state' and the 'rule of law state'. The thesis that the positive law can be legitimate only if it conforms with values external to positive legality can easily be turned into the view that it may well be sufficient for the legitimacy of exercises of political power that they are motivated by the right kind of moral reasons.[77] Lawfulness, under such a view, is at best a circumstantial attribute of the legitimacy of exercises of political power. If one's actions are taken in the name of a higher moral ideal, compliance with positive legal norms may seem unimportant from a normative point of view. If one is a positivist claiming to act on behalf of such ideals, one will be on guard against 'obsequious quietism'; if one is a natural lawyer, on Kelsen's understanding, one will take the view that the positive legal order one feels morally entitled to disrespect lacks the quality of genuine law. But the practical consequences of both views are likely to be very similar.

Kelsen, I will argue, was afraid of such an attitude because he believed that it incapacitates the essential function of positive law. Positive law, in Kelsen's view, is at bottom an instrument for the peaceful and legitimate arbitration of social conflicts in a pluralist society. But positive law cannot play this role if its authority is perceived to be dependent upon external moral or political sources of value. Kelsen was concerned to deny a necessary relation between legality and justice because he wanted to attack the idea that positive law is legitimate, that it merits respect, only as long as its content conforms to some absolute standard of justice external to positive law. Kelsen's denial of a necessary connection between legality and external justice, in other words, serves to protect an autonomous relation between positive legality and political legitimacy.

Kelsen invested the pure theory with the hope that its adoption as a conceptual framework to think about state and law would increase the availability and attractiveness of peaceful solutions to political conflicts. The reason for this hope is that the separation between the relation of legality and legitimacy and the relation of legality and justice cuts two ways. It does not just attempt to affirm that legality is intrinsically valuable. It also opens the law for peaceful legislative reform by severing the tight connection between justified normativity and substantive justice that

[77] The classical formulation for such a position is Locke's definition of prerogative as 'power to act according to discretion, for the publick good, without the prescription of the Law, and sometimes even against it' (John Locke, *Two Treatises of Government*, edited by Peter Laslett (Cambridge, 1988) 375.) In fairness to Locke, it has to be stressed that prerogative is clearly limited to action in particular instances not sufficiently provided for by general laws. But the idea can clearly be given a much wider application once the internal relation between the rule of law and the liberal reading of the public good is severed. See for a historical account of this process Carl Schmitt, *Die Diktatur. Von den Anfängen des modernen Souveränitätsgedankens bis zum proletarischen Klassenkampf* (Berlin, 1928).

Kelsen takes to be characteristic of natural law theory. And insofar as the preservation of legal order and continuity is always valuable in some respects, jurisprudence should approach the choice between legality and illegality from a particular perspective. It ought to, or so Kelsen believed, put the burden of proof on the advocate of illegality instead of pretending that the value of legality is a mere function of how well it serves some substantive conception of the good.

I readily admit that Kelsen's own description of his legal-theoretical project, a description that puts heavy emphasis on the idea that the pure theory is a science of the law, would appear to conflict with my approach. I am not making the claim, consequently, to be offering a definitive exegesis that provides the closest possible approximation to what Kelsen really meant to say. But I hope to be able to show that my interpretation has a firm basis in Kelsen's work. I also believe that my reading of the pure theory exhibits the virtue of interpretive charity in one important respect. It allows us to understand Kelsen's political interventions and his work in constitutional theory as based on his legal theory and it thus discharges him from the accusations of inconsistency or dishonesty that are frequently leveled at his political interventions. We are not forced to choose, in my view, between Kelsen the legal theorist and Kelsen the political theorist. I will argue that the position one arrives at by rejecting the choice, even if it forces us to discard some elements of Kelsen's self-understanding as a legal scientist, is philosophically interesting in its own right. It shows how the different strands that drive the positivist project can be reintegrated into a powerful theory of political legitimacy capable of standing on its own feet.[78]

Democracy, constitutionalism, and legal peace in Kelsen's utopia of legality

Kelsen's strong principle of legality, I have claimed in the previous section, cannot be defended on the basis of the idea that illegal acts of state are inconceivable. However, I contend that Kelsen's political works—in particular his works in the theory of democracy, his defense of constitutional adjudication, and his advocacy of 'peace through law' in the international sphere—contain the materials for an alternative defense of the strong principle of legality and of the version of the identity thesis that goes along with it.

---

[78] Stanley Paulson has remarked that Kelsen's 'is a corpus of writings rich enough to sustain an array of readings, reflecting different philosophical interests and persuasions' (Paulson, 'The Weak Reading of Authority' (n 49 above) 171.) I will focus on Kelsen's work during the 1920s and 1930s, but I will occasionally make use of earlier and later works. I will not, however, include any discussion of Kelsen's late skeptical phase after 1960. Moreover, I will not make any attempt to enter debates about the periodization of Kelsen's work. I will assume, rather, that the pre-1960 works can, for my purposes, be treated as a unity. The relative continuity of Kelsen's work up to 1960 is emphasized by Stanley Paulson, 'Four Phases in Hans Kelsen's Legal Theory? Reflections on a Periodization' in *Oxford Journal of Legal Studies* 18 (1998) 153–66.

This alternative defense aims to show that the strong principle of legality forms the cornerstone of an internally coherent and highly attractive constitutional ideal that I will call the 'utopia of legality'. The utopia of legality is a constitutional system in which the legality, in the non-trivial sense of the term, of an act of state that enacts or executes a legal norm is ordinarily sufficient to make that norm (or act of execution) fully legitimate, to constitute a duty on the part of the subjects of the law to defer to and to obey it. The reason for this is that the utopia of legality is a system in which people are subject, as far as this is possible, only to the objective rule of laws, and not to the rule of men.

When Kelsen claims that the pure theory is adequate to the idea of the rule of law he ought to be interpreted as saying that the pure theory is adequate to the aim of realizing a utopia of legality. There is no conclusive reason to accept Kelsen's understanding of legal normativity unless one is committed to the ideal of realizing a utopia of legality. Conversely, if the utopia of legality is a coherent and viable ideal, and if it is indeed considered to be morally attractive, one will have reason to adopt a Kelsenian understanding of legal normativity since such an understanding serves the realization of the ideal. Kelsen's political works, in their relation to the legal-theoretical works, can fruitfully be read as an attempt to establish that the utopia of legality is indeed a viable and attractive constitutional ideal whose realization would be served by the adoption of a Kelsenian understanding of legal normativity.

The structure of this book is governed by its main ambition, to spell out the different elements of Kelsen's utopia of legality and to show how they relate to each other. In Chapter 2, I will attempt to analyze Kelsen's claim that the pure theory is an autonomous science of the law. This chapter has a largely negative and agenda-setting function. It aims to show that the autonomy of jurisprudence in Kelsen cannot meaningfully be understood as a purely 'epistemological' or 'methodological' principle. The assumption of the autonomy of jurisprudence, expressed in the act of the presupposition of a basic norm, can be justified only if we can reasonably make general attributions of justified normativity to the positive law qua positive law, only if it is possible reasonably to assume the existence of internal values of legality independent of substantive justice.

Kelsen's *Reine Rechtslehre* does not develop a positive account of the features of legality that make the act of presupposing a basic norm reasonable. But the resources for such an account can be found elsewhere in Kelsen's oeuvre. In Chapter 3, I will argue that Kelsen's development of the thesis of the identity of law and state is committed to a strong principle of legality. This principle provides the foundation for an account of the rule of law that explains how conformity with the law can contribute to the legitimacy of exercises of political power. In its primary form the principle claims that any purported act of state that does not fully comply with all legal norms which bear on the kind of exercise of public power in question is therefore null and void, even if it was performed by a person designated as a bearer of public authority. But in this form, the principle of legality is clearly impracticable, as it would seem to empower each individual subject of the law to consider any purported exercise of public power whose perfect legality is, according to the subject, open to doubt to be null and void. The principle can become practicable only if it is transformed into the demand that all alleged exercises of public authority be reviewable by independent courts endowed with the power to void any exercise of public power not judged to be perfectly legal.

A commitment to this principle, however, is in itself insufficient fully to realize a utopia of legality and to justify the normative claims of the law. In Chapter 4, I propose the view that Kelsen's theory of democracy is best understood as a reaction to this insufficiency. The normative intuition that underpins Kelsen's commitment to a strong principle of legality is the idea that those who are subject to public power are not therefore subject to the personal whim of those who happen to exercise public power but only to the laws that authorize bearers of public power, guide their decisions, and delimit their proper sphere of authority. But the enforcement of this distinction through the application of a strict principle of legality will have to fall short of achieving its intended aim, to protect us from arbitrary exercises of personal power, as long as legislation is organized in an autocratic fashion, as long as general laws are potentially no more than projections of the partial interest of one person or of some tiny social elite. The introduction of democracy, defined by Kelsen as participation of the subjects of the law in its creation, is a necessary step towards the completion of the normative ideal implicit in Kelsen's reading of the identity thesis.

Kelsen's theory of democracy, though generally neglected in scholarly debate, is interesting in its own right and apart from the role it plays within the attempt to explain the pure theory's adequacy to the idea of the rule of law. Kelsen offers a highly unusual justification of majoritarian democracy that is based on the value of freedom and not on the value of equality. The majority rule, Kelsen claims, is preferable to any other mode of taking legislative decisions because it allows the largest possible number of subjects of the law to remain free in society, to avoid conflict between their personal will and the demands of the law. Kelsen claims, moreover, that this thin justification suffices to reconcile members of an outvoted minority to the decisions lawfully taken by a democratic majority and even to give them grounds to identify with general norms created against their will. The interest in freedom, Kelsen assumes, is an interest that is shared even by members of groups that are radically divided in their ideals of social justice. If the process of the democratic creation of general law can be justified on the basis of the value of freedom, Kelsen hopes, that process will be able peacefully to arbitrate conflicts about justice amongst ideologically divided groups. Democracy does not presuppose a prior agreement on the structure of a just society. Rather, it allows a society to function, and to function legitimately, without such agreement.

The problem with Kelsen's line of argument is obvious. The freedom-based justification of the majority rule seems incapable, at first glance, to shoulder the legitimatory and reconciliatory burden Kelsen wants to impose on it. Let us assume it is true that, in a majoritarian democracy, the largest possible number of people will find their personal interest served by the law. It is unclear, to say the least, why those whose interests are not reflected in the law created by a majority ought to consider this truth to have any reconciliatory value. It would appear that a more substantive justification of democracy is needed, then, which is unlikely to remain neutral amongst competing conceptions of a just society. Part of my project in Chapter 4 is to show that Kelsen's freedom-based justification of majoritarian democracy does not have to fall to this criticism. A charitable reconstruction, rather, establishes that a modified version of Kelsen's argument might well be able to make good on its promises.

In Chapter 5, I turn to another important theme in Kelsen's political works, his advocacy of the institution of a constitutional court endowed with the power to strike down unconstitutional law and to invalidate unconstitutional acts of the highest organs of government. In one sense, this advocacy is just the application of Kelsen's strict principle of legality to questions of constitutional legality. According to the strict principle of constitutional legality, full conformity with constitutional law is a necessary requirement of the validity of an act of legislation or any other act of an organ of state that directly executes the constitution. And if the demand for such conformity cannot be enforced against the legislator and other highest organs of government by an independent court, constitutional law will remain a defective form of law the validity of which is potentially in doubt.

Kelsen's argument for a constitutional court, though, appears to be entangled in an intractable difficulty. Kelsen admits that general legal norms are typically unable uniquely to determine a correct answer to a legal question to be decided by a court. If this problem applies to constitutional laws, the constitution will be unable uniquely to determine correct solutions to constitutional disputes such as disputes over the constitutionality of acts of legislation. As a result, it would seem to make little sense for Kelsen to claim that a constitutional court can act as a guardian of constitutional legality. Kelsen's general view of adjudication appears to entail that a constitutional court will inevitably take discretionary political decisions that determine the meaning of the constitution instead of enforcing objective limits of political authority. Our commitment to democracy, however, would seem to provide strong reasons for thinking that purely political disputes concerning the meaning of the constitution ought to be decided by democratically elected political organs and not by courts.

My argument in Chapter 5 tries to show that it is possible, despite these difficulties, to understand Kelsen's conception of constitutional review as a conception of guardianship and to integrate it with a Kelsenian understanding of democracy. Democracy and constitutional review, on a Kelsenian conception, not only turn out not to conflict. They turn out to be mutually supportive institutions both of which are needed to realize the constitutional ideal of a utopia of legality.

Finally, Chapter 6 offers an outlook on Kelsen's theory of international law. In contrast to other legal positivists, Kelsen devoted a considerable part of his work to questions of international law, and in particular to an attack on the effects of law-state

dualism in international law. That the pure theory is meant to be adequate to a normative ideal of legality is nowhere more obvious than in Kelsen's dismissal of the concept of sovereignty as the 'principal instrument of imperialistic ideology directed
against international law'.[79] The elimination of the concept of sovereignty from the
vocabulary of international law, Kelsen hoped, would remove one of the major intellectual obstacles to the realization of a global legal order enabling states to settle their
conflicts in a peaceful way.

However, Kelsen's arguments for an abandonment of the concept of sovereignty
in international law run into problems not altogether dissimilar to the problems
that afflict his official reading of the adequacy thesis. Kelsen claims that the only
theoretical alternative to a radical denial of international law consists in the view
that all national legal systems form dependent parts of a single global legal order.
This view is based on the 'scientific' claim that the coexistence of several valid yet
normatively unrelated legal systems is jurisprudentially inconceivable. But as it
stands, this claim seems to be as implausible as the view that it is impossible to
conceive of an illegal act of state. I will therefore try to defend Kelsen's views on
international law by emphasizing that they are adequate to an important moral
ambition, namely to create an international utopia of legality that effectively
serves the value of the preservation of peace.

In the concluding chapter, I will once again take up the discussion of Kelsen's
relation to contemporary positivism and ask what general contribution his legal
theory might make to current jurisprudential debates. My conclusion will be that
the choice of a Kelsenian understanding of legal normativity might well be justifiable in the light of the constitutional ideal to which that understanding is adequate
since that ideal is both coherent and, on the face of it, morally attractive. I will
argue as well that other theories of the nature of law are expressive of different constitutional ideals. The choice of a concept of law is therefore inseparable from political-theoretical questions about the best form of government.

[79] Kelsen, *Introduction to the Problems of Legal Theory* (n 41 above) 124.

2

The Pure Theory of Law—Science or Political Theory?

The preface to the first edition of the *Reine Rechtslehre* declares that the primary aim of the pure theory of law is to raise jurisprudence to the level of an independent science, a science characterized by the hallmarks of objectivity and exactitude. The pure theory is concerned to describe the law as it is, not to tell us how it ought to be. It is thus based on a methodological principle that, Kelsen argues, should 'appear obvious' but that has nevertheless so far been neglected: We have to free legal cognition of all 'foreign elements', 'to eliminate from this cognition everything not belonging to the object of cognition precisely specified as law'.[1]

However, the sense in which this methodological principle is uncontroversial is unlikely to mark the difference between the pure theory and other jurisprudential approaches and to explain the superiority of the former over the latter. Legal theorists of different stripes disagree, as we have seen, over what is to count as 'the object of cognition' specifiable as law. The methodological claim that legal theory should focus on analysis of the law and exclude from its view everything not belonging to that object of cognition cannot preempt such debates. It presupposes an answer to them. The claim that legal theory must be both scientific and independent from other sciences can become an operative methodological principle only once we know its object and once we know that this object requires jurisprudence to be an independent science. Kelsen, by contrast, typically argues that what counts as law is what the pure theory will identify as such since all other ways of identifying the law fail to treat it as the object of an independent science.[2] One is tempted to conclude that Kelsen's pretension to have offered a legal science simply begs the question. Before we accept this verdict, however, we are obliged, as charitable

---

[1] Hans Kelsen, *Introduction to the Problems of Legal Theory. A Translation of the First Edition of the Reine Rechtslehre of Pure Theory of Law*, translated and edited by Bonnie Litschewski-Paulson and Stanley L Paulson (Oxford, 1992) 1.

[2] See for a similar observation Joseph Raz, 'The Problem about the Nature of Law' in Joseph Raz, *Ethics in the Public Domain. Essays in the Morality of Law and Politics* (Oxford, 1995) 195–209, at 202 and Joseph Raz, 'The Purity of the Pure Theory' in Richard Tur and William Twining (eds), *Essays on Kelsen* (Oxford, 1986) 79–97, at 83: 'Kelsen's defence of the sources thesis is largely dependent on the view that the "scientific" study of law would not be possible if the identification of law turned on moral argument. But this argument is clearly fallacious. The study of law must be adjusted to its object. If its object cannot be studied "scientifically" then its study should not strive to be scientific.'

interpreters, to take a closer look at the features that, in Kelsen's view, make the pure theory scientific. These features might, after all, be necessary to meet standards of adequacy for a legal theory that are defensible on independent grounds.

Kelsen's claim that the pure theory is an independent science of law, on closer inspection, refers to three distinct characteristics: first, the fact that the pure theory is a normative science and hence independent from any natural science, second the pure theory's separation from the theory of justice, and finally the fact that it is a general legal theory that describes a structure common to all legal systems.

Kelsen's conception of natural science is very broad. It encompasses all forms of inquiry, including the empirical social and human sciences, that aim to unearth causal regularities and explain and predict observable events on the basis of these regularities.[3] Jurisprudence, by contrast, is a normative science that describes the structure and the content of a certain species of normative system. Kelsen claims that one can engage in a normative science only if one is entitled to presuppose the objective validity of the norms one is analyzing. Objective validity, the mode of existence of norms, is not explicable in terms of empirical facts. Jurisprudence, therefore, has to be distinguished clearly from any form of empirical cognition of the law if it is to be adequate to its object.[4]

Legal theory, second, in order to achieve scientific status, must be separated from moral theory or, as Kelsen often puts it, the theory of justice.[5] The frequent emphasis on the separation of law from justice in Kelsen's works is aligned with a distinction between legal form and legal content. A satisfactory conception of the validity of a legal norm, Kelsen claims, must be fully dissociated from any normative evaluation of the content of that norm. Kelsen usually explains this requirement as a condition of objectivity. Theories of justice, or of the moral correctness of the content of law, he frequently suggests, are mere expressions of subjective interests. Hence, the pure theory, as a theory concerned to focus solely on the objective cognition of the law, must cleanse its concept of legality from assessments of the moral quality of legal content lest its claim to objectivity be undermined.[6]

The third characteristic of the pure theory as a science is its aim to be a 'general legal theory',[7] a theory of law as such, not of any particular legal system. Of course, Kelsen does not want to suggest that there is a set of universally and intrinsically valid norms that necessarily form part of the content of every legal system. Such a view is the identifying mark of natural law theory. Rather, he claims that all legal systems necessarily share certain structural properties that can be outlined in a

---

[3] See Kelsen, *Introduction to the Problems of Legal Theory* (n 1 above) 13–14 and Hans Kelsen, *Der soziologische und der juristische Staatsbegriff. Kritische Untersuchung des Verhältnisses von Recht und Staat* (Tübingen, 1928) 1–74.

[4] Kelsen, *Introduction to the Problems of Legal Theory* (n 1 above) 23–5.   [5] Ibid, 15–19.

[6] Ibid, 16: the content of justice 'cannot be determined by the Pure Theory of Law or, indeed, arrived at by way of rational cognition at all—as the history of human intellectual endeavour demonstrates, with its failure over a millennium to resolve this problem'.   [7] Ibid, 7.

universal jurisprudential conceptual framework. The pure theory as a science aims to offer such an outline of the structural properties shared by all positive legal systems. The point of this endeavor is to purify legal concepts of all elements that are projections of practical interests only *contingently* related to the necessary structure of legality.

This thumbnail sketch makes it clear that Kelsen's defense of the pure theory cannot appeal to any generally accepted understanding of what it means for a theory of law to be scientific. An analysis of the pure theory, instead of trying to make sense of the abstract claim that jurisprudence would not be scientific if it were impure, should therefore ask whether there are any good independent reasons to accept the three characteristics of the pure theory as necessary conditions of adequacy for a jurisprudential theory. If there are such reasons, the analysis should go on to ascertain how the pure theory tries to answer to these standards of adequacy and to assess whether it is successful in doing so.

In this chapter, I will try to explore the possibility of offering a defense of the pure theory along these lines. My result will be that it might be possible to offer such a defense, but not in a way that will allow us to hold on to the idea that the pure theory is a purely descriptive theory. I will argue that Kelsen's emphasis on the double purity of jurisprudence from both empirical social science and substantive theory of justice makes sense only if we take jurisprudence to be grounded in the normative assumption that there are autonomous values of legality. The possibility of reasonably assuming that such values exist makes a normative legal science possible. The independence, and, from a legal point of view, the normative priority of legality's value from controversial conceptions of substantive social justice, makes it necessary to insulate the identification of valid law from judgments of justice. These observations entail that we have sufficient reason to accept Kelsen's double demand for purity as a standard of adequacy for legal theory only if we commit to a normative ideal of the rule of law that, as I will argue, is served by acceptance of the demand for purity. There is no defense of the pure theory, then, which is independent of a commitment to this ideal. The attempt to justify Kelsen's conditions of adequacy for a legal theory must therefore lead into Kelsen's political theory, which will be the subject of subsequent chapters of this thesis.

In this chapter, I will proceed by discussing Kelsen's two conditions of purity, the distinction of legal theory from the theory of justice and the distinction of legal theory and empirical science, starting with the latter. Kelsen's descriptions of the general structure of legal system will be brought into play as needed to make the argument. My aim, in the discussion of both conditions of purity, is to question Kelsen's 'official' arguments that attempt to defend the pure theory on a purely methodological or epistemological basis. I believe that these official arguments, so to speak, fail to show the pure theory itself in its best light. They conceal an underlying theory of the value of legality that needs to be set free from Kelsen's occasionally unhelpful scientist rhetoric.

I Law and Nature—Subjective and Objective Legal Meaning

The main intuition driving Kelsen's view that legal normativity cannot be analyzed in terms of social fact and that a satisfactory legal theory therefore has to be a normative as opposed to an empirical science is the distinction between the subjective and the objective legal meaning of human actions.[8] Kelsen argues that any legal theory must be based on an acknowledgement of the need to draw this distinction. He goes on to claim that the presupposition of a basic norm that is irreducible to social fact and that provides all the laws that have membership in a legal system with objective normative force is necessary to draw a distinction between objective and subjective legal meaning. However, Kelsen's argument suffers from the fact that his presentation of the distinction between objective and subjective legal meaning is none too clear. It appears to draw into one several different understandings of objectivity that ought to be kept apart.

Kelsen introduces the distinction between objective and subjective meaning by referring to a number of examples of legal acts: 'a parliamentary enactment, say, or an administrative act, a judicial decision, a private law transaction, a delict'.[9] He observes that such acts can be described from two different points of view or under two different aspects. On the one hand, they are instances of mere behavior; they are observable external events taking place in time and space that are subject to some kind of causal explanation. On the other hand, they can be interpreted as meaningful *actions* that have 'a sense that is, so to speak, immanent in or attached to the act or event'.[10]

The meaning or sense of an act, Kelsen claims, cannot derive from its position in a chain of causes and effects; it does not attach to the act insofar as it is an externally observable natural event. Rather, it stems from the fact that the act falls under legal norms that attribute a normative significance to human actions. Some piece of behavior can count as a case of theft only if there is a legal rule that classifies certain kinds of behavior as theft. Some behavior can count as the enactment of a law only if there is a legal rule that determines that behavior of a certain kind is to count as an act of legislation, and so forth. Such rules, in Kelsen's view, function as 'schemata of interpretation' that provide what would otherwise be mere instances of externally observable behavior with an immanent meaning.[11]

---

[8] Kelsen, *Introduction to the Problems of Legal Theory* (n 1 above) 9–10 and Hans Kelsen, *Reine Rechtslehre* (2nd ed, Wien, 1960) 1–3. The distinction figures prominently in many of Kelsen's works. See for example Hans Kelsen, *Vom Wesen und Wert der Demokratie* (Tübingen, 1929) 7–8; Kelsen, *Der soziologische und der juristische Staatsbegriff* (n 3 above) 44–5.

[9] Kelsen, *Introduction to the Problems of Legal Theory* (n 1 above) 8.

[10] Ibid: 'People assemble in a hall, they give speeches, some rise, others remain seated—this is the external event. Its meaning: that a statute is enacted. Or, a man dressed in robes says certain words from a platform, addressing someone standing before him. This external event has as its meaning a judicial decision.'   [11] Ibid, 10.

Kelsen appears to suggest, at least in some of his works, that this simple contrast is sufficient to justify the claim that legal theory must be a normative science; the suggestion being that we can describe human behavior as socially meaningful only if we interpret it from the point of view of a normative legal science.[12] This argument is highly dubious for two reasons. First, Kelsen seems to overlook that we can certainly describe pieces of human behavior as socially meaningful without subsuming them under legal rules. Secondly, even if we accepted the more limited claim that human actions can have a specifically legal meaning only insofar as they fall under objectively valid legal norms, we would certainly not have shown that the existence of such norms cannot be explained in terms of a social practice of one kind or another.[13]

Some of Kelsen's remarks, in any case, make it clear that the distinction between objective and subjective legal meaning responds to a much narrower concern than the explanation of social meaning in general. According to Kelsen, the human actions that we interpret as legally relevant events typically carry a 'self-interpretation'; they are taken to have a certain legal meaning by those who perform them. What Kelsen calls the 'subjective legal meaning' of an act is a self-interpretation of the legal meaning of one's own acts.[14] In other words, it is the legal meaning that an agent intending to perform a legal act attaches to that act, in virtue of his own understanding of the legal norms that apply to the situation in which he acts. Legislators raising their arms do not just happen to enact a law while they scratch their heads. They believe that they are enacting a law, usually motivated by some set of ulterior concerns, and make it known that this is what they take themselves to be doing. Generally speaking, people living under a legal order constantly engage in or avoid actions because they assume that these actions have certain legal consequences and because they expect others to interpret their actions and to react to them accordingly.

However, Kelsen points out that it is often wrong to take subjective legal meaning at face value. People may be mistaken about the legal significance of their own or other's actions. The members of a legislature, for example, may believe that their hand-raising amounted to the enactment of a law. But this belief can clearly be false, say for want of observance of some procedural norm. Needless to say, people's perceptions and public representations of legal meaning may also be distorted by their wants and interests. What is more, some people may have reason deliberately to misrepresent the legal meaning of their acts to others. Finally, even well-intentioned and well-informed agents will, on occasion, disagree about the legal meaning of certain acts. For all these reasons, legal science needs to be able to distinguish between what people believe or claim is the legal meaning of an act and

---

[12] See for an example Kelsen, *Der soziologische und der juristische Staatsbegriff* (n 3 above) 156–70.
[13] See for a detailed critique along these lines Weyma Lübbe, *Legitimität kraft Legalität. Sinnverstehen und Institutionenanalyse bei Max Weber und seinen Kritikern* (Tübingen, 1991) 25–61.
[14] Kelsen, *Introduction to the Problems of Legal Theory* (n 1 above) 9–10.

its true or objective legal meaning.[15] Surely, human actions cannot have whatever normative meaning individual subjects of the law pretend, believe or want them to have if there is to be legal order. Whether an intended legal act objectively succeeds to accomplish its goal, Kelsen argues, must depend on whether a system of valid legal norms does, in fact, attribute a suitable objective meaning to it.[16]

If understood in the narrow fashion just outlined, the need to draw a distinction between objective and subjective legal meaning will hardly be controversial. It is not quite clear, however, exactly what further conclusions we are entitled to draw from this observation. Kelsen argues that a legal theory necessarily has to be a normative science, based on the presupposition of an objectively valid basic norm, in order to be able to draw a successful distinction between subjective and objective legal meaning. The pure theory of law, Kelsen argues, is the only legal theory that lives up to this criterion of adequacy. Forms of positivism that try to explain legal validity in terms of social fact, on the other hand, necessarily fail on this score.[17]

In order to assess the strength of this argument, it is helpful to compare Kelsen's pure theory with Hart's positivism. Hart argues that legal rules are a form of social rules and that their validity is ultimately grounded in a complex matter of social fact.[18] A primary social rule exists, in Hart's view, if and only if the following conditions are met: it is regularly observed by the members of a society; non-compliance is typically met with critical reactions by one's peers; and the rule is used to justify one's own behavior or to criticize that of others. People believe that it is improper not to take off one's hat in church, they regularly do so, they somehow socially sanction those who don't, and they justify this attitude with reference to the rule that one ought to take off one's hat in church. Given these empirical conditions, we can say that the rule that one ought to take off one's hat in church *exists*.[19]

Hart expands this basic account of social rules into a theory of legal system by introducing the concept of a rule of recognition. A rule of recognition provides a conventional standard for the identification of *legally valid* primary rules of obligation as well as for the identification of secondary rules conferring legislative and adjudicative powers. While non-legal social rules exist only if they are practiced as a matter of fact, a legal rule that can be identified in terms of the rule of recognition is *valid*, even if it lacks full social effectiveness, provided it passes the test of validity established by the rule of recognition.[20] The rule of recognition itself, however, exists in much the same way as a simple primary social rule. Hart describes it as 'a complex, but normally concordant, practice of the court's, officials, and private persons in identifying the law by reference to certain criteria'.[21] The claim that

---

[15] Ibid, 9.

[16] See ibid, 11 and 13–14. The pure theory is not concerned with people's intentional attitudes towards valid norms and neither is it to be confused with a legal sociology 'whose task is to enquire into the causes and effects of those natural events that, interpreted by way of legal cognition, are represented as legal acts' (ibid, 13).   [17] See Kelsen, *Reine Rechtslehre* (n 8 above) 4–9, 196–7.

[18] See H L A Hart, *The Concept of Law*, 2nd ed, edited by Penelope Bulloch and Joseph Raz (Oxford, 1994).   [19] See ibid, 54–6.

[20] See ibid, 99–107.   [21] Ibid, 107.

there is a rule of recognition, and hence that there is law, simply states an observable empirical social fact.[22]

Since it conceives of the highest rule of legal system as a de facto social practice and not as an objectively valid norm, Hart's theory fails to qualify as a normative science in Kelsen's sense of the term. But it seems doubtful whether Kelsen is entitled to claim that the theory therefore fails to make sense of the distinction between objective and subjective legal meaning. Hart would presumably agree that the existence of legal order requires that the members of a society or at least its legal officials have the ability to distinguish successfully between what individual subjects of the law claim or believe is the legal meaning of their actions and some socially recognized or 'official' legal meaning of these actions. In fact, the need to draw the distinction motivates Hart's claim that a regime of primary social rules will acquire the status of a legal system only once it is supplemented by secondary rules, including both special rules for the identification of law and rules conferring powers of adjudication. Wherever such rules are available, Hart argues in effect, the requirement of objectivity is satisfied to a sufficient degree.[23]

A Kelsenian is likely to reply that this observation misses part of the point of the distinction between subjective and objective legal meaning. The distinction is not merely concerned with what allows us to *identify* the objective legal meaning of an act. It is also concerned with explaining the normative import of legal acts. To say that a legal act is objectively and not just subjectively valid, according to Kelsen, is to say that it succeeded to enact an 'objectively valid norm that imposes obligations and confers rights upon individuals'.[24] If I succeed, for example, to establish a valid contract I will be objectively justified, in some yet to be specified sense, in raising certain normative claims against the other party. A legal theory that identifies normative analysis with sociological description, according to Kelsen, cannot form the basis of jurisprudence since it will necessarily misrepresent the normative nature of legal discourse in which such claims are raised:

If one deprives the norm or the 'ought' of meaning, then there will be no meaning in the assertions that something is legally allowed, something is legally proscribed, this belongs to me, that belongs to you, X has a right to do this, Y is obligated to do that, and so on. In short, all the thousands of statements in which the life of the law is manifest daily will have lost their significance. For it is one thing to say that A is legally obligated to turn over 1000 talers to B, and quite another to say that there is a certain chance that A will in fact turn over 1000 talers to B. And it is one thing to say that, in terms of a statute, certain behavior is a delict and, in conformity with the statute, is to be punished, and quite another to say that whoever has behaved in this way will in all probability be punished.[25]

---

[22] See for a recent analysis and defense: Jules Coleman, *The Practice of Principle. In Defense of a Pragmatist Approach to Legal Theory* (Oxford, 2001) 74–102.

[23] See Hart, *The Concept of Law* (n 18 above) 89–96.

[24] Hans Kelsen, *The Pure Theory of Law. Translated from the second German edition by Max Knight* (Berkeley, 1970) 103.

[25] Kelsen, *Introduction to the Problems of Legal Theory* (n 1 above) 33.

We may grant Kelsen that the claim that 'A will be forced to pay' does not have the same meaning as the claim that 'A ought to pay'. This argument, however, appears to be insufficient as a criticism of Hart's conception of law since the latter can easily accommodate the irreducibility of statements about valid legal norms to statements about causal relationships. It is only the rule of recognition, according to Hart, that exists as a matter of social fact, as a concordant practice of the identification of law amongst legal officials. The other rules of a legal system are valid in virtue of being identifiable on the basis of the rule of recognition. These dependent norms, moreover, need not be perfectly effective. They remain in force, even if subjects of the law quite regularly violate them, as long as the rule of recognition continues to exist. Hence, when legal practitioners issue statements about such norms, on the basis of the rule of recognition, they do not make causal predictions.[26] Kelsen, I conclude, is not entitled to claim that a practice-based legal theory like Hart's fails to make *any* sense of the normative import of the distinction between objective and subjective legal meaning. Insofar as the necessity for drawing it is uncontroversial, Hart's view appears able to do so. Kelsen is not in a position to claim, therefore, that the pure theory is the only non-naturalist legal theory that will avoid crude reductionism about legal normativity.[27]

However, the fact that an intuitively uncontroversial understanding of the distinction between objective and subjective legal meaning fails to support the pure theory over a Hartian approach does not suffice to establish that Kelsen's understanding of legal normativity lacks adequate motivation. Kelsen, as we will see, reads the distinction in a much more ambitious sense than seems required by the simple and uncontroversial need to avoid total subjectivism about legal meaning. And this more ambitious reading of legal objectivity might yet turn out to be defensible on the basis of a more specific understanding of the point of the distinction between subjective and objective legal meaning.

In what ways, then, is Kelsen's conception of legal normativity ambitious beyond the measure required for drawing a basic objectivity/subjectivity distinction? According to Kelsen, the objective legal meaning of an act needs to be distinguished not just from what this or that individual or group subject to the law takes it to be. Objective legal meaning or the objective validity of legal norms is not explicable in terms of any set of beliefs, attitudes or practices, however widely shared amongst the members of a society or its legal professionals. Someone who assumes the existence of a basic norm is not stating the empirical fact that there is a social practice,

---

[26] See the discussion of the 'idea of obligation' in Hart, *The Concept of Law* (n 18 above) 79–88. Hart acknowledges that 'the predictive interpretation obscures the fact that, where rules exist, deviations from them are not merely grounds for a prediction that hostile reactions will follow or that a court will apply sanctions to those who break them, but are also a reason or justification for such reaction and for applying the sanctions' (ibid, 82).

[27] Stanley L Paulson, 'Introduction' in Kelsen, *Introduction to the Problems of Legal Theory* (n 1 above) xlii. See also Stanley L Paulson, 'The Neo-Kantian Dimension in Kelsen's Pure Theory of Law' in *Oxford Journal of Legal Studies* 12 (1992) 311–32.

in some society, of using rules identified in a certain conventional way as standards of legal evaluation. He is assuming that the basic norm itself—which is not a positive norm since it is not 'created in a legal process, not issued or set'—is objectively valid. What is more, he is assuming that the fact that it validates all other legal norms explains why these norms give rise to obligations while the demands made by a gang of robbers don't.[28] Kelsen claims, moreover, that any legal order possesses a property of completeness. All disputes about the objective legal meaning of human acts falling into the temporal and geographical sphere of validity of a legal order can be decided on the basis of the legal norms contained in that order.[29]

Kelsen clearly has a practical interest in making these two claims. He is interested in defending the absolute normative objectivity and completeness of law because he is worried by the way in which a Hartian legal theory tries to deal with what Hart calls the 'open texture of law'.[30] Hart assumes that the validity of the legal rules that confer legal meaning on particular acts is based on a complex form of de facto agreement concerning the methods of identification and application of law amongst legal practitioners. This agreement may at times fail to provide a clear and agreed-upon answer to the question as to how to legally deal with a particular case. In such a situation, Hart admits, we simply cannot meaningfully distinguish between the subjective and the objective sense of an act on the basis of the law. An exercise of political discretion on the part of judges is needed to fix the legal meaning of acts that take place in a penumbra of uncertainty.[31]

The need for recourse to such discretion may not seem very problematic as long as one is dealing with minor problems that arise from the interpretation of legal rules that undeniably form part of the legal system. But Hart acknowledges, in *The Concept of Law*, that problems of indeterminacy may afflict the rule of recognition itself and thus make it impossible to decide on legal grounds whether, for example, the enactment of a certain kind of statute would be unconstitutional or not.[32] Such cases of constitutional conflict, if they fall into a penumbra of 'uncertainty', will inevitably raise the question of who has the political legitimacy that is needed to exercise the required discretionary authority. And Hart's view, insofar as it suggests that there are no legal answers in such cases, seems to cast a cloud of suspicion on the idea that such a conflict could be decided in the way in which legal conflicts are ordinarily decided, namely by a court *that is taking a legal decision*. Hart believes that

---

[28] See Kelsen, *Introduction to the Problems of Legal Theory* (n 1 above) 56–8; Kelsen, *Reine Rechtslehre* (n 8 above) 45–51.

[29] See ibid, 84–6; Hans Kelsen, 'On the Theory of Interpretation', translated by Bonnie Litschewski-Paulson and Stanley L Paulson, in *Legal Studies* 10 (1990) 127–35, at 132–3; Hans Kelsen, *Law and Peace in International Relations. The Oliver Wendell Holmes Lectures, 1940–41* (Cambridge/Mass, 1942) 159–67; Hans Kelsen, 'Wer soll der Hüter der Verfassung sein?' in Hans Klecatsky, René Marcić, and Herbert Schambeck (eds), *Die Wiener rechtstheoretische Schule. Ausgewählte Schriften von Hans Kelsen, Adolf Julius Merkl und Alfred Verdross* (Wien, 1968) vol II, 1873–912, at 1882–4.

[30] See Hart, *The Concept of Law* (n 18 above) 121–32.   [31] Ibid, 132.

[32] Ibid, 144–50.

such matters 'can be settled only by a choice, made by someone to whose choices in this matter authority is eventually accorded'.[33]

Kelsen's claim that all human acts falling into the temporal and geographical sphere of validity of some legal order have an objective legal meaning entails that none of these acts can bring about any legal effect unless it objectively complies with a norm that attributes that effect to that act. The pure theory denies that any human act or set of human acts can be legally self-certifying.[34] From a Kelsenian perspective, the person in Hart's account 'to whose choices in this matter authority is eventually accorded' must claim to have or at least successfully to exercise the power to turn her own *subjective* intentions into valid law. She must take the view that her decisions have legislative power despite the fact that there is no prior legal rule objectively authorizing that exercise.

Kelsen claims that such exercises of authority—exercises that are not legally authorized yet claim to have legislative power—are inconceivable from a jurisprudential point of view since jurisprudence has to assume, in order to be scientific, that the law comprehensively regulates its own creation and application. Legal theory would not be 'scientific', according to Kelsen, if it gave up on this assumption, just as natural science would cease to be scientific if it started to explain events that do not seem to fit any established theory as discretionary divine interventions into the ordinary natural run of things.[35] Hart's legal theory entails that jurisprudence must accept that an exercise of mere de facto power can have legislative force. When Hart says that, in a constitutional conflict over the meaning of the rule of recognition, 'all that succeeds is success',[36] he is implicitly affirming the dualist idea of a distinction between law and state and thus affirming the view that legal order is not just dependent on, but inevitably subject to the incursions of, a meta-legal purely political power.[37]

The claim of the availability of a legal answer to any dispute falling within the sphere of validity of a legal order is particularly relevant in two areas of law Kelsen was especially concerned with: constitutional law and international law. Kelsen's ambition is to show that there are no jurisprudential reasons to think that some actions of state cannot be fully subjected to the rule of law. He argues that when a state is making the claim that its actions are not justiciable—either in the internal or in the international context—its rulers are merely expressing their unwillingness to accept subjection to the law: an unwillingness that is veiled by an ungrounded appeal to the claim that, unfortunately, the law fails to provide clear guidance. But the claim that the law has 'run out' is never a sufficient reason, Kelsen aims to

---

[33] Ibid, 146.
[34] See Bert Van Roermund, 'Authority and Authorization' in *Law and Philosophy* 19 (2000) 201–22, at 215–19.   [35] See Kelsen, *Der soziologische und der juristische Staatsbegriff* (n 3 above) 219–53.
[36] Hart, *The Concept of Law* (n 18 above) 149.
[37] Kelsen admits that a certain degree of overall effectiveness is a necessary condition for the existence of a legal system. See Kelsen, *Introduction to the Problems of Legal Theory* (n 1 above) 60–3. What he rejects, though, is the idea that there could be valid particular legislative acts that are not authorized by a legal norm.

show, for rejecting submission to legal arbitration since such arbitration is always in principle available once there is a legal order.[38]

Kelsen's standard of legal objectivity, therefore, clearly carries normative implications. Apart from denying the possibility of legally self-certifying powers, it claims that the law contains the resources to settle any social dispute on a legal basis. What is more, it claims that the settlement to be given on a legal basis is not just the settlement that some powerful individual member of society or some powerful group of individual members of society want to see enforced. It is the settlement provided by the law as an objective normative order.

All this raises the question, of course, whether Kelsen is really entitled to reject Hart's view of the limitations of legal order *as a positivist*. It would appear that the pure theory, in order to achieve its aims, will either have to claim that positive law is perfectly determinate, that there is no problem of open texture, or it will have to accept that meta-positive moral standards must necessarily govern our concept of legality whenever open-textured positive rules alone would not be able to ground an objective and determinate legal meaning or an act. Kelsen, needless to say, attempts to reject both options. But is there a third?

Kelsen's theory of legal order

Kelsen's account of legal validity officially rests on the view that causality and normativity are two categorically different yet structurally analogous forms of lawful relatedness of events that constitute two separate realms of reality. Causal or natural laws connect events as causes and effects. To assert that there is some causal law is to say that if an event of a certain kind takes place another event of a certain kind *will* take place. Norms, on the other hand, constitute normative connections between events. To say that a norm exists is to say that if a certain kind of event takes place another event of a certain kind *ought* to take place. Normative assertions, in contrast to causal claims, are not falsified by a failure of the normative consequence to actually obtain. This fundamental categorical distinction between causality and normative attribution or 'imputation', Kelsen claims, is immediately given to consciousness. It is therefore self-evidently impossible to reduce statements about norms to statements about natural laws or to derive 'ought' from 'is'.[39]

Kelsen argues that it is a consequence of the underivability of 'ought' from 'is' that there are only two ways to establish the validity of norms: a norm can be valid in virtue of a validating relation to some other norm, in virtue of its place in a system of norms, or it can be intrinsically valid. All systems of norms, both moral and legal, according to Kelsen, have a hierarchical structure. At the apex of every system of norms we find a basic norm that individuates the system and provides all norms that have membership in the system with normative force. Basic norms are

---

[38] See Kelsen, *Law and Peace in International Relations* (n 29 above) 163–7; Kelsen, 'Wer soll der Hüter der Verfassung sein?' (n 29 above) 1882–4.
[39] See Kelsen, *Introduction to the Problems of Legal Theory* (n 1 above) 22–5.

not dependent on other norms and neither are they reducible to empirical fact. They possess intrinsic validity. The validity, and hence the normativity, of all other norms of a normative system is directly or indirectly dependent on the system's basic norm.[40] The dependence of lower-order on higher-order norms, however, is not of the same kind in moral and legal systems. In the case of a moral system, all norms that form part of the system, Kelsen thinks, are logically entailed by a basic norm that takes the form of some fundamental moral principle treated as a necessary truth, in virtue of its content, by the moral theorist. This means, of course, that in the case of a moral system, it is really the system as a whole that is intrinsically or necessarily valid.[41]

In a legal system, on the other hand, the dependence-relations between the basic norm and the lower order norms are genetic and contingent. A legal system is a dynamic chain of creation ('*Erzeugungszusammenhang*').[42] The basic norm of a legal system, in contrast to the basic norm of a moral system, is not a substantive principle but rather a blanket authorization of the legal system's fundamental legislative procedures.[43] Kelsen emphasizes that the basic norm itself imposes no substantive constraints on the content of the law. It has a 'thoroughly formal, dynamic character'. He claims, moreover, that it is impossible logically to deduce any particular norm that has membership in a legal system from that system's basic norm or from the fundamental legislative procedures it authorizes. Legal norms 'must be created by way of a special act issuing or setting them, an act not of the intellect but of the will'. They are valid if and only if they can be shown to have been enacted in accordance with the basic norm and with the fundamental legislative procedures authorized by it.[44] Since all legal norms other than the basic norm are results of actual exercises of will, Kelsen claims that 'any content whatsoever can be law', regardless of its substantive moral quality.[45]

The basic norm itself, of course, cannot be the result of an enactment since the possibility of valid enactment presupposes authorization given by a norm. Kelsen argues that its objective validity must be assumed or presupposed in order for legal cognition to be possible, in order for it to be possible to interpret the law as normative. To presuppose a basic norm is to accept that the historically first constitution to which the norms of a legal order that is by and large effective can be traced back through an unbroken chain of validity has to be considered as objectively

---

[40] See ibid, 55–8 and Kelsen, *Reine Rechtslehre* (n 8 above) 196–227.

[41] Kelsen, *Introduction to the Problems of Legal Theory* (n 1 above) 55.

[42] Ibid, 56–7. For a very helpful analysis of Kelsen's theory of the structure of legal systems see Joseph Raz, 'Kelsen's Theory of the Basic Norm' in Joseph Raz, *The Authority of Law. Essays on Law and Morality* (Oxford, 1979) 122–45, at 122–7.

[43] See Kelsen, *Introduction to the Problems of Legal Theory* (n 1 above) 56–7.   [44] Ibid, 56.

[45] Ibid. This claim has to be read with care. Kelsen does not assert that any legal system can take any content. Some legal systems may contain unamendable constitutional restrictions that effectively limit the permissible content of the system. Kelsen argues, rather, that any content could become law in some possible legal system. See Hans Kelsen, *Das Problem der Souveränität und die Theorie des Völkerrechts* (Tübingen, 1920) 47–53.

valid and as validating all norms that were created in accordance with it. The basic norm itself demands that coercive force be exercised 'as determined by the framers of the first constitution', namely in accordance with legal rules contained in or derived from the first constitution.[46]

Let us note some important consequences of this picture. Kelsen's theory of the basic norm plays a double role. The basic norm grounds the unity of a legal system and it is the source of the normativity of all norms belonging to the system. Objective validity, or membership in a normative system individuated by a basic norm, is the specific mode of existence of all norms. To say that a norm is valid is to say that it has been enacted in accordance with the legislative procedures authorized by the basic norm. And this is the same thing as to say that it exists, in the only sense in which norms can be said to exist.[47]

Moreover, to show that some directive is a legally valid norm is to give an answer to the question why one ought to act in accordance with the directive, at least on the condition that the validity of the basic norm is presupposed. The recourse to the basic norm provides at least a conditional justification for the demand raised by the validated norm.[48] As Joseph Raz aptly put it, Kelsen's theory of legal validity conceives of legal validity as a species of justified normativity.[49] A conception of legal validity that identifies validity with a form of justified normativity rejects the claim that standards of behavior can be considered as norms regardless of whether they have genuine normative force. Instead, it assumes that 'legal standards of behavior are norms only if and in so far as they are justified'.[50]

However, the thumbnail sketch of Kelsen's theory of legal system offered so far does not explain what sense of 'justification' is in play in the idea of conditional justification just outlined. Moreover, it is hard to see how the basic norm's discharge of either of its two functions helps to sustain Kelsen's claim that the existence of a legal system will endow all human acts falling within its temporal and geographical sphere of validity with an objective legal meaning and hence make all social disputes decidable on a legal basis. The presupposition of the basic norm does not, as

---

[46] See Kelsen, *Introduction to the Problems of Legal Theory* (n 1 above) 56–8 and Kelsen, *Reine Rechtslehre* (n 8 above) 203–4. For a discussion of different interpretations of the act of presupposing a basic norm see Uta Bindreiter, 'Presupposing the Basic Norm' in *Ratio Juris* 14 (2001) 143–75.

[47] Kelsen, *Introduction to the Problems of Legal Theory* (n 1 above) 12.

[48] See ibid, 58 and Kelsen, *Reine Rechtslehre* (n 8 above) 198–200, 202–4.

[49] Raz, *Kelsen's Theory of the Basic Norm* (n 41 above) 134.

[50] Ibid, 134. Raz goes on to claim that Kelsen is committed to the following three claims: 1. Legal validity is a form of justified normativity; 2. an individual subject of the law can consider the law as normative/justified 'only if he endorses it as morally just and good'; and 3. legal science 'considers legal systems as normative in the same sense of 'normative' but in a different sense of 'consider' which does not commit it to accepting the laws as just (134–5). I agree that Kelsen indeed makes the first claim. (For a different view see Bindreiter, 'Presupposing the Basic Norm' (n 46 above) 155–60.) In my view, however, Kelsen does not take it that to consider law as valid is to consider it as 'just and good'. He argues that it is to consider it as *legitimate*. It is true, then, that legal science considers the law as normative in the same sense of 'normative' as the individual. But legal science also considers the law as normative in the same sense of 'consider', namely in a sense that commits it to accepting the law as legitimate, though not as just and good.

Hart pointed out, appear to provide us with any additional criteria, with criteria over and above those contained in a system's rule of recognition or first constitution, for identifying valid law. It therefore seems that the basic norm cannot help us, even if we accept its normative claims, to determine the objective legal meaning of an act where the positive law, as identified along Hartian lines, fails to do so.[51]

Kelsen's theory of legal order, I will now argue, contains a reply to this latter criticism. This reply, I believe, also helps explain what it means to justify a norm by showing its validity. In order to see what the reply is, we need to take a step back from the theory of the basic norm and take a closer look at Kelsen's theory of the structure of legal norms and his conception of legal order.

As we have just seen, the content of the basic norm of a legal system can be expressed, according to Kelsen, by saying that 'coercive force ought to be applied under the conditions and in the manner determined by the framers of the first constitution or by the authorities to whom they have delegated legislative powers'.[52] The specific difference between legal and moral norms, Kelsen claims, is that legal norms authorize the use of coercive force.[53] A complete statement of a legal norm, therefore, is a hypothetical whose antecedent lists the conditions that are legally sufficient for the application of a sanction to some subject of the law and whose consequent specifies the sanction. Legal norms, in their primary form, are not imperatives that directly express the legal duties of subjects of the law. Rather, they are authorizations for the use of coercive force on the part of a society against its individual members that are addressed to legal officials.[54]

Legal duties as we ordinarily understand them are defined by Kelsen in terms of sanction-authorizing norms. Subjects of the law have a legal duty not to perform actions that are conditions for the application of a sanction.[55] All actions that are not explicitly designated as conditions of the application of a sanction are permissible. This view is at least in part motivated by the idea that the law can take any content. It expresses the claim that, from a legal scientific point of view, all illegal actions are illicit because they are forbidden, not forbidden because they are illicit. However, there is one crucial exception to this principle. In many of his writings, Kelsen asserts that the law necessarily claims a monopoly of legitimate force, that it claims that all uses of coercive force not authorized by the law are legally impermissible.[56] Subjects of a legal system are under a general duty to abstain from

---

[51] See H L A Hart, 'Kelsen's Doctrine of the Unity of Law' in H L A Hart, *Essays in Jurisprudence and Philosophy* (Oxford, 1983) 309–48, at 338–9.

[52] Kelsen, *Introduction to the Problems of Legal Theory* (n 1 above) 57–8.

[53] See ibid, 26. For criticism see H L A Hart, 'Kelsen Visited' in H L A Hart, *Essays in Jurisprudence and Philosophy* (n 51 above) 286–308, at 295–301.

[54] Kelsen, *Introduction to the Problems of Legal Theory* (n 1 above) 26. See for further discussion Stanley L Paulson, 'The Weak Reading of Authority in Hans Kelsen's Pure Theory of Law' in *Law and Philosophy* 19 (2000), 131–71, at 139–55.

[55] Kelsen, *Introduction to the Problems of Legal Theory* (n 1 above) 29–30.

[56] See Kelsen, *Law and Peace in International Relations* (n 29 above) 13; Hans Kelsen, *Principles of International Law* (New York, 1952) 13–18; Hans Kelsen, *Peace through Law* (Chapel Hill, 1944) 3–4. Kelsen rejected the view in the second edition of the *Reine Rechtslehre* (n 8 above) 37–8.

unilateral violence against each other. An endorsement of the basic norm of a legal system, thus, is an endorsement of the view that the employment of coercive power is justified if and only if it is authorized by a valid legal norm, by a norm created in accordance with the fundamental constitutional rules mentioned by the basic norm as well as in accordance with the lower-order legal rules dependent on them.

This unstated prohibition of all unauthorized violence, Kelsen argues, grounds the property of completeness. All actions within some legal system's personal, temporal and geographical sphere of authority are either legally permissible, in the sense of not being the condition of the application of a sanction, or impermissible, that is subject to a sanction. There is no such thing as conduct that is permissible in virtue of being exempted from legal regulation; the liberty of subjects of the law depends on the silence of the law. If a legal system exists—however rudimentary and imperfect its body of positive norms—all social disputes are therefore, according to Kelsen, decidable on a legal basis.[57] If faced with a plaintiff's claim, a judge will either determine that there is a positive norm that sustains the claim, ie he will find that some prior action of the defendant fulfills the antecedent of a legal norm and that force ought therefore to be applied against the defendant. Alternatively, the judge will find that there is no such rule and dismiss the claim on the basis of the principle that the law permits everything it does not explicitly forbid. In the face of such a rebuttal, the plaintiff may not take any further action of his own to press his claim against the defendant since all use of force that is not authorized by the legal order is taken to be impermissible.

This notion of completeness needs to be interpreted in the light of Kelsen's account of the *Stufenbau* or hierarchical structure of legal order, a conception that emphasizes the genetic character of the validating relations between norms belonging to a legal system.[58] The doctrine of legal hierarchy portrays legal order, in its dynamic aspect, as a continuous process of law-creation that starts out with the enactment of general legal norms, in accordance with the constitutional rules directly authorized by the basic norm, and that is continued by administrative or judicial decisions which apply the general legal norms enacted by the legislator to particular cases by enacting particular norms. Legal science, when trying to validate a normative legal statement, works in the reverse direction. It traces the particular norms of a legal system back to higher authorizing norms and finally to the basic norm.[59]

The theory of the *Stufenbau* makes two key claims. The first is that the legal content on any level of the legal hierarchy—legislative or adjudicative/administrative—can never be derived from the content of the norms on the higher levels by way of a logical operation. In a legal system, any step from one level of the hierarchy down to the one below, from relative generality to relative particularity, is essentially dependent on actual concretizing human decisions. Legal norms on a higher rung

---

[57] See Kelsen, *Law and Peace in International Relations* (n 29 above) 163–4; Kelsen, *Introduction to the Problems of Legal Theory* (n 1 above) 84–6; Kelsen, 'On the Theory of Interpretation' (n 29 above) 132–3.   [58] See Kelsen, *Introduction to the Problems of Legal Theory* (n 1 above) 55–75.   [59] See ibid, 57.

of the pyramid never fully determine the content of the lower-order norms whose enactment they authorize. They only lay down procedural and material boundary conditions for the valid enactment of lower-order norms. The content of lower-order legal norms is therefore always partly dependent on how the people authorized to apply some set of higher order norms have *chosen* to exercise discretionary powers conferred upon them by legal order. According to Kelsen, this need for discretion characterizes legal systems *all the way down* from the most general constitutional norms to simple administrative orders or particular judicial decisions.[60]

The second, corresponding key claim of the theory of legal hierarchy is that all exercises of power on any level of the hierarchy are, despite their partly discretionary character, governed by authorizing legal norms. Even a legislature can create valid law only by objectively complying with the constitutional rules authorized by the basic norm. Its position, Kelsen claims, does not differ qualitatively from that of a judge who is enacting a particular norm, on the basis of a general legal norm he is authorized to apply to particular cases. The difference between the two cases is one of degree. The legislature has a comparatively larger sphere of freedom of decision. But this does not mean that its acts are not controlled by the law. Valid exercises of authority are always legally limited, since an action can be a valid exercise of authority only as long as it objectively complies with the boundary conditions set by authorizing higher order legal norms.[61]

Since all steps from one level of legal hierarchy down to the next require exercises of authority, legal science cannot determine how the top-down process of law-creation is to unfold. For it to attempt to do so would amount to a confusion of scientific judgment with legislative authority. However, what legal science can do, according to Kelsen, is to ascertain whether a decision proposed or taken by a legislator, judge, or administrator as a matter of fact respects the limits of authority implied by the higher order legal norms under whose authorization the decision maker claims to be acting. A decision is to be considered valid, irrespective of its content, if and only if the decision taker objectively acted within the limits of his authority as defined by the higher-order norms he claims to apply. Kelsen's existence/validity thesis entails that a legal norm can only either be valid, and hence be normative, since it has been enacted in conformity with the norms that authorize its enactment or be null, ie non-existent, for failure of the alleged act of enactment to comply with the applicable authorizing norms. Legal science, then, deals with the question whether purported enactments of norms are successful or not, not with the question whether some authorized decision is a correct or a mistaken exercise of the discretionary element involved in any legal decision.

---

[60] See ibid, 67–8.

[61] See ibid, 70 and Kelsen, *Reine Rechtslehre* (n 8 above) 197: 'Only a competent authority can enact valid norms; and such competence can only be based on a norm that authorizes the enactment of other norms. The authority empowered to enact norms is subject to the norm that empowers it, as much as the individuals who are under an obligation to obey the norms the authority enacts.' [my translation]

Let me now take a second stab at the question I raised at the end of the previous section. As we have seen, Kelsen works with a notion of legal objectivity that claims that *all* disputes about the objective legal meaning of acts taking place in the temporal and geographical sphere of authority of a legal system, and not just those easily subsumable under determinate material norms, can be decided on a legal basis. The theory of the basic norm on its own, however, seemed to provide no help in understanding this claim. Our analysis of the doctrine of legal hierarchy, I will now argue, puts us into a better position to see how the pure theory wants to sustain its strong conception of objective legal meaning.

It is clear that Kelsen does not defend completeness either by making the claim that the positive law as a system of general rules is perfectly determinate or by embracing a view that allows judges to rely on moral principles that cannot be shown to have been enacted as law. Rather, what might have seemed to be a claim to perfect determinacy of legal meaning turns out, on closer inspection, to be a claim to the perfect *determinability* of legal meaning through the progressively concrete and always partly discretionary decisions enacted by a hierarchy of decision-takers corresponding to the hierarchy of legal norms. The objectivity of legal meaning is guaranteed by the fact that any dispute about the legal meaning of a human act is decidable under proper authorization from the basic norm. The open texture of law, then, does not impose an outer limit on the scope of legal objectivity, as suggested by theories that distinguish between adjudicative activity in a core of determinacy, in which judges enforce objective material legal standards, and adjudicative activity in a penumbra of uncertainty in which judges make law under the formal authority conferred by jurisdictional norms. The open texture of law, rather, is grist for the mill of the exercise of the legislative powers conferred by the first constitution, that exercise being understood as a process of progressive concretization of law that routinely takes place on all levels of legal hierarchy.

These observations, I believe, provide us with a clue as to the nature of the relation between validity and justification that guides Kelsen's seemingly extravagant reading of the objectivity/subjectivity distinction. Kelsen made the claim, to recall, that only his normative science of law is able to make sense of normative statements like 'A is legally obligated to pay 1,000 talers to B'. Taking into account the theory of legal hierarchy, I now want to contrast Kelsen's understanding of the normative import of such statements with Hart's as well as Raz's by asking what makes such a statement true in each view.

Hart's account of what it means for A to be under a legal obligation to pay would presumably focus on the general material legal rule that is applied in a court's judgment that A ought to pay. What it means to say that A is under a legal obligation to pay is that there is a valid legal rule, identifiable on the basis of the rule of recognition, from which a judge can infer with sufficient clarity that A, given the situation at hand, is legally required to make the payment. Given the existence of such a sufficiently determinate rule, the existence of the obligation is not dependent on whether a judge in fact orders A to pay the money. If the judge takes a decision determined by a general legal rule he is not exercising authority or discretion. Rather, the judge's decision will be legally correct or mistaken depending on whether it tracks or fails to track A's obligations. In the rare cases in which a sufficiently determinate rule does not exist, the discretionary decision the judge ends up taking will not be interpretable as the enforcement of a legal duty. While it may be formally legal in virtue of the fact that the judge is institutionally empowered to decide the issue, his decision will, in effect, create law.[62]

The fact that a decision has been taken in accordance with a sufficiently determinate general rule, however, tells us little, according to Hart, about the question whether the decision is morally justified.[63] Should it turn out to be true that A ought to perform his legal obligation to pay, all things considered, this will be so only because the rule happens to be morally justifiable from an external perspective. If a judge decides a case that is not determined by a general rule, the normative quality of his decision will depend on the soundness of his moral judgment. But in neither case will the material or formal legality of the judge's decision be sufficient to morally justify its content.

In Raz's view, the normativity of the law is a particular instance of the wider phenomenon of practical authority. A person will have practical authority over another, according to Raz, if their relationship satisfies the 'normal justification thesis', ie if it is the case that 'the alleged subject is likely better to comply with reasons which apply to him (other than the alleged authoritative directives) if he accepts the directives of the alleged authority as authoritatively binding and tries to follow them, rather than by trying to follow the reasons which apply to him directly'.[64]

If applied to the law, Raz argues, this general conception of authority can explain (as Hart's, according to Raz, cannot)[65] how the fact that a course of action is required by a legally valid directive can make a practical difference to those subject to the law. A norm is legally valid, according to Raz, if and only if it has membership, as determined on the basis of social sources, in a legal system. The law, moreover, necessarily claims that all legally valid norms are the results of valid exercises of practical authority. This claim need not always be justified. But to the extent that it is, the fact of the existence of a legally valid norm will constitute an exclusionary reason for action applying to some subject of the law, a reason that would not exist were it not for the actual enactment of the norm.[66]

Raz's normal justification thesis implicitly claims that the ultimate source of justified legal authority is always a person or institution whose decisions are identifiable, on the basis of a source-based test, as valid legal norms. To say that the law claims or possesses authority can only mean that the persons or institutions who

---

[62] See H L A Hart, 'Positivism and the Separation of Law and Morals' in H L A Hart, *Essays in Jurisprudence and Philosophy* (Oxford, 1983) 49–87, at 62–72.

[63] See ibid, 72–8.   [64] Joseph Raz, *The Morality of Freedom* (Oxford, 1986) 53.

[65] See Joseph Raz, *Practical Reason and Norms* (Princeton, 1990) 56–8.

[66] See ibid, 127–9.

enact the law claim or possess authority since only persons or institutions can make practical judgments on our behalf and take decisions on the basis of these judgments. For this reason, I will henceforth refer to Raz's conception of authority as a personal conception of authority.[67]

Whether persons or institutions enacting law possess justified authority depends, according to the normal justification thesis, on whether their decisions are more likely to lead us to conformity with the demands of reason than would decisions taken by ourselves. Let us assume that the normal justification thesis is justified with respect to the relationship between some person or institution formally authorized to enact law and some subject or group of subjects of the law. In this case, positive standards of legal validity will be needed to identify valid exclusionary reasons for action that apply to subjects of the law. But the fact that some decision was taken in accordance with the legal standards that allow us to identify its outcome as *legally valid* does not suffice to establish the existence of a valid exclusionary reason unless the normal justification thesis is satisfied on independent grounds. Legality, in other words, mediates antecedent relationships of authority between persons or persons and institutions, but it does not by itself constitute a ground of justified normativity.

The statement that A, according to the law, ought to pay 1,000 talers to B, is true, according to Raz, if there is a legally valid norm applicable to the situation from which we can infer, with sufficient determinacy, that A ought to pay. The statement will express a valid exclusionary reason, and thus make a practical difference, if the legislator who enacted the law has personal authority with respect to the persons affected by the law. As in Hart, a judge applying the law to the particular case is not, at least not usually, exercising authority. He is guided by the law in the same way as its primary subjects. If we are faced with cases in which a judge cannot arrive at a determinate decision on the basis of already existing law, we may have to ask whether the judge himself has personal authority with respect to the particular decisions he is to take. But such cases are, once again, considered untypical. In neither case, however, is legality itself a source of justified normative authority. It never does more than to communicate directives of persons or institutions whose status as practical authorities needs to be established on independent grounds.

Kelsen's conception of legal order leads to a picture different from both Hart's and Raz's view. For Kelsen, A's legal obligation to pay 1,000 talers to B exists *because* a particular norm ordering him to pay has been *validly enacted* by a judge and thus forms part of the legal system. The enactment of this particular norm is authorized by some more general norm under which the judge subsumes the case at hand, a

---

[67] See the personalist formulations of the normal justification thesis in Raz, *The Morality of Freedom* (n 64 above) 53 and Raz, 'Authority, Law, and Morality' in Joseph Raz, *Ethics in the Public Domain* (n 2 above) 210–37, at 214. For a defense of Raz's personalist approach to authority see Andrei Marmor, 'Authority and Authorship' in Andrei Marmor, *Positive Law and Objective Values* (Oxford, 2001) 89–111.

norm whose creation can, in turn, be traced back to the basic norm. But since any step from one level of legal hierarchy to the next in turn involves a fresh exercise of authority, the existence of A's legal obligation can never exclusively depend, as it usually will in Hart, on the content of the general legal rule applied by the court. Rather, Kelsen's theory of legal order emphasizes that the particular norm as well as the more general norm that authorized its enactment are both members of a chain of partly discretionary yet legally limited decisions that were taken in accordance with the basic norm, and thus in accordance with a comprehensive normative scheme for regulating the use of coercive force in a society.

This thesis has implications for the relation of validity and justification. For Hart, as we have seen, the moral justification of a legal obligation enforced or created by a particular decision can be reduced to an assessment of the substantive moral quality of the political decisions of a legislator or of the judge, if the latter is deciding in the penumbra. Kelsen's rejection of a qualitative distinction between legislation and application of law, however, entails that we can never reduce our justificatory assessment of the particular decision ordering A to pay to an assessment of either the moral quality of the content of the general norm it applies or the moral quality of an exercise of discretion on the part of the judge. The first reduction is impossible because the content of the higher order general norm does not fully determine the particular decision. The higher order norm, moreover, is not a pure exercise of political power. It was itself enacted in accordance with yet higher constitutional norms that forge a link to the basic norm. The general law's constitutional legality may therefore bear on its justification, and thus indirectly on the justification of any particular enactment authorized by it. The reduction to the moral quality of a judge's exercise of discretion is impossible because any particular decision, even while being legally underdetermined, is taking place within a guiding and authorizing framework set by higher order norms.

In other words, our assessment of the normative quality of any particular decision cannot abstract from the fact that the norm in question forms part of a legal system, that it was enacted in accordance with the conditions set by all higher order legal norms that form part of the chain leading back to the basic norm. When we say, on Kelsenian grounds, that A ought to pay 1,000 talers to B, and when we validate this claim by recourse to a basic norm, we bring into play the legal system as a whole, as well as the fact of membership of the particular norm in that whole. We make the claim, in other words, that the norm's membership in a legal system always has a *sui generis*, content-independent significance from a normative point of view. Kelsen's claim to completeness, raised on behalf of legal order, and his idea of justification through recourse to a basic norm, thus, are linked in the following way: Someone who presupposes a basic norm accepts the claim that any valid legal norm, including any valid particular norm, ought to be considered as justified, regardless of its content, in virtue of the fact that its enactment took place in accordance with the conditions which higher order legal norms impose upon the possibility of tracing it back to the basic norm.

Kelsen's understanding of the normativity of law, needless to say, marks a distinction not just from Hart but also from Raz. Both views overlap to some extent insofar as they both claim that the fact of membership of a norm in a legal system, as ascertained on the basis of pedigree, may have a *sui generis* normative significance. But while Raz claims that legal norms have authority if they are enacted by persons or institutions who do not just claim but who actually possess practical authority on independent grounds, Kelsen argues that decisions taken by persons and institutions are justified, regardless of their content, as long as legal science can show them to have been properly authorized by a basic norm. If they are so authorized they give rise to obligations regardless of whether those who validly enacted any of the norms involved in the relevant chain of validity possess personal authority in a Razian sense. For Kelsen, it is legality itself that transfers content-independent normativity on decisions taken in accordance with the basic norm instead of merely transmitting a personal authority attributable to those who enact the law. The normative authority of persons and institutions depends on the law and not the other way around.

Hart's and Raz's views are animated by a conventional distinction between political and legal decisions Kelsen consciously rejects. According to this conventional view, law is *created* by political decision-takers in the form of general rules and then *applied* by judges who, at least in the large majority of cases, need not and ought not engage in political decision taking. What happens once we move outside of the core of determinate relationships between a general rule and its particular instantiations is only of limited jurisprudential concern. What justified normativity we can attribute to particular decisions determined by general norms, on the other hand, will for the most part result from either the substantive moral correctness of the general norm or from the personal authority of the legislator. Any story about the justification of the law will have to be located on the political side of the legal-political divide. Legal order itself, to the extent that general law is determinate, can do little more than to preserve whatever normativity legislative decisions possess in virtue of their moral correctness or in virtue of their having been enacted by personal authorities.

Kelsen's project, by contrast, aims to domesticate politics by integrating it fully into a legal framework, a framework that at least has the potential to ensure that political decisions will be more than mere exercises of arbitrary power.[68] The pure

---

[68] For a different reading of Kelsen's theory of legal hierarchy and his conception of the structure of legal norms see Paulson, 'The Weak Reading of Authority' (n 54 above) 139–55. Paulson takes the view that Kelsen's empowerment conception of legal norms tends to conflict with his normativism. Legal norms, in their primary form as authorizations for the use of coercive force, are addressed to legal officials. Yet, Kelsen normativism is clearly assuming that norms, in some sense, bind or oblige subjects of the law. But they certainly cannot have that force if all they do is to authorize officials to apply sanctions. The approach proposed here assumes that authorizing norms do not just empower officials. They also, at least potentially, put limitations on exercises of authority that can play a power-constraining role. Insofar as they do, they are not just addressed to officials but also to citizens who have an interest in the question whether exercises of official power remain within their proper constraints. A conception of

theory as a normative science, as we will see, is *needed* to make sense of the normative claims of the sovereign state, understood as a legal hierarchy, to the obedience
of its subjects *as claims grounded in legality*. The pure theory is *possible*; it is more
than a mere ideology, if we can reasonably assume that legality is at least potentially more than an instrument of power and hence capable of sustaining the normative authority of the state. Kelsen, on the interpretation I will offer, argues that
the state's claim to obedience can make sense only if we understand that claim as a
claim based on an appeal to an ideal of the rule of law.

Kelsen and theoretical anarchism: The pure theory as critique of ideology

Let me try to further support my claim that Kelsen is committed to offering a normative argument about the justificatory power of the rule of law by taking a look
at Kelsen's defense of the pure theory against theoretical anarchism or the 'denial
of the ought'. This defense, I will now argue, will only make sense if it is understood as part of a normative political-theoretical argument.

A denier of the ought, Kelsen claims, tries to reduce the existence of a legal
norm, for example of the norm forbidding theft, to a set of 'determinations of fact'.
These include the observation that 'some people try to induce others to forbear
from theft or to punish thieves, and that people, by and large, do forbear from theft
and do punish thieves'. Kelsen says, in almost Fullerian language, that this perspective 'sees in the law (as in the connection between human beings who make the
law and who carry it out) an enterprise comparable, say, to that of a hunter who
sets out bait to lure game into a trap' and he claims that such a view 'consciously
ignores the normative meaning that accompanies lawmaking acts'.[69]

According to the denier, the use of normative legal language has to be considered
as 'ideological' and 'unscientific' because there is no normative meaning of lawmaking acts. The denier claims that 'as "reality"—and so as the object of scientific
cognition—there is only the physico-psychical event subject to the law of cause
and effect, that is to say, there is only nature'.[70] Kelsen acknowledges that legal
norms would not exist, in his technical sense that equates existence with validity, if
we could not reasonably attribute a normative meaning to lawmaking acts. Such
a normative meaning, as we have seen, cannot be grounded in natural reality. But
if legal norms did not exist in the mode of objective validity, there could be no
autonomous legal science that describes the objective normative meaning of human
acts falling under valid legal norms.

---

obligation can be developed indirectly: the rights and duties of subjects of the law that are implied by
primary sanction authorizing norms will bind to the extent that the primary norms constitute a system
of constraints on the official exercise of coercive power that legitimizes properly authorized exercises of
power.

[69] Kelsen, *Introduction to the Problems of Legal Theory* (n 1 above) 32. See also Hans Kelsen, *Reine
Rechtslehre* (n 8 above) 107–13.

[70] Kelsen, *Introduction to the Problems of Legal Theory* (n 1 above) 33.

This may at first glance seem somewhat too sweeping an argument to be all that interesting. But the denier of legal normativity does not claim that we cannot reasonably talk about norms from a scientific point of view because all that really exists are particles of matter in motion. Recall Kelsen's broad notion of natural science. It encompasses all sciences that work with the category of causality, and Kelsen himself clearly includes in this category disciplines like empirical sociology and psychology. The denier is fully entitled to draw upon the resources of these sciences in formulating his attack. Hence, he should not have a problem admitting that what we call 'law' exists as a social practice in something like the Hartian sense. His challenge arises from the fact that law that exists as an actual social practice can be described from two different perspectives: an empirical socio-psychological perspective based on the category of causality and a normative perspective based on the postulation of a basic norm. The denier's attack draws its strength from the suspicion that the descriptions offered from these two perspectives might turn out to be incompatible.

A scientist analyzing law from a naturalist perspective will try to offer a causal explanation for why people engage in the social practice that we commonly think of as a legal practice. What the denier claims when he says that normative legal science is an ideology is that the best causal explanation for the existence of legal practices available to us may turn out to make it impossible for someone who accepts it as true to continue reasonably to apply Kelsen's normative perspective to legal phenomena. A causal explanation of legal practices will not just refer to the kinds of facts that Hart claims *define* what it means for a social practice of law to exist. The explanation will also address the motivating beliefs held by the participants in the practice and employ them to causally explain their rule-following behavior.[71] The problem of incompatibility arises because we cannot rule out that this inquiry into the genesis of the beliefs that underpin people's actual law-abiding behavior will lead to the conclusion that the best causal explanation for why people hold these beliefs and hence engage in legal practices is one that will show these beliefs to be a form of false consciousness. In this case, Kelsen seems to assume, the denier would be justified in his refusal to see in the law 'anything but naked power'.[72]

Let us assume that we are looking at a society in which de facto power and access to opportunities and goods are distributed unequally between a favored and a disfavored group.[73] Let us assume further that the members of the disfavored group nevertheless accept the legitimacy of the system. They may believe that the system treats them unjustly, but they also acknowledge that they are under an obligation to obey the system's laws. The favored group is playing by some set of legal rules that are, for the most part, impartially applied and that are justified by a justificatory

---

[71] See ibid, 13–14 and 31.

[72] Ibid, 34. See also Kelsen, *Reine Rechtslehre* (n 68 above) 107–8, where the denier is identified as a Marxist legal sociologist who claims that the normative interpretation of law serves a class-interest.

[73] The following is inspired by Bernard Williams, *Truth and Truthfulness. An Essay in Genealogy* (Princeton, 2002) 225–32.

narrative that enjoys a certain degree of acceptance even amongst members of the disfavored group.

A critic might suspect that the disfavored group's acceptance of the idea that it has an obligation to obey the law is nothing but a result of the unequal distribution of power and hence of no legitimating effect. The acceptance may, for example, be a causal effect of indoctrination that objectively serves the interests of the powerful. That a belief in the legitimacy of the system is a causal effect of indoctrination does not entail, one might reply, that the belief must be false. Let us therefore assume further that there is no remotely plausible explanation of the acceptance, on the part of members of the disfavored group, of a belief in the law's normativity which does not involve the fact that this belief has the causal effect of stabilizing the unequal distribution of power. Members of the disfavored group couldn't have acquired a belief in the system's legitimacy in any other way than through indoctrination that serves the ruling class's interest. Those who accept the normativity of law under these conditions as members of a disfavored group, we can assume, would not do so if they were aware of these causal facts or if they were psychologically capable to face up to them.

Kelsen's denier claims that any normative interpretation of a legal system must fail this test. He is not just saying that some legal systems are predominantly unjust instruments of arbitrary power and that part of the reason why they are nevertheless stable is that they are bolstered by ideologies that engender irrational obedience to their law. The denier claims that legal science itself is an ideology because the legal systems to which it invariably attributes normativity are nothing but structures of domination that systematically favor the subjective interest of one group over that of another. The pure theory's normative interpretation of the law, hence, never offers more than a veneer of respectability for unjustifiable brute facts of power.

The most obvious positivist strategy for defending legal science against this claim, of course, is to argue that legal science only describes but does not endorse the normative claims of the law. If one takes such a view one can go on to argue that the anarchist may be right in his assessment that any explicit or implicit appeal to a general duty to obey the law (that is to paper over disagreement about the law's lack of substantive merits) is ideological in character. The fact that a system, just or unjust, can be described as normative from an 'internal point of view' has no bearings on the moral question whether its decisions are to be considered as justifiable exercises of political power and it is therefore wrong to claim that legal science will necessarily be complicit in whatever injustice the described system may happen to be guilty of.

It is not quite clear whether Kelsen adopts this standard positivist reply. At least on the face of it, there seems to be a good reason not to attribute it to him. The standard positivist solution just outlined makes theoretical anarchism fully compatible with a non-reductive account of legal normativity. But once the two positions are taken to be compatible, the fact that it is possible or even necessary to describe law as normative from some internal perspective will not suffice to show that there is anything wrong with thinking of law, at the same time, as the practice of setting out bait to lure people into a trap.[74]

Kelsen, however, clearly does believe that the challenge of the theoretical anarchist needs to be taken more seriously than this. He clearly takes it that legal science will be more than an ideology only if it is entitled to make a general attribution of justified normativity to the law. And it is hard to see how the claim that legal science is so entitled could fail to carry a commitment to the view that the law itself is something more than the mere expression of a will to power, that any political system—insofar as it can coherently be described as a legal order—embeds considerable moral value.

Let us take a closer look, then, at Kelsen's defense of the pure theory against the charge that it is an ideology. This defense draws a distinction between two different senses of the term 'ideology'. On the one hand, the term may be used to describe a gap between natural and normative reality. The pure theory is concerned with the immanent meaning, the '*Eigengesetzlichkeit*' or internal lawful structure, of systems of norms. This makes it into an ideology, Kelsen admits, insofar as it is concerned with a system of normative facts to which natural reality will never fully correspond. In a second, pejorative sense the term 'ideology' refers to a system of thought that is rooted 'in will, not in cognition'.[75] In this second sense, an ideology does not refer to anything that has objective reality. Rather, it 'veils reality by transfiguring or distorting it'. The denier of the ought, of course, claims that the pure theory is an ideology in this second sense. He claims that its conception of objective legal meaning does not refer to anything real. It merely serves the interests of a ruling class that wants to see the social status quo protected. But this, Kelsen claims, is an unconvincing charge against the pure theory.

Kelsen presents two main arguments to rebut charge that the pure theory is an ideology in the pejorative sense. First, he points out that a normative science of law serves a legitimate intellectual purpose. As long as there is law, there is a legitimate need for a dogmatic jurisprudence serving legal professionals. This dogmatic jurisprudence is a normative discourse, describing people's legal rights and obligations, which cannot be reduced to a legal sociology. But the denier of the 'ought', it seems, is barred from participating in this discourse. He cannot describe the normative situation that obtains in our example by saying that 'A ought to pay 1,000 talers to B' because he claims to know that statements like this cannot possibly be true. What it means for such a statement to be true, in Kelsen's view, is that A ought to pay 1,000 talers to B because this is required by a valid legal norm. But the denier takes the view that it cannot be the case that one ought to do something because it is required by the law since there are no legal norms that exist in the mode of validity.[76]

---

[74] See Matthew Kramer, *In Defense of Legal Positivism. Law without Trimmings* (Oxford, 1999) 78–112.
[75] Kelsen, *Introduction to the Problems of Legal Theory* (n 1 above) 19.   [76] See ibid, 34–5.

Kelsen's second reply to the charge of ideology is to put emphasis on the fact that the pure theory is a positive theory of law. As a theory of positive law, the pure theory 'preserves its anti-ideological stance by seeking to isolate representations of the positive law from every natural law ideology of justice'.[77] The pure theory, Kelsen explains, describes the law as it is, not as it ought to be, and it refrains from evaluating the content of the law in the light of any substantive conception of justice. It therefore prevents an uncritical identification of existing law with a higher, morally correct law. The fact that the pure theory's attribution of normativity to the law does not justify the content of the law as just and good, then, saves it from the charge of being a mere ideology.

Do these arguments show that Kelsen was embracing the standard positivist solution I outlined above, namely that legal science cannot be called an ideology because it only describes, while it does not endorse, the normative claims of the law? Or do they suggest that the pure theory must be based on the assumption that there is necessarily some value in legal normativity?

With respect to the first argument, the answer depends on whether or not the use of normative legal language, the participation in a normative legal discourse, must go along with an endorsement of the normative claims of the law. If so, the claim that there is a demand for a dogmatic jurisprudence as long as there is law will not suffice to rebut the challenge of the denier. After all, the denier argues that the law itself is nothing but an instrument of unjust oppression and that we would be better off without it. Hence, he should not be worried by the fact that his view bars him from participating in a discourse that maintains the fiction that law is something other than an expression of unjust power. This challenge can only be met by a substantive argument that shows that the law is not merely an instrument of oppression and that there are reasonable grounds to endorse its normative claims and to presuppose a basic norm.

One might argue, in reply, that the use of normative legal language does not necessarily have to go along with an endorsement of the law's normative claims. Even while normative legal language is ordinarily used in ways that express endorsement, legal science uses normative legal language in a special, normatively uncommitted way. Hence, it cannot be accused of being an ideology that lends a helping hand to an unjust system of power. This solution has undoubted support in Kelsen's oeuvre. The clearest instance is Kelsen's claim, in the second edition of the *Reine Rechtslehre*, that there could be an anarchist law professor who uses normative legal language without endorsing the law's normativity. This professor might explicitly tell his students that he believes that no legal system's normative claims could ever merit endorsement. But he could still be a competent teacher of the law, using normative legal statements in a detached sense or from a 'legal point of view' while teaching the internal workings of the law.[78]

---

[77] Ibid, 35–6.   [78] See Kelsen, *Reine Rechtslehre* (n 68 above) 224.

This argument is clearly insufficient to defend the pure theory as a science separable from all evaluative concerns. The anarchist professor is committed to the view that the ordinary practice of using normative legal statements, which endorses the claims of the law, is fundamentally misguided. He takes it that it is ideological in the pejorative sense and that our society would therefore be better off if it were altogether discontinued. He believes that the true meaning of the practice is not what ordinary people take it to be and that they would stop to use normative legal statements if they understood this. And if people stopped to continue the practice, there would of course no longer be any occasion for a scientist to use normative legal statements in a detached or uncommitted sense. These facts put considerable pressure on the idea that the pure theory can be defended against the charge of being ideological by withdrawing from any endorsement of the normative claims it attributes to the law.

To use Kelsen's own analogy, there could be an anarchist law professor only in the sense in which there could be a competent teacher of dogmatic theology at some Catholic university who believed that Catholic theology, despite its admirable internal coherence, is ultimately nothing but a silly superstition derived from a series of literary forgeries. The religious practice based on this superstition might well have need of a dogmatic theology, just as the law has a need of dogmatic jurisprudence. But our professor would presumably nevertheless believe that everyone would be better off if they came to acknowledge the fictitious nature of this dogmatic theology. He would certainly not think of himself as teaching a science and he would not believe that the fact that Catholic theology possesses some measure of internal coherence suffices to protect it from the charge of being an ideology. What is more, he would have to ask himself whether he is not contributing, against his will, to the preservation of a system of belief which undermines people's autonomy.

The same considerations apply to the anarchist law professor. There could be an anarchist who is a competent teacher of law. But if his view of the law were correct, he could not take himself to be teaching a science. The anarchist professor's own activity of analyzing the internal workings of the law would be parasitical, in his view, on the regrettable fact that ordinary members of his society continue to believe in the objective existence of entities (valid norms) that are no more real than witches and fairies. Hence, the defense of the pure theory from the charge of ideology cannot proceed from his perspective. It will still have to come to rest on an argument that shows that we can reasonably attribute justified normativity to the law by presupposing a basic norm.

Kelsen's second rebuttal of the charge of ideology, I believe, can be read in a way that supports this conclusion. At first glance, this may seem to be a surprising claim. Kelsen argues that his version of the separation of law and morality insulates the pure theory from the denier's attack. But Kelsen's point here, as we will see, need not be that we can save legal theory from the charge of being complicit in whatever abuses take place by the use of legal means by denying that the law has any normative authority. Rather, Kelsen can be interpreted as saying that it is possible to attribute normativity to the form of law without having to claim that its content conforms to some controversial conception of substantive justice. That a norm has been enacted as law does not establish that it is substantively just. Conversely, that an enacted norm is unjust does not speak against its validity or normativity. The core of Kelsen's separation thesis, under this interpretation, is not that law cannot claim any normative authority. It is that one can consider legal norms as normative, in virtue of the fact that they can be traced back to a basic norm, without considering them as just and good.

Let me conclude. If Kelsen is concerned to give a satisfactory answer to the theoretical anarchist, he must provide some positive explanation of why we are justified to presuppose a basic norm and to endorse the normative authority this presupposition attributes to the form of law. This positive explanation, I believe, can only be based on the contribution that legality makes to the legitimacy of political power exercised in lawful fashion. Kelsen's argument against the denier of the ought, then, is inseparable from his positive political-theoretical project.

Conclusions on Law and Nature

The interpretation of Kelsen's analysis of legal validity offered here has stressed that the strong notion of legal objectivity which the pure theory attributes to the law results from the ambition to offer an account of the legitimate state. It is meaningful only if we can reasonably attribute to legal order the claim to be a justified comprehensive ordering of the social use of coercive force. To presuppose a basic norm, in short, is to postulate that exercises of coercive force that take place under the authorization of that basic norm are, in some sense and to some extent, morally justified. Without this assumption, Kelsenian normative legal science would be pointless.

I have emphasized that something is amiss with what I have called Kelsen's official defense of the theory of the basic norm. It is undeniable that Kelsen sometimes argues in a way that seems designed to avoid having to defend the normative commitments that appear to be implicit in his criticism of the theoretical anarchist. Kelsen's official argument, as we have seen, starts out from the claim that we need to draw a distinction between the subjective and the objective legal meaning of human acts as well as between causal and normative reality. It claims that assuming an objectively valid basic norm is the only possible means of drawing these distinctions and hence a necessary condition of the possibility of legal 'cognition'. The anarchist denies that there is legal cognition, but there is legal cognition, therefore the anarchist is wrong.

But of course, all depends on what we understand by 'legal cognition'. When Kelsen says that law does not exist from the point of view of someone who refuses to assume the validity of a basic norm, he cannot really be making the claim that such a person would not be able to recognize as such what we would consider the legal practices of a society. The problem raised by the 'denier of the ought' can arise only if we are in a position to make sense of the alternative of either attributing or refusing to attribute normative authority to a social practice that we can already identify as legal from a descriptive point of view. But if we can already make sense of some practice as legal from a descriptive point of view, we will be able to operate with *some* distinction between individual subjective and socially recognized legal meaning and it will hence appear that the theory of the basic norm is not needed to make sense of the objectivity of law. Or, put more precisely, it will appear so unless we attribute to the law a normative ambition that positivists are usually unwilling to embrace.

Hart assumes, just like the theoretical anarchist, that we can identify legal practices on the basis of an empirical concept of law that refers to certain kinds of social facts. But he rejects an assumption that Kelsen and his theoretical anarchist share, namely the view that we must be able to make a general attribution of justified normativity to the law and show that this attribution stands up to a critique of ideology in order for legal science to be possible and for legal practice to be meaningful. For Hart, the question whether a reasonable citizen should endorse the law or not is contingent on the moral quality of the goals it is made to serve by those who determine its content. The anarchist's problem, therefore, does not even arise since Hart's concept of law no longer attributes normative authority to the law *qua* law. Analogous observations apply, as we have seen, to Raz's conception of legal normativity as personal authority. In both conceptions, the question of justification is outsourced from jurisprudence to normative political theory.

But the comparison so far between Kelsen and Hart/Raz suggests that this outsourcing comes at a price. Hart's and Raz's views implicitly entail an approval of the dualist separation of law and state or between the law as a system of norms and the institutions that bindingly apply those norms. A theory of the law, Hart and Raz claim, cannot also be a theory of the state because the unity of legal order presupposes the prior unity of state.[79] Both thus give up on an ambition Kelsen thinks we must attribute to the law in order to engage in legal science, namely that positive legal order, by providing a comprehensive organization of power that prevents arbitrary exercises of power, can generate a framework for the legitimate settlement of *all* social disputes. Dualist theories of the law-state relationship assume, by contrast, that positivist jurisprudence rests on the presupposition that the fundamental 'problem of social order' has already been solved and the law, in any case, cannot contribute to its solution.[80]

The proposal I want to make is that Kelsen's legal theory must be understood as a refusal to accept this limitation. The pure theory contains a genuinely normative strand of thought not based on the implausible idea that the basic norm is needed to establish the possibility of the cognition of the law as an actual social practice.

---

[79] See Hart, *Kelsen's Doctrine of the Unity of Law* (n 50 above) 335–6 and Joseph Raz, 'The Identity of Legal Systems' in Joseph Raz, *The Authority of Law. Essays on Law and Morality* (Oxford, 1979) 78–102, at 97–100.

[80] See David Dyzenhaus, *Legality and Legitimacy. Carl Schmitt, Hans Kelsen, and Hermann Heller in Weimar* (Oxford, 1997) 16.

According to this strand, the presupposition of a basic norm is needed not to allow us to recognize law from a descriptive point of view but rather to make sense of what Kelsen takes to be its normative aspirations.

Nothing I have said so far, I hasten to add, should be considered as an argument for the view that a legal theory must accept the view of the normativity of law that I take to be implicit in Kelsen's approach. The defense of the pure theory's conception of legal normativity ultimately rests on the way in which Kelsen integrated it with a theory of the rule of law, of democracy, and of adjudication. In the upcoming chapters, I want to focus on this attempt to integrate legal and political theory, at the expense of what I have called Kelsen's 'official' view. But before I can do so, I have to answer two obvious questions. What remains of Kelsen's positivism, of his separation of law and justice, once one adopts the normative reading of the pure theory I proposed? Second, what is the exact sense in which law is, according to Kelsen, normative?

II Law and Morality

Kelsen claims that legal norms exist insofar as they are valid. He believes, according to the reading I suggested, that the validity of a norm entails that it is, in some sense, justifiable. This view, of course, would appear to conflict openly with Kelsen's second condition of purity or scientific standing, the separation of law and morality. In what follows, I want to argue that my interpretation can leave room for Kelsen's understanding of the separation of law and morality. The pure theory's separation of law and morality, or, as Kelsen frequently puts it, of law and absolute justice, has a much more limited meaning than to deny any necessary relation between law and morality. But this limited meaning suffices to explain why Kelsen put heavy emphasis on the *positivity* of law, on the idea that all valid legal norms other than the basic norm are enacted or posited norms whose validity can be ascertained without reliance on assessments of substantive justice.

Some interpreters who acknowledge that Kelsen's views make sense only if they are read from a normative perspective have noted that Kelsen appears to reject natural law theory only because he was in the grips of a crude ethical relativism. Once we reject this relativism, they argue, we are free to reinterpret Kelsen's basic norm as making a claim to substantive justice with respect to the content of the laws it purports to authorize. In Robert Alexy's view, for example, Kelsen's analysis of the structure of legal system is basically sound and can more or less be left in place. All we need to do to turn the pure theory into an acceptable explanation of the normativity of law is to replace Kelsen's 'analytical basic norm' with some substantive moral principle that can serve as a 'normative basic norm' underwriting a claim to 'practical correctness' of all norms that depend on it.[81]

---

[81] See Robert Alexy, *Begriff und Geltung des Rechts* (Freiburg/München, 1994) 154–97.

In what follows, I want to argue that Kelsen's emphasis on the positivity of law should not be so easily thrown overboard since it has a deeper motivation than skepticism about moral truth. Kelsen's separation thesis serves to drive home the point that the normativity we attribute to a norm insofar as it is legally valid is categorically different from and independent of assessments of the substantive justice of its content. The law will not be able to serve what Kelsen takes to be its main function if we obfuscate this difference. To distinguish Kelsenian legal normativity clearly from substantive justice, I will from now on refer to the normativity a basic norm attributes to all norms that have membership in a legal system as *legitimacy*.

I will begin by providing a formal description of legitimacy that aims to highlight the differences between legitimacy and substantive justice. I will then go on to interpret Kelsen's separation thesis in the light of the social function of legitimacy. Finally, I will address the worry that a general attribution of legitimacy to the law is likely to engender an uncritical attitude towards unjust law.

The pure theory as a theory of legal legitimacy

I should emphasize right away that Kelsen himself does not employ the term 'legitimacy' to characterize the normativity the pure theory attributes to the law. What is more, he sometimes actively disparages the idea that the law can legitimize political power.[82] So the claim that the pure theory ought to be read as a theory of legitimacy seems to be a non-starter. I can only ask the reader to bear with me for a moment. Needless to say, the term 'legitimacy' is used in a number of different senses. It will therefore be necessary to explain my use of the concept. Once this use is explained, I hope, it will be possible to make good on the claim that the term 'legitimacy' is an adequate label for Kelsen's conception of legal normativity.

The understanding of the term I will be working with here assumes that legitimacy, in its primary sense, is a property of political decisions, including decisions to enact general or particular legal norms. The core intuition guiding my use of the term is the idea that a political decision can be legitimate, in virtue of its pedigree, without being or being accepted as substantively just. Accordingly, if we say that some political decision is legitimate we do not necessarily express approval of its substantive merits. What we are saying is that whoever took the decision was entitled to take the decision on the basis of *his* assessment of the situation or problem to which the decision responds. The claim that some decision is legitimate typically goes along with the view that a certain number of other decisions would have been equally legitimate, regardless of their content, had they been taken by the decision taker in question.

The fact that we accept a decision as legitimate does not necessarily mean that we will no longer form a judgment of its substantive quality. Neither, therefore,

---

[82] Kelsen, *Introduction to the Problems of Legal Theory* (n 1 above) 37–8, 104–6. Kelsen's disparagements of legitimacy usually appear in the specific context of the rejection of law-state dualism, ie of the idea that a state separate from law and conceived of as an order of power can legitimate itself by a voluntary and defeasible commitment to legality.

does it mean that there are no practical standards to which a decision that we will accept as legitimate, irrespective of its content, ought to conform. We may often come to believe that a legitimate decision is bad in substantive quality since the relevant decision taker exercised his powers badly, in a fashion not properly responsive to the reasons we think ought to have guided his decision. But we acknowledge, nevertheless, that the fact that the decision was taken by a person or institution competent to take it constitutes a reason for action in conformity with the decision that possesses at least some degree of exclusionary force.[83] We accept that we are, to some extent, bound by the decision, even if it is not the decision we believe, perhaps with good reason, would have been the right one to take.[84] The aim to find grounds of decisional legitimacy, then, can be regarded as a reaction to what is, according to Jeremy Waldron, the fundamental predicament of politics in a modern society: the pervasiveness of disagreement about the common good.[85]

It is necessary to distinguish between de facto and de jure legitimacy. De facto legitimacy exists wherever the decisions taken by some decision taker are, as a matter of fact, considered to be legitimate, accepted as having some degree of exclusionary force, by those to whom they are addressed. De jure legitimacy obtains wherever such acceptance ought to be forthcoming from a reasonable person. At least in the realm of the political, de facto and de jure legitimacy are intimately related, as Kelsen acknowledges. The conditions for it to be the case that one ought to attribute a measure of legitimacy to some political system must include the requirement that the system be by and large effective, that it is willing and capable to consistently enforce its rulings even against de facto dissent. This requirement, however, is unlikely to be satisfied unless the decisions attributable to the system are, as a matter of fact, treated as legitimate by a sufficient number of its subjects.[86]

De jure legitimacy, then, presupposes de facto legitimacy. But the relationship cannot be reversed. Mistaken or ill-motivated de facto acceptance of claims to legitimacy, based on ideology or myth, constitutes one of the key stabilizing foundations

---

[83] I am using the term in the Razian sense. I will assume, however, that exclusionary force has a dimension of weight. See n 105 below.

[84] See for a similar use of the term 'legitimacy': John Rawls, 'Reply to Habermas' in John Rawls, *Political Liberalism* (New York, 1996) 372–434, at 427–8. The conception of legitimacy I want to attribute to Kelsen has roots in Max Weber's classification of forms of legitimacy. See Max Weber, *Wirtschaft und Gesellschaft. Grundriß der verstehenden Soziologie*, edited by Johannes Winckelmann (Tübingen, 1980) 16–20 and 122–30 as well as Joseph Raz's conception of authority. See Joseph Raz, 'Law and Authority' in Raz, *The Authority of Law* (n 42 above) 3–33.

[85] See Jeremy Waldron, *Law and Disagreement* (Oxford, 1999).

[86] I am suggesting this as an interpretation of Kelsen's view of the relation between legal validity and the effectiveness of law. Kelsen consistently maintained that a sufficient degree of effectiveness of a legal order was a requirement for the presupposition of a basic norm. If the basic norm itself has a normative, and not merely an epistemological significance, the same must be true of the requirement of effectiveness. See for the relation between validity and effectiveness: Kelsen, *Introduction to the Problems of Legal Theory* (n 1 above) 59–61; Kelsen, *Das Problem der Souveränität* (n 45 above) 94–101. Some of Kelsen's shorter pieces on natural law and legal positivism come quite close the normative reading of the relationship I propose. See Hans Kelsen, 'Die philosophischen Grundlagen der Naturrechtslehre und des Rechtspositivismus' in *Die Wiener rechtstheoretische Schule* (n 29 above) vol I, 281–350, at 337–9.

of despotic systems of governance which treat the ruled as mere instruments of the private interests of the rulers. Political systems which rest on such ill-motivated acceptance of legitimacy will typically not just be despotic in substance. They will also deny their subjects full freedom of thought and expression in order to stabilize the legitimating ideology and the power of the rulers. These observations lead to the question whether de facto belief in the general legitimacy of a political system can take a reasonable form, a form that is sufficient to ensure social stability, yet minimally dependent on myth or ideology. A political system that matches this standard would clearly be a strong candidate for possessing a degree of de jure legitimacy.

The pure theory of law, once it is read in the light of Kelsen's political theory, can be understood as a theory of political legitimacy that tries to address the question just outlined. First, the normativity attributed by Kelsenian legal science to all norms that have membership in a legal system can be interpreted as a form of de jure legitimacy which I will call 'legal legitimacy', to be carefully distinguished from substantive justice. Kelsen's reasons for distinguishing legitimacy from justice will occupy us in the next section. The second key claim made by the pure theory as a normative science, to be discussed in this section, is the claim that legality is not just a necessary condition of political legitimacy. It is also the only valid source of de jure legitimacy. Belief in legal legitimacy, according to Kelsen, is the only reasonable form of acceptance of claims to political legitimacy because it is the only form of belief in political legitimacy that does not depend on ideology. Hence, the claims of states or political systems to the obedience of their citizens will be justified to the extent that these claims can be supported by an appeal to legal legitimacy.

These claims need some further explanation. I do not mean to suggest that legality is the only source of practical justification for political decisions. Of course, we often have reason to conform to political decisions that have nothing to do with considerations of legitimacy. If a political decision is acknowledged to be good, considerations of legitimacy will not be needed to motivate reasonable compliance. The claim is, rather, that legality is the only valid source of reasons with exclusionary force for conformity with political decisions that, from the perspective of the subject, appear to lack sufficient substantive quality.

Moreover, I do not claim that the legality of a political decision will always be sufficient to exclude or outweigh content related practical considerations speaking against conformity with the demands it raises. The justificatory force of legal legitimacy is a matter of degree. Whether the legality of a political decision is a strong enough reason of legitimacy to justify the state's unconditional demand for conformity with that decision will depend on how well the state in question approximates the constitutional ideal of a utopia of legality to be discussed in the remaining chapters of this book.

In order to explain why legality, according to Kelsen, is the only valid source of de jure legitimacy, it will be helpful to take a look at a primitive species of de facto legitimacy that is not in any way related to legality.[87] The charismatic leader of a spontaneously arising political movement is considered by his followers to possess legitimate political power insofar as they treat his decisions as binding regardless of their assessment of the merits of those decisions. Legitimacy grounded in charisma can be described as a form of personal authority (though it differs, of course, from Razian personal authority with respect to its justificatory basis). Those who subject themselves to charisma aim to become part of 'something bigger' or to attain salvation through unconditional loyalty, even if that means that they will have to leave their individuality behind. The followers of a charismatic leader, in keeping with this ambition, do not think of the leader's capacity to take binding decisions as being dependent on their consent or on any formal authorization. Rather, they take it to flow from the leader's exceptional personal qualities or from his privileged contact with higher powers. As a result, belief in charisma as a source of legitimacy is not easily reconciled with the impression that the leader is no longer favored by the Gods. Continuing support for charismatic leadership usually depends at least on the illusion of success.

At first, the group of followers will typically be a fluid mass and not a formal organization and the paradigmatic form of exercise of authority will be the personal appearance and address of the leader. As soon as a political movement acquires some complexity, de facto legitimacy grounded in personal charisma will, of course, have to be channeled through some formalized structure of authority. The charismatic leader will, for practical reasons, need to delegate some of his powers, to communicate with and direct followers in other ways than by meeting them in person, and so on. But this formalized structure will remain a mere instrument for the transmission of the content of his personal decisions. He will retain the authority to bypass it, if he so chooses, to make exemptions to previously announced rules, or to reassert his authority by revoking delegated powers and appearing *in propria persona*. In other words, the formalized structure of authority may help the followers, in many cases, to identify the will of the charismatic leader. It may even be practically indispensable. But the fact that the leader's authority is normally exercised through the structure is considered irrelevant from a justificatory point of view. The leader's charismatic personality is considered to be the only genuine *source* of legitimacy and it can interfere in the constituted order at will.

Kelsen, of course, is committed to a rejection of any such view by the general structure of his theory. The pure theory is unable to describe a polity based on the charismatic model, if there is such a thing, as a legal order. The identity thesis claims that personal acts can be described as exercises of public authority only insofar as they are legally authorized. The charismatic model, however, rejects the view that the authority of the political leader depends on legal authorization. It claims that acts that violate whatever rules may have been introduced for purposes of

---

[87] The following is inspired by Max Weber. See Weber, *Wirtschaft und Gesellschaft* (n 84 above) 654–87.

convenience, or that have no basis in such rules, may nevertheless turn out to be legitimate exercises of political authority if they directly proceed from a charismatic leader. The ideology of charisma, hence, justifies what is in substance a relationship of arbitrary power and it can do so only by demanding the sacrifice of the intellect.

Political structures based on charismatic authority, however, are seldom stable in the long run, at least not in a pure form. Let us assume that our charismatic polity has solidified into an absolute monarchy that is based on a fundamental constitutional rule of rightful inheritance of the title to govern. The main difference between the charismatic structure and the absolutist system is that a monarch's authority, contrary to that of the charismatic leader, depends on the legal authorization provided by the rule of succession, however substantively unrestricted it may otherwise appear to be. Absolutist constitutional orders, moreover, typically acknowledged a distinction between actions the monarch takes in his official or political capacity and actions he takes as a natural person. Further legal rules are necessary to maintain any such distinction and such rules may well take on considerable complexity. Conformity with these rules, finally, is no longer taken to be a matter of mere convenience. Rather, it is seen as a requirement of the bindingness of any decision since decisions will not be attributable to the monarch in his official capacity, and hence to the state, unless they are legal. The typical form taken by de facto belief in the legitimacy of absolutism thus forges a firm link between legality and legitimacy. It assumes that the legitimacy of the actions of the absolutist king essentially depends on a notion of legality, however thin in content.

Of course, the pure theory would, in describing the absolutist system as a legal order, abstract from the standard justification for why subjects ought to defer to the system's laws. This standard justification claims that those who are designated to rule by the rule of inheritance are divinely appointed and must be obeyed, even if they act unjustly, since they perform the function of punishing us for our sins.[88] Note that subjects who accept this justificatory narrative will nevertheless rely on the law to identify the directives they take themselves to be bound by. They will believe that the authority of the natural person who exercises kingly powers is dependent on the inheritance rule, and not on personal qualities. This belief entails that the king, in contrast to the charismatic leader, necessarily has to act through formal legal channels, however rudimentary, in order for his commands to be considered as public acts and thus as legitimate.

---

[88] See for an example of this view: 'An Homily against Disobedience and Wylful Rebellion' (1570) in David Wootton, *Divine Right and Democracy. An Anthology of Political Writing in Stuart England* (London, 1986) 94–8, at 97–8: 'Unto the which similitude of heavenly government, the nearer and nearer that an earthly prince does come in his regiment, the greater the blessing of God's mercy is he unto that country and people over whom he reigns. And the further and further that an earthly prince does swerve from the example of heavenly government, the greater plague he is of God's wrath, and punishment by God's justice, unto that country and people over whom God for their sins has placed such a prince and governor.'

The belief in the legitimacy of decisions so identified, moreover, will acquire a new feature that was lacking from charismatic legitimacy. The believer in the divine right of kings can accept that legally valid decisions need to be obeyed even if they are unjust or ill-considered since he will treat the legality of a decision as a reason for obedience that is independent of an assessment of the substantive quality of the king's decisions. The doctrine of the divine right of kings is not making the claim that there are no practical standards to which kingly decisions ought to conform. Its point, rather, is that the king is responsible only to God for how he discharges his moral duty to act in accordance with these standards. As long as a subject accepts the doctrine of divine right, he can combine the belief that a decision taken by the ruler is substantively unjust with an endorsement of the decision's legitimacy. The doctrine, hence, at least carves out the space for what one might call a private tribunal in which the ruler's actions are subject to the citizen's silent criticism, even if that criticism has no public effect.

However, neither the fact that the decisions of the absolute monarch will be considered as legitimate only if they are legal nor the fact that the monarch's decisions are, at least in principle, subject to a standard of criticism, will suffice to prevent governance that is despotic in substance. A ruler's failure to comply with his moral duties, according to divine right, does not take anything away from the subject's unconditional duty of obedience. In other words, acceptance of the doctrine potentially creates a total separation between the purported ground of the legitimacy of the ruler's decisions and the degree to which these decisions exhibit concern for the interests of the governed. A subject's only consolation is the belief that a tyrannical king will be punished by God.

The possibility that such separation will occur, and yet fail to endanger the stability of the state, is clearly dependent on acceptance of the doctrine of divine right. I have pointed out that the believer in the divine right of kings, just like the legal scientist, operates with a basic norm and identifies his legal duties on its basis. But his act of presupposition differs crucially from that of the legal scientist. It is impure insofar as it is motivated by belief in a non-scientific, a non-jurisprudential ideology. The believer in the divine right of kings accepts that only legally authorized acts can be attributed to the monarch in his official capacity and hence be binding. But he does not accept the view that the legality of these acts explains why they are to be considered as legitimate. The justificatory force of the basic norm, from the point of view of the believer in the divine right of kings, is absolutely justifiable in terms of a meta-legal theological narrative. What is more, the strength of the justificatory force of the basic norm, from the point of view of this theological narrative, is completely independent both of the substantive moral quality of the particular legal norms that come to depend on it as well as on the question how they come to depend on it. The believer's ultimate explanation for why legally valid decisions are legitimate takes the form of a simple reference to the idea that the basic norm of the legal system is grounded in a divine command. This reference, as far as he is concerned, withstands any further questioning.

The mode of justification employed by the believer in the divine right of kings is a one-way projection of justificatory force from the basic norm to all norms that depend on it.[89] Such a one-way projection will, of course, have a strong tendency to favor autocratic structures of government. Legality is needed, at the end of the day, only to allow the believer to identify the content of God's will (since we assume that it is God's will that we obey the ruler unconditionally). But in order to serve this function or to serve it well, there is no need for legal order to contain, on any of its levels, legal norms that would put any interesting constraints on the unilateral exercise of political power by formally authorized organs of state.

The Kelsenian legal scientist presupposing a basic norm would not refer to the divine right of kings in stating the absolutist system's basic norm. According to the standard positivist interpretation of Kelsen's theory of the basic norm, this is a simple consequence of the fact that the pure theory does not endorse the normativity it attributes to the legal system.[90] Our previous arguments about the character of Kelsenian legal science, however, suggest a different explanation for why legal science, in stating the basic norm of our absolute monarchy, abstracts from the official justificatory ground of the system. Kelsen claims that the pure theory is more than an ideology that veils reality in order to serve some will to power, despite the fact that it makes a general attribution of justified normativity to the law. Kelsen is committed, it would therefore seem, to the view that it has to be possible *reasonably* to make a general attribution of justified normativity to the legal system by presupposing the basic norm.

This minimally includes the requirement that it has to be possible to attribute normativity to the law *without* resorting to an ideological fiction like the divine right of kings. In other words, a proponent of the pure theory, if forced to describe our absolutist state, would refuse to treat the doctrine of the divine right of kings as part of the constitutional law of the realm since he is committed to the view that the normativity we attribute to the norms that have membership in a legal system will show itself to be something more than a veil for a naked claim to power even after our legal-scientific description has stripped the system of the cover provided by the theological argument. But the pure theory does not thereby lose its critical force. It is also committed to the view that the absolutist state's law will show itself to be something less than the believer in the divine right of kings assumes once it is stripped of its cover.

The transition from charismatic leadership to the absolutist state is a transition into legal order or statehood as such. And this transition inevitably subjects exercises of authority to a weak rationalizing force of legality that confers at least some degree of legitimacy upon them. However, the legitimacy that absolutist governance possesses in virtue of being legal falls far short of being a sufficient ground for an

[89] I am borrowing the term from Lon L Fuller, 'A Reply to Critics', in Lon L Fuller, *The Morality of Law. Revised Edition* (New Haven, 1964) 187–242, at 191–7.
[90] See Raz, *Kelsen's Theory of the Basic Norm* (n 42 above) 134–43.

unconditional duty of obedience to the law. The Kelsenian refuses, though, to conclude from this observation that no legal order, *qua legal order*, could ever give rise to duties of obedience that come reasonably close to justifying the claims of the state. He rejects the view, in other words, that all differences in moral quality between our absolutist system and other, less autocratic systems will have to be explicated as differences in the moral quality of the law's content.

This refusal commits the Kelsenian to a positive project. He will have to show that there could be legal orders that can justifiably make a claim to legitimacy, on behalf of all norms that have membership, which is strong enough approximately to justify a general duty to obey the law. But this claim must not be based on some absolute justification of the basic norm that is ultimately dependent, as the divine right of kings, on an ideological narrative drawn from non-jurisprudential sources. The Kelsenian will have to show, moreover, that such an ideal legal order would realize an aspiration of legality to which other legal orders that fall considerably short of realizing it can nevertheless already be taken to be committed.

I believe that this argumentative burden can be shouldered by exploiting the identity thesis. The identity thesis claims that only legally authorized acts are attributable to the state. Read in terms of Kelsen's theory of legal hierarchy, the thesis states that decisions taken on any level of legal hierarchy will be exercises of public power attributable to the state only if they objectively conform to the higher order legal norms providing their conditions of authorization. The claim that positive legal validity is internally related to justified normativity can be cashed out by an argument that tries to show how legitimating constraints can be packed into the positive legal conditions for the identification of acts as acts of state.

The pure theory, in other words, portrays the claim to legitimacy raised by the basic norm on behalf of a legal system as a self-referential claim, as a claim about the nature of the relation between the legal system as a whole and its parts and not as a one way projection of justificatory force. In presupposing a basic norm, the pure theorist takes the view that it is the way in which the enactment of law takes place— the way in which particular legal norms, directly or indirectly, depend on the basic norm—that legitimates the law, instead of merely *transmitting* an absolute legitimacy attributed to the basic norm (or to those whom it empowers to legislate) on ideological and non-jurisprudential grounds. Only by focusing on this form of legitimacy do we enter the sphere of legal legitimacy proper and therefore of a kind of legitimacy that can withstand disagreement about the substantive merits of policies while not being dependent on irrational myth. It is for this reason that legality is to be considered as the only source of de jure legitimacy.

Note that the project outlined here takes it that the capacity of a legal system to endow decisions lawfully taken with legitimacy can differ in strength. Any legal system possesses some legitimating capacity, but many will not possess a whole lot. Legal legitimacy will frequently fall far short of providing a full justification for the unconditional claim to obedience that is typically raised by states. There are three basic features of legal order, however, that can gradually strengthen a legality-based claim to legitimacy: the impartial administration of the law, the democratic creation of general legal norms, and the protection of individual and minority interests by formal constitutionalism. The more strongly the method of norm-enactment in a legal order is characterized by these features, the more legal legitimacy will come to approximate a full justification of the state's claims. The availability of an ideal of legality that would approximately justify the state's claims, in turn, makes it reasonable to treat all instances of legal order both as inevitably possessing some measure of legitimating force and as being defective in the light of an ideal to the realization of which they are necessarily committed.

Given full institutional realization of the legitimacy enhancing features, it will be unlikely that a system's decisions will fail to exhibit proper concern for the interests of all its subjects. However, the Kelsenian theory of legal legitimacy, as we will see, does not aim to provide an instrumental justification for the three legitimacy-enhancing features just listed. Their role is not to ensure that actions of state conform to some comprehensive theory of political justice that determines the substantive content of the proper concern citizens are owed by the state. As grounds of legitimacy they remain parts of an open-ended legal method for taking collectively binding decisions that transfers legitimacy on its outcomes instead of guaranteeing outcomes that we independently know to be correct.[91] For this reason, Kelsen's overall argument is best described as an argument about legitimacy.

Kelsen and the separation of law and morality

Let us now go back to the main topic of this chapter and take a look, in the light of the conception of legitimacy just outlined, at Kelsen's defense of a separation of moral and legal theory as a condition of the possibility of legal science. Kelsen's separation thesis, I will try to show, makes sense only if interpreted as a limited claim to the independence of legal legitimacy from assessments of the substantive moral quality of the law's content, and not as a general denial of any necessary relation between law and morality.

On the face of it, Kelsen rests his case for the separation thesis on a crude skeptical argument about morality: moral attitudes and beliefs are nothing but expressions of subjective interests. Hence, there can be no such thing as a science of morals because

---

[91] Let me briefly point out why I do not consider Razian authority to be a species of legitimacy. Raz's normal justification thesis seems to entail that I can come to acknowledge some person or institution as having authority over me only if the authority and I share a view as to how to define the set of first order reasons on the basis of which the authority is to decide in my place. But this appears to make it difficult for Razian authority to function in situations where an authority and I run into normative disagreement. Such disagreements will typically involve disagreements about what kinds of reasons ought to guide political decisions, and not just a lack of knowledge, on the part of the guided person, of what specific reasons of a certain kind there are and what they require. If we accept this point, the scope of Razian legal authority must turn out to be very limited as it will turn out to be unable to deal with the problem of normative disagreement between citizens. See for thoughts along similar lines Philip Soper, *The Ethics of Deference. Learning from Law's Morals* (Cambridge, 2002) 43–7. Appeals to legitimacy, however, are usually taken to be able to exclude, and thus to bridge, normative disagreement between citizens.

moral norms lack objective validity. Normative legal statements, in Kelsen's view, have to be capable of objective truth and falsity if there is to be a legal science. Jurisprudence, since it aspires to be scientific, therefore has to be autonomous from morality lest it be infected by the subjectivity characterizing moral claims.[92]

The problem with this argument from skepticism for a separation of law and morality, or more exactly, of law and moral opinion, is that there seems to be no reason for someone who denies that his moral views lack objectivity to accept it. It seems that if I believe that there are objectively valid moral norms there will be no reason for me, given Kelsen's conception of normative science, to accept the claim that legal norms can only be validated by the genetic recourse to a basic norm and not by direct reliance on moral argument. Kelsen himself admits the point. The existence of positive law, of law that claims to be valid in virtue of historical origin and not in virtue of content, would be 'entirely incomprehensible', in his view, if there were 'an absolutely good social order emerging from nature, reason, or divine will'.[93] The way in which Kelsen phrases his admission, however, suggests that we should not jump to the conclusion that he has no reason other than an implausible meta-ethical view for wanting to keep legal theory separate from morality too fast.

The pure theory, Kelsen claims, assumes that there is no absolute standard of good or just social order deriving from nature, reason, or divine will.[94] But this view is clearly ambiguous. It might be taken to mean that there is no objective standard of justice and that all opinions about justice are therefore mere expressions of subjective taste or preference. But it might as well refer to the view that we have no absolutely reliable cognitive access to a standard of justice, as would be provided by direct knowledge of God's will or intuitive insight into a transcendent idea of the good, such that the standard in question could not reasonably be challenged or be subject to disagreement. Much of what Kelsen has to say about justice is clearly concerned with the consequences of this epistemic thesis or its rejection for our understanding of normative disagreement.

After having argued that any notion of justice which claims 'absolute validity' would have to be a 'transcendent thing in itself' situated 'beyond all experience', Kelsen makes the following statement:

Seen from the standpoint of rational cognition, there are only interests and thus conflicts of interests, which are resolved by way of an ordering of interests that either satisfies the one at the expense of the other, or establishes a balance, a compromise between the opposing

---

[92] See Kelsen, *Introduction to the Problems of Legal Theory* (n 1 above) 15–18. Of course, I am already committed to a rejection of this view in virtue of my claim that the pure theory ought to be read as a theory of legitimacy. What I want to do here is to show that Kelsen's understanding of the relation of law and morality can be interpreted so as to make room for this claim.   [93] Ibid, 17.

[94] Kelsen usually refers to such standards specifically as theories of justice and expresses his separation thesis by arguing that legal theory is separate from the theory of justice. See for example Hans Kelsen, 'Die Idee des Naturrechts' in *Die Wiener rechtstheoretische Schule* (n 29 above) vol I, 245–80, at 246–8; Kelsen, 'Die philosophischen Grundlagen der Naturrechtslehre und des Rechtspositivismus' ibid 281–350, at 341–5.

interests. That only one ordering of interests has absolute value (which really means, 'is just') cannot be accounted for by way of rational cognition. If there were justice in the sense in which one usually appeals to it when one wants to assert certain interests over others, then the positive law would be completely superfluous, its existence entirely incomprehensible. Given an absolutely good social order emerging from nature, reason, or divine will, the activity of the legislator would be as foolish as artificial illumination in the brightest sunlight.[95]

What Kelsen appears to be saying here is that societies often experience conflicts of interest in which both parties tend to think of their demands as requirements of 'absolute' justice. These conflicts can be solved only in either of two ways: by giving unconditional preference to one of the competing interests, endorsing its claim that its demands are required by absolute justice, or by finding some kind of compromise that tries, to the extent possible, to cater to the interests of both parties because one regards them both as entitled to concern even while refusing to grant to either the status of a requirement of absolute justice.

Kelsen clearly assumes that the project of a legal science as a normative science distinct from any doctrine of absolute justice is intimately related to the second form of conflict-management. The essential function of positive legal order, of legislation and adjudication, is to bring about a compromise of social interests in the absence of an agreed upon conception of 'absolutely good social order'. Kelsen claims that the first form of conflict resolution will appear rational only to those who are willing to claim to be in secure possession of an absolute conception of justice no one could reasonably disagree with.[96] The rationality of the first method presupposes, further, that one has to claim perfect insight into how one's absolute ideal of justice applies to concrete circumstances.[97] Given these two conditions, legal legitimacy, as a distinctive resource of conflict resolution, would neither be needed nor be justifiable. But if one believes that these two conditions are not satisfied (and that those who believe they are satisfied are deluding themselves) one should clearly be concerned to preserve the law's capacity to function as a framework for finding compromise.

In the light of this concern, Kelsen's argument for the separation thesis need not be understood as a consequence of a questionable meta-ethical relativism that is combined with a sterile and unmotivated demand for a scientific jurisprudence. Rather, it can be understood as motivated by the practical interest to establish that the law's normative authority, and hence its capacity to bridge differences and induce compromise, is independent of differing assessments of the justice of its content. What is more, this interest would explain why the law must be identifiable on the basis of its pedigree and without recourse to people's opinions about justice. But it would not entail, finally, that there is no necessary relation between legality and legitimacy.

[95] Kelsen, *Introduction to the Problems of Legal Theory* (n 1 above) 17.
[96] See Kelsen, *Vom Wesen und Wert der Demokratie* (n 8 above) 98–104.
[97] See Kelsen, 'Die Idee des Naturrechts' (n 94 above) 257–74.

Much of what Kelsen says about the character of natural law theory fits this interpretation of his separation thesis rather well. As we have seen, Kelsen claims that legal validity is internally related to a form of justified normativity. At times, Kelsen goes so far as to say that the positivity of law consists in the fact that the normativity of law is grounded in an autonomous source of normativity. Natural law theory, in turn, is conceived of as a view that denies that legal normativity is based in an autonomous source of normativity.[98]

Natural law theorists claim, according to Kelsen, that 'the law as such is part of morality', of a theory of justice.[99] This description must be interpreted in the light of Kelsen's view of normative systems. Recall that this view distinguishes between two different senses of intrinsic validity in order to account for the validity of moral and legal basic norms, respectively. The basic norm of a moral system is a necessary truth, in virtue of its content, whereas the basic norm of a legal system is a necessary condition of interpreting human acts as having objective legal significance. Recall as well that Kelsen distinguished between two correspondingly different ways in which norms relate to a basic norm in moral and legal normative systems. In a moral system the relations are logical and static; in a legal system they are genetic and dynamic. Dependent *legal* norms are valid in virtue of the historical fact that they happen to have been enacted in a way that is authorized by the basic norm. Dependent *moral* norms are valid, according to the natural law theorist, if they are logically entailed by the basic norm of a moral system into whose timeless truth the natural law theorist claims to have certain insight.[100]

To say that the law is part of morality, given this picture, is to say that the ultimate basic norm of a justified legal system must be a substantive moral norm that possesses necessary validity and that provides the content for an absolute ideal of justice. Enacted norms of a positive legal system that is to be integrated into the moral system individuated by some moral basic norm will be valid and hence possess normativity only if their content does not conflict with the moral basic norm or any other moral norm that is logically entailed by it. Since natural law theory treats the moral basic norm as the ground of the normativity of the law, and since the law, in Kelsen's view, is valid only insofar as it is normative, any judgment on

---

[98] See Kelsen, *Das Problem der Souveränität* (n 45 above) 92–4.

[99] Kelsen, *Introduction to the Problems of Legal Theory* (n 1 above) 15.

[100] A somewhat similar contrast is drawn by Scott Shapiro, 'On Hart's Way Out' in Jules Coleman (ed), *Hart's Postscript. Essays on the Postscript to the 'Concept of Law'* (Oxford, 2001) 177–82. Shapiro argues that the inclusion of morality in a rule of recognition makes that rule and hence the legal system itself, at least in part, static. Shapiro thinks that, as a result, moral norms validated by an inclusive rule of recognition cannot exercise guidance or make a practical difference in virtue of their dependence on the rule of recognition. The reason is that we will have to assess the validity of such norms in terms of their content before we can grant them membership in the legal system. A dependence relation between a norm and a validating norm can practically matter only if it is forged by an actual decision under a dynamic authorizing rule. Kelsen, of course, draws much more ambitious conclusions from the contrast between static morality and dynamic positive law and he tries to integrate them into a normative argument that is concerned not with guidance per se but with legitimate guidance. But Kelsen is in perfect agreement, as far as I can see, with Shapiro's more limited claims against inclusive positivism.

the conformity of the content of an enacted law with the natural law standard must at the same time be a judgment of the legal validity of that law. It will therefore be impossible for the natural lawyer to accept any particular positive law as valid if he believes that its content is morally incorrect.

A natural law theorist, Kelsen goes on to argue, could not even authorize a person or institution to enact binding interpretations of the law of nature.[101] As soon as he takes the modest step of empowering someone else to judge whether some action conforms with the standards of natural law, the decisions taken by that judge will have to be valid in virtue of some other criterion than their perceived conformity in content with the demands of natural law, in order to be able to serve any of the functions that might conceivably motivate such empowerment. This alternative standard can only be the fact that the decision taken by the judge is identifiable, without resort to any assessment of the moral quality of the content of the decision, as a properly authorized decision. But if validity is to remain connected to justified normativity, this different standard must be an autonomous source of content-independent normativity that can legitimately exclude the subject's understanding of the demands of natural law. The conditions sufficient to establish that a judicial decision was properly authorized must also suffice to endow these decisions with a degree of legitimacy, regardless of their content.

Kelsen adds a further twist to his argument by claiming that natural law theory can take two different forms, both of which make the peaceful solution of social conflict through law impossible.[102] A conservative natural law theorist, arguing against the possibility of legitimate legal change, will claim that some existing positive legal order is indeed part of some absolute moral order. Its norms, therefore, are to be considered as substantively just and not just as legitimate. Such a view will be forced to assume that those who criticize the existing law as unjust in content must be morally wrong. As a result, it will have a tendency to deny to dissenters the status of practical agents fully capable of autonomous moral judgment and to severely limit the possibility of public criticism. A revolutionary natural law theorist or anarchist rightly insists on the inalienability of his capacity of moral judgment. He goes on to attack the normativity of the existing legal order by denying that it conforms in content to the standards of true justice. Laws *qua* laws, he claims, cannot possess any content-independent normativity whatsoever and should therefore not be considered authoritative unless they are perfectly just. The fact that some action is illegal, the revolutionary concludes, can never be a reason not to perform it, given that the action can be expected to bring about what he sees as a net gain in justice.

Kelsen's separation thesis attempts to steer a middle course between these two views, a course that is respectful of the individual's claim to autonomous moral judgment while not leading to anarchist consequences. Kelsen's separation thesis

---

does not, therefore, aim to separate the link between legality and legitimacy. Rather, it tries to show that the link is, at least to some extent, independent of assessments of the substantive moral quality of the content of law in the light of meta-positive ideals of justice and that it can therefore exert a mediating function even in the absence of social agreement on any such ideal. Kelsen's second condition of the autonomy of legal science, the separation of law and morality, follows from the principle that the legitimacy of law has to rest on structural features of legal order itself. We need not, therefore, suppose that Kelsen's separation thesis is motivated by an emotivist theory of moral judgment that clashes with an obsession with scientific tidiness. Kelsen's separation of legality and substantive justice, rather, can be understood as being grounded in an attempt to defend the autonomous value of positive legality.

Further questions

Let me recapitulate some of the steps so far in our reconstruction of Kelsen's position. The legal scientist, in presupposing the basic norm of some legal system makes a general attribution of justified normativity to all legal norms depending on that basic norm. The identity thesis entails that we must give this claim a political reading. According to the identity thesis, a human act can be attributed to the state only if it is a valid exercise of a power conferred by law. Hence, the presupposition of a basic norm attributes justified normativity to all acts of a state. The political dimension of Kelsen's understanding of legal order is also obvious in the idea that the law is complete, that there is always a legal basis to decide any social dispute wherever there is law.

I have described the relation of legal science to these claims by introducing the notion of legal legitimacy. The legal scientist, in presupposing a basic norm, is making a general attribution of legitimacy to the state as legal order. Since legitimacy comes in degrees, this attribution does not necessarily amount to a full endorsement of the normative claims of the state. However, Kelsen's position, as I have interpreted it, does entail that any legal order, even our absolutist state, possesses some degree of general legitimacy, due to the fact that all its acts are filtered through a legal hierarchy.

This conclusion immediately raises a worry. One might suspect that it is guilty of favoring dangerous habits of uncritical deference to bad laws. Many legal systems, after all, are obnoxiously unjust and undeserving of obedience. A legal theory that claims to be a form of anti-authoritarian social criticism should, so one might argue, avoid any normative commitment of the kind entailed by the presupposition of a basic norm. It should not foster the illusion that even obnoxiously unjust states merit to be respected, to some extent, merely because they are instances of legal order. This, needless to say, is the worry that animated Hart's version of the separation thesis in the first place. And it applies with full force to Kelsen, since Kelsen is not discounting wicked legal systems as instances of legal order. The aim to provide a general theory of law on the one hand and the aim to make a general attribution of justified normativity to the legal system as a whole seem to pull us into different and irreconcilable directions.[103]

I would certainly be overstating my case if I claimed that Kelsen had ever mounted an explicit defense of the idea of legal legitimacy against this criticism. But I hope to show in the remainder of this book that his account of legal order contains the resources to give a reply. To set the stage for the further chapters in this thesis, let me offer, in broad outline, a possible Kelsenian answer to the worry.

Kelsen would agree, I have already claimed, that the fact that all legal systems possess some degree of legitimacy does not entail that a reasonable person subject to some legal system necessarily ought to do as the law demands, all things considered. Hart is clearly right to say that the threshold conditions which a political system must pass in order to qualify as a legal order are much too weak to rule out the possibility of great iniquity that makes a state unworthy of obedience. But it is important to keep in mind that there are systems of domination that fail to meet the threshold of legality, that cannot be interpreted as legal structures, and that there are forms of iniquity that do not easily lend themselves to legal organization. It is important to keep in mind as well that Hart's observation leaves open two different ways of thinking about the excellence of legal systems.

Hart's view seems to boil down the idea that the excellence of a legal system would mainly consist in the fact that its laws happen not to be iniquitous in content. This situation will obtain if those who have legislative power enact laws that are morally good in content. The likelihood of such good legislation being enacted, finally, is increased by the open criticism of the law's authority invited by Hartian positivism. Kelsen, as we will see, adheres to a different understanding of the excellence of law. The pure theory's legal-scientific perspective, in addition to claiming that all legal systems possess some rudimentary legitimacy, assumes that legal legitimacy is a potentially sufficient ground to underwrite the state's claims to obedience. In other words, legal science attributes to the state as legal order a normative aspiration of a certain kind. It claims that a state could cultivate legitimacy-enhancing features of legality to such an extent that the legality of its acts would become a sufficient ground for acceptance, on the part of reasonable subjects, of the state's claim to be able to decide bindingly all social disputes arising amongst them. The act of presupposing a basic norm, hence, is a way of expressing allegiance to the ambition of

---

[103] Hart was puzzled by Kelsen's account of the relation of law and morality. See Hart, 'Kelsen Visited' (n 53 above) 301–8. Hart takes issue with Kelsen's claim that 'it is logically impossible to regard a particular rule of law as valid and at the same time to accept, as morally binding, a moral rule forbidding the behaviour required by the legal rule'. (Hart, *The Concept of Law* [n 18 above] 293.) Given the interpretation offered in the previous section, Kelsen's puzzling claim can be understood as a thesis about the relation of positive and natural law. Kelsen is rejecting the natural lawyer's view that a positive law cannot be legally valid if it conflicts with an absolute ideal of social justice. This view does not entail that it is impossible to hold the belief that some law is materially incorrect in the light of one's own understanding of justice. Of course, since Kelsenian validity is a form of justified normativity, Kelsen is committed to the view that a law's material incorrectness does not establish its illegitimacy. But this commitment does not entail the absurd view that it is impossible to conceive of conflicts between law and morality.

creating what I will call a *utopia of legality*. Legal science can justifiably abstract from
all sources of justification other than legality and pretend, so to speak, that legality
fully justifies acts of state as long as the hope for this utopia is reasonable.[104]

The conception of a utopia of legality is an exceedingly modest social ideal. Kelsen
acknowledges, as we will see, that the main interest citizens take in the state's decisions is an interest in the content of those decisions and in how that content affects
their personal plans. But in a state that has fully developed the legitimacy enhancing features of legality, reasonable citizens will always be able to live with decisions the content of which does not fully cater to their interests or align with their
moral beliefs because the legal legitimacy of these decisions will be strong enough
to motivate reasonable deference to these decisions. In a utopia of legality legal
legitimacy can always step in for other reasons for conformity with the state's
demands, for example belief in the substantive rightness of the decisions, trust in the
moral integrity and practical expertise of the rulers, or a shared conception of good
governance, should these latter motivations prove unavailable. And insofar as legal
legitimacy can step in for such reasons, it will make possible the peaceful coexistence between morally divided groups in a pluralist society.

The answer to the question of the weight we ought to give to the legal legitimacy
of the state's decisions is dependent on the degree to which the system approximates
a utopia of legality. This weight may turn out to be insufficient to preempt substantive moral reasons for not paying respect to the law. It is up to the subjects of
the law to determine whether this is the case or not and thus to adjudicate on the
limits of their duty to defer to the judgments of the state. What the pure theory
does claim, however, is that someone who is not willing to give any exclusionary
force whatsoever, in his practical deliberations, to the fact that a political decision
he is expected to defer to has been filtered through legal order is acting in a morally
blameworthy fashion since he expresses a principled unwillingness to subject his
normative conflicts with others to legal arbitration.[105] The same is true of someone who is not willing to be responsive, in his judgments of weight, to the degree

---

[104] The conception I am attributing to Kelsen here bears some resemblance to Lon Fuller's distinction between a legal morality of duty and a legal morality of aspiration. See Lon Fuller, *The Morality of
Law* (n 89 above) 3–32. The difference between the two conceptions is that Kelsen has a more modest
view of the legitimating capacities of the threshold level that determines whether we are faced with a
legal system. His conception of law's ambitions, on the other hand, includes political elements that are
missing from Fuller's conception. Fuller sometimes sounds like a law-state dualist who continues to
think of the law as mediating a pre-legal political relationship between ruler and ruled. Rex, throughout his misadventures, failed to govern through law. But Fuller's story seems to entail that the basic
ruler-ruled relationship between Rex and his unfortunate subjects was never in question. Fuller, inter-
estingly, was directly influenced by the German dualist doctrine of state Kelsen's identity thesis is
meant to debunk. His idea of reciprocity between government and citizen is influenced by the sociologist Georg Simmel (see ibid, 39–40) who forms one of Kelsen's main targets of attack in *Der soziologische und der juristische Staatsbegriff* (n 3 above) 4–11.

[105] This picture of the relation between legitimate law and individual decision rejects Raz's view
that valid reasons with exclusionary force must invariably prevail over the reasons they replace. For a
general defense of the idea of weight of exclusionary force see Frederick Schauer, *Playing by the Rules.
A Philosophical Examination of Rule-Based Decision-Making in Law and Life* (Oxford, 1991) 88–92

to which a state approximates a utopia of legality. The pure theory as a normative science of the law, then, rests on the assumption that the stance of the natural lawyer, as described above, is morally indefensible.

The legitimate state, in Kelsen's view, is essentially an arbitrator amongst morally divided social groups. Kelsen therefore believes that the discharge of the arbitrating function of the state takes normative precedence over any other function. Insofar as a political order can be described as a legal system, from a legal scientific perspective, it inevitably has already *begun* to play the role of an arbitrator, even if its decisions are not yet fully justifiable on the basis of an ideal of fair arbitration. The pure theory is a legal theory adequate to the ideal of the rule of law insofar as it clears the way for the fullest possible realization of this essential function of legal order.

So what about the Hartian complaint we started out from? Does Kelsen's claim that even an absolutist state, in virtue of being a legal order, possesses some degree of general legitimacy create a problem for the idea that jurisprudence can conceive of law only *sub specie justificationis*? Kelsen, to repeat, would agree that a legal order, and in particular a legal order of the absolutist or 'autocratic' kind, can be wicked in the sense of containing egregiously unjust laws that do not, all things considered, merit to be obeyed. But he would not agree with the view that the best way to prevent such iniquity is to reject the idea that legality has a general legitimating force. A wicked legal system's moral shortcomings are not shortcomings that it is afflicted with insofar as it exhibits, to some extent, the structure of legal order but rather shortcomings it exhibits insofar as it fails to be a fully developed legal order that could effectively constrain morally terrible abuses of the law. For Kelsen, the fact that some legal systems are wicked is less important, in terms of how to generally characterize legality and its normative aspirations, than the fact that legality always constrains political power to some degree and that the kind of constraint we find, at least in a nascent form, in all legal systems can be developed and institutionally explicated in a way that empowers legality to act as a potent source of legitimacy. It would therefore be wrong to think that we can only choose between a view that uncritically affirms the claims of the state and a view that altogether denies that legality possesses legitimating powers.

Of course, the view I have attributed to Kelsen is so far nothing more than a promise. Whether it is to be preferred to conventional forms of positivism cannot

and Soper, *The Ethics of Deference* (n 91 above) 45. Raz's demand that exclusionary reasons always prevail over all reasons they purport to exclude stacks the deck against Kelsenian legal science. Raz observes that 'while it is true that legal requirements are not, in law, absolute, the law itself claims to determine their proper import, to fix the conditions in which they are overridden'. (Joseph Raz, 'The Obligation to Obey the Law' in Raz, *The Authority of Law* [n 42 above] 233–49, at 236.) If this is a true description of scope of the law's claims and if it is true as well that valid exclusionary reasons always prevail over the excluded reasons, the Kelsenian legal scientist must be committed to endorsing the view that the law's final decisions always exclude *all* reasons against obedience. This, however, is a claim that cannot possibly be true. Hence, legal science cannot possibly be normative. If Schauer and Soper are right to reject the view that exclusionary reasons always beat the reasons they purport to exclude, this problem can be avoided.

be decided in the abstract. Kelsen will have to show that his conception of legal legitimacy can be given positive content by a theory of the rule of law, of democracy, and of constitutionalism. If Kelsen can show that the pure theory can coherently interpret these features of political order as excellences of legality that will have iniquity-preventing effects, positivists who deny any interesting general link between legality and legitimacy on practical grounds will at least be under pressure to explain why we ought to prefer a conception of law based on such denial to the pure theory. The answer to this question, moreover, is likely to turn on competing general ideals of good social order and of the role that the law can play in achieving and maintaining them.

Kelsen's political writings, to which I will now turn, can be read as an attempt to explicate the promised relationship between legality and legitimacy indirectly. They rely on two conceptions that Kelsen himself does not make fully explicit. These are the conception of a reasonable person and the conception of the law-abiding citizen.

The reasonable person is simply a person who, in trying to find a viable form of coexistence with others, takes what Kelsen calls 'the standpoint of rational cognition'. She rejects any legitimating myth and aspires to live a life of autonomy. This stance, as we will see, should not be taken to entail, as Kelsen sometimes suggests, that the reasonable person has to think of her own substantive beliefs about justice as mere projections of brute subjective preference. Rather, a person taking the standpoint of rational cognition is a person who considers her own views as to how the content of positive law ideally ought to look like as fallible. She acknowledges that reasonable disagreement about such matters is possible and that her own views therefore must be open to the criticisms of others. As a result, the reasonable person is willing to accept that her political goals can justifiably be subjected to a suitably constructed institutionalized process of social arbitration.

The law-abiding citizen, in turn, is a subject of the law who acts in conformity with any decision taken under the authority of the basic norm, barring exceptional circumstances, because he takes the legality of such decisions to be an ordinarily sufficient reason not to act on his own moral beliefs should they be in conflict with a legally authorized decision.

The ideal of the utopia of legality is an attempt to outline the conditions under which a reasonable person, a person who is adopting 'the standpoint of rational cognition', can take the stance of a law-abiding citizen. Or, put differently, it is an attempt to outline the conditions under which acceptance of the general claim to obedience made by a legally organized state can take the form of genuine law-abidingness. In a utopia of legality, Kelsen claims, exercises of political power that exhibit full legality will typically possess a legitimacy strong enough to motivate reasonable deference, regardless of how those who are legally authorized to take political decisions choose to exercise their powers. Its legal 'methods' for arriving at solutions to conflicts of interest are such that reasonable persons would not reject their outcomes since they could not reasonably claim that their interests have been unduly neglected or not been given the respect they deserve from other reasonable persons.

In what follows, I want to trace the different steps of development from a simple autocratic system to a utopia of legality. These steps mark the gradual transition from a primitive political system in which the positive legal order primarily facilitates the implementation of a particular 'absolutist' view of the correct ordering of interests to a system in which legality constrains political power in a way that allows all citizens to identify with the results of its valid exercise. Insofar as a legal system goes through this transition, law is working itself pure, in the eyes of the reasonable citizen, by coming to rely less and less on external sources of normative support. Legality progressively realizes the potential strength of its own legitimating powers and finally turns into the only source of justification needed to sustain the political system.

3

Kelsen's Principles of Legality

In this section, I will outline the fundamental structure of Kelsen's account of the rule of law which is based on the thesis of the identity of law and state, on the view that it is impossible to attribute an act performed by a human being to the state unless that act is legal. The claim that it is possible to base a conception of the rule of law on the identity thesis, of course, needs some defense. As I have argued in the introduction, there are strong intuitive reasons to believe that the identity thesis can be true only if it is interpreted in a way that trivializes the ideal of the rule of law.

The problem, in a nutshell, is this. Public officials who claim to exercise powers conferred by legal order often appear to act in ways that we believe violate constraints of legality. Kelsen's identity thesis, however, makes it impossible to describe such situations by saying that the state or those acting on its behalf violated the law. The only two possible descriptions of the situation, given the identity thesis, are the following: Either the fact that I believe an act of a public official to have been legally defective in some way or other must entitle me to conclude that the act, though taken by a person who holds public office, was null, not an act of state and therefore not binding, because it was, in my view, not perfectly legal. This first way of interpreting the identity thesis would, for obvious reasons, completely undermine the possibility of legal authority.

The second option is the view that all decisions identifiable as decisions taken by public officials on the basis of some lesser standard than perfect legality are to be considered as legally valid, in virtue of having been taken by public officials, regardless of whether they conform in substance to all the laws they claim to apply. This second approach to the identity thesis, by contrast, fails to impose any constraints on the power of public officials to act as they see fit. The resulting position amounts to law-state dualism in effect, if not in name.

The way in which Kelsen dealt with this problem in the *Introduction to the Problems of Legal Theory* strongly suggests that he adopted the second option by embracing what is called the doctrine of 'normative alternatives'.[1] The doctrine of normative alternatives claims that norms on a higher level of the legal hierarchy

---

[1] Hans Kelsen, *Introduction to the Problems of Legal Theory. A Translation of the First Edition of the Reine Rechtslehre or Pure Theory of Law*, translated and edited by Bonnie Litschewsky-Paulson and Stanley L Paulson (Oxford, 1992) 71–7. See also Hans Kelsen, *Reine Rechtslehre* (2nd ed, Wien, 1960) 271–4.

provide not only for the validity of lower-level norms that conform in procedure and substance to the requirements of legality intended by the higher-level norms. They also provide for the validity of lower-level norms violating those intended requirements. The consistency of legal order is preserved, therefore, even in case officials exercise power in ways that violate higher-order legal norms. Kelsen himself describes the doctrine, with respect to a judicial decision applying a statute to a particular case, as follows:

The statute does not provide simply that the judicial decision [...] should be created in a certain way and have a certain content; it also provides, alternatively, that even an individual norm created in another way or having another content should be valid until it is overturned, in a certain procedure, on the basis of its conflict with the first provision of the statute. Once the procedure is exhausted, or if no appropriate procedure is provided for at all, then the doctrine of finality applies, and the force of law accrues to the lower-level norm as against the higher-level norm. This means that the lower-level norm, notwithstanding the fact that its content runs counter to the higher-level norm, remains valid—indeed, it remains valid owing to a principle established by the higher-level norm itself, namely, the doctrine of finality.[2]

It seems hard to avoid the conclusion that Kelsen is in effect saying that those who are authorized to take any legal decision have the power freely to choose to either apply the law or to decide according to their personal discretion. The claim that the state cannot act illegally, hence, would be trivially true. And this trivial truth would do little more than to mask an unfettered discretionary regime of those who wield the powers of the state.[3] Kelsen's claim that the pure theory is adequate to the ideal of the rule of law would turn out to be altogether meaningless.

In what follows I will try to show that the pure theory contains the resources to respond to this problem, by analyzing Kelsen's conceptions of nullity and voidability of legal norms. The purpose of these conceptions, I will argue, is to develop a

---

[2] See Kelsen, *Introduction to the Problems of Legal Theory* (n 1 above) 73–4. Similar considerations apply on all levels of legal hierarchy, for example to the relation between the enactment of a statute and the constitutional norms governing the legality of such enactments.

[3] This interpretation of normative alternatives has been put forward by J W Harris, 'Kelsen's Concept of Authority' in *Cambridge Law Journal* 36 (1977) 353–63. The problem for Kelsen is succinctly summarized by J W Harris, 'Kelsen and Normative Consistency' in Richard Tur and William Twining (eds), *Essays on Kelsen* (Oxford, 1986) 201–28, at 217: '... given Kelsen's dogmatic assumption that all valid legal norms (except the basic norm) must have been authorized by a pre-existing norm, it follows that the law always, by virtue of alternative authorization, confers on norm-authorities the choice to follow the substantive content of higher norms or to ignore it.' The solution to the problem, Harris argues, is to let go of the identity thesis. See for other instances of this interpretation Carlos Santiago Nino, 'Some Confusions Surrounding Kelsen's Concept of Validity' in Stanley Paulson and Bonnie Litschewski-Paulson (eds), *Normativity and Norms. Critical Perspectives on Kelsenian Themes* (Oxford, 1998) 253–61; David Dyzenhaus, *Legality and Legitimacy. Carl Schmitt, Hans Kelsen, and Hermann Heller in Weimar* (Oxford, 1997) 155–7. Stanley Paulson defended Kelsen's conception against the charge that it leaves judges and other public officials free to decide whether to apply the law or not in Stanley Paulson, 'Material and Formal Authorisation in Kelsen's Pure Theory' in *Cambridge Law Journal* 39 (1980) 172–93. My interpretation can be read as a defense of Paulson's conclusions, though it rejects his distinction between formal and material authorization.

version of the identity thesis that steers a middle course between the two problematic interpretations of the thesis outlined, a course that accepts the conceptual
primacy of the first of the two interpretations of the identity thesis just outlined but
that tries to mitigate its anarchic consequences. The middle course is meant to
explicate the potentially anarchic idea of legal objectivity in terms of a set of claims
about the necessary internal institutional structure of a legal order that can justifiably claim to be entitled bindingly to interpret the law. This explication provides
the formal elements of the utopia of legality. Kelsen argues that those who claim to
be acting in an official capacity or on behalf of the state can justifiably invoke a
presumption of legality, and hence some measure of legitimacy, for their acts only
if the legal order fully submits these acts to independent judicial review. In other
words, normative alternatives can exist only where the legal order itself offers redress
against decisions that are suspected of being legally defective. That legal order realizes this 'guarantee of legality', I will argue, is a necessary though not a sufficient
condition of the reasonableness of the perspective of a law-abiding citizen.[4]

Legal hierarchy and depersonalization of the state

In order to understand the first step of Kelsen's argument about legal legitimacy, it
is crucial to take another look at some implications of the theory of legal hierarchy.[5]
Kelsen's theory of legal hierarchy is best described as an attempt to undermine our
intuitive tendency to distinguish sharply between legal and political decisions as
well as to question the constitutional-theoretical consequences we tend to infer
from it. Let me briefly characterize the intuition and its consequences in order to
provide a contrasting background for Kelsen's argument.

[4] Throughout this chapter, I will mainly rely on Hans Kelsen, 'Über Staatsunrecht' in Hans
Klecatsky, René Marcić, and Herbert Schambeck (eds), *Die Wiener rechtstheoretische Schule. Ausgewählte
Schriften von Hans Kelsen, Adolf Julius Merkl und Alfred Verdross* (Wien, 1968), vol I, 957–1214 and Hans
Kelsen, *Allgemeine Staatslehre* (Berlin, 1925) 285–301. The article on 'Staatsunrecht' (on 'state illegal-
ity') provides essential political-theoretical context to Kelsen's general argument about normative alter-
natives that is missing from the *Introduction*.

[5] At this point, a note on periodization is necessary. My main source for this chapter, Kelsen's article
'Über Staatsunrecht' was published in 1914, at a point when Kelsen had not yet adopted the doctrine
of legal hierarchy. See Stanley L Paulson, 'Four Phases in Hans Kelsen's Legal Theory? Reflections on a
Periodization' in *Oxford Journal of Legal Studies* 18 (1998) 153–66, at 164–6. Paulson takes the view
that the doctrine of legal hierarchy is at odds with the 'normative' Kelsen since it treats legal norms as
mere empowerments and not as constraints on official power. See Stanley L Paulson, 'The Weak
Reading of Authority in Hans Kelsen's Pure Theory of Law' in *Law and Philosophy* 19 (2000) 131–71,
at 150–2. If one takes this view, one might be inclined to interpret the doctrine of hierarchy as an
implicit repudiation of the themes of 'Über Staatsunrecht'. I will take a different route and attempt to
interpret the doctrine of legal hierarchy as well as Kelsen's earlier reflections on state illegality as part of a
single position. Kelsen, apparently, did not think his 1914 position conflicted with the doctrine of
legal hierarchy. He approvingly cited 'Über Staatsunrecht' in later works that postdate his adoption of
the doctrine of legal hierarchy. See Kelsen, *Allgemeine Staatslehre* (n 4 above) 388 and Hans Kelsen,
*Der soziologische und der juristische Staatsbegriff. Kritische Untersuchung des Verhältnisses von Staat und
Recht* (Tübingen, 1928) 233–7. We are therefore at least entitled to make an attempt to read the doctrine of legal hierarchy and the theory of state illegality as complementary.

Legislative decisions are commonly thought of as the paradigmatic form of political decisions. While the norms created by valid legislative decisions are identified with recourse to other legal rules we do not generally think of legislative decisions as legal decisions. The reason seems to be that the rules that allow us to identify valid legislative decisions are predominantly procedural. They allocate normative powers to decision-takers but do not determine the content of the decisions to be taken. The legislators are free to exercise the normative powers allocated by the procedural rules they work under as they see fit, to turn into law the rules they deem most reasonable on substantive grounds. At least in modern constitutional contexts, this legislative freedom is usually justified on the basis of the idea that the legislators are democratically elected representatives of the people who exercise the powers of the popular sovereign and who take political responsibility for how they exercise those powers.

Judicial decisions, on the other hand, are the paradigm of legal decisions. They typically do not themselves create law but rather apply law created by the legislators. Judges who have to decide a case do not have the discretion to take the decision they deem most reasonable. Rather, they are bound to the norms enacted by the legislature and their decisions are considered to be legitimate to the extent that they faithfully apply these already existing legal norms. Judges are institutionally independent, ie they are not subject to the direct orders of any other organ of government. This independence enables them to resist pressures to bend the law to the interests of powerful parties whose interests are at stake in a given case. But it is not a license for failing to exhibit deference to the laws enacted by the legislator. The independence of judges would turn into a form of unjustifiable privilege if judges usurped the political powers of the legislator. Such powers can be exercised legitimately only by those who can be held politically accountable.

Kelsen's conception of legal hierarchy implies that this picture is in important respects misleading. Kelsen rejects the idea that there is a sharp qualitative distinction between legal and political decision taking.[6] He believes not just that the distinction is unwarranted from the perspective of legal theory. He also thinks, as we will see, that overemphasizing the sharpness of the distinction will inevitably undersell or even deny the resources of legitimacy internal to legal order.[7] Drawing a sharp distinction between legal and political decisions suggests that the legitimacy of political decisions is ultimately not to be sought in their legality. It also suggests that legal decision-taking is mere execution of political decisions already taken and thus incapable of enforcing standards of legitimacy that justify political decisions. Positive legality, according to the picture just outlined, cannot function as a legitimating condition on the exercise of political power and as long as legality cannot

---

[6] The denial of a qualitative distinction between legal and political decisions is a constant refrain in Kelsen's works. See for example Kelsen, *Introduction to the Problems of Legal Theory* (n 1 above) 70–1; Kelsen, *Allgemeine Staatslehre* (n 4 above) 233–4; Kelsen, 'Die Lehre von den drei Gewalten oder Funktionen des Staates' in *Die Wiener rechtstheoretische Schule* (n 4 above) vol II, 1625–60, at 1633–4.
[7] See Kelsen, *Allgemeine Staatslehre* (n 4 above) 255–61.

function in a legitimating role the perspective of the law-abiding citizen will remain quixotic.

Kelsen's notion of legal hierarchy attacks the standard distinction between legal and political decisions by emphasizing three interrelated aspects of positive legal order. The first is the thoroughly decisionist character of legal order. Kelsen claims that, with the exception of the basic norm itself, all legal norms, general laws, as well as individual norms enacted by judges as decisions in particular cases, are the result of human decisions. All these decisions are, in Kelsen's view, to a larger or lesser degree discretionary. A legal norm, on any level of the hierarchy, has normative force, according to the pure theory, because it was enacted in accordance with the applicable higher order norms authorizing its enactment. But these authorizing norms always leave open several possible decisions on the lower level. As long as those who enact a norm remain *within the limits* of their authorization there is no further question of legal correctness. The normative force of legal norms thus depends *solely* on their enactment in accordance with a 'method' authorized by the basic norm. If a norm was enacted in conformity with the rules authorized by the basic norm, if it exists at all, it has normative force whatever its content may be.[8]

The second feature of legal order that Kelsen's theory of legal hierarchy is concerned to drive home is the claim that, on any level of the hierarchy, valid authority to take decisions that others have to accept as binding is *always* conferred by higher order legal norms. The pure theory denies that there can be such a thing as 'natural' authority to take decisions others ought to submit to in virtue of personal wisdom, deeper moral insight, charisma, the raw power to exercise successful leadership, or any other personal characteristic that is not attributed by the law. More importantly, the pure theory denies that there is any particular organ of state, on any level of the legal hierarchy, that can make a more direct claim to represent 'the people' or 'the state' than any other.[9] Legal authority, according to the pure theory, is not grounded in some purely political source of authority external to the positive law. It is attributed to the system as a whole by presupposing a basic norm. Hence, a legal decision taker can exercise legitimate authority over someone else only by objectively complying with some authorizing legal rule or set of legal rules on a higher level of the hierarchy.

Finally, it is a crucial element of Kelsen's view of authorization that the legal hierarchy is more than just a jurisdictional hierarchy. While legal order can be portrayed as a layered system of authorizing norms, the material norms on any given

---

[8] Kelsen, *Introduction to the Problems of Legal Theory* (n 1 above) 63–4: '... the law governs its own creation. In particular, it is a legal norm that governs the process whereby another legal norm is created, and also governs—to a [varying degree]—the content of the norm to be created. Given the dynamic character of the law, a norm is valid because and in so far as it was created in a certain way, that is, in the way determined by another norm; and this latter norm, then, represents the basis of the validity of the former norm.'

[9] See the attacks on the 'fiction of representation' in Kelsen, *Allgemeine Staatslehre* (n 4 above) 312–17 and the discussion of 'the people' in Hans Kelsen, *Vom Wesen und Wert der Demokratie* (Tübingen, 1929) 14–25.

level of the hierarchy form an inseparable part of the authorizing conditions for valid exercises of legal power on the lower levels.[10] Kelsen's primary idea of authorization, then, is not that those who are formally authorized to take decisions on any level of the hierarchy have a power to take decisions that are binding even if they violate material law. Rather, it is given by what I have called a strong principle of legality. Decisions taken by legal officials are authoritative only if they are taken in *full* compliance with *all* relevant higher order legal norms, including all applicable higher-order material norms.

Kelsen's rejection of the view that formally authorized decisions have legal force even if they violate material law, however, is not merely motivated by an interest in bringing material constraints of legality to bear on acts of state. Kelsen also believes that the question whether an act was formally authorized will in many cases be as controversial as any dispute about the material legality of an alleged act of state.[11] In other words, Kelsen does not work with a distinction between formal and material legality as much as he works with a distinction between defective legal norms and legal norms that exhibit full conformity with the laws that authorized their enactment. A piece of legislation or a judicial or administrative decision, though, can be defective not just in virtue of violating a material legal constraint but also in virtue of violating some procedural constraint.[12] And insofar as procedural constraints often entrench a division of powers or accord rights of participation to minorities, a group that controls the core of the legislative or administrative process may have as much of an incentive to play fast and loose with procedural provisions as it may be tempted to disregard material law.

The theory of legal hierarchy, then, is committed to a substantive conception of legality. Unless we are dealing with rare limiting cases in which there are no material norms relevant to the decision at hand, legality includes, but is not limited to, material legality.[13] When Kelsen claims that legal decisions are valid, irrespective

[10] Kelsen believes, for example, that a general law forbidding theft that is applied by a judge to a particular case authorizes the particular norm enacted by the judge. The relevant chain of validity, in other words, runs through the material norm against theft. See Kelsen, 'Die Lehre von den drei Gewalten' (n 6 above) 1632–3.

[11] The examples of legal conflicts Kelsen invokes in his arguments for judicial review mainly concern conflicts of competence. Kelsen talks at length about conflicts concerning the validity of acts of legislation lacking parliamentary consent in a constitutional monarchy. The question of the conditions of the rightful exercise and of the scope of the powers of the president of the Weimar Republic, especially of the powers under the emergency provisions of art 48 of the Weimar constitution, are likewise issues of formal authority. Kelsen clearly did not think, then, that the enforcement of full or substantive procedural legality is any less important politically than the defense of material individual rights.

[12] This is indicated by Kelsen's way of phrasing the problem of the relation between norms on different levels of legal hierarchy. See for example Kelsen, *Introduction to the Problems of Legal Theory* (n 1 above) 72: 'If, for example, an unconstitutional statute is possible—that is, a valid statute that either in the manner of its creation or in its content fails to conform to the provisions of the prevailing constitution...' This passage clearly implies that a statute that is valid in virtue of the doctrine of normative alternatives can be defective either procedurally or materially. Hence, the alternative between a defective and non-defective norm cannot overlap with the distinction between formal and material legality.

[13] For example legislative acts in absolute monarchies that have no 'formal constitution', ie no constitution that involves several organs in the process of legislation or that restricts the permissible

of their content, if they have been enacted in accordance with the method or in the way that is authorized by the basic norm he does not want to express approval of the view that they are valid on formal grounds even if they are materially mistaken. Rather, to say that a decision was taken in accordance with the way or method authorized by the basic norm is to say that the decision is both formally and materially correct.

The reason why Kelsen continues to speak in proceduralist terms like 'way' or 'method' in order to characterize his overall conception of legality, even while he rejects a distinction between formal and material authorization, is straightforward enough. In Kelsen's view, a legal decision can be both procedurally and materially correct without being uniquely determined by the higher-order legal norms that condition its legality. This is quite obvious in the case of legislative enactments that are both procedurally valid and that comply with all material constitutional norms. The content of such legislative enactments is obviously underdetermined even by a combination of perfect procedural and material constitutionality. In Kelsen's view, the same is true, though to a lesser degree, of any administrative or judicial decision. All legal norms, with the exception of particular norms enacted on the lowest level of legal hierarchy, play a double role. They authorize all decisions that can reasonably be interpreted as decisions falling under them. At the same time, however, they limit the authority they confer to a larger or lesser extent. In Kelsenian legal order, there is no 'raw' or unlimited authority since all authority depends on prior authorization by legal rules and all legal rules, procedural and material, have the tendency to constrain. At the same time, there is never such a thing as a decision that does not involve an exercise of authority, however limited.

A legal decision, then, simply is a legally authorized decision. This feature, however, does not distinguish 'legal' from 'political' decisions. Of course, Kelsen admits that there are important differences between legislation and adjudication or administration. But he claims that these differences can be explained as differences of degree or quantity, not of quality. The decisions of judges and administrators are, relatively speaking, more restricted by already existing legal norms than those of a legislature. But for Kelsen, this just means that the conditions on the valid exercise of authority tend to become more specific and determinate the further down the hierarchy of the 'Stufenbau' we move.[14]

Kelsen's theory of legal hierarchy has an important implication for the relations between the decision takers on different levels of the hierarchy, namely that it is fundamentally misguided to conceive of the enactment of a norm on any level of the hierarchy as the issuing of an order or a command to decision takers on a lower level. Legislators can enact general norms that impact on the conditions under which other officials can legitimately exercise their authority to decide particular

content of legislation. In such systems, however, formal constraints are very likely to be less developed as well.

[14] See Kelsen, *Introduction to the Problems of Legal Theory* (n 1 above) 63–71.

cases. But they can do so only by *objectively* complying with whatever higher-order constitutional norms authorize and govern legislation.[15] Hence, it is incompatible with the legal-scientific point of view to assume that the legislature possesses a political authority which entitles it to think of its laws as standing orders to lower-level officials. Such officials will consider themselves subject to the actual intentions or the 'subjective' will of the legislators, as expressed in a general norm, only insofar as *they* judge that the norm objectively complies with the legal conditions authorizing legislative acts. They are subject only to the law itself, not to those who make it.[16]

This position of lower-level officials with respect to the legislator is only a special case of a more general phenomenon. The same principles apply to any relation between decision takers on a relatively higher and a relatively lower level of the legal hierarchy. Most importantly, they apply, as Kelsen emphasizes explicitly, to the relation of the individual subject of the law to the institutionalized legal system as a whole. The final addressees of the law's claim to obedience are individual subjects of the law who are called upon to perform a legal duty created by the legal system. And it is the perspective of the subject to which Kelsen's argument about legal legitimacy is primarily addressed.[17]

This conclusion is reinforced by a second important consequence of Kelsen's theory of legal hierarchy. The theory of legal hierarchy implies that the pure theory as legal science cannot precisely tell a legal decision maker on any level of the hierarchy, from a prospective point of view, what decision he ought to take *within* the bounds of his authorization. Kelsen's distinction between objective and subjective legal meaning assumes, however, that it is possible for legal science to assess the legality of any decision proposed as a means of filling out the frame left open by higher-order norms. Jurisprudence can give an answer to the question whether a decision that is to be taken or that has been taken is in full compliance with the relevant authorizing legal conditions or not. And it is precisely this question that needs to be answerable for the perspective of the law-abiding citizen to be meaningful.

Another way to put this point is to say that the pure theory, as legal 'science', is primarily a theory of the review of decisions taken by those who claim to be authorized by legal order to take decisions binding on others. And this review, in its most fundamental form, is the prerogative of the law-abiding citizen who, while he acknowledges that he is subject to the law, wants to determine what his concrete legal duties are. The law-abiding citizen, by definition, accepts that he has to do whatever validly enacted law requires him to do. But he also insists that he is subject only to the objective meaning of the law and not to the subjective intentions of the persons the law authorizes to enact positive norms.[18]

---

[15] See Kelsen, *Allgemeine Staatslehre* (n 4 above) 287–9.   [16] See ibid, 285–301.

[17] See Kelsen, *Über Staatsunrecht* (n 4 above) 1031–9 and Kelsen, *Allgemeine Staatslehre* (n 4 above) 287–8.

[18] See for further explicit affirmations of this idea Kelsen, *Der soziologische und der juristische Staatsbegriff* (n 5 above) 91; Kelsen, *Das Problem der Souveränität und die Theorie des Völkerrechts. Beitrag zu einer reinen Rechtslehre* (Tübingen, 1920) 8, 17, and 267.

Kelsen's principle of legality I: Nullity

According to the primary understanding of the identity thesis, acts performed by natural persons can be interpreted as acts of state and hence be considered as valid exercises of public power only if they can be shown to have been legally authorized. Otherwise they are mere private acts for which those who performed them bear personal responsibility. Kelsen's official arguments in defense of the identity thesis can be summed up briefly.[19] What we call the person of the state cannot possibly be a sociological or psychological reality. If we talk of the person of the state or if we attribute to that person a will of the state we are dealing in a jurisprudential idealization or fiction. This fiction is a useful shorthand way of referring to the fact that we consider certain human acts or decisions as enactments of norms because they are properly authorized by higher order norms that we acknowledge as valid grounds of authority. But once we take the fiction to refer to a real person or a real or 'subjective' will behind the positive law we are engaging in an unjustifiable 'hypostatization'.[20]

If the unity of the state is to be identified with the unity of legal order, any attempt to grasp the unity of the state must be bound to a 'principle of legality'[21] which states that in order for an act to count as an act of state that act must be legal. But this principle, as a restatement of the identity thesis, does not put the state under any duties. The state as a normative order cannot be subject to the principle of legality because the state as normative order does not have the capacity to act illegally.[22] We have already encountered this thesis in a different form. Kelsen, as we have seen, claims that the objective validity of a norm must be equated with its existence. If all existing norms are objectively valid and hence binding, it must be impossible for the state to enact a norm that lacks objective validity.

That the state lacks the power to act illegally, however, does not entail that the identity thesis is normatively empty, as is often supposed by authors who overlook that Kelsenian legality is substantive.[23] It means that whoever claims to be authorized by the legal order to take binding decisions, whether he be a legislator, administrator, or a judge, will fail to actually do so, will fail to enact a valid norm, if he exceeds the limits of his authority: an authority whose scope is conditioned by the combination of all applicable procedural and material norms. The fact that the principle of legality entails that all acts of state are legal, therefore, must not be understood as an endorsement of the arbitrary and unlimited power of those who claim to act in the state's name. It is directed against the view that an act which

---

[19] See Kelsen, 'Über Staatsunrecht' (n 4 above) 960–72. See also Kelsen, *Der soziologische und der juristische Staatsbegriff* (n 5 above) 114–204; Kelsen, *Introduction to the Problems of Legal Theory* (n 1 above) 97–106.

[20] See Kelsen, *Der soziologische und der juristische Staatsbegriff* (n 5 above) 251–3.

[21] I am borrowing this term from Dyzenhaus, *Legality and Legitimacy* (n 3 above) 116.

[22] See Kelsen, 'Über Staatsunrecht' (n 4 above) 986.

[23] For a typical instance see the references to Kelsen in Lon L Fuller, 'A Reply to Critics' in Lon L Fuller, *The Morality of Law. Revised Edition* (New Haven, 1964) 187–242.

falls short of perfect legality is valid, and hence binding on subjects, since it is still attributable, despite its imperfect legality, to the state.[24]

The idea that we can attribute an act to the state only insofar as we can identify it as legal entails, according to Kelsen, that a *judgment of attribution* is presupposed in any characterization of an act as an act of state. A judgment of attribution is not itself an exercise of legal authority but rather an exercise of jurisprudential or legal scientific understanding. It follows that the addressees of any act that purports to be an enactment of a binding norm have to have the power to form a judgment of attribution before they can come to the conclusion that the act is objectively authorized, an act of state, and therefore binding. This holds true even of the law-abiding citizen who has already acknowledged a duty to defer to all decisions that can be attributed to the state. If addressees cannot make a judgment of attribution, they will have to assume that the act is only 'subjectively' but not objectively an exercise of legal authority and the norm it purports to have created therefore *null*.[25]

Kelsen's favorite example of a clear situation of nullity is the affair of the Hauptmann von Köpenick.[26] The Hauptmann was an imposter who put on the uniform of a colonel, walked into the Prussian town of Köpenick, and started to issue orders to local citizens and administrative officials. Since people took his uniform as sufficient proof of his status he was able to get people to obey him and ultimately to make off with the city's tax money that had been kept in a locked box in the town hall.[27]

Kelsen acknowledges, of course, that in most situations in which the legality of an act that claims to be an act of state is in doubt matters will be significantly more complicated. In most interesting cases, the people whose actions are in question

[24] See Kelsen, *Der soziologische und der juristische Staatsbegriff* (n 5 above) 136–40.

[25] Kelsen, 'Über Staatsunrecht' (n 4 above) 1034, claims that judgments of attribution pertain by default to the 'logical authority of the individual'. See also Kelsen, *Allgemeine Staatslehre* (n 4 above) 277–8. This view explicitly rejects the distinction between the 'individual point of view' and the 'legal point of view' that Raz (See Joseph Raz, 'Kelsen's Theory of the Basic Norm' in Joseph Raz, *The Authority of Law. Essays on Law and Morality* (Oxford, 1979) 122–45, at 140) attributes to Kelsen. Kelsen makes it quite clear that logical authority, in contrast to decisional authority, pertains to every subject of the law. Raz claims that 'there is, for Kelsen, a great difference between a personal point of view and the scientific point of view' (ibid). This is correct only if we understand the distinction between the personal and the scientific point of view as a distinction between two different evaluative perspectives, namely between one's substantive conception of justice on the one hand and one's attribution of content-independent legitimacy to valid law on the other. But it is false if the scientific or legal point of view is understood as a non-evaluative point of view.

[26] See Kelsen, *Introduction to the Problems of Legal Theory* (n 1 above) 9; Kelsen, 'Über Staatsunrecht' (n 4 above) 1008.

[27] Note three important features of this story. First, it is usually read as an exemplification of the uncritical veneration of authority that was typical of Wilhelmine Germany. It illustrates the cultural power of the presumption of the legality of authority. Second, it re-emphasizes Kelsen's point that ordinary citizens are the final addressees of the argument about state illegality. The story, after all, is one about direct interaction between authority and the actual human beings who were, as the ultimate addressees of the state's claims, expected to obey. Finally, the defectiveness of the Colonel's acts was clearly one in formal authority which reaffirms our point that Kelsen does not believe that formal authority is less problematic than material legality.

will be people who can at least make a plausible prima facie claim to be acting in a public capacity. It will usually not be in question that they are authorized by the law to enact certain decisions, in compliance with rules that constitute and limit, to a larger or lesser extent, their authority and that if they successfully do so citizens will be subject to their decisions. What is more, those who are authorized to exercise legal authority will naturally have to claim that their decisions are valid exercises of public authority if they are to decide at all. But Kelsen emphasizes that the argument about nullity is perfectly general. The acts of a 'real' public official are as liable to nullity, if they exceed the authority conferred by legal order, as those of an imposter like the Hauptmann von Köpenick who does not possess any authority to begin with.

An act of state that is null is non-existing as an act of state from a legal-logical perspective. Everyone is entitled to refuse to attribute such an act that occurs with the claim to be an act of state. It is incapable of bringing forth the legal effects that the legal order connects to acts of state. A special official procedure to ascertain nullity is not needed. The question whether we are faced with a case of nullity or not is a legal-logical question. Such questions are decided by the understanding of each judging individual, not by the authority of the state.[28]

Note that this is a very radical view. Any act that turns out to be non-authorized under retrospective review, a review that any ordinary subject of the law is entitled to perform, is to be considered null. Note as well that the review does not end at the point at which someone who is formally identifiable as a public official declares his decision. It clearly includes a real scrutiny of the question whether the decision taken is properly authorized by all procedural and material norms it claims to apply. In other words, one cannot arrive at the conclusion that the public official has acted in a public capacity unless one is willing to accept that his decision is a reasonable way of applying or interpreting the legal norms on the basis of which he claims to act. The review is thus inevitably a review for the validity of the decision since actions outside of the bounds of proper authority result in nullity.

The notion of nullity is obviously related to the pure theory's insistence on the irreducible objectivity of the basic norm and the norms deriving from it.[29] This insistence expresses the regulative jurisprudential assumption that it is always meaningful to distinguish between the subjective and the objective meaning of *all* acts that claim to be exercises of official power. It cannot be the case that alleged enactments of norms are objectively valid merely because those who are authorized to take legislative, adjudicative, or administrative decisions within proper limits *say so*. That the pure theory is a science, or a function of cognition and not of the will, as Kelsen sometimes puts it,[30] *means* that those who are authorized to decide under some power-conferring rule cannot also have an authority to *decide*, with a binding effect on the addressees, that what they intend to be an enactment of a norm

[28] Kelsen, 'Über Staatsunrecht' (n 4 above) 1004.
[29] See Kelsen, *Allgemeine Staatslehre* (n 4 above) 278.
[30] See Kelsen, *Introduction to the Problems of Legal Theory* (n 1 above) 18–19.

must be considered by others as having objectively complied with the relevant power-conferring rules. The claim on the part of an authority to have the power to preempt judgments of attribution is nonsensical because any claim to deference presupposes that those who make the claim have already been identified as organs of the state. It is therefore impossible to subject the prior judgment of attribution to a duty of deference. The judgment whether some alleged act of state is properly authorized and therefore legally binding or not rests, by default, with those to whom the act is addressed.[31]

Kelsen consequently rejects the view that administrative acts, in contrast to legal acts of private citizens that are to be assessed under private law, can claim a presumption of validity in virtue of being acts of state, that 'the state's power, manifesting itself in the administrative act, testifies to its own legality'. Kelsen replies that this is true only 'if the state's power does, indeed, manifest itself in the administrative act. But the state's power itself cannot testify to whether it does appear in the administrative act, ie to whether we are even faced with an administrative act.'[32] The question cannot be decided by the state acting as a supreme authority. It is a matter of legal science, and hence, as we have seen, a judgment up to each individual citizen. Finally, Kelsen argues that a positive legal order need not explicitly incorporate an enumeration of grounds of nullity in order to empower citizens to arrive at judgments of nullity. Such provisions can, at best, have declaratory force.[33] The subject's power to issue a judgment of nullity, as we will now see, can only be overturned by the introduction of enumerated conditions of voidability.

Kelsen's principle of legality II: Voidability

Kelsen's general argument about nullity would seem to lead into a potentially dangerous standoff between subjects of the law and legal decision makers.[34] That no public official can have the legal authority to make his decisions binding on others in any other way than by objectively complying with all norms that authorize and guide him does not change the fact that officials who have to take legal decisions will inevitably have to proceed on the basis of the claim that they are complying with the authorizing rules if they are to decide at all. Even if decision-makers cannot and do not claim to have a legal power to self-validate their own acts, and even if they try in good faith to comply with the rules authorizing them, they cannot possibly accept the view that the question whether their acts bind the addressees is contingent on whether the addressees, as a matter of fact, recognize their acts to be valid.

Note that the objectivist reading of the claim that a decision is binding if and only if it was taken in accordance with the proper authorizing rules would appear

[31] See Kelsen, *Allgemeine Staatslehre* (n 4 above) 289–90.
[32] Kelsen, 'Über Staatsunrecht' (n 4 above) 1027–8 [my translation]. See also Kelsen, *Allgemeine Staatslehre* (n 4 above) 295–7.   [33] See Kelsen, 'Über Staatsunrecht' (n 4 above) 1031–5.
[34] See Kelsen, *Allgemeine Staatslehre* (n 4 above) 297–9.

to entail that an addressee of the enactment may be just as wrong, misguided, or self-interested in claiming that some alleged exercise of authority is null as the officials claiming to have acted as organs of the state may be in arguing that it is valid. As a subject of the law I will, of course, have to form a belief about whether a claimed exercise of public power succeeded to enact an objectively valid norm or not. But the fact that I believe that some attempted enactment did not result in a valid norm (which is, for practical purposes, indistinguishable from my claim to have this belief) clearly should not suffice to excuse my illegal behavior if I am wrong. A legal order cannot adopt the principle that anyone's mere claim to have doubts about the validity of a norm suffices to free that person from any legal obligation. Such a rule could obviously be abused by subjects of the law who are interested to shrug off any legal obligation at their pleasure. These observations are nothing but the flip side of the claim that persons charged with the exercise of official power cannot self-validate their acts. The ideal of the rule of law differs not only from the rule of men, it also differs from the freedom of unrestricted self-government.[35]

The law-abiding citizen does not dispute this implication of the idea of legal objectivity. He will claim that he can only act on his own judgments of attribution. But he will accept that this judgment is an intellectual operation, a function of the understanding, not an exercise of legal authority. He will accept, consequently, that he cannot claim a subjective right to decide not to obey a valid legal norm. What is more, the law-abiding citizen, since he believes, by definition, that deference is reasonably owed to legal order (though not to the persons who execute it), will acknowledge an interest in seeing the law fully executed. In other words, he will take the view that the state must not acknowledge anyone else's claims to be the final judge of his or her legal obligations.

Kelsen believes that this description of the point of view of the law-abiding citizen suggests that the law-abiding citizen should be willing to accept a partial transfer of his powers of primary review to adjudicative institutions authorized to scrutinize the legality of acts of enactment or exercises of political power.[36] The simple standoff between the claims of officialdom and the point of view of the subject of the law must and can be mediated, Kelsen believes, by the explicit introduction of system-internal institutions of review or guarantees of legality.[37] The introduction of such system-internal mechanisms of review gives rise to the category of *voidable* norms. And in a well-developed legal order, the voidability of norms will largely replace citizen-judgments of nullity.[38]

A voidable norm is a norm that has been enacted in a way that gives us at least a prima facie reason to believe that it is legal, for example because it was enacted by

---

[35] See Kelsen, 'Über Staatsunrecht' (n 4 above) 1039; Kelsen, *Vom Wesen und Wert der Demokratie* (n 9 above) 4–9; Kelsen, *Allgemeine Staatslehre* (n 4 above) 250–1.

[36] See Kelsen, 'Über Staatsunrecht' (n 4 above) 1037–9.

[37] See Kelsen, 'Wesen und Entwicklung der Staatsgerichtsbarkeit' in *Die Wiener rechtstheoretische Schule* (n 4 above) vol II, 1813–71, at 1826–34.

[38] See Kelsen, *Allgemeine Staatslehre* (n 4 above) 277–8; Kelsen, *Introduction to the Problems of Legal Theory* (n 1 above) 71–5.

decision takers who have formal competence with respect to the matter at hand, but that is suspected to be legally defective because it violates a material or procedural higher-order norm that is part of the full set of conditions authorizing the acts of the relevant organ of state. However, a voidable norm is legally valid and thus binding until it is officially repealed by an organ of state that has been endowed, by positive law, with the authority to review the decisions of those who enacted it.

The introduction of the category of voidability of course raises the question how we are to distinguish between nullity and voidability. Kelsen discusses several proposals that he thinks are typical examples of the misguidedness of natural law theory. For example, Kelsen attacks the view that the distinction between nullity and voidability can be related to that between private and public law.[39] According to such a view, legal defects of acts of private citizens always entail nullity while acts of state that have an appearance of legality are always fully valid unless the state itself decides to retract them. This presumption, Kelsen thinks, is a piece of authoritarian ideology that does not stand up to the demands of a legal science. Legal science has to start out from the opposite presumption that all legal acts, including acts of state, which are in any way legally defective are null. This presumption stands until the positive law explicitly declares that a certain kind of defect does not automatically invalidate a norm and provides for a system-internal mechanism of repeal. Voidable norms, in other words, can exist only where the positive law explicitly provides for a mechanism of repeal.[40]

By putting into place a system-internal mechanism of review, the legal order, or the state, is taking away the judgment on whether a legal defect afflicts a legal decision from the individual subject of the law. And such internalization has the effect that a decision which is suspected to be defective is to be considered valid by those not entitled to review until it is repealed. The size of the category of voidable norms, of the norms that can claim a presumptive validity, therefore depends on the positive law, on the extent to which the legal system provides subjects with institutionalized means to challenge the legality of norms that are suspected of being defective.

While Kelsen believes that the distinction between nullity and voidability is dependent on the content of the positive law, he observes that most legal orders tend to draw the line in a certain way. Kelsen claims that it is theoretically possible for there to be a primitive legal system that does not contain any voidable norms because it has not yet started to 'internalize' disputes about the legality of acts allegedly authorized by law. On the other hand, one could imagine a system that tried to preempt judgments of nullity on the part of the citizens as far as possible. But such a system would be impracticable, according to Kelsen, since it would entail that citizens would have to give the benefit of the doubt even to imposters like the

---

[39] See Kelsen, 'Über Staatsunrecht' (n 4 above) 1023–31. The attack on the distinction between private and public law is, of course, only a special instance of the general attack on the law-state dualism. See also Kelsen, *Introduction to the Problems of Legal Theory* (n 1 above) 97–106.

[40] See Kelsen, 'Wesen und Entwicklung der Staatsgerichtsbarkeit' (n 37 above) 1828.

Hauptmann von Köpenick until their acts have been invalidated by a court. Actual legal orders usually distinguish between formal and substantive legality and restrict the category of nullity to more obvious cases of formal invalidity while they tend to refer all questions of material legality to the courts. But this way of drawing the distinction is not in any way necessary or 'natural'. It is merely the most practical way of organizing voidability.[41]

One important consequence of this view is that it entails a certain picture of the role of courts endowed with powers of review. Kelsen, as we have seen, is committed to the idea that no organ of the state can self-certify its claimed exercises of authority. We have also seen that review for authority is always substantive review, at least if there are any material norms that condition the authority of some organ of state. This suggests rather strongly that a system-internal replacement for primary review, as exercised by law-abiding subjects, has to come in the form of institutions that are *independent* of the organs who took the decisions that are challenged by a subject.[42] Secondly, these independent organs of review have to have the power to engage in *meaningful review* of the material correctness of the decisions under scrutiny; they cannot simply stop at an inquiry into the formal validity of official acts or adopt a policy of deference to the claim to legality inevitably made by the organ under review. If they so restricted themselves, they would be meaningless institutions incapable of offering a replacement for the primary review exercised by the law-abiding citizen.[43]

Kelsen's argument seems to entail as well that the law-creating organs whose decisions are to be reviewed cannot legitimately use their powers to attempt to bypass or switch off judicial review. To claim such a power would be equivalent to claiming the power to preempt the law-abiding citizen's judgments of attribution. But such a claim cannot coherently be made by rulers who claim that their authority is based on the law and who claim that their subjects therefore ought to adopt the deferential posture of a law-abiding citizen. From the perspective of the law-abiding citizen, a presumption of validity enjoyed by formally valid acts of state can be bought only at the price of making available a mechanism of independent review that searchingly scrutinizes the way in which the substantive legal norms purportedly authorizing organs of state have been applied by these organs.[44]

---

[41] See Kelsen, 'Über Staatsunrecht' (n 4 above) 1033–5.

[42] See Kelsen, 'Wesen und Entwicklung der Staatsgerichtsbarkeit' (n 37 above) 1836; Kelsen, 'Wer soll der Hüter der Verfassung sein?' in *Die Wiener rechtstheoretische Schule* (n 4 above) vol II, 1873–912, at 1874: 'There is no technical legal principle that commands as wide an agreement as the principle that no one ought to be judge in his own cause.' [my translation]

[43] See Hans Kelsen, 'Das Urteil des Staatsgerichtshofs vom 25. Oktober 1932' in *Die Justiz* 8 (1932–1933) 65–91, at 70.

[44] This interpretation may be suspected of illegitimately introducing a Fullerian flair into Kelsen's conception of legal order. But it finds independent support in Kelsen's theory of constitutional adjudication which will be discussed below in Chapter 5. Kelsen argues explicitly that constitutional norms which can be bypassed by government lack full legal force and acquire it only once they are guaranteed by an independent constitutional court. See Kelsen, 'Wesen und Entwicklung der Staatsgerichtsbarkeit' (n 37 above). The general idea is that a norm whose observance is merely optional

Due to the introduction of voidability, the idea that the state can do no wrong has been split up into a set of choices. That it is impossible for the state to act illegally, either means that ordinary subjects of the law have the power to refuse to attribute what they perceive as illegal acts to the state or it has to mean that the state must be willing to institute system-internal guarantees of legality that live up to the three conditions just outlined. If a legal order embraces the second option, it will generate a new version of the principle of legality. This new version of the principle is no longer bound to the simple alternative of validity vs nullity. Rather, it makes the aspirational claim that legally defective decisions by officials should be reduced as far as possible. Review by independent courts is the technical means by which a state can document its commitment to this principle and hence make bearable the fact that decision-takers will inevitably have to proceed on the assumption that their decisions exhibit legality.[45]

Under this transformed reading, the identity thesis expresses a normative ideal governing the exercise of public power, and not just an empty conceptual truth. Public officials exercise their powers under legal authorization. They claim, and law-abiding citizens accept, that the legality of a decision taken by a public official is a ground of legitimacy. If this idea is to have any bite, it cannot be that the deciding officials themselves get to have the final say on what the law is authorizing them to do. Precisely the same principle, of course, applies to all legal acts of private persons, like the drawing up of a testament or the making of a private contract. Kelsen's point is that there is no interesting difference, from a legal-theoretical point of view, between these two situations. If the rules of contract, in order to be effective, require adjudication, the same goes for the rules that authorize public officials to take binding decisions. Hence, such decisions should be open to precisely the same kind of judicial scrutiny, undertaken on behalf of affected citizens.

Of course, Kelsen's way of presenting the introduction of the transformed principle of legality is getting things backwards, in a sense. Almost all of us are born into already existing states and we are never offered a choice between exercising our rights of review for ourselves and transferring them to special institutions. Already existing states will, as a matter of fact, claim absolute authority to decide all social disputes and as long as they exist they will be able to enforce their rulings. Kelsen does not deny any of these facts.[46] His argument so far can nevertheless be read as part of an overall argument about the conditions under which a state can legitimately expect its subjects to adopt the posture of law-abiding citizens. It provides one crucial necessary condition for a state's being able to appeal to the legality of

for government is not, strictly speaking, a valid legal norm. This, however, seems just another way of making Fuller's point that the enactment of legal norms is meaningful only if the state undertakes a commitment to bring about congruence between the law and official acts. See Lon L Fuller, *The Morality of Law* (n 23 above) 81–91.

[45] The import of the transformed version of the principle of legality is cashed out in Kelsen's notion of 'guarantees of legality'. See Kelsen, 'Wesen und Entwicklung der Staatsgerichtsbarkeit' (n 37 above) 1826–34.   [46] See for example Kelsen, *Vom Wesen und Wert der Demokratie* (n 9 above) 8–9.

its acts as a resource of legitimacy, as a ground of the claim that its subjects ought to respect its rulings, even if they don't agree on the merits, because those rulings are controlled by constraints of legality. Such an appeal makes sense, according to Kelsen, only if a state fully commits itself to the second, internalized variant of the principle of legality. If the state did not make this commitment, citizens would not be in a position to think of the duties of obedience the state takes them to be under in terms of subjection to the law.[47] Rather, citizens would have to accept a duty to defer to the personal authority or subjective will of those who exercise political power in order to rationalize obedience since the power-holders would, as a matter of fact, be the final judges of what the laws that purport to control their exercises of power mean. A state's willingness to commit to the transformed principle of legality is therefore a necessary condition of the possibility of reasonable adoption of the perspective of the law-abiding citizen on the part of subjects.

The sovereignty of law: The doctrine of normative alternatives reconsidered

A critic might complain that we are still basically in the same standoff between the individual subject and the institutionalized legal system we started out from. After all, isn't the legal order as a whole, including the courts, doing what Kelsen thinks no individual organ of state can do? Isn't it perfectly possible to envisage a situation in which an independent reviewing court has searchingly scrutinized a judicial, administrative or legislative decision, has decided that the decision should stand, but has nevertheless, in our view, made a mistake in not voiding the decision under review? If such mistaken decisions stand, are we not ultimately displacing substantive with formal authority, the rule of law with an appeal to the state's power?[48]

It would appear that there are only two alternatives for Kelsen. The first is to say that the judgment is null since it is legally mistaken. The other is to say that whatever particular norm the system finally settles on, after it has gone through all its internal motions, is valid regardless of what we perceive as the substantive legal merits of the final decision. Even if we are ultimately subjected to an interpretation of the law we do not agree with, we have at least been able to avail ourselves of a searching review of the original decision in front of an independent court.

---

[47] Kelsen's attacks on the distinction of law and state as an 'ideology of legitimacy' (see Kelsen, *Introduction to the Problems of Legal Theory* [n 1 above] 98–9 and 106–7) are directed against states that (or more precisely: whose governing elites) are not willing to fully commit to the internalized principle of legality but who are nevertheless trying to justify their rule in terms of a conditional commitment to legality. It is this constellation that allows the state to justify itself 'by way of the law or, what comes to the same thing, to justify the law by way of the state' (ibid, 106).

[48] See for a detailed statement of this charge Paulson, 'Material and Formal Authorization in Kelsen's Pure Theory' (n 3 above) 183–8. A similar line of argument appears to underpin Jeremy Waldron's attack on the principle that no one ought to be a judge in his own cause. See Jeremy Waldron, *Law and Disagreement* (Oxford, 1999) 296–8.

A system that internalizes procedures of review will be entitled to claim that its final decisions are objectively valid. Nullity is not completely out of the picture. First, subjects of the law will still have to be able to identify the decisions as decisions taken by competent organs. Second, the reviewing organ that takes the final decision must presumably act in a way that is not obviously incompatible with the claim to legality that Kelsen, as we have seen, takes to be a characteristic of all exercises of public power. But the legal system, given fulfillment of these conditions, will completely preempt a subject's judgment on all substantive legal reasons by claiming an authoritative power to decide what norms will finally stand, even if this means that some defective decisions will acquire legal force.

Kelsen signals his approval of the second option by saying that the decisions of a reviewing court are inevitably constitutive and not declarative.[49] He observes that questions of material legality as well as complex procedural issues are usually difficult to answer. In most interesting cases where material legality is an issue we are faced with the possibility of reasonable disagreement; even legal experts often fail to arrive at a clear consensus as to how to deal with hard cases. What is more, the possibilities for disagreement are not limited to questions of material legality. The question whether some act of state that has an appearance of legality, but whose legality is nevertheless subject to disagreement, fulfills all authorizing conditions, Kelsen argues, is hardly ever answerable 'with the same degree of objective certainty and exactitude as the question whether something is an acid or a base'.[50] It is only to be expected, given these conditions, that the legal system will give preference to its own assertions in the cases that are most likely to lead to disagreement. Kelsen admits that the state or legal system is, in adopting this stance, 'putting its own authority above that of the individual'. But he argues that it cannot be reasonable to accept the stance of the law-abiding citizen while refusing to accept the legal system's claim to final authority, at least as long as the internal mechanisms of review possess the features that make them an adequate replacement for individual judgments of nullity.[51]

Kelsen's doctrine of finality thus amounts to a claim to sovereignty of the legal order as a whole. In the final resort, the law is whatever the state, the institutionalized legal system, says it is. Once all material legal constraints on official action have been turned into conditions of voidability, the legal system, taken as a whole, acquires legal infallibility. But Kelsen does not take the view that the final decision of the final court of appeal is binding even if it is mistaken, if it fails to overturn a defective norm enacted by some other organ of state.[52] Rather, the final refusal to

---

[49] See Kelsen, 'Wesen und Entwicklung der Staatsgerichtsbarkeit' (n 37 above) 1854–7; Kelsen, 'Das Urteil des Staatsgerichtshofs' (n 43 above) 82–91.

[50] Kelsen, 'Über Staatsunrecht' (n 4 above) 1037–8 [my translation].   [51] Ibid, 1038–9.

[52] Joseph Raz, *Practical Reason and Norms* (Princeton, 1990) 134–5 writes: 'Courts have the power to make an authoritative determination of people's legal situation. Private individuals may express their opinions on the subject but their views are not binding. The fact that a court can make a binding decision does not mean that it cannot err. It means that its decision is binding even if it is mistaken.' J W Harris takes a similar line in 'Kelsen's Concept of Authority' (n 3 above) 359. Such a view is not

overturn a decision that has an appearance of legality but whose perfect legality is nevertheless in doubt has the constitutive effect of healing any legal defect we might have attributed to the norm in advance of the final decision.[53] A judicial decision that purports to be final can lack validity only if it is null, but it can be null only if it is obviously violating fundamental material or formal constraints. This, however, is unlikely ever to be the case in a well-developed modern legal system. A fully developed legal system rightfully claims to have the power to finally determine what its norms mean with respect to any particular dispute. The law, in other words, is a law unto itself.[54]

Kelsen believes that the state, the legal order personified, necessarily has to claim to be a law unto itself, if there is to be social order at all. If we did not sustain the state's claim to sovereignty in this abstract sense, we would have to 'put the individual' or groups of like minded individuals 'above the state' and allow individuals or groups to be judges in their own cause and to impose their subjective intentions onto others. But this situation would not be much preferable to one in which the state refused to commit to a strong principle of legality and turned into the instrument of the interest of one particular group. The sovereignty of the state or legal order, then, is a necessary condition of the realization of a rule of law, as opposed to a rule of men. That avoidance of the danger of a rule of men is the point of the

---

an option for Kelsen, as we have seen, because he does not think we can separate the authority of the institutions applying the law from the demands of the law itself.

[53] See Kelsen, 'Über Staatsunrecht' (n 4 above) 1057 where Kelsen speaks of the infallibility of the final decision. Kelsen, *Introduction to the Problems of Legal Theory* (n 1 above) 73 defines defectiveness as voidability. To say that a norm is defective is to say that it is valid for the time being but that it can still be overturned in a process of review. It follows that if this process has run its course and not led to a repeal of the norm whose legality was in doubt, the norm is no longer voidable and hence no longer defective. Paulson, *Material and Formal Authorisation in Kelsen's Pure Theory* (n 3 above) 180–3 thus goes wrong in claiming that Kelsen would describe a case like *Korematsu v United States* as a case in which formal authorization makes up for a lack of material authorization (= for material illegality) of the decision, namely to uphold the internment of Japanese US citizens. What Kelsen would say, it seems to me, is that the legislative and executive decisions that led to internment had an appearance of legality, that there was disagreement about the full legality of these acts, but that their legality was put beyond doubt by the US Supreme Court. The Court, in other words, did not replace material legality with formal authority. Rather, it authoritatively settled a disagreement over the meaning of a material legal norm. Paulson, understandably, wants to make room for the possibility of saying, within a Kelsenian scheme, that even a final decision of Supreme Court may be legally defective, despite the fact that it acquires finality in virtue of formal authorization. The desire to make room for this possibility, in turn, is motivated by the aim to deny that Kelsen's doctrine of normative alternatives entails that judges are under no duty to apply the law. I agree with this last point, but I do not think Paulson's distinction between formal and material authorization is needed to make it. What is more, I suspect that Kelsen would have been quite unhappy with the idea that formal legality can be invoked as a remedy for a lack of material legality. The point of his guarantees of legality, rather, is to maximize both formal and material legality at the same time in order to allow the state to defend its normative claims on the basis of an appeal to the idea that is has done its utmost to ensure the substantive legality of its acts. It seems to me that Paulson's distinction undermines that ambition and implicitly slides back into a form of law-state dualism. See his conclusion ibid, 193.

[54] Kelsen's preferred manner of expressing this point is to say that the sovereignty of the state is the same as the positivity of the law. See Kelsen, *Der soziologische und der juristische Staatsbegriff* (n 5 above) 84–91; Kelsen, *Das Problem der Souveränität* (n 18 above) 85–101.

state's claim to sovereignty entails, however, that the claim to sovereignty can be justified only through full adherence to the aspirations implicit in the ideal of legal objectivity on the part of all public officials who are charged with creating and executing the law.[55]

I want to conclude by returning to the doctrine of normative alternatives. At the outset, I referred to the view that the doctrine entails that judges or other officials charged with exercising powers conferred by the law have a free choice either to apply the law or to decide as they see fit since the doctrine provides for the legality of acts that do not conform with all of the authorizing legal norms. Our interpretation of Kelsen's treatment of the problem in *Über Staatsunrecht* clearly shows this view to be mistaken. As we have seen, Kelsen's argument operates on the basis of a number of background assumptions which explain why the two alternatives cannot have the same status.[56] Kelsen assumes, first, that objectively valid law is normative, that it is binding on its subjects. Law-abiding citizens, second, accept a duty to defer to objectively valid law, but not to the personal opinions or the will of those who are empowered by law to take binding decisions. Decision-takers, in turn, make a claim to legality on behalf of their decisions. This claim is made because it is understood that the objective or full legality of a decision can legitimize its content.

Given these assumptions, we are left with the limited problem that disagreements over the legality of acts of state are bound to arise even between law-abiding citizens and public officials who claim to be acting legally. It is these disagreements which are to be and which can be settled through internalized processes of review or guarantees of legality that lead to final decisions that heal any suspicion of illegality. If both the citizen and the official or public agency appeal to a notion of objective legality, Kelsen assumes, they cannot coherently reject the idea of impartial arbitration of disputes over the meaning of that notion with respect to a particular dispute. It would be pragmatically inconsistent, Kelsen at times suggests, for the parties to a dispute to adopt the view that legality matters and to reject the idea that the objective meaning of one's legal rights and duties is legitimately determinable by independent courts.[57] Kelsen's background assumptions are incompatible, I conclude, with the idea that the doctrine of normative alternatives offers public officials an open choice between legality and illegality. Such a reading would make a mockery of the assumption, shared between the law-abiding citizen and the conscientious public

[55] Another way of making the same point is to say that Hobbes's regress argument, the view that the relation between sovereign and subject cannot be subjected to the arbitration of a third party since that third party would then become a new sovereign, suffices to establish only that the law must be a law unto itself. It does not suffice to establish, *pace* Waldron (see n 48 above), that it is futile to subject conflicts between citizens and particular organs of state to impartial arbitration.

[56] For Kelsen's claim that they cannot have the same status see Kelsen, *Introduction to the Problems of Legal Theory* (n 1 above) 73 and Kelsen, *Reine Rechtslehre* (n 1 above) 278.

[57] See Kelsen, 'Wer soll der Hüter der Verfassung sein?' (n 42 above) 1882–4; Kelsen, *Law and Peace in International Relations. The Oliver Wendell Holmes Lectures, 1940–1941* (Cambridge/ Mass, 1942) 165.

official, that addressees of the law's demands have a duty to obey objectively valid law but not those who make or apply it.

Further questions

Kelsen's argument so far does not offer a full statement of the conditions under which it is reasonable to adopt the perspective of the law-abiding citizen. What Kelsen claims to have shown by now is only that it would not be possible reasonably to adopt that perspective if those who claim to exercise public power cannot be held to account, by independent courts, for non-compliance with the positive legal rules that authorize them. But the existence of formal 'Rechtsstaatlichkeit' cannot be a sufficient condition for the reasonableness of the total deference to positive legality that is entailed by adoption of the law-abiding stance. The law-abiding person accepts subjection to the law, objectively understood, though not subjection to the persons who make or apply it. But why, we must now ask, ought a person to accept that she is obliged to defer to the law, objectively understood? It would seem to be clear that even perfect fulfillment of Kelsen's principle of legality on the part of some positive legal system ought not to be regarded as a sufficient answer to this question.

A political system could make this commitment and remain a legislative autocracy in which a monarch's personal will authoritatively determines the content of all general legal norms. Such a political system, insofar as it is a legal order in Kelsen's sense, would exhibit many features that would entitle it to some respect on the basis of the legality of its actions: all particular exercises of state power would take place on the basis of general norms and conformity of those particular exercises with the general norms authorizing them would be open to independent judicial review. Moreover, the fact that subordinate actors are bound to higher-order laws but not to commands directly issued by higher-order power-holders would have effects not dissimilar to those of a constitutionally more explicit division of powers.

Another way to put this point is to say that Kelsen's argument so far expresses intuitions akin to those that drive Lon Fuller's fable of the hapless king REX.[58] But his view is open to a criticism that is equally applicable to Fuller's conception. Nothing in Fuller's story suggests that REX's failures to enact valid law have anything to do with the fact that he is an absolute monarch. For all we know, he could, according to Fuller, enact valid law by conforming to Fuller's eight principles of legality. And if he did, his subjects would be under a duty to respect his laws as legitimate and to consider them something more than 'one way projections of authority'.[59]

---

[58] See Lon L Fuller, *The Morality of Law* (n 23 above) 33–93. Fuller claims that any attempt on the part of a ruler to rule through legal rules inevitably commits the ruler to a list of principles of legality, the most important of which is the congruence between declared law and official act, ie the willingness on the part of government to act in accordance with its own rules.   [59] See ibid, 192.

Kelsen, it seems to me, would agree with Fuller's view that respect for the principles of legality is necessary for legitimacy. But he would deny that it is sufficient reasonably to motivate adoption of the point of view of the law-abiding citizen. Let us assume that I am a convinced socialist who believes that the system of private property is a system of organized exploitation. REX, while conforming to the principles of legality, consistently supports the system of private property and it is clear that he will not change his mind. Kelsen's argument so far seems powerless to provide me with a sufficient reason from legality to accept the legitimacy of REX's laws protecting private property. Nothing in the way in which these laws came about gives me a reason to discount my disapproval of their content.

One might argue, of course, that it is wrong to blame a conception of legality for not being able to offer an answer to this challenge. A conception of legality will only be able to shoulder part of the justificatory burden that needs to be shouldered to fully justify the claims of, for example, a capitalist state. At some point, it would seem, we need to supplement our ideal of the rule of law with a substantive account of the good state in order to arrive at full justification. Reasons of legitimacy drawn from a conception of legality alone cannot reconcile a socialist with capitalism. This admission, of course, would spell defeat for the ideal of a utopia of legality. Kelsen is unwilling to concede such defeat. He acknowledges that the criticism of the socialist is well taken. But for reasons already discussed, he does not want to supplement his basic account of legality with a substantive theory of political justice. Rather, he thinks that the ideal of legality itself can be extended in a way that provides an answer to the question raised by the socialist or by others in a comparable situation.

The question, then, is whether it is possible to give more normative substance to the law's legitimacy by refining the procedures of enactment of law in the right way. Kelsen, I will argue in the next chapter, attempts to give an affirmative answer to this question. Democracy and constitutionalism, he believes, can be reconstructed as methods or procedures for the exercise of legislative authority that make the distinction between subjection to the law and subjection to those who make it applicable on the level of legislation. However, since the understanding of democracy and constitutionalism remains procedural, the argument as a whole stays within the confines of a conception of legal legitimacy and does not turn into or rest on a full-blown conception of justice.

This may appear to be an implausibly ambitious conception of legality. But there are two important considerations that seem to support the project.

The first is the fact that if we do not defend the utopia of legality, we will have a much harder time defending the basic level of legality against politically motivated encroachments. Abandoning the utopia of legality is tantamount to admitting that the 'Rechtsstaat' cannot claim an unconditional normative priority over a managerial state that justifies itself by the efficient and benevolent pursuit of a substantive common good, the ethnic nation state that justifies itself by expressing a cultural identity, or any other state that essentially draws upon sources of justification alien to the ideal of the rule of law. But if other reasons are, in any case, needed and available to defend the authority of the state, it seems impossible to claim that public power is constituted by legality and outright dogmatic not to contemplate the possibility that these other reasons might require restrictions of the 'formal' rule of law in some cases, whether in the form of general suspensions of legal order or in the form of intra-legal tradeoffs between the rule of law and substantive policy goals.

The second and closely related consideration in support of the utopia of legality is that it is the only possible reaction to a situation of deep antagonism between competing social groups. The alternatives to the utopia of legality, insofar as they would have to rely on a substantive conception of the good state to justify duties of obedience, all seem to presuppose a social consensus of some kind on the values and goals the state ought to serve. But Kelsen found himself in a social situation in which tensions between ideologically divided political groups were so deep that an appeal to such shared values was unlikely to carry much force. In such conditions there is no option other than to try to extend the reach of the rule of law into politics, unless one is willing to accept the Schmittian claim that deep social antagonisms have to be fought out violently before legality can meaningfully govern a society.

4

Kelsen's Theory of Democracy—
Reconciliation with Social Order

The purpose of this chapter is to show how Kelsen's theory of democracy builds on and develops the general argument about legal legitimacy I attributed to him in the previous chapter. The law-abiding citizen, as we have seen, takes himself to be subject to the law, understood as a set of objective authorizing rules, but he rejects the idea that he is subject to the personal will of those whom the law authorizes to take decisions that bind him. We have seen how this idea is cashed out by Kelsen in terms of a principle of legality that refuses to accept any self-certification of power and that tries to make sure that all exercises of political power fully respect the procedural and substantive higher order legal norms that ground their authority.

But the bare notion of legal objectivity and the formal account of the rule of law based on it are insufficient fully to motivate reasonable acceptance of the point of view of the law-abiding citizen. The distinction drawn by the law-abiding citizen between subjection to the objective normativity of the law and subjection to the subjective will of those whom the law authorizes to take decisions does not explain why there is a reason to subject oneself to the objective law in the first place. As we have seen, nothing in Kelsen's general conception of legal order seems to rule out the possibility that the basic norm may, for example, confer substantively unlimited legislative powers on an absolute monarch or a small social elite. Under such circumstances, the distinction between the objective demands of the law and the subjective intentions of the legislator, as well as its effective enforcement by independent courts, could only be of limited normative relevance. It would not be able to ground a justified expectation that reasonable subjects will wholeheartedly adopt the point of view of the law-abiding citizen. Kelsen will thus have to show that his basic account of the rule of law can be extended from the bottom to the top of the legal hierarchy so as to cover the decisions that we ordinarily think of as legislative. However, he will have to do so without relying on a natural law theory or a substantive theory of political justice since such reliance would make it impossible for him to maintain the project of a theory of legal legitimacy. In other words, Kelsen needs to argue that there is some way or method for enacting general law such that the full legality of claimed exercises of legislative power under that method can legitimize these exercises of legislative power even in the absence of agreement about their substantive merits.

Kelsen, I will argue in this chapter, claims that a democratic constitution, and only a democratic constitution, is able to perform this legitimizing function, a function which is needed to fill the gap in the formal conception of the rule of law and to realize the utopia of legality. A democratic constitution differs from an autocratic constitution, according to Kelsen, in that it subjects acts of legislation to conditions of legality that constrain exercises of legislative power in a way which ensures that the content of general law will turn out to be more than the unfiltered expression of the subjective will of a single ruler or a mere faction. The conditions of legality imposed by a democratic constitution, however, nevertheless remain ideologically neutral with respect to all normative disputes about the optimal content of positive law that can arise amongst democratic citizens. This neutrality allows democratic legality to mediate in political disputes amongst democratic citizens.

As a matter of fact, Kelsen is making a somewhat stronger claim than this. The stronger claim is that subjecting acts of legislation to legitimizing conditions of legality is the essential purpose of democracy. According to Kelsen, there is no way to understand democracy as it actually exists as an intrinsically meaningful institution unless we accept this description of democracy's essential purpose. A state whose claims to authority cannot reasonably be understood as based on a discharge of this purpose cannot be a true democracy, even if it claims to be committed to the principle of popular sovereignty. The project to offer a pure theory of legal legitimacy postulates a mutual dependence between the rule of law and democracy. The basic conception of legal objectivity outlined in the previous chapter is alone insufficient fully to realize its promise to replace the rule of men with the rule of law. Democratic creation of general laws is needed to perfect a system committed to Kelsen's principles of legality into a utopia of legality. Democracy, on the other hand, can claim to be a form of constitutional order distinct from autocracy only insofar as it realizes the normative ambition implicit in Kelsen's notion of legal objectivity.

The earliest comprehensive development of Kelsen's theory of democracy is to be found in *Vom Wesen und Wert der Demokratie* ('The Nature and Value of Democracy'), a short as yet untranslated monograph, largely apologetic in character.[1] The

---

[1] Hans Kelsen, *Vom Wesen und Wert der Demokratie. Neudruck der zweiten umgearbeiteten Auflage von 1929* (Aalen, 1963). Other important sources for Kelsen's theory of democracy are Hans Kelsen, *Allgemeine Staatslehre* (Berlin, 1925) 320–75; Hans Kelsen, 'Verteidigung der Demokratie' in Hans Kelsen, *Demokratie und Sozialismus. Ausgewählte Aufsätze*, edited by Norbert Leser (Wien, 1967) 60–8; Hans Kelsen, 'Foundations of Democracy' in *Ethics* 66 (1955) 1–101. Kelsen's theory of democracy has so far attracted relatively little attention. But see Andreas Kalyvas, 'The Basic Norm and Democracy in Hans Kelsen's Legal and Political Theory' in *Philosophy and Social Criticism* 32 (2006) 573–99; Horst Dreier, *Rechtslehre, Staatssoziologie und Demokratietheorie bei Hans Kelsen* (Baden-Baden, 1986) 249–94 and David Dyzenhaus, *Legality and Legitimacy. Carl Schmitt, Hans Kelsen, and Hermann Heller in Weimar* (Oxford, 1997) 132–49. There are some interesting parallels between Kelsen's view and the approach defended in Thomas Christiano, 'The Authority of Democracy' in *The Journal of Political Philosophy* 13 (2004) 266–90.

kind of democracy Kelsen is defending in that book is an ideal-type, in the Weberian sense, of the actual constitutional system that has achieved a more or less quasi-paradigmatic status in the western world: a political system based on a universal franchise, in which general legislative decisions are taken by majority vote of the people or by majority vote of their elected representatives, that is committed to the rule of law, and that includes a written constitution protecting individual rights and rights of minority groups.

Kelsen's argument about the nature and value of this ideal type of actual democracy primarily aims to defend the claim that actual democracy has a unified nature, that the combination of features which characterize it can be understood as serving one and the same value. Actual democracy, Kelsen claims, preserves individual freedom to the largest extent possible in a social context and it does so in virtue of its central feature, the taking of legislative decisions through majority vote. All other features of the ideal type, Kelsen claims, can be interpreted as conditions of the well-functioning of majority rule. If such an interpretation is possible, Kelsen believes, we will be able to reject the view that 'true' democracy, understood as the authentic self-government of the people, on the one hand and a state's commitment to principles of legality and to formal constitutionalism on the other hand serve different values that may turn out to be irreconcilable in situations of crisis and thus force us into a choice between democracy and the rule of law.[2]

The implicit context of Kelsen's argument is the political conflict between capitalism and socialism.[3] Kelsen observes that the demand for a realization of the ideal type of actual democracy enjoyed almost universal approval throughout the 19th century. Both bourgeois liberals and socialists tended to think of their own views as intimately related to this ideal type. They shared a common front against constitutional monarchy, the typical form of government on the continent in 19th century Europe, and both hoped that a combination of representative democracy and the rule of law would inevitably tend to help realize their ideas of good social order. But Kelsen observes, writing in the 1920s, that the alignment between actual democracy and socialism has become tenuous. A new form of socialism openly advocates dictatorship because it no longer sees a parliamentary democracy committed to the rule of law as an efficient vehicle for the realization of socialist goals and of true democracy. The pressure exercised by communism, moreover, has given rise to a corresponding 'anti-democratic attitude of the bourgeoisie', an attitude that finds its most radical practical expression in Italian fascism, but that is based on the more general view that the system of actual democracy may not legitimately be used, as

---

[2] This view was taken by Kelsen's most important interlocutor in the Weimar period. See Carl Schmitt, *Die geistesgeschichtliche Lage des heutigen Parlamentarismus* (Berlin, 1926); Carl Schmitt, *Verfassungslehre* (Berlin, 1928) 221–82 and 303–19. The idea that democracy essentially conflicts with formal constitutionalism has recently been defended by Jeremy Waldron, *Law and Disagreement* (Oxford, 1999) 255–312.

[3] See Kelsen, *Vom Wesen und Wert der Demokratie* (n 1 above) 1–2; Kelsen, 'Verteidigung der Demokratie' (n 1 above) 60–1; Kelsen, 'Foundations of Democracy' (n 1 above) 1–2 and 68–86.

reformist socialists had hoped, to peacefully and legally transform a society based on private property rights into a socialist society.[4]

Kelsen's outline of the nature and value of democracy is a reaction to this situation. It attempts to argue that the unifying value of democracy, the protection of individual freedom to the largest possible extent, is independent of and normatively prior to the values which animate both socialism and capitalism as comprehensive conceptions of good social order.[5] Kelsen argues that the conflict between socialism and a capitalism tempted to turn to fascism is therefore less fundamental than the choice between political democracy, which can in principle accommodate both socialism and capitalism while preserving individual freedom, and either the socialist or the fascist form of autocracy or dictatorship. Actual democracy, hence, is the political system that makes it possible for the conflict between socialists and capitalists, and other possible conflicts over the best form of social order, to take a peaceful form.

Kelsen on the 'torment of heteronomy'

Kelsen's analysis of the nature and value of democracy starts out from a fundamental assumption that we have already encountered, but that is expressed in much more explicit terms here than in any of his legal-theoretical works. According to Kelsen, there is an unbridgeable opposition between individual freedom and social order.[6] Kelsen uses the phrase 'social order' interchangeably with 'legal order'. If there is to be social order there has to be a positive legal system that successfully regulates all human conduct through coercive rules that it creates, applies, and enforces by itself. Social order as legal order is opposed to the anarchy of a state of nature in which people are subject to nothing but their own will. Echoing his legal-theoretical distinction between the subjective and the objective legal meaning of human acts, Kelsen attributes to social order an 'objective validity' that is independent of and superior to the subjective 'will of the norm subject'.[7] The possibility of conflict between subjective individual will and objective social or legal order therefore inevitably leads to a 'torment of heteronomy'.[8]

Our desire for natural freedom, understood as the absence of subjection to normative authority, Kelsen claims, must undergo a fundamental metamorphosis, it must be transformed into an acceptance of some form of political freedom, for social order to be possible.[9] The question Kelsen is concerned with is whether such

[4] Kelsen, *Vom Wesen und Wert der Demokratie* (n 1 above) 2.
[5] See Kelsen, 'Foundations of Democracy' (n 1 above) 68: 'The following analysis tends to show that neither capitalism nor socialism is essentially, that is to say, by their very nature, connected with a definite political system. Each of them can be established under a democratic as well as an autocratic regime. [...] there is no necessary relationship between a definite political and a definite economic system.'   [6] See Kelsen, *Vom Wesen und Wert der Demokratie* (n 1 above) 2–13.
[7] Ibid, 7. See also Kelsen, 'Foundations of Democracy' (n 1 above) 22.
[8] Kelsen, *Vom Wesen und Wert der Demokratie* (n 1 above) 3; 'Foundations of Democracy' (n 1 above) 18.   [9] Ibid, 18–19.

a metamorphosis can take a reasonable form. Kelsen's argument for democracy, in a nutshell, claims that democracy, while being a species of objective social order and hence as likely to give rise to conflicts between individual will and the legally organized claims of society as any other form of social order, is capable of bringing about at least a limited reconciliation between the aspiration to individual freedom and the demands of the law. Democracy, Kelsen claims, is a transformation of natural freedom that preserves what is valuable in natural freedom by allowing subjects of the law to participate in its creation.[10] This capability for reconciliation distinguishes democracy from all non-democratic or 'autocratic' forms of social order which exclude the large majority of subjects of the law from participation in its creation.[11]

While Kelsen clearly suggests that democracy can be justified as the only form of political order able to play the reconciliatory role just outlined, he does not explain the structure of the conflict between individual freedom and social order very clearly. At times, he appears to imply that the conflict is nothing but a simple standoff between brute individual desire determined by laws of nature and the objective normativity of legal command.[12] What is more, Kelsen tends to present the argument for democracy as reconciliation in what I believe are misleadingly simplistic terms. He suggests that democracy is preferable to autocratic forms of government simply because it allows a greater number of subjects of social order to satisfy their subjective preferences,[13] a claim that is hardly going to provide much comfort to members of a minority.[14]

I believe that Kelsen's real argument for democracy is more interesting. But in order to get at its hidden complexity we have to take a closer look at the notions of freedom and heteronomy *presupposed* by it. Drawing upon and widening our earlier analysis, I will therefore try to sketch a somewhat richer interpretation of the problem of the 'torment of heteronomy' than is explicitly offered by Kelsen himself to provide a background for his main argument for democracy.

In order to understand why social order allegedly subjects us to a torment of heteronomy we must first take a look at what it means, according to Kelsen, for an objective social or legal order to exist. As we have seen, Kelsen claims that legal norms exist in the mode of objective validity and that the objective validity or existence of all norms belonging to a legal system depends on the presupposition of a basic norm that confers validity on all norms authorized by it. The normativity of

---

[10] See ibid, 27.

[11] Ibid, 4: 'If there is to be society, if there is to be a state, there has to be a binding order of the reciprocal conduct of human beings, there has to be political rule. But if it is necessary for us to be ruled, we at least want to make sure that we are ruled only by ourselves. Social or political freedom thus separates itself from natural freedom. Politically free is he who, while subject, is subject only to his own but not to someone else's will. This opens up the fundamental distinction between the forms of state and society.' See as well Kelsen, *Allgemeine Staatslehre* (n 1 above) 321–2.

[12] See Kelsen, *Vom Wesen und Wert der Demokratie* (n 1 above) 4–6.   [13] See ibid, 9–10.

[14] Apart from the fact that it may well run into the well-known problems afflicting aggregation of preferences. See Frank Cunningham, *Theories of Democracy* (London, 2002) 66–8.

norms, we were told, is irreducible to causal relations of any kind. However, Kelsen emphasizes in all his major works that the existence of a legal system is bound to a threshold condition of effectiveness.[15] A system of social relationships can be interpreted as a legal order, it can carry the attribution of a basic norm, only if the actual behavior of the people involved by and large corresponds with the normative order constituted by the presupposition of the basic norm. And as long as this threshold of effectiveness is met, subjects of the law must expect that laws are likely to be enforced, regardless of whether they are universally recognized as legitimate, against those who break them. The existence of a legal system as a normative order, in other words, is inseparable from the fact that its addressees are subject to a threat of force.

Kelsen himself claims not to be much interested in people's motivations for acting in accordance with the law. He emphasizes that they vary greatly and that the psychological question why people obey the law is of no concern to the jurist.[16] Kelsen is certainly right to point to the multiplicity of possible motivations for conformity with the law. In a large number of cases, the fact that some action is the action required by law will play no motivational role whatsoever. One may believe that what is required by the law is the right thing to do, on independent grounds, perhaps even without being aware of the precise structure of the relevant legal demand. One may simply follow a social custom that has been positivized without making any conscious distinction between following the law and a habit of doing as others do. We can distinguish such cases from instances of law-conforming behavior that are motivated by the fact that the law requires a certain course of action.

This is a wide category that in turn includes a number of rather different items. But two species of action falling into this wider genus are particularly salient. First, there are actions motivated by a fear of the sanctions the law puts on transgressions of legal norms and, second, there are actions motivated by acceptance of the legitimacy of the norms enacted by the legally organized political system. Kelsen, it should be noted, accepts the importance of both of these species.[17] The actions falling into these two categories have in common that they are typically experienced as actions taken under a restraint on our freedom, a restraint that is imposed by the law against our will and that is often considered undesirable.[18]

---

[15] See Hans Kelsen, *Introduction to the Problems of Legal Theory. A Translation of the First Edition of the Reine Rechtslehre or Pure Theory of Law*, translated and edited by Bonnie Litschewski-Paulson and Stanley L Paulson (Oxford, 1992) 60–3; Kelsen, 'Foundations of Democracy' (n 1 above) 11: '... the legal order constituting the state is valid only if it is, by and large, effective, that is to say, obeyed by the individuals whose behavior it regulates'.   [16] See ibid, 31–2.

[17] See Kelsen, *Introduction to the Problems of Legal Theory* (n 15 above) 26 and 28–9. The centrality of belief in legitimacy is implicitly recognized in Kelsen's attack on 'ideologies of legitimacy', in particular in his attack on law-state dualism.

[18] Actions undertaken in the belief that the law has authority in a Razian sense are a third category of actions motivated by the fact that the law requires some course of action. But they differ from actions caused by fear of sanction or by acceptance of legitimacy in that they do not have to be experienced as constraints of our freedom.

It is a sociological truism, a truism that Kelsen, I assume, would not have denied that actions motivated by fear of sanctions and actions motivated by acceptance of legitimacy have a central importance for the stability of a legal-political order.[19] It is likely to be the case, in any political system, that sufficient compliance with the demands of the law will at least sometimes have to depend on motivations other than spontaneous moral agreement with the content of law or simple habit, namely on fear of sanctions or on acceptance of legitimacy. However, these two forms of motivation for action in accordance with the law can hardly have equal standing. No normative system could be stable if threats of punishment were its primary resource for dealing with disagreement over the substantive merits of the positive law. A sufficient number of subjects of a legal system have to accept that they have a duty to defer to decisions that are legally valid in order for the system to be stable. In other words, a system's stability depends on whether a sufficient number of subjects are willing to accept the system's normative claim to obedience, which of course raises the question whether (or under what conditions) such acceptance can be reasonable. Reconciliation with the claims of the law will be possible insofar as a satisfactory answer to this question is available.

As we have seen, Kelsen's principles of legality provide only a partial answer to this question, an answer that is not strong enough to come reasonably close to a full justification of the state's claims on the basis of legal legitimacy. Kelsen's theory of democracy claims that the enactment of general legal norms in accordance with democratic procedure, together with a commitment to the principles of legality, will make it fully reasonable to adopt the stance of a law-abiding citizen. In a democracy, therefore, fulfillment of the sociological condition of stability, namely that there be a sufficient number of citizens accepting the legitimacy of legally valid norms, is not dependent on attitudes of subjects that are inherently unreasonable. The belief that the legitimizing power of democratic legality is strong enough approximately to justify the claims of the state does not require an abdication of reasonable self-government.

It must be admitted that Kelsen himself never explicitly defends his theory of democracy in these terms.[20] My claim is an extrapolation from Kelsen's views the steps of which I now want to trace. What we do know is that Kelsen thinks democracy is some form of remedy for the 'torment of heteronomy' that we undergo in social order. Democracy, however, could only be a remedy for the 'torment of

---

[19] See Max Weber, *Wirtschaft und Gesellschaft. Grundriß der verstehenden Soziologie*, edited by Johannes Winckelmann (Tübingen, 1980) 16 and 122–4. Kelsen never expressly signs on to this truism. But Kelsen's view of democracy, as I will argue shortly, would make no sense unless we assume that he accepted it.

[20] However, he comes close at times. See Kelsen, 'Foundations of Democracy' (n 1 above) 29: 'The rationalistic character of democracy manifests itself especially in the tendency to establish the legal order of the state as a system of general norms created by a procedure well-organized for this purpose. [...] The ideal of legality plays a decisive role: it is assumed that the individual acts of state may be justified by their conformity with the general norms of the law.'

heteronomy' if we conceive of the conflict between individual will and social order in a certain way.

Let us look at a first, simple picture of the conflict that seems to follow directly from the combination of Kelsen's analysis of the existent conditions of legal systems with what might appear to be his 'official' view of practical reason. Kelsen at times appears to claim that reason is the slave of desire, that all action is motivated by brute inclination and subjective preference.[21] The torment suffered by individuals, then, must be a simple clash of individual desire with the demands of objective social order. Social order subjects us to a torment of heteronomy simply because its sanction-backed rules force us to do things we would otherwise prefer not to do or because its rules stop us from doing things we would otherwise prefer to do. The system, as long as it exists, will impose its demands upon us regardless of whether they overlap with our personal wants. Hence, it forces us to act against our 'subjective will' more often than not.

The problem with this view is that it suggests that all forms of acceptance of legitimacy are equally irrational. A reasonable individual ought to try to maximize satisfaction of individual preferences and acceptance of the legitimacy of imposed normative constraints is never a way to do so. This is not necessarily to deny that a reasonable individual would prefer to live in a democracy and not in an autocracy. It might be reasonable to expect that democratic law is less likely to conflict with one's personal wants than autocratic law. But if the law does so conflict, my reasons for complying with its demands will stem exclusively from the threat of sanction attached to the law. The simple picture of the torment of heteronomy given so far could therefore never lead to the conclusion that the fact that some action is demanded by law binds us to the performance of that action. By implication, the view has no room for the idea that the reasonableness of acceptance of the legitimacy of law is dependent on constitutional form, on the choice between democracy and autocracy.

Some of Kelsen's remarks, however, do not portray the distinction between personal will and social order primarily in terms of a distinction between brute subjective preference and the brute coercive power of an institutionalized and sanction-backed legal system. They suggest, rather, that the problem of torment arises from the fact that legal order makes normative claims, from the fact that the norms it produces are taken to be binding irrespective of what the subjects happen to believe about their merits.[22] The source of the problem of torment, then, is that legislators as well as subjects of the law are capable of forming beliefs about the practical merits of acts of legislation that at least purport to be objective and that do not directly boil down to how these decisions affect their purely subjective wants.[23]

---

[21] See for example Hans Kelsen, *Reine Rechtslehre* (2nd ed, Wien, 1960) 62.

[22] For a fuller discussion see the last section in this chapter.

[23] See Hans Kelsen, 'Value Judgments in the Science of Law' in Hans Kelsen, *What is Justice? Justice, Law, and Politics in the Mirror of Science* (Berkeley, 1957) 209–30, at 227–8.

The conflict between legal order and those subject to it, thus, will be a conflict that arises from the fact that those who enact legal norms and those who are subject to them take different views about the merits of the law. If the law makes normative claims, the addressees of the law, it seems, must assume that the law's claim to be binding is conditional on a sufficient practical quality of its content or, in the case of particular applicative decisions, of sufficient legal correctness. But according to the pure theory, any final decision attributable to a legal system is valid and enforceable as long as the legal system exists, regardless of de facto dissent, however well justified such dissent may be in terms of the standards of goodness of legislation or legal correctness that ought to govern official decisions.

We can conclude that a conflict between the personal will of an agent capable of forming a conception of justice and willing to act on that conception, even if doing so may require accepting constraints on the satisfaction of his desires, on the one hand and the claims of social order on the other will be as unbridgeable as the conflict between social order and the will of a pure utility-maximizer. Even if I subscribe to a view of social justice that entails that I have objectively valid obligations towards others I will claim, as a self-governing person, to be the final judge of what these standards are and of what they mean. But the objectivity of legal order entails that my judgment cannot have any effect if it conflicts with a decision produced by the legal system.

In keeping with this idea, Kelsen emphasizes that the torment of heteronomy has the character of an insult to our aspiration to self-government. The subjection to someone else's will, he emphasizes, is scandalous particularly insofar as it is a subjection to someone else's *judgment*.[24] This reading of the torment is further corroborated by Kelsen's claim that the torment of heteronomy is connected to the idea of natural equality.[25] As a believer in natural equality, I will think that the fact that positive legal order puts someone else in a position to give me directives does not reflect any natural hierarchy of authority or difference of quality amongst us that would justify the idea that I ought to subject to that other person's judgments. But if this is true, how could the claim that I am bound to defer to his judgment ever be justifiable?

We started out from a crude interpretation of the sources of the torment of heteronomy as a clash between subjective desire and social order that appeared to leave no role to democracy in the solution to the problem. We have now offered an alternative account of the sources of the torment that involves a very different picture of the person subject to the torment, namely that of a person capable of

[24] See Kelsen, *Vom Wesen und Wert der Demokratie* (n 1 above) 3 and 11–12; Kelsen, 'Über Staatsunrecht' in Hans Klecatsky, René Marcić, and Herbert Schambeck (eds), *Die Wiener rechtstheoretische Schule. Ausgewählte Schriften von Hans Kelsen, Adolf Julius Merkl und Alfred Verdross* (Wien, 1968) vol I, 957–1057, at 1038: 'We can say that the essence of the state's authority, the meaning of the subjection of the individual to the state is manifested not so much in the exercise of the state's power of coercion, not so much in the subjection of the individual will, as it is manifested in the subjection of individual thought and judgment.' [my translation]

[25] See Kelsen, *Vom Wesen und Wert der Demokratie* (n 1 above) 3.

forming a conception of the justice of laws and willing to act in accordance with it, but subject to the sanction-backed normative claims of a legal order that will potentially pay no heed to her conception of legal justice. The torment suffered by this person arises not simply from a restriction of her ability to satisfy her subjective preferences. Rather, it is the result of a comparison of the law she is actually subjected to with her ideal of a just legal order. The actual legal order, as a result of what she sees as other people's misguided judgments, either puts her under obligations she would not be under in what she considers a substantively just legal order or it withholds from her what she believes she is entitled to.

Let us now consider whether this second account of the sources of the torment puts us into a better position to make sense of the idea that democracy may provide some kind of solution to the problem of torment. In answering this question, we need to distinguish between two different possible kinds of solution. Democracy may either promise to *deliver* us from the torment of heteronomy or it may promise to *reconcile* us with it. The distinction is best explained by the use of an earlier example.

Let us assume I steadfastly believe, submitting to the authority of the bible or the church, in the theological doctrines that bolster the divine right of kings. I believe that I will have to obey even a ruler who has turned into a tyrant since such rulers are God's punishment for our wickedness. Of course, my personal plans are liable to suffer frustration at the hands of such authority. But I will patiently endure these frustrations as punishment for my sins and I will take it on faith that obedience to the commands of rightfully constituted authority is a divine command and will ultimately set me free. I will thus consider myself obliged to obey my ruler's directives even if I rightly judge that they are deeply immoral and unjust in content.

Would it be right to say that I am suffering the torment of heteronomy? In one sense, the answer must be affirmative. It is compatible with my view of political authority to believe that the ruler himself has a moral obligation, though unenforceable, not to act like a tyrant. In obeying my ruler's directives, I am not surrendering my judgment on the substantive quality of those directives. I do not have to surrender my judgment on the substantive quality of my ruler's directives, in order to obey, because my faith provides me with a categorical reason to obey his directives that is not dependent on my assessment of quality. While I am subject to a torment of heteronomy in the sense that I am restrained by norms whose content I experience as unreasonable, I am nevertheless reconciled, through my faith, to the social order that inflicts that torment.

This reconciliation, however, would appear to be unavailable for persons who aspire to full individual autonomy, understood as the idea that one's own reason, and not the authority claimed by a revealed system of religious belief, ought to have the final judgment in all practical matters. For a fully self-governing person, the question whether she ought to obey a directive on some content-independent ground could not be totally divorced, it seems, from the question whether that directive is a good directive.

An autonomous person living under an absolutist regime based on the divine right of kings will, of course, always be able to distance herself from the normative claims of the social order she is subjected to. The regime, after all, cannot force her to accept that its norms are binding. The autonomous person will nevertheless often have reason to conform to the law in outer act. She might happen to agree with at least some of the decisions taken by the state on the merits and be motivated to comply with the law in virtue of this agreement on the merits. She may even reasonably come to believe that the law has some authority in a Razian sense, based on the expertise of lawmakers or on their capacity to provide a framework for coordination. She may judge, finally, in cases in which neither of these two grounds of compliance are applicable, that it is reasonable to act as the law demands since it is reasonable to avoid the punishment for breaking the law. In all these cases, the autonomous person can reasonably act in compliance with the law, without attributing any legitimacy to the law.

It would be wrong, however, to conclude from this that one can escape the torment of heteronomy through a simple inner refusal to accept any claims to legitimacy. The first and second motivations for compliance just listed will often not be available, and if they are available they will be available only circumstantially. Hence, the autonomous person living in an absolutist state will often end up in situations where the only thing that can reasonably motivate compliance with the law is the threat of a sanction. If she finds herself in this situation, she will suffer from a torment of heteronomy without being reconciled to social order. If the autonomous person is confronted with a law she deems unreasonable, she cannot, in contrast to the believer in some legitimating myth, supply a reason for deference from a background theory that rationalizes deference to bad law. To her, the unreasonable demand must appear as a naked exercise of arbitrary power.

If democracy is to provide a solution to this problem, it must ensure that subjects of a democracy will never end up in a situation where an interest in the avoidance of sanctions is the only reasonable motivation for conformity with the law's demands. Given this requirement, we might expect an argument for democracy, or for some form of democracy, to show that democracy is the social order the institutional structure of which *guarantees* that the freedom of reasonable persons will never be subject to unreasonable restriction by positive laws. In other words, in order to deliver ourselves from the problem of heteronomy we need to create a society in which reasonable persons will be subject only to laws they can fully identify with, accept as substantively just, as self-governing autonomous persons. Democracy, or some form of it, we would have to claim, is that society. In a democracy, the reasonable person's compliance with law would therefore never have to be motivated by fear of sanctions but neither would it ever rest on acceptance of a claim to legitimacy. The law's coercive force would be employed only against unreasonable persons or as a counter to unreasonable and unethical motivations that may afflict even reasonable persons. But the law would never function as a constraint on the measure of freedom that persons may reasonably believe they are entitled to under a just scheme of the distribution of freedom. The democratic metamorphosis of natural into social freedom, under such a view, would perfectly correspond to the transformation of the individual from a desire-driven creature into an autonomous moral agent.

Kelsen, as we will see, rejects this defense of democracy as too ambitious. Under conditions of pluralism democracy can at best promise reconciliation with, not deliverance from, the torment of heteronomy. Democracy, as the cornerstone of the utopia of legality, is a secular replacement—not reliant on irrational myth and thus not incompatible with our aspiration to autonomy—for the form of reconciliation that our religious believer relied on to rationalize his obedience to an absolute monarch. Democracy, of course, will leave much less room for arbitrary power than the divine right of kings since its legislative procedures ensure that the content of the law is influenced by the citizen's conceptions of justice. But the argument for democracy nevertheless remains an argument about legitimacy, an argument that is meant to justify imposed restraints on conduct whose substantive reasonableness may reasonably be doubted.

Kelsen fears that if we attribute to the democratic ideal the ambition to do away with the torment of heteronomy altogether we will put intolerable stress on democracy as it actually exists, warts and all. If we set our sights too high, we are likely to end up with the assessment that actual democracy, as opposed to some yet to be realized ideal democratic state that would allegedly guarantee total deliverance from heteronomy, does not differ qualitatively from non-democratic positive constitutions since both fail to fully realize the emancipatory ambition of 'true democracy'. It is only a short step from this conclusion to the call for a revolutionary dictatorship supposed to create the conditions of an authentic democracy. Actual democracy, consequently, would not be able to contribute to the pacification of a social conflict as deep as that between capitalism and socialism since its proper functioning would be seen to depend on a prior choice for either capitalism or socialism that will have to be implemented through some form of transitional violence.

The opposite danger, of course, is that a democratic theory that lowers its sights will slide down a slippery slope towards a lesser form of reconciliation that may be achieved by systems far more authoritarian than the ideal type of actual democracy. The reasonable person, Kelsen assumes, is aware of the difference between existing social order and a state of nature and she will acknowledge that the state of nature cannot be preferable to social order.[26] The reason for this is clear, at least under the second interpretation of the torment of heteronomy. Reasonable persons will, of course, be able to exercise reasonable self-government in a state of nature. But they will not be able successfully to act on their conceptions of the good in any coherent fashion since their actions will largely be driven by fear of others and take the form of ad hoc attempts to react to perceived threats. But Kelsen cannot be content

---

[26] Kelsen's support of this view is evident in his emphasis on the centrality of the value of peace, both within and between states. See for example Kelsen, *Vom Wesen und Wert der Demokratie* (n 1 above) 68.

to leave matters at a Hobbesian level,[27] to replace belief in the divine right of kings with a general fear of the state of nature. If this first step toward reconciliation were sufficient to reconcile us to social order there could be no further argument for actual democracy since any constitutional form would be as good as any other as long as it constituted a sovereign state, or, in Kelsen's terminology, an objective social order.

The two extremes of Hobbesianism and full deliverance from heteronomy are the poles between which Kelsen's reconciliatory argument must move if it is to be successful. The argument has to show that democracy can bring about a stronger form of reconciliation than any form of autocracy because it respects our claim to autonomy, in a way in which autocratic political systems do not, even while it legitimately subjects us, from time to time, to the torment of heteronomy.

The failure of the argument from deliverance

Kelsen's argument for democracy picks up on and reinterprets a key theme of Rousseau's theory of democracy. Rousseau famously searched for a social order 'by means of which each one, while uniting with all, nevertheless obeys only himself and remains as free as before'.[28] Kelsen's theory of democracy, put differently, tries to offer an interpretation of Rousseau's idea of democracy as an identity of ruler and ruled. Democracy is the result of a 'metamorphosis of the idea of freedom' that replaces natural freedom, the freedom to act unrestricted by an external normative authority, with political freedom.[29] Kelsen defines political freedom as follows: 'Politically free is he who, while being subject, is subject only to his own but not subject to an alien will.'[30] Democracy, understood as the rule of laws enacted by a majority, ensures that the people rule themselves by participating in the formation of the will of the state.[31]

Kelsen makes it quite clear that what he means by participation in the formation of the ruling will of the state is participation in the determination of the content of general laws, not merely the power to appoint and recall members of a political elite who will lead and legislate as they see fit once they are elected.[32] Kelsen contrasts democracy as 'government by the people' with what he calls 'government for the people'.[33] A government for the people is a government that claims to be

[27] I do not intend to commit myself here to any view as to whether the standard interpretation of Hobbes I rely on here is defensible or not. See for a different view David Dyzenhaus, 'Hobbes and the Legitimacy of Law' in *Law and Philosophy* 20 (2001) 461–98.

[28] J J Rousseau, 'On the Social Contract' in *Classics of Moral and Political Theory*, edited by Michael L Morgan (Indianapolis, 1992) 771–830 at 776.

[29] Kelsen, *Vom Wesen und Wert der Demokratie* (n 1 above) 3–13.   [30] Ibid, 4.

[31] Ibid, 14: 'The idea of democracy is that of a form of state or society in which the will of the community, or, put without resort to imagery, the social order is created by those subject to it: by the people. Democracy means identity of leader and led, subject and object of rule, means rule of the people over the people'. [my translation] It should be noted that Carl Schmitt employed the same definition of democracy. See Schmitt, *Verfassungslehre* (n 2 above) 234–5.

[32] Kelsen explicitly rejects Joseph Schumpeter's elitist view of democracy. See Kelsen, 'Foundations of Democracy' (n 1 above) 84–5.   [33] See ibid, 1.

acting in the interest of the citizens but that excludes most citizens from participation in the formation of the will of the state. Every government, Kelsen argues, at least claims to be a government for the people. What distinguishes democracy is the fact that the majority of the subjects of the law themselves, either directly or through representatives, determine the content of the general legal rules they have to obey.

Kelsen's acceptance of an ideal of participatory democracy is subject, however, to some important qualifications. Rousseau conceived of the social contract as a total alienation of natural freedom through which we undergo a wholesale transformation of practical identity. The freedom we receive in a democratic order differs in quality from the freedom we gave up when we entered it from a state of nature. The democratic state, as Rousseau points out, does not preserve our natural freedom to a larger extent than any other state. Its authority is just as unlimited as that of any other political order. Citizens of a democracy are nevertheless perfectly free since they can, as *citoyens*, reasonably identify with the general will. If I am forced, against my inclinations, to obey the rulings of the general will, as expressed in a majority vote, I am forced to be free. My disagreements with the general will, should I have any, only go to show that I have been mistaken about the content of the will of the people.[34]

Kelsen adopts this conception of democracy only in part. He agrees that the authority of the democratic state is as unlimited as that of any other; this much is implicit in his conception of social order. However, Kelsen rejects Rousseau's idea of what it means for the people to rule themselves through taking majority votes. He does not conceive of the democratic metamorphosis of freedom as a process that transforms our practical identities, as an ascent to a higher ideal of civic virtue that leaves our individuality behind. Kelsen's reinterpretation of the claim that, in a democracy, I am subject to my own will in being subject to the will of the state is meant to be compatible with the individualist assumption that my own will or my own practical identity are in principle distinct from the will of any state, including the democratic state. The reason for this distinctness is not that my own will is private, but rather that it is expressive of my inalienable capability to form a conception of the good, including a conception of justice, on the basis of an autonomous exercise of my own cognitive and moral powers.[35]

The freedom to act on that conception, while being subject to as little interference as possible, is the freedom the autonomous person is interested in and the infringement of which by social order gives rise to the problem of torment. Kelsen's democratic state, as we will see, is legitimate because it can respect this freedom in a way in which an autocracy could not.[36] Kelsen therefore rejects Rousseau's idea that I have been mistaken about the content of what ought to have been my own

---

[34] See Rousseau, *On the Social Contract* (n 28 above) 780–3 and 814–16.

[35] This is why Kelsen rejects the final step in the metamorphosis of freedom, ie the uncritical personification of the state. See Kelsen, *Vom Wesen und Wert der Demokratie* (n 1 above) 11–13 and 98–104.

[36] See Kelsen, 'Foundations of Democracy' (n 1 above) 27.

will if I am outvoted in a truly democratic vote. But he nevertheless wants to hold on to a weaker version of the idea that I am subject only to my own will in being subjected to the decision of a democratic majority of which I did not form a part. Kelsen's metamorphosis of natural into social freedom, hence, must preserve a continuity between a reflective aspiration to freedom on my part that is based on an autonomous exercise of my cognitive and moral powers and the political freedom afforded by a majoritarian democracy. This continuity must affirm my distinctness as a self-governing moral agent while allowing me to identify with democratically enacted laws even if I don't agree with them on the merits.

Kelsen's reasons for adopting this stance result from the failure of arguments that read democracy as promising deliverance from the torment of heteronomy. This failure can be brought out by asking what it means for the will of the ruler and the ruled to be identical. A first, trivial proposal would be the following. I can be said to be subject only to my own will if the will of the state, as expressed in its laws, conforms in content to my own will. The laws have the content I think they ought to have, in the light of my conception of the good, and they consequently facilitate and support my plans instead of restricting and frustrating them.

This trivial sense of identity cannot be all we mean when we say that one is subject only to one's own will in a democracy. The substantive content of the laws, after all, could be in line with my personal beliefs as to what it ought to be even in an absolute monarchy as long as the monarch chose to enact laws that happen to conform to my conception of the good. However, the relation between my freedom and the form of government would be wholly contingent since the monarch might just as well choose to enact norms that do not serve my views. Something more than the mere circumstantial overlap in content between my will and the law is needed to make sense of the democratic claim that I am subject only to my own will in being subject to a democratically created will of state.

What makes a democratic system based on majority rule different from an autocracy, one might go on to argue, is that, in a democracy, the question whether the laws serve the subjects' interests is not contingent upon the wisdom, virtue, or benevolence of a single person or small group of persons who exercise legislative power. In a system with democratic legislation, in contrast to an autocracy, the people, a majority of the subjects of the law or of their representatives, have to give their consent to acts of legislation. Hence, it is unlikely that the system will produce legislation that systematically violates the interests of the people by preferring the partial interests of a small minority or governing elite over the common good, at least if we can assume that we are dealing with a citizenry made up of reasonable individuals. Government on the basis of the majority rule, direct or representative, thus makes sure that the chance to enjoy laws that tend to serve the shared interests of the citizens is non-contingently related to the form of government.

As we will see, Kelsen defends a variant of this view. However, the justification of democracy just outlined is open to two different interpretations. It can be read as an argument from deliverance or as an argument from reconciliation. If read as an argument from deliverance, the claim that democracy forges a non-contingent relation between the content of the law and the reasonable interests of all subjects assumes that 'the people' share a common interest against those who rule over them and might be tempted to abuse that rule in their purely private or sectarian interest. Put differently, the picture presupposes the existence of an objective commonality of interest amongst citizens that is in need of political protection against potentially tyrannical rulers (and self-interested defectors). Since the illicit maximization of private interest is the only conceivable motivation for defection from the common good and since no purely private interest will ever be able to attain a legislative majority, the participation of the people in the formation of the will of the state will ensure that the laws will be in line with what reasonable citizens recognize as the common good. Democracy answers not to the problem of how to settle disputes over the fundamental meaning of terms like 'common good' or 'public interest'. Its function, rather, is to prevent both defection from and tyrannical corruption of a standard of common interest already acknowledged as correct on independent grounds.

Kelsen believes that an argument of this kind is not acceptable as a defense of modern democracy since it fails to take account of the problem of pluralism. He emphasizes that there is reasonable disagreement about the good amongst the differing groups who have acquired rights of participation in the formation of the will of the state in modern pluralist democracies.[37] We can no longer assume that there is a pre-established harmony between some common interest and that of a legislative majority. The question whether the laws reliably serve any individual's conception of the good will once again be contingent upon how a potentially alien will, now that of the majority, chooses to decide. The principle of majority rule, therefore, is powerless, in a pluralist society, to guarantee a non-circumstantial identity in content between the wills of ruler and ruled.

It is tempting to conclude further that the failure of majoritarianism, under conditions of pluralism, to guarantee identity in content between the ruling will and the will of the reasonable citizen is an unavoidable consequence of a characteristic that is necessarily shared by *all* forms of social order in the Kelsenian sense. Kelsen himself certainly suggests such a view in discussing Rousseau's claim that a genuine democracy cannot be representative. Rousseau famously argued that the English people are free only while they are voting but that they are subject to their rulers in much the same way as the subjects of an absolute monarch at any other time.[38] Kelsen expresses agreement with this assessment. But he does not think that we should conclude that democracy ought to be direct. Rather, he claims that Rousseau's complaint necessarily applies to all forms of democracy.[39]

---

[37] See Kelsen, *Vom Wesen und Wert der Demokratie* (n 1 above) 14–25.
[38] See Rousseau, *On the Social Contract* (n 28 above) 810.
[39] See Kelsen, *Vom Wesen und Wert der Demokratie* (n 1 above) 6–11 and 16–20; Kelsen, 'Foundations of Democracy' (n 1 above) 21–4.

Even in a direct democracy, Kelsen argues, there will be ample room for divergence between the content of one's own will and that of the will of state. One's own will is identical with that of the state only as long as one is voting with the majority. An attempt to solve this problem by introducing a strict requirement of unanimity would simply shift the issue to another level. Even a unanimous decision claims to bind those who consented until the decision is officially overturned. But people may change their minds concerning the reasonableness of a legislative decision after the decision has been taken. If they do so, they will once again find themselves at odds with social order. If a requirement of unanimity is imposed on any amendment of previously agreed upon law, and if a majority of voters subsequently change their mind about some previously enacted law, the requirement may even come to frustrate the aspirations of a much larger number of persons than continue to agree with the content of the law.

One might deny, by way of reaction to this problem, that a unanimous decision ought to have the power to continue to bind those who once consented if their will, their opinion of the merits of the legislative decision, changes later on. If one believes that unanimity is required for the legitimate enactment of a law, Kelsen hypothesizes, it seems altogether reasonable to conclude that the law can remain valid only as long as all those who once consented continue to agree with it.[40] But if we make this admission, we are endowing the individual with a right to opt out of social order at her personal discretion. Adoption of this view would empty the basic norm of social order of all normative meaning. It would no longer define a method for taking collectively binding decisions, and if it didn't, social order would lack objective normativity. In order to be a form of effective social order, Kelsen concludes, even the most radically democratic state will have to stop short of this dissolution. But this inevitably entails that even the most radically democratic state cannot ensure full identity in content between the wills of rulers and ruled or between the people as subject and the people as object of political rule. Despite our rights of participation in the creation of a collective will some of us will find themselves, at least some of the time, in the role of *subjects* who are categorically bound, whether they like it or not, to decisions they do not support.[41]

If we accept this argument we are forced, it would seem, to conclude that what is more important than the differences between different constitutions authorized by different basic norms is what they all have in common. All basic norms introduce a distinction between rulers and ruled insofar as they all empower some to take decisions that claim to be categorically binding on others and that are, if necessary, forcibly imposed upon individual subjects or groups of subjects who happen to disagree with their merits. Political unity is not expressed by but rather brought about by subjection to the will of state, as identified by some basic procedure for taking collectively binding decisions. Any legal system, as long as it forms an objective social order, potentially serves the transcendent interest of avoiding the state

---

[40] Ibid, 22.   [41] See Kelsen, *Vom Wesen und Wert der Demokratie* (n 1 above) 6–8.

of nature equally well. Any morally relevant differences between legal systems, therefore, depend on how well these systems happen to serve some meta-legal conception of political justice. The ideology of democracy is a myth since no form of organizing the practice of the taking of binding collective decisions is closer than any other to realizing an actual identity between the will of the rulers and that of all the ruled. There is no distinction between 'government by the people' and 'government for the people'.

The defense of majoritarian democracy from deliverance thus ends up in a dilemma. Majoritarian democracy, in order to live up to its promise that it will not subject us to an alien will, either presupposes a shared conception of the good on the part of the individuals forming a commonwealth or it does not qualitatively differ from autocratic forms of government in which the content of the public good is determined by the legislative fiat of a sovereign whose will simply displaces that of dissenting citizens.

The answer to the question whether this dilemma is a problem for democracy, of course, depends on what conception of democracy we are working with and on what we want it to do. One might try to defend democracy as the identity of ruler and ruled by reading the dilemma as proof of the claim that a true identity of ruler and ruled presupposes a substantive ethical homogeneity of the people, a homogeneity that finds its most authentic expression in legally unregulated dictatorial acts of popular sovereignty that take place in a state of exception and not in a system of formal majority rule committed to the principle of legality.[42] Alternatively, one might adopt the view that majoritarian democracy is a potentially dangerous form of government that needs to be tempered by a substantive liberal constitutionalism which imposes external normative limits on the powers of the democratic legislator.

But neither of these solutions to the dilemma is available to Kelsen. Schmitt's version of the identity thesis replaces reconciliation with violent exclusion. It unilaterally subjects individual autonomy to a definition of the common good offered by the strongest social group, the group likely to prevail in a civil war. The liberal solution, on the other hand, presupposes a way of drawing a distinction between the public and the private that is likely to be fundamentally controversial, at least if our society is ravaged by a conflict as profound as that between capitalists and socialists. Kelsen's idea of democracy as the cornerstone of a utopia of legality was supposed to subject such conflicts to peaceful arbitration under the law. But neither the Schmittian nor the liberal option seem to leave any room for the idea that democratic legality could play such a bridging function since they both assume that the norms enacted through a scheme of democratic legality can only be justified if they conform to either a people's substantive homogeneity or the meta-legal moral principles informing the idea of a liberal constitution.

While Kelsen acknowledges that majoritarian democracy is not capable of bringing about a perfect identity of the will of rulers and ruled, he must hold on to

---

[42] See Schmitt, *Verfassungslehre* (n 2 above) 235.

some weaker variant of the identity thesis to make the utopia of legality work. This weaker variant of the identity thesis, I will now argue, is supplied by an argument from reconciliation.

Kelsen's defense of majority rule: The argument from reconciliation

A guarantee of perfect overlap between the content of the will of any reasonable subject and the content of a will of state formed by majority decision is an unrealistic ideal. But majoritarian democracy, Kelsen believes, can nevertheless be justified in terms of the idea of an identity between ruler and ruled, namely as the best approximation to the ideal of freedom from subjection to an alien will that is possible in a pluralist social context.[43] Kelsen's official argument for this view is rather simple and it fails, on the face of it, to do full justice to the real complexities of the problem it is supposed to tackle. But it can be amended if read in the light of the revised understanding of the sources of the torment of heteronomy I offered earlier on.

Kelsen's argument is based on the claim that even the most democratic state will still have to be an instance of objective social order that subjects us to a mode of collective decision-taking the results of which are taken to be binding and which are enforced, as long as the system exists, against all de facto resistance. The only alternative is absence of social order, a state of nature. Given that social order is necessary the question we must ask is which form of social order best preserves or protects the freedom of a reasonable person, her capacity successfully to act in accordance with her autonomously formed conception of the good, a conception that includes a standard of social justice or of the practical excellence of laws.

Kelsen's explanation for why majority rule is better than any other rule for taking collectively binding decisions, despite the fact that no such rule will fully eliminate the gap between the will of rulers and ruled, is the following:

Only the claim that as many people as possible ought to be free, that as few people as possible ought to end up in a contradiction between their own will and the general will of the social order—given that total freedom is impossible—provides a reasonable path to the principle of majority rule.[44]

Requirements for qualified majorities or even for unanimity, Kelsen explains, protect individual freedom only in advance of the decision. But they put a straightjacket on any later attempt to change or amend the content of social order. Hence, they make it more difficult for the content of the law to reflect changes in the prevailing attitudes and ambitions of the subjects. A requirement of unanimity in a direct democracy, to mention the most extreme case, would empower a single individual to frustrate the aims of all other members of society should they seek amendment of a previously decided upon rule. To allow a minority to take or amend collectively

---

[43] See Kelsen, *Vom Wesen und Wert der Demokratie* (n 1 above) 9–10.
[44] Ibid, 9. [my translation]

binding decisions, on the other hand, would openly fly in the face of the democratic principle of equality, interpreted as the claim that each citizen's individual interest in freedom, in not having his personal will frustrated by a contradiction with social order, should be given equal weight.[45] The majoritarian principle, hence, strikes the best balance between the interest in individual freedom and the necessity for a binding social order.[46]

The aim of this argument, clearly, is to reconcile the members of an outvoted minority to the results of majority rule. But it seems, at first glance, that it obviously fails to do so. My individual interests may happen to overlap with the content of the law or they may not, depending on whether I am a member of the majority or not. But if I am a member of a minority, the content of social order will not conform to my personal view of the common good and I will be relatively unfree for the simple reason that a majority has decided to act on a conception of the common good different from my own. The fact that majority rule ensures that as many people as possible are free, in the sense of achieving overlap in content between their will and the general will, is unlikely to reconcile me fully with the torment of heteronomy I have to bear.

However, Kelsen's argument does not boil down to the simple claim that majoritarian democracy maximizes the identity in content between the will of the state and the wills of the subjects of the law. It implicitly rests on a richer conception of well-functioning democracy. This richer conception introduces a number of qualifications to simple majoritarianism. These qualifications are best described as conditions that must be fulfilled for an appeal to majoritarianism to carry any legitimatory weight in the eyes of the outvoted.[47]

First, a democracy can be well-functioning only if we do not find ourselves in a situation where the different political parties or camps in a society are fundamentally divided by permanently fixed political identities that do not allow individuals to cross over from one group to another and that make it all but impossible for members of the two groups to think of themselves as members of a community constituted by pursuit of a shared good. Examples of such constellations would include Protestants and Catholics in Northern Ireland or Serbs and Muslims in Bosnia. Majorities, in such a situation have an overriding incentive permanently to entrench their status and to exploit their position of power to exclude the opposition from any present or future position of influence. It would obviously not be reasonable for members of a minority to accept as legitimate the outcomes of a system of majority voting if they can expect to be permanently excluded from any influence on the lawmaking power, on the basis of the majority's implicit claim

---

[45] Kelsen, 'Foundations of Democracy' (n 1 above) 25: 'For the view that the degree of freedom is proportionate to the number of free individuals implies that all individuals are of equal political value and that everybody has the same claim to freedom.'

[46] See Kelsen, *Vom Wesen und Wert der Demokratie* (n 1 above) 9–10. See for a rather similar view Ian Shapiro, *The State of Democratic Theory* (Princeton, 2003) 10–34.

[47] See Kelsen, *Vom Wesen und Wert der Demokratie* (n 1 above) 55–66.

that the minority's identity is alien to the ethical nature of the community. What a minority should be interested in, short of trying to secede, is to acquire veto rights or protective privileges disabling the powers of a potentially hostile democratic majority.

Genuine democracy, Kelsen claims, 'conceptually presupposes the existence of a minority. Hence, the right of the majority presupposes the legitimate existence of a minority'.[48] In other words, a majority can meaningfully be considered a *democratic* majority only as long as it is faced by a minority that is a majority in waiting and that puts forward a different interpretation of the common good to which it hopes to convert a majority of voters.[49] Members of a majority in the democratic sense ought to consider the fact that they are, for now, members of a majority as being in a certain sense circumstantial. They ought to think of their own present account of the common good as a tentative and revisable proposal and they should take into account the possibility that they may not want to continue to endorse it in the future, perhaps as a result of a minority's well-taken criticisms.[50]

In a well-functioning democracy, then, citizens will be attached to different conceptions of the common good, but they will consider these conceptions as inclusive conceptions of the common good. A temporary majority will at least claim to make a proposal that is addressed to all citizens and that takes into account the interests of those who disagree. This willingness is likely to be the stronger, the more the momentary dividing lines between the competing parties are permeable, the more the grouping of citizens into political parties turns out to be a function of their disagreement about the best inclusive conception of the common good and not the result of a prior difference in identity of class or ethnicity that is perceived as unbridgeable by any peaceful means.

In line with this idea, Kelsen's argument emphasizes the possibility of change in the subjective will of the citizens.[51] Kelsen's argument portrays good democratic citizens as persons who will continually reconsider their practical commitments in the light of an ongoing political process.[52] In other words, the idea that there is no permanent boundary between a majority and minority holding different inclusive conceptions of the good at some particular time is related to the view that a reasonable citizen will not adopt an unquestioning commitment to a particular conception of the good. Rather, a good democratic citizen will be willing critically to re-evaluate his own beliefs in the light of ongoing public debate. And if one assumes, as a good democratic citizen, that such debate can potentially lead one to change one's mind, one cannot reasonably take an interest in irrevocably binding one's own future self to one's decisions in the present. This picture provides a missing rationale for the majoritarian argument whose crude variant we rejected as insufficient. The idea that changes in prevalent opinion amongst good democratic citizens should be reflected in the content of the will of the state with as little delay as possible, in

---

48 Ibid, 53.   49 Ibid, 56–7.   50 See ibid, 98–104.   51 See ibid, 6–9.
52 See Kelsen's insistence that democracy requires a 'relativist' worldview. Ibid, 100–3.

order to allow the highest possible number of citizens achieve overlap in content between their conception of the good and the will of the state at any given time, assumes that the opinions reflected in the will of the majority have a rational basis in continuing public discussion about the best inclusive conception of the good.

This conception of a well-functioning democracy entails, as Kelsen acknowledges, a second crucial qualification of simple majoritarianism. A democratic community must pay principled respect to a list of essential democratic freedoms. Since 'democracy is discussion', Kelsen argues, a democratic system must accept that 'freedom of religion, freedom of opinion and press, belong to the essence of democracy'.[53] Democracy, moreover, must be based on the ideal that all citizens are to have full and equal access to rights of political participation. Democratic elections, Kelsen claims, 'are those which are based on universal, equal, free, and secret suffrage'.[54] Systems which fall far short of a universal franchise, therefore, are to be considered defective from the point of view of democratic theory.

Kelsen's claim here is not that such freedoms must necessarily be formally entrenched in a written constitution. His general point, rather, is that a political system in which major players flagrantly failed to respect these fundamental rights would no longer deserve to be called a well-functioning democracy. This would be true, for example of a system in which a majority started to disenfranchise enough members of the minority to ensure itself against any future loss of legislative power or of a system in which a minority opposed the majority's decisions on the basis of the claim that true democracy is possible only in a socialist (or vice versa, a capitalist) state.

In a well-functioning democracy, any individual who is outvoted can reasonably have the expectation of being part of the majority at some future point, either because the majority can be convinced to change its mind or because he changes his mind or due to a combination of both. A temporary majority, on the other hand, will not think of its own laws as final determinations of the community's conception of the common good. The principle of revisability and the notion of community going along with it thus make it possible for the outvoted person to see her own interest in freedom reflected in a social will created according to the majority rule even if the content of that will does not, for now, match her own will. Members of a minority will thus be able to identify with the present general will even if they disagree with its content on the merits.

In order to understand how this picture of democracy tries to reconcile the individualist nature of the aspiration to freedom with the idea of an identity of the will of rulers and ruled, we must recall the factors that gave rise to the torment of heteronomy. As self-governing persons, we reject the idea that we could ever reasonably surrender our moral judgment, including our capacity to form a conception of the common good, to an external practical authority. Unless we are willing to accept as sufficient a purely Hobbesian reconciliation with authority, we will therefore

---

[53] Kelsen, *Foundations of Democracy* (n 1 above) 28.   [54] Ibid, 3.

also believe that the justifiability of a government's actions must ultimately depend on whether these actions can be expected to serve the implementation of what we think of as a good community. We suffer torment if the state subjects us to decisions that we believe do not conform to a defensible notion of the common good. Democracy as unqualified majority rule, however, seemed unable to guarantee such conformity or identity. As a result, it seemed unclear whether it had anything more to offer than could, in any case, be delivered by an absolutist scheme that conforms with a Hobbesian conception of the unity of state.

Does Kelsen's reformulated conception of identity provide a way out of this problem? Let us note first that Kelsen's well-functioning democracy does not require surrender of judgment to the will of the majority. As a member of an outvoted minority in Kelsenian democracy, I remain free (like the supporter of the divine right of kings) to believe that the legislator's decisions are substantively wrong since they are based on a conception of the good that I disagree with and that I believe my fellow citizens should not endorse. But this freedom is publicly honored, as it is not in an absolute monarchy, in democracy's acceptance of my right to dissent publicly and to try to bring about revision of past legislative acts. For the time being, the fact that all citizens were allowed to participate in the discussion leading up to the decision, that all had their vote, as well as the decision's openness for future revision, provides me with a reason to defer to the majority's decision even if I do not agree with it on the merits.

Democratic reconciliation, moreover, does not rest solely on this proceduralist argument. Given a healthy political culture, characterized by the interplay between a democratic majority and a democratic minority, the right to bring about change translates into real chance to do so. Moreover, an inclusive conception of the good adopted by a temporary majority, since it is a result of genuine public debate, is unlikely altogether to fail to reflect the views and interests of the outvoted citizens. While the argument for democracy remains an argument for legitimacy, and hence for reconciliation only, the torment of heteronomy arising from subjection to a democratic majority will therefore usually take a relatively mild form.

In a well-functioning democracy the autonomous person, even while being subject to laws that do not fully express her conception of the common good, will thus be able to motivate her law-abiding behavior on grounds that do not boil down to fear of coercion or fear of the state of nature. Acceptance of the legitimacy of the laws of a well-functioning democracy, we can conclude, is a reasonable, autonomy-preserving habit of deference to social order. Given that social order is necessary and given that full identity in content between the will of all subjects and the will of the state is to be hoped for only under the unrealistic assumption of perfect normative agreement, a democratically formed will of state is the best mechanism of legislation we could reasonably expect.

Given the existence of a well-functioning democracy, the theory of democratic legitimacy holds that my fellow citizens are entitled to my deference if I find myself in a minority, just as I am entitled to theirs in case my view should, for now, win out. In obeying democratically enacted law we do not agree with, we are deferring to our fellow citizens who for now form the majority. But in deferring to their view, we are subjecting ourselves to the will of a temporally extended community of which we can meaningfully consider ourselves a part. This identity, in turn, is what makes it possible to treat democratically enacted laws as instances of objective normativity, as laws that can reasonably be regarded as something more than mere expressions of some person's or some group's subjective will and hence provide the stance of the law-abiding citizen with meaning.

Freedom and compromise: Democracy and constitutional entrenchment

Kelsen's general argument for the democratic utopia of legality stands in tension with a core element of most modern democratic constitutions, with the fact that these constitutions usually entrench a set of individual rights or rights of minority groups: typically by providing for special amendment-procedures that require super-majoritarian approval. The reason for this tension is a latent conflict between the strategy of constitutional entrenchment and the idea of legal legitimacy. Kelsen's qualified majoritarianism, as outlined so far, is fully compatible with the idea of legal legitimacy. The qualifications, as we have seen, are necessary to endow formally democratic processes of legislation with a higher legitimizing force than can be claimed by autocratic forms of legislation. But the qualifications do not directly figure in the criteria of validity of democratic law and they do not directly restrict the possible outcomes of democratic legislation. Consequently, we can, given fulfillment of the qualifications, treat the positive legality of a democratically enacted law as a source of legitimacy.

Constitutional entrenchment, however, seems to be hard to reconcile with the idea of legal legitimacy, especially in the case of rights not essential to democracy. As we have seen, Kelsen wants his theory of democracy to mediate between socialists and capitalists. In keeping with this ambition, Kelsen's majoritarianism denies that a right to private property in means of production (or the absence of such a right) is a necessary element of a democratic constitution since he wants to maintain the possibility that a democracy could be either socialist or capitalist.[55] A democratic legislator can legitimately decide, under the condition that any such decision be revisable, whether society ought to be socialist or capitalist. Those outvoted, Kelsen suggests, ought to accept the adopted framework as legitimate, for the time being, in virtue of the fact that the issue was decided democratically. But the idea that majoritarian democracy is to play this legitimizing role strongly suggests, given Kelsen's own understanding of the virtues of the majority rule, that the decision taken should either not be entrenched or that it cannot, in case it is entrenched, be convincingly justified on the basis of an understanding of democracy as majority rule.[56]

[55] See the discussion of Hayek in Kelsen, *Foundations of Democracy* (n 1 above) 77–84.
[56] See for a forceful statement of this argument Carl Schmitt, *Legalität und Legitimität* (Berlin, 1932) 38–57.

Entrenchment, one might go on to argue, would hardly make sense unless we take it that the function of the entrenchment is to subject majoritarian legislation, even if it otherwise conforms with Kelsen's qualifications, to a list of external substantive restrictions on permissible outcomes. But once we accept this view, we appear to be committed to the belief that majoritarian democracy, even in its qualified form, can be said to legitimize its outcomes only under some prior substantive restraint, a restraint expressed in an entrenched constitutional choice for a capitalist or a socialist society. As a result, we will either have to reject formal constitutionalism or we will have to admit that democratic legality cannot mediate between capitalists and socialists. Actual democracy, would, from the perspective of justification, have to be read as expressing the recognition of a substantive moral condition on justifiable governance.

Kelsen is a defender of constitutional entrenchment and even of a strong conception of constitutional review.[57] But he refuses to acknowledge any fundamental tension between his general argument for democratic majoritarianism and the constitutional practice of entrenching rights against ordinary legislative majorities. He argues, rather, that modern constitutionalism, far from being incompatible with democratic majoritarianism, can be interpreted as making a necessary contribution to the project of a utopia of legality.[58]

Before we take a look at his reasons for taking this stance, it should be noted that Kelsen is committed to rejecting one standard strategy for making constitutionally entrenched rights compatible with democracy, namely theories of constituent power. According to theories of constituent power, constitutions containing entrenched rights can themselves be interpreted as the result of exercises of a higher form of popular sovereignty that manifests itself either in the meta-legal political acts which lead to the revolutionary creation of a constitution or in the heightened political mobilization that is necessary to push a proposal for constitutional amendment past supermajoritarian hurdles. Constitutionally entrenched rights, under such a view, express the will of the people even while they are shielded from ordinary majorities.[59]

Kelsen's theory of legal order is committed to rejecting theories of constituent power in both these forms. According to the theory of legal hierarchy, a right enjoys the status of a constitutional right because it happens to be protected by a special, supermajoritarian procedure for amendment, and not because its entrenchment expresses a higher will of the people.[60] The special procedure governing the enactment as well as the abrogation of constitutional laws, in turn, is valid because it is authorized by a basic norm. The basic norm, finally, cannot itself be the result of an enactment since all valid enactment, according to Kelsen, presupposes the prior validity of an authorizing norm. The theory of the basic norm, in other words, entails that the validity of a constitution or a constitutional law cannot be conceived

---

57 See Chapter 5 below.
58 See Kelsen, *Vom Wesen und Wert der Demokratie* (n 1 above) 53–5 and 75–6.
59 See Bruce Ackerman, *We the People: Foundations* (Cambridge/Mass, 1991).
60 See Kelsen, *Vom Wesen und Wert der Demokratie* (n 1 above) 53–4.

of as the result of an enactment performed by a popular sovereign, acting as constituent power. The pure theory therefore makes it impossible to portray entrenched constitutional rights as the results of a choice taken by a higher will of the people.

Such a higher will, according to Kelsen, does not exist. To believe that popular sovereignty could consist in anything other than in an identity of ruler and ruled which is brought about *under and by* the procedures determined by the constitution is a potentially dangerous autocratic fiction. A democratic constitution, for Kelsen, cannot be an expression of a moral identity of the people that transcends ordinary, legally organized pluralist politics. It is like a ship that we rebuild plank by plank to keep it afloat and to make it better suited to our changing and developing views of the good.[61]

Kelsen's defense of the claim that constitutional entrenchment can be explained as a corollary of majoritarian democracy has a relatively uncontroversial and a controversial part. Given Kelsen's general understanding of majoritarianism, entrenchment of rights essential to democracy poses no special problems of justification. No one who accepts the qualifications on crude majoritarianism that alone make democracy meaningful, it would seem, could have a reason to oppose explicit protection of rights essential to democracy.[62] Explaining entrenchment of rights not essential to democracy, however, will be much harder. Kelsen will have to argue for the justifiability of the entrenchment of constitutional rights not essential to democracy on grounds of a theory of democratic legitimacy.

Kelsen's strategy for walking this tightrope flows from his account of well-functioning democracy. This account implies that majoritarianism has legitimizing powers only if it is practiced in a spirit of reconciliation and mutual respect between majority and minority. But if practiced in such a spirit, Kelsen argues, majoritarianism will protect freedom not simply by making sure that the greatest possible number of people have their way. It will also tend to produce legislative solutions that both majority and minority can recognize as acceptable *compromises* reflecting a wider range of interests than just those of the members of the current majority.

The constitutional entrenchment of non-essential rights can be seen as being conducive to this aspect of the well-functioning of democracy. The existence of constitutional constraints protecting minority interests, especially if they are enforced by a constitutional court endowed with the power to strike down unconstitutional laws, provides increased incentives to a temporary majority to compromise with a temporary minority, to legislate in a way that stays clear of conflicts over the constitutionality of laws enacted by the majority. Constitutional rights protecting basic interests of minorities, Kelsen concludes, need not be understood as an extraneous limitation of democratic majoritarianism. Rather, they can be seen as

---

[61] See ibid, 14–25. For a more critical perspective on Kelsen's denial of constituent power see Kalyvas, 'The Basic Norm and Democracy' (n 1 above).

[62] However, see Waldron, *Law and Disagreement* (n 2 above) 295–6.

complementing its basic purpose: to maximize the degree of freedom enjoyed by subjects of the law.[63]

This view is backed up by an account of the changing structure and political function of liberal rights in constitutional history. Kelsen claims that liberal rights originated as protections of individual interests against arbitrary interference by the executive of an absolutist state. Absolutist monarchies claimed to have the power to exercise administrative acts without a formal legal basis in general laws, if the public good, as interpreted by the executive, was perceived to necessitate such action. The emerging liberal public tried to protect itself against discretionary executive action by attempting to subject all interferences with a standard list of basic rights and freedoms to the requirement that they have a basis in standing and general legal rules enacted with the approval of a parliament. This understanding of the structure of liberal rights is animated by the idea that the threat to individual liberty emanates primarily from the executive, illegitimately exploiting the cover provided by prerogative power to act for the common good so as to satisfy private desires for glory or gain of a monarch and his court. The 'people' represented by parliament were seen as sharing an easily discernable common interest in preventing such arbitrary domination and exploitation at the hands of a monarch. Enforcing a proviso of legality for interferences with individual freedoms, subjecting these interferences to the rule of law to which parliament had given assent, was thus considered a sufficient protection of individual interests since it was assumed that a representative parliament would not have an interest in legitimizing unreasonable interferences with individual liberty.[64]

A Kelsenian democracy, of course, trivially fulfills this standard. All general laws are enacted by the people or their representatives. The system, moreover, is bound to the principles of legality stemming from Kelsen's thesis of the identity of law and state. According to the identity thesis, all alleged exercises of administrative or executive authority must substantially conform to all positive legal norms in force in order to count as genuine exercises of public power. However, Kelsen is aware of the fact that the problem of the protection of subjects of the law against governmental tyranny reappears in the context of a democratic order in a new form. While a majoritarian democracy committed to formal principles of legality offers relatively effective protection of individual interests against a tyrannical executive, one may fear that it will offer insufficient protection of minority groups against the whims of a parliamentary majority. And this potential insufficiency must become a pressing problem as soon as the old coalition of democratic forces arrayed against monarchy disintegrates into a competition amongst ideologically divided parties in a pluralist democracy.

In a fully democratized state, constitutional rights therefore acquire a new significance and they need to be given a new form. The new significance is that of a protection of the interests of minorities against majorities. The new form is the

---

[63] See Kelsen, *Vom Wesen und Wert der Demokratie* (n 1 above) 53–68.   [64] See ibid, 53–4.

differentiation, in positive constitutional law, between ordinary laws and constitutional laws. Kelsen defines constitutional laws as positive legal norms that can be amended or abrogated only through a special legislative procedure that usually requires a qualified majority. He argues that in a modern pluralist democracy, basic interests of minorities ought to be protected in this special way in order for minorities to enjoy effective safeguards against the potential tyranny of majorities.[65]

This line of argument can be applied both to rights essential to democracy and to rights not essential to democracy. The rights Kelsen deems essential to any democracy, as we have seen, are rights of access to the public sphere and rights to participation in the formation of the content of law. Preservation of these rights must be the most fundamental political interest of a minority, whatever other basic interests it might happen to have. Disenfranchisement, after all, is only the most radical form of disregard of a minority's views or interests. Access to the public sphere and rights of participation are valuable from a minority's point of view mainly because they allow it to exercise at least some influence on the formation of the will of the state to which it will be subjected. A majority, on the other hand, will take itself to have reason to pay unconditional respect to the rights of access essential to democracy only if it accepts that the minority has legitimate interests and views, interests and views that ought to be taken into account and to be reflected in the law to some extent.

It would therefore be wrong to think of the added pressure towards respect for minority interests that results from formal constitutionalism as a device that is alien to ordinary majoritarian democracy. Even a simple majoritarian system, as we have seen, is not supposed to function as a dictatorship of the majority. The entrenchment of basic minority interests as constitutional rights, Kelsen claims, will have the practical effect of increasing the chance that both parties will be willing and able to stay clear of a 'winner takes all' politics and instead adopt a strategy of legislative compromise.[66] He goes on to point out that the content of a compromise is not to be confused with 'a higher, an absolute truth or an absolute value standing above the group interests'.[67] The claim that a compromise is not expressive of an absolute truth, however, should not be read as saying that a compromise is nothing but a bargain reflecting a balance of power. A democratic majority and a democratic minority acknowledge that they are embarked on a common project of living together that makes sense only on the basis of a sufficient degree of mutual respect for one another's interests. Constitutionally entrenched rights strengthen the tendency towards compromise between majority and minority that should, in any case, characterize all well-functioning democratic systems by tempering the danger of inconsiderate and disrespectful rashness in the majority's decisions.

---

[65] See ibid, 54–5.

[66] Ibid, 57–8: 'Compromise means: the parties leave behind what divides them and emphasize what unites them. Every exchange, every contract, is a compromise. To compromise means to find a way to get along with each other. [...] If the procedures of a parliament have a deeper meaning, it can only be that a synthesis can somehow arise from the opposition of thesis and antithesis of differing political interests.'   [67] Ibid, 58.

Once these principles are recognized, the reasons for entrenching rights essential to democracy equally allow for the entrenchment of a *revisable* set of non-essential rights. The members of a democratic majority who are hampered in the pursuit of their present interests by constitutionally entrenched rights would thus be wrong to interpret those restrictions as unjustifiable privileges that illegitimately constrain the general will. They could take such a view only if they were willing to adopt the unqualified reading of the democratic identity between ruler and ruled preferred by Rousseau according to which an outvoted minority has simply been mistaken about the content of the general will. But if all citizens accept the assumption that the function of the majority rule is that of forming a will of state with which all their fellows can reasonably identify, even if they do not fully agree with its content on the merits, a majority cannot possibly arrive at the conclusion that the constitutional entrenchment of a revisable set of minority interests not essential to democracy is undemocratic.

This reading of constitutional rights is compatible with the idea of legal legitimacy since it manages to explain and justify the existence of constitutionally entrenched rights not essential to democracy in a way that does not oblige us to read the constitution as a permanent commitment to a list of substantive moral principles not essential to democracy that take normative priority over constituted democratic legality. Instead, it emphasizes the revisability of these constitutional rights, while showing how they enhance the well-functioning of majoritarian democracy.

I certainly would not want to claim that this argument is without its problems. One obvious line of criticism can be developed from the perspective of Jeremy Waldron's legislation-centered democratic jurisprudence. Waldron agrees with Kelsen that a well-functioning democracy necessarily requires a political culture of mutual respect between majority and minority. But once there is such a culture, he goes on to argue, there is no further need for a constitutional or even a constitutional court endowed with the power to strike down unconstitutional legislation.[68]

Waldron claims—and Kelsen, as we have seen, would not disagree—that modern societies are characterized by pervasive disagreement about the good. Such disagreement includes disagreement about the precise content of the respect that democratic citizens owe to each other, even of rights essential to democracy. Once we assume that we find ourselves in healthy political culture, we are obliged to assume as well that legislators, as fellow citizens, are trying to answer such questions as best as they can and in good faith. On the other hand, however, we are not entitled to assume that a written constitution entrenching rights would end disagreement about their meaning. What is more, we are not entitled to expect that judges wouldn't disagree in much the same way as citizens or to expect that they would be more likely to act in good faith than legislators. Hence, we should default to the

---

[68] See Waldron, *Law and Disagreement* (n 2 above) 221–3 and 282–312.

principle that, in a democracy, conflicts about the meaning of rights that demo-cratic citizens owe to each other should be determined by the democratic legislator. To leave such decisions to a politically unaccountable judiciary engaged in inter-preting a vague constitutional document, Waldron fears, may corrupt the political culture essential to a well-functioning democracy instead of supporting it.

It seems to me that the differences between Waldron's and Kelsen's views are not particularly profound. Insofar as Waldron is concerned to argue against an understanding of constitutionalism that turns the constitution into an open-ended mandate to a small judicial elite to transform the law in accordance with its moral predilections, Kelsen, as we shall see in the next chapter, would agree with the basic thrust of his polemic. However, Kelsen might nevertheless be right to claim that a formal constitution enforced by a court operating on a more modest understand-ing of its role could have beneficial effects on the maintenance of a healthy demo-cratic political culture. The idealizing assumptions that Waldron applies to the process of parliamentary legislation clearly do not always hold in reality. We know (even though we believe that one can reasonably disagree about almost everything) that legislative majorities will sometimes be inclined not to settle disputes con-cerning the rights that democratic citizens must grant to each other in good faith, but rather in such a way as to enhance their power.

Constitutional restraints enforceable by a court are likely to inhibit such tenden-cies, sometimes for quite pedestrian reasons. Political parties, to name only one such reason, are under pressure to satisfy their actual or potential voters, a group that is likely not to encompass the whole citizenry. The presence of enforceable constitutional restraints may well make it easier for politicians to justify an absten-tion from maximalist legislative strategies to their own electorate. Such effects do not presuppose that judges have a moral expertise that legislators inevitably lack or that they will always be of one opinion. They are likely to obtain, as Kelsen points out, as soon as courts possess institutional independence and are staffed by trained legal specialists.[69]

More generally speaking, a healthy political culture need not result exclusively from the personal virtue of legislators and individual citizens. It may draw additional support from the constitutionally required co-operation of different organs of state that lessens the demand for virtuous habits on the part of individual actors, be they citizens, legislators, or judges.[70] Kelsen's argument for constitutionalism, then, can be rephrased as making the rather commonsensical claim that constitutionalism, rightly understood, might well favor the chance that the political system as a whole will exhibit the virtues of mutual respect that Waldron, in an effort to counter Dworkin's idealization of the judiciary, attributes to legislatures.

---

[69] See Hans Kelsen, *Allgemeine Staatslehre* (n 1 above) 298.

[70] For a general argument that realization of the ideal of the rule of law requires co-operation between all three branches of the constitution see David Dyzenhaus, *The Constitution of Law. Legality in a Time of Emergency* (Cambridge, 2006).

Kelsen's argument, though, is open to a more specific criticism. One might argue that it fudges the distinction between rights that are essential and rights that are not essential to democracy. Kelsen ultimately seems to argue that the fact that an entrenched right can be amended by a suitably large majority is sufficient for claiming that the right's status poses no special problems from the point of view of democratic theory. This claim appears to overlook that the practical barriers faced by any attempt to bring together a supermajority are usually so high that it seems more appropriate to assimilate entrenchment on the basis of supermajoritarian requirements to complete disabilities on ordinary legislative power than to suggest that they are a variation of the rules guiding ordinary majoritarianism.[71] If this perspective is appropriate, entrenchment of rights not essential to democracy will not be justifiable in a way that saves Kelsen's utopia of legality.

This criticism can be strengthened by an observation about Kelsen's general conception of legal order, namely that it is unable to mark any distinction between different kinds of entrenched rights (or of ordinary rights, for that matter). As we have seen, Kelsen takes the view that basic interests acquire the status of formal constitutional rights insofar as they happen to enjoy special protection through an amendment procedure that requires a legislative supermajority, not because their content requires entrenchment. But this would seem to entail that any justification for entrenchment Kelsen could possibly offer, as part of a theory of legal legitimacy, must be blind to the distinction between rights essential and rights not essential to democracy.

This attack is certainly to be taken seriously. But it does not establish that Kelsen must fail to give *any* weight to the distinction between essential and non-essential rights. It may be helpful to take note of the way in which the distinction applies to a system that has not entrenched any rights. Kelsen admits that a democracy of this type can, through a majority-decision, lawfully be turned into an autocracy, for example by disenfranchising a large part of the population.[72] But even while such a law would not be formally illegal, it will clearly reduce dramatically the legitimizing power of any appeal to the system's legality. The same considerations would apply if an attempt to disenfranchise a group of citizens found the support of a supermajority in a system with entrenched rights, even though the practical hurdles would, thankfully, be much higher.

A piece of legislation or a constitutional amendment changing non-essential rights, on the other hand, need not have any direct consequences for the status of the system as a democracy and hence for its capability to appeal to democratic legality as a source of legitimacy. This way of drawing a distinction between essential and non-essential rights clearly has a strong practical importance for subjects of the law, subjects who need to decide how far it is possible for them reasonably to

---

[71] See Schmitt, *Legalität und Legitimität* (n 56 above) 38–57; Gopal Sreenivasan, 'Does Today's International Trade Agreement Bind Tomorrow's Citizens?' in *Chicago Kent Law Review* 81 (2006) 119–49, at I§ 1–2 and III§ 4.   [72] See Kelsen, 'Verteidigung der Demokratie' (n 1 above) 68.

exhibit genuine law-abidingness. As we will see in the next chapter, the distinction also has important practical consequences for Kelsen's conception of constitutional adjudication. It would therefore be wrong to claim that Kelsen's overall argument is unable to take any account of the difference between essential and non-essential rights.

The position that there is no morally relevant practical difference between the imposition of a strict disability and the imposition of supermajoritarian requirement, moreover, has problems of its own. The view is based on the intuition that any plausible justification for the imposition of a supermajoritarian requirement must equally justify the imposition of a strict disability. Hence, it comes close to saying that supermajoritarian requirements are, strictly speaking, a meaningless institution since they might as well be replaced with strict disabilities wherever they are justified. But this conclusion would appear to make it difficult to make sense of much Western constitutional history and practice. To claim that supermajoritarian requirements effectively block democratic change of constitutionally entrenched rights, or to deny that they can be helpful in enhancing the legitimacy of changes that affect fundamental elements of social structure, seems to be a contestable reading of the historical record. But if this is true, the same must go for the claim that the distinction between strict disabilities and supermajoritarian requirements lacks a justifiable rationale.[73]

Kelsen's emphasis on the revisability of non-entrenched rights is connected to the claim that the constitution should not be conceived of as being permanently wedded to any particular interpretation of the moral identity of the people. The point of democracy, in Kelsen's view, is that it allows us peacefully to work out disputes about the moral identity of our community through a process that tests its own limits and transforms identities. Of course, such a process needs to start somewhere, it presupposes that the groups in a society mutually respect each other and thus have the ability and willingness to talk. But the chances that we will be able to find provisional common ground are increased by the open admission of the contingent nature, from the legal point of view, of the material content of the legal system, including the revisable content of the constitution. In a well-functioning democratic system, reconciliation is brought about by the reciprocal acknowledgement between the political camps that the current legal content need not be permanent, that it is legitimate to challenge it publicly, and to try to radically transform it by going through the necessary legislative motions. A normatively more committed reading of the constitution will be superfluous, Kelsen believes, as long as the citizens of a democratic state are able to maintain proper respect for each other's views. Where they are unwilling to do so, it is unlikely to be of much help.[74]

---

[73] The German *Grundgesetz* (in article 79 §3) even draws an explicit distinction between unamendable constitutional provisions and entrenched constitutional provisions.

[74] See Kelsen, 'Verteidigung der Demokratie' (n 1 above) 65–6.

In line with this understanding of democracy, Kelsen's constitutional theory takes an affirmative stance towards what Carl Schmitt considered to be the Weimar constitution's fatal flaw, namely the fact that it did not appear clearly to decide the question whether Germany would be a capitalist or a socialist country by leaving the matter open to future legislative supermajorities.[75] In Kelsen's view, such openness is a virtue of a democratic constitution since it is the function of a democratic constitution to provide a legal framework for the peaceful and legitimate regulation of conflict about such issues. This point comes out very clearly in what Kelsen says about the conflict between capitalism and socialism:

And if there is any form that offers the possibility to arbitrate this enormous contradiction— a contradiction one might regret but whose existence cannot be denied—in a peaceful and gradual fashion, instead of letting it degenerate into a revolutionary catastrophe with much bloodshed, it is the form of parliamentary democracy whose ideology may be a freedom that is not fully attainable in social reality but whose reality is peace.[76]

A revolutionary socialist, in other words, does not just reject capitalism. He also rejects a democratic solution to what he perceives as the injustice of capitalism. Of course, the socialist could not be expected to accept the priority of democracy as a binding side constraint on his pursuit of socialist goals if the constitutional system weren't in principle open to those goals. Neither could he be expected to accept the normative priority of democratic legality over his substantive conception of the good (at least not on any other than crudely Hobbesian grounds) if he knew that the bourgeois side unconditionally prefers civil war over a democracy that realizes socialist goals. But there is a real difference, in Kelsen's view, between taking the view that one cannot be expected to accept the sovereignty of democratic procedure if it is clear that the opposing party is unwilling to do the same (or at least unwilling to abstain from abusive uses of that procedure) and taking the view that true democracy is not possible in a social system that is still, for the time being, giving prominent place to private property in means of production.

The *revolutionary* socialist, just like the capitalist natural lawyer, refuses to consider as normative any law that fails to express his substantive conception of good social order. This stance amounts to a refusal to acknowledge that democratic legality can be a source of legitimacy, that the conflict between socialism and capitalism, or any other two mutually opposed conceptions of the public good, may be amenable to legitimate arbitration through the rule of democratic positive law.[77] This refusal, Kelsen's believes, is motivated by the view that the freedom which a democratic utopia of legality would afford to all its citizens has no genuine and independent value that could reconcile a citizen whose social ideals are not perfectly realized to its normative claims. It also denies that we have a duty to respect

[75] See Schmitt, *Legalität und Legitimität* (n 56 above) 82–91.
[76] Kelsen, *Vom Wesen und Wert der Demokratie* (n 1 above) 68.
[77] See ibid, 66–8 and 93–7.

the freedom the utopia affords to those who disagree with us. Someone who accepts these claims, Kelsen believes, is likely to prefer some form of dictatorship of class, at least for a transitional period, to the legitimacy of democratic legality.

Kelsen does not argue directly against the choice for dictatorship. But he claims that it can appear to be justified only if one believes that the relatively mild torment of heteronomy inflicted by a constitutional democracy is altogether intolerable and that one may therefore legitimately seek deliverance from one's own torment by imposing one's conception of the good social order on others by the use of violence. Someone who takes such a position has to deny that the pluralism of conceptions of the common good that characterizes modern societies is a natural consequence of the autonomous exercise of the freedoms granted by a democratic society. Only thus will he be able to conclude that one can force people to be free by coercing them into subjection to one's own conception of the good or that one can create a perfectly identitarian democracy, as Schmitt believed, by eliminating the internal enemy. Such projects, Kelsen is concerned to show, cannot justify themselves by appealing to an ideal of 'true democracy', if the term 'democracy' is to have any distinctive meaning.

Kelsen's relativism

Kelsen closes his argument for democracy by emphasizing that acceptance of the normative priority of democratic legality over one's substantive conception of the public good makes sense only from a 'relativist' point of view.[78] However, what Kelsen has to say about relativism and its relation to democracy is perplexing and difficult to understand. It is hard to avoid the conclusion that Kelsen based his theory of democracy on the incoherent idea that 'truth claims have to be checked at the door of politics' in order to 'preserve democratic politics by not insisting on the rightness of a set of values'.[79]

In what follows, I want to try to assess Kelsen's thesis that democracy is based on relativism as charitably as possible. But I should say at the outset that I do not believe that one can understand everything Kelsen says about relativism and democracy in his political works as part of one coherent view. Some of Kelsen's claims about relativism and democracy, if read charitably, can be interpreted in a meaningful and attractive way if we rely on the resources we have established so far in this chapter. But some conflict with his political project and should therefore be discarded by those who are attracted to a Kelsenian understanding of democracy. What I will try to establish is that there is an adequate understanding of the relation between democracy and relativism which does not lead to the conclusion that moral truth-claims

[78] See ibid, 98–104; Kelsen, 'Foundations of Democracy' (n 1 above) 14–18; Hans Kelsen, 'Staatsform und Weltanschauung' in Kelsen, *Demokratie und Sozialismus* (n 1 above) 40–59; Hans Kelsen, 'What is Justice?' in Hans Kelsen, *What is Justice? Justice, Law, and Politics in the Mirror of Science. Collected Essays by Hans Kelsen* (Berkeley, 1957) 1–24, at 22–4.
[79] Dyzenhaus, *Legality and Legitimacy* (n 1 above) 234–5.

must be checked at the door of politics. That Kelsen may not have managed to articulate it clearly enough certainly does not undermine the attractiveness of his conception of democracy.

Any discussion of Kelsen's claim that democracy is based on relativism should start out from the observation that Kelsen uses the term 'relativism' in a number of different senses all of which he took to bear, apparently, on the general claim that democracy presupposes relativism. These usages, I will try to show, are hard to reconcile with each other.[80] Any interpretation of the claim that democracy is based on relativism will therefore have to choose between different understandings of 'relativism'. Our task, then, can only be to find the understanding most adequate to the political project of democracy, as described in the previous sections of this chapter.

In a first sense, Kelsen uses the term 'relativism' to express allegiance to an emotivist conception of moral judgment.[81] According to this conception, it is impossible to 'decide between two conflicting judgments of value in a rational scientific way' since judgments of moral value merely express our differing subjective emotional and volitional reactions to external objects. Even though they purport to be objective, moral value judgments therefore fail to describe genuine properties of the valued objects.[82] This subjectivity of judgments of value contrasts with the objectivity of theoretical scientific judgments which are 'about reality' and 'verifiable by experiment'.[83]

If Kelsen's relativism is at the core an affirmation of the view that moral judgments are mere expressions of subjective desire, it seems hard to avoid the suspicion that the view that democracy presupposes relativism must be based on a mistaken inference from the claim that there are no objective moral values to the claim that one ought to pay respect to everyone else's opinions about value since no one's opinions about value are better than anyone else's. Such a view, needless to say, could not possibly ground the theory of democracy I have attributed to Kelsen. Unfortunately, it seems undeniable that Kelsen is, at times, explicitly drawing this fallacious inference.[84]

However, Kelsen also employs the term 'relativism' to refer to a general philosophical 'Weltanschauung' that contrasts with an equally general 'Weltanschauung'

---

[80] See Jes Bjarup, 'Kelsen's Theory of Law and Philosophy of Justice' in William Twining and Richard Tur (eds), *Essays on Kelsen* (Oxford, 1986) 273–303.

[81] See for example Kelsen, 'Foundations of Democracy' (n 1 above) 17: 'Philosophical relativism, on the other hand, as antimetaphysical empiricism (or positivism), insists upon a clear separation of reality and value and distinguishes between propositions about reality and genuine value judgments, which, in the last analysis, are not based on a rational cognition of reality but on the emotional factors of human consciousness, on man's wishes and fears. Since they do not refer to values immanent in absolute reality, they cannot establish absolute, but only relative, values.'

[82] Kelsen, 'What is Justice?' (n 78 above) 5.   [83] Ibid.

[84] Kelsen, *Vom Wesen und Wert der Demokratie* (n 1 above) 101 and Kelsen, 'What is Justice' (n 78 above) 22–4. See also Kelsen, 'Foundations of Democracy' (n 1 above) 61: 'Tolerance presupposes the relativity of the truth maintained or the value postulated; and the relativity of a truth or value implies that the opposite truth or value is not entirely excluded. This is the reason why the expression of an opposite truth or propaganda for the opposite value must not be suppressed.'

of 'absolutism'. The absolutist claims to have certain intuitive insight into the structure of reality as it is in itself, including an idea of the good, while the relativist
admits that human cognition is essentially limited to what we can experience in
space and time and therefore fallible.[85] Acceptance of democracy, Kelsen claims,
presupposes that one has adopted a relativist 'Weltanschauung'. Support for autocracy, on the other hand, is typically related to philosophical absolutism.[86]

Kelsen agrees that if some person or some group had infallible intuitive insight
into an unchanging idea of the good, while the other members of society lack it,
that person or group ought to take all legislative decisions in an autocratic fashion.
To take decisions in any other way, after all, could only make them worse in substantive quality. But from a relativist point of view, claims to infallible insight into
the good are unsustainable. The relativist takes it, rather, that an absolute justification of policies is unavailable. No opinion about the good, however well tested, is
forever beyond challenge since all our opinions are fallible. Hence, legislative decisions ought not to be taken in an autocratic fashion.

Note that this second understanding of relativism does not, as such, mark any
difference between the theoretical and the practical since it claims that theoretical
scientific judgments, as much as judgments of value, lack a basis in an absolute
conception of reality and are fallible. And to say that judgments of value are fallible does not imply, of course, that they are mere projections of subjective emotions.
So there is a potential tension between the first usage of 'relativism' and the second.
Of course, we cannot yet infer that they necessarily conflict. It would seem to be
possible, after all, to reject an absolutist conception of theoretical truth and to claim
that judgments of value are relative to those who make them in a more thorough-
going way than theoretical judgments.[87] It should be noted, though, that some of
the things Kelsen says when drawing a contrast between relativism and absolutism
as general worldviews do not really sit too well with such a view. The problem can
be brought out by taking a look at a quotation that is characteristic of Kelsen's
attempts to relate democracy to a relativist worldview:

If, however, it is recognized that only relative values are accessible to human knowledge and
human will, then it is justifiable to enforce a social order against reluctant individuals only
if this order is in harmony with the greatest possible number of equal individuals, that is to
say, with the will of the majority. It may be that the opinion of the minority, and not the

---

[85] Kelsen, 'Foundations of Democracy' (n 1 above) 16 defines 'relativism' and 'absolutism' as follows:
'Philosophical absolutism is the view that there is an absolute reality, ie, a reality that exists independently of human cognition. Hence its existence is beyond space and time, to which human cognition is
restricted. Philosophical relativism, on the other hand, advocates the empirical doctrine that reality
exists only within human cognition, and that, as the object of cognition, reality is relative to the knowing subject. The absolute, the thing in itself, is beyond human experience; it is inaccessible to human
knowledge and therefore unknowable. To the assumption of absolute existence corresponds the possibility of absolute truth and absolute values, denied by philosophical relativism, which recognizes only
relative truth and relative values.'

[86] See Kelsen, *Vom Wesen und Wert der Demokratie* (n 1 above) 98–104.

[87] See Philip Pettit, 'Kelsen on Justice: A Charitable Reading' in *Essays on Kelsen* (n 80 above) 305–18.

opinion of the majority, is correct. Solely because of this possibility, which only philosophical relativism can admit—that what is right today may be wrong tomorrow—the minority must have a chance to express freely their opinion and must have full opportunity of becoming a majority. Only if it is not possible to decide in an absolute way what is right and what is wrong is it advisable to discuss the issue and, after discussion, to submit to a compromise.[88]

Kelsen's line of argument here clearly presupposes that it actually makes sense, even for the proponent of relativist worldview, to look for a correct solution to a problem of policy, with what limited and essentially fallible discursive means are available to us. On a purely emotivist account of value, we could not say that the opinions of the minority may be correct and it would not be clear why it should be advisable to discuss.

The idea that a relativist worldview supports democracy, then, appears to be based, on the one hand, on a rejection of the idea that there could be social elites that possess an infallible and exclusive insight into the good and that are therefore entitled to lord it over the rest. But it also presupposes, on the other hand, that debates about what policies ought to be adopted by the community, about what values are defensible grounds of policy, are at least meaningful practices, that they offer a better chance than any other mode of decision-taking that we will arrive at morally defensible laws.[89] At least once we take into account the political use Kelsen wants to make of the contrast between absolutism and relativism as worldviews, the second use of 'relativism' therefore turns out to be irreconcilable with the first.

In a third use of 'relativism', Kelsen claims that he is only offering a conditional or a relative, but not an absolute justification of democracy. Democracy, Kelsen takes himself to have established, is internally related to the value of freedom since democracy, if defined as 'a political method by which the social order is created and applied by those subject to the order', will 'necessarily, always and everywhere, serve this ideal of political freedom'.[90] But his theory of democracy remains relativist, Kelsen claims, insofar as it does not commit those who accept it as an account of the nature of democracy to the normative claim that our social order ought to be organized democratically. It only commits us to the view that there is an internal relation between democracy and Kelsen's ideal of freedom under social order, such that this ideal can only be realized through democracy.

[88] Kelsen, 'Absolutism and Relativism in Philosophy and Politics' in Kelsen, *What is Justice?* (n 78 above) 198–208, at 206–7.

[89] To be sure, Kelsen frequently emphasizes that disputes about justice can have no rational solution since all abstract conceptions of equality are empty. See for example Kelsen, 'What is Justice?' in Kelsen, *What is Justice* (n 78 above) and Hans Kelsen, 'Vom Wesen der Gerechtigkeit' in Kelsen, *Reine Rechtslehre* (2nd ed, Wien, 1960) 357–444. But these claims are themselves explicitly put forward as claims about 'absolute justice' and they are typically tempered by the claim that conflicts of interest become amenable to compromise once they are no longer seen as conflicts between absolute conceptions of justice. Such claims make little sense unless we suppose that to strike a balance between competing interests is a normatively superior way of resolving conflicts.

[90] Kelsen, 'Foundations of Democracy' (n 1 above) 4.

Kelsen cautions that we must not confuse the question 'whether democracy can necessarily serve a certain ideal with the question as to whether democracy can be itself an absolute ideal'.[91] The first question, he implies, is answerable on scientific grounds whereas the second is not. Accordingly, Kelsen's theory of democracy will commit one to the view that democracy is the best form of government if and only if one has already accepted the idea that the freedom which it realizes is the supreme social ideal or value. But this ethical commitment, and here the first understanding of 'relativism' once again raises its head, is not one that could be justified on scientific grounds.

However, Kelsen's claim that his theory of democracy is a scientific theory, since it is not committed to the view that democracy is the best form of government, still carries the suggestion that even someone who rejects the view that the freedom served by democracy ought to be the highest social value is obliged to accept Kelsen's concept of democracy as descriptively adequate. And this 'scientific' result would already sustain one of Kelsen's main critical intentions, namely to make sure that defenders of dictatorship are stopped from invoking the ideal of democracy in peddling their cause, that they will be forced to present their views as views that oppose democracy.

But this clearly will not do. Perhaps there are defenders of dictatorship who would be willing to accept Kelsen's theory of democracy as descriptively adequate, and yet reject the view that democracy is the best form of government, on the basis of the argument that the value of freedom is less important than other values such as security, order, or solidarity. But they are certainly more likely to try to reclaim the concept of democracy and it is hard to see how Kelsen can stop them from doing so, given that he offers what is clearly a value-laden and contestable description of democracy.

Kelsen's definition of democracy, as we have seen, focuses on the fact that at least the general laws of legal order are enacted on the basis of majority votes of either the whole electorate or its representatives and it interprets this institutional fact as a realization, however modest and approximate, of the idea that the people rule themselves and thus enjoy a freedom they could not enjoy in an autocracy. However, there are definitions of democracy, as Kelsen was well aware, that give prominence to other characteristics, for example the fact that there are regular elections such that rulers, even while they govern autocratically once in office, can be recalled by an electorate. Empirically speaking, this feature may well be as characteristic, perhaps more characteristic, of the systems we intuitively think of as democracies as the Kelsenian ideal of self-rule of the people. It would seem that Kelsen can justify a rejection of theories of democracy that focus on this latter feature, to the exclusion of the idea that democracy is the self-rule of the people, only on the basis of a prior answer to the question of what values democracy ought to serve. Competing theories, in turn, are likely to express different views of the essence and value of

[91] Ibid.

democracy. Kelsen would clearly be right to suspect that such competing theories will sever the connection between democracy and his understanding of freedom. But what could it mean for a positivist to claim that such attempts at redefinition can be ruled out on strictly scientific grounds?

It seems hard to avoid the conclusion that Kelsen's approach in democratic theory mirrors his approach to legal normativity in general. Kelsen claims that his approach to democracy is the only one that will allow us to understand democracy as a meaningful institution, just as he claims that the pure theory is the only theory of law that will allow us to understand law as normative. But he is open to the obvious objection that the point of democracy can be interpreted in many different ways, just as his general theory of law is open to the charge that it can claim to be the only theory that allows us to interpret law as normative only once we presuppose a rather peculiar and contested view of what it means to interpret law as normative.[92]

Let me point to another interesting analogy between Kelsen's concept of democracy and his concept of law, as I have interpreted it. Kelsen's concept of democracy aims to be general but it is at the same time aspirational. It entails that a polity could be more or less democratic.[93] I will name only three clear instances of this perfectionism: First, Kelsen believes that a democracy is the more democratic the wider its franchise, the more closely the overlap between citizens and subjects of the legal system.[94] Secondly, Kelsen is convinced that in a representative democracy, proportional representation is to be preferred to a 'first past the post' system.[95] Third, Kelsen is clearly committed to the view that there is a strong relation between democracy and the rule of law.[96] The upshot of these observations is that the concept of democracy, while aspiring to descriptive generality, is also an ideal. Hence, there will be many systems that we can describe as democracies because they exhibit the core feature, self-rule of the people, to some extent but that will be deficient from the point of view of democracy's ideal. But in this respect, the concept of democracy, it seems, is perfectly analogous to the concept of law if our earlier analysis of the thesis of the identity of law and state is correct.

All this strongly suggests that Kelsen's conception of democracy, just like his conception of legal normativity in general, is meaningful only once we endorse the normative ideal the conception is supposed to serve. There would be no pressing reason to define democracy as Kelsen does, and hence to conclude that what I have called actual democracy is the authentic form of democracy, if one did not accept the idea that freedom ought to be the supreme value of a well-ordered society. In the same way, there would be no pressing reason, as we have seen, to adopt the normative perspective of the pure theory unless one endorsed the ideal of legality implicit in Kelsen's understanding of legal objectivity.

---

[92] This analogy finds support in the fact that Kelsen argues that legal-scientific judgments are relative value-judgments that depend on the presupposition of the basic norm. See Kelsen, 'Value Judgments in the Science of Law' in Kelsen, *What is Justice?* (n 78 above) 209–30.
[93] See Kelsen, 'Foundations of Democracy' (n 1 above) 3.   [94] See ibid.
[95] See ibid, 84.   [96] See ibid, 29–30.

Note that I am not claiming that Kelsen is wrong to take the view that there is an internal relation between the value of freedom and the institutional system of actual democracy as defined at the outset. Actual democracy may well be the indispensable institutional and cultural embodiment of a distinctive ideal of freedom in legal order. If this claim holds true, Kelsen's views about the nature of democracy are more than arbitrary terminological stipulations. They would be claims about the nature of one social institution and it would be true that any choice against the form of order represented by that institution entails a choice against the value realized by and only by that institution. My claim is that this result does not suffice to show that it would be illicit to decide to apply the name 'democracy' to a different institution, on the basis of an analysis of the value of democracy grounded in an ultimate value other than freedom.

In other words, even the 'scientific' part of Kelsen's analysis will have no apologetic value; it will not suffice to show that we should understand by 'democracy' the set of institutions that secures freedom, unless one assumes that the preservation of the largest measure of freedom compatible with social order is rightly considered to be the highest political value. In the light of this analysis, it is rather unfortunate that Kelsen tends to lapse back into the first, emotivist sense of 'relativism' as soon as he talks about his attachment to the value of freedom that is presupposed in his conditional justification of democracy. Kelsen's theory of democracy is ultimately uninteresting if we do not accept a commitment to defend our attachment to that value on the basis of reasoned argument. Of course, if we are relativists in the second of the three senses defined here, we will not try to offer a justification of our commitment to freedom that is based on appeals to an exclusive and non-discursive insight into a transcendent ideal of the good. Instead, we will try to make our case by appeal to experiences and interests that others share or can be brought to share through discussion. But we will not therefore think that our commitments to freedom and democracy are a matter of mere subjective taste or that one might as well commit to autocratic views.

Let me sum up the results of the comparison of Kelsen's different senses of 'relativism' and their relation to the justification of democracy. The first of these senses, general subjectivism about value, cannot figure in a defense of democracy since any such defense would involve a mistaken inference from subjectivism about value to the demand for tolerance. It is also in conflict with the second sense, the idea that democracy presupposes a rejection of claims to infallible *a priori* insight into the good on the part of a social elite and that it is based on acceptance of a fallibilist conception of moral judgment that makes public discussion about the good meaningful. The third sense, the idea of a conditional or relative justification of democracy, rests on an unsustainable attempt to distinguish between moral and 'scientific' reasoning about democracy. Moreover, it seems wedded to the problematic first sense of 'relativism'.

If there is a defensible core in Kelsen's talk about relativism, I conclude, it is to be found in the second of the three understandings of relativism. Kelsen's statements on the relation between value relativism and democracy should be read as reflections on the attitude that is required of someone who adopts the point of view of a law-abiding citizen in a democratic state.

Let us assume we accept the idea of freedom that is realized by a democracy as the supreme social ideal. We can do so only if we believe that fully developed democratic legality makes legislative decisions legitimate, that it justifies legislative decisions even if they do not overlap in content with our own substantive ideals of justice or good legal content. The ethical core of this belief is the idea that we have a duty, under certain conditions, to defer to our fellow citizens' view of the substantive merits of some policy even if we disagree with that view in the sense that we think it leads to a decision which is morally suboptimal. Deference, of course, does not require that the democratic majority's opinion as to what constitutes a good decision has to be accepted as superior to one's own. But it has to be possible for us to accept that it is reasonable to defer to the judgment of the majority as a temporary determination of the content of legal order and hence of our actual legal obligations.

The second sense of 'relativism' emphasizes that we can be reconciled to social order in this way by democracy only if we are able to think of genuine democracy as a rational process through which we potentially learn something, through which our own ideals undergo development in virtue of an exchange of opinion with our fellow citizens. As members of an outvoted minority, we have to be able to accept that the majority's legislative proposals stem from an inclusive conception of the good that may contain insights and reflect experiences missing from our own. But it would not be possible for us to take this view of a majority's decisions if we believed that we had received full notice of the morally optimal content of positive law from divine revelation, from some form of a priori intuition, or from a scientific understanding of human history.

If we took such a view, democratic legislation could at best reproduce what we already know to be morally correct. If it failed to do so, the fact that the decision was taken democratically would not provide us with any further non-Hobbesian reason to consider them justified. In other words, Kelsen should be read as claiming that, as democratic citizens, we have to be fallibilists with respect to our own conception of substantive justice or good legal content. But if we thought of our own opinions about justice as mere subjective preferences, we would be as incapable of taking the stance that Kelsen thinks is required for a democracy to function as we would if we took ourselves to be in possession of an unchallengeable ideal of justice.

The interpretation of Kelsen's relativism I just offered serves to rebut the charge that the Kelsenian would want truth-claims to be kept out of politics. It is true, of course, that Kelsen's theory of the democratic state, and his conception of law in general, are committed to a principle of moral neutrality as a reaction to the fact of pluralism. But in order properly to assess Kelsen's position it is important to see that the principle does not operate in quite the same ways as the most popular contemporary principles of liberal neutrality. Contemporary accounts of liberal neutrality usually try directly or indirectly to restrict the morally or politically permissible *content* of democratically created positive law. They assume, in other words, that the fact that a law was enacted democratically cannot be a sufficient condition of its legitimacy unless further criteria of neutrality or epistemic abstinence are satisfied.

Rawls, for example, assumes that it is illegitimate to legislate on the basis of a 'comprehensive' conception of the good about which there is reasonable disagreement (in the Rawlsian sense) since doing so would violate obligations of mutual respect for differing practical identities that hold amongst citizens. Arguments *de lege ferenda*, Rawls claims, have to be couched in terms of public reasons that do not entail a denial of the truth of any 'reasonable' comprehensive conception of the good since no group of citizens could reasonably be expected to endorse a policy that is based on a rejection of the truth of its comprehensive conception of the good.[97]

It is instructive to compare this conception of neutrality to Kelsen's. Kelsenian democracy is committed to moral neutrality, but only on the level of constitutional form, not on the level of legal content. Kelsen's argument for the legitimacy of any democratically created content assumes that no particular content, ordinary or constitutional, is ever to be looked upon as a final and unchangeable expression of the community's moral identity. In order for the identity thesis to make any sense, the people, and that means, the actual people subjected to the law at any given moment, have to remain sovereign in the sense of retaining the power to change and amend any legal content through the employment of the democratic method. An adequate understanding of a democratic constitution, then, must remain neutral among the differing conceptions of good legislative content that can be entertained by democratic citizens.

But this neutrality on the constitutional level opens up the possibility of taking decisions about revisable legislative content in the light of comprehensive conceptions of the good that are reasonably rejected by some citizens. The whole point and purpose of an argument about legal legitimacy is to establish that pieces of legislation (and constitutional legislation) may justifiably be based on the conception of moral truth held by the legislative majority because their *legitimacy*, in a well-functioning democracy, does not have to be defended in terms of those truth-claims. The availability of democratic legitimacy makes it possible for citizens and legislators to engage in uninhibited and critical discussion of different views of the public good as well as to decide, for now, on the basis of the revisable outcomes of such discussion.

The availability of Kelsenian democratic legitimacy, moreover, is clearly premised on a certain 'theory of the truth of moral judgments', namely one that rejects the force of appeals to religious authority or intuitive insight into a transcendental good. The democratic method, in Kelsen's view, encourages all comprehensive conceptions of the good to bring themselves fully into play when it comes to determining

---

[97] See John Rawls, *Political Liberalism* (New York, 1996) xliv–xlv.

the content of the law. But it rejects the view that we must pay any further respect to practical identities based on absolutist worldviews. Kelsenian citizens owe each other open access to public debate, equal participation in political rights, and a willingness to enter into a real argument. A majority has to be ready to argue for the truth of its position in good faith and to treat the minority as an interlocutor and an addressee of its arguments. Under circumstances of relativism, this duty entails that the opposing side is being given a fair hearing, that it is considered as a voice that can make a valuable contribution to a rational decision on the content of the law. But it does not entail that the majority is under a duty to refrain from acting on its own beliefs only to spare the sensibilities of those who consider their moral views to be non-negotiable and who are therefore unwilling to put them to the test of public discussion.

Some remarks of Kelsen's clearly suggest that this stance is itself based on an attachment to the liberal value of autonomy that the later Rawls would consider to be inappropriate in political liberalism. Kelsen argues that moral 'absolutism' is popular because it allows people to avoid taking responsibility for their own moral beliefs. In other words, moral absolutism liberates people from the burdensome attempt to make use of their own understanding in forming opinions about value and from the danger of getting it wrong.[98] But the capacity to form one's own conception of the good is what provides human beings with the interest in the kind of freedom that a state, according to Kelsen, must respect if it wants to be fully legitimate.

It is wrong, I conclude, to treat Kelsen's theory of democracy as a close relation of a Rawlsian political conception of liberalism.[99] Kelsenian neutrality tries to divorce jurisprudence from theories of justice, understood as theories about the best design of the content of positive law. But the reflections about democracy make it perfectly clear that this neutralization is not meant to deny that legality, and in particular democratic legality, has normative value. It is an attempt to argue that the values internally related to legality should be kept apart from, and be treated as prior to, judgments of substantive justice. In a democratic system, the autonomy of the jurisprudential perspective comes into its own, so to speak, insofar as the internal legitimizing values of legality can—since the people are governing themselves—justifiably claim to preempt individual judgments based on comprehensive conceptions of the good.

Relativism in the second of the three senses discussed above fosters acceptance of this priority thesis since relativists will not tend to think of themselves as those

---

[98] To be sure, Kelsen, echoing Max Weber, expresses this idea in a misleading existentialist fashion when he writes that '. . . relativism imposes upon the individual the difficult tasks of deciding for himself what is right and what is wrong. This, of course, implies a very serious responsibility, the most serious moral responsibility a man can assume. If men are too weak to bear this responsibility, they shift it to an authority above them, to the government and, in the last instance, to God.' (Kelsen, 'What is Justice?' in Kelsen, *What is Justice* [n. 78 above] 22).

[99] Dyzenhaus, *Legality and Legitimacy* (n 1 above) 218–58.

who bring salvation, if necessary with fire and sword, to their fellow citizens. They accept the view that a democratic legal order that possesses integrity should command respect even if its material content is not in line with one's personal opinions about how the ideal social order would look like. But it is precisely this acknowledgement, the fact that relativists are psychologically equipped to deal with the fact of *pro tempore* subjection to laws whose practical quality they deem to be controversial, that makes it possible to fully unleash open democratic deliberation about the best content of the law and to finally separate the state's claim to legitimacy from all claims to moral authority.

5

Democratic Constitutionalism—Kelsen's Theory of Constitutional Review

Kelsen claims, as we have seen, that the pure theory is a legal theory adequate to the rule of law. One of the most important implications of this adequacy, in Kelsen's view, is that it provides the basis for a defense of constitutional review. Kelsen believes that the pure theory undermines the common assumption that the practice of constitutional adjudication is at least potentially in tension with democratic politics.[1] If understood in the light of the pure theory, democracy and the practice of judicial review of the constitutionality of all acts of the highest organs of government as well as of the legislature will be seen as mutually supporting institutions. Both democracy and constitutionalism are needed to provide a full institutional explication of the idea of legal objectivity and to realize the utopia of legality. Democracy, insofar as it is defined by its opposition to autocracy, is strengthened by constitutionalism and constitutionalism, as serving the purpose of the protection of minority interests, is meaningful only if we accept the legitimacy of constitutional review.[2]

Kelsen's argument is addressing a specific situation in positive constitutional law that was typical of many inter-war continental European polities. Most of these states were parliamentary democracies, committed to the principle of popular sovereignty. They were usually endowed, moreover, with written constitutions determining the fundamental procedures of legislation and protecting basic civil (and in some cases basic social) rights. However, they usually did not possess a constitutional court endowed with the power to strike down unconstitutional legislation. To the contrary, many of the constitutions in question, Kelsen observes, explicitly refused to grant courts the authority to review laws for their constitutionality and

---

[1] See for the most important recent development of the theme Jeremy Waldron, *Law and Disagreement* (Oxford, 1999) 211–312. The view tends to linger on even where constitutional review is an accepted practice, in the form of theories of adjudication that deny judges the power to enforce constitutional values against the original intent of the framers of the constitution. See Antonin Scalia, *A Matter of Interpretation. Federal Courts and the Law*, edited by Amy Gutmann (Princeton, 1997) 3–47.

[2] The sources for Kelsen's view of constitutional adjudication are: Hans Kelsen, 'Wesen und Entwicklung der Staatsgerichtsbarkeit' in Hans Klecatsky, René Marcić, and Herbert Schambeck (eds), *Die Wiener rechtstheoretische Schule. Ausgewählte Schriften von Hans Kelsen, Adolf Julius Merkl und Alfred Verdross* (Wien, 1968), vol II, 1813–71; Hans Kelsen, 'Wer soll der Hüter der Verfassung sein?' in ibid, 1873–922. See also Hans Kelsen, *Allgemeine Staatslehre* (Berlin, 1925) 248–55 and 285–301.

to treat them as null, ie not to apply them, should they deem them unconstitutional.[3] Kelsen's defense of constitutional adjudication is meant to advocate the creation of a constitutional court in a polity that is ostensibly committed, in virtue of a positive constitution, to democracy *and* constitutionalism, yet lacks the institution of a court equipped with the power to review the constitutionality of the acts of the highest organs of government, in particular those of the legislature, and authoritatively to invalidate them.[4]

Kelsen's argument, in a nutshell, is that a 'formal constitution'[5] governing ordinary legislation and other acts of highest organs of government remains a defective form of law unless it is enforced against these organs by an independent court providing a 'guarantee of legality' of legislative acts and other acts of the highest organs of government.[6] His basic reason for this claim is an application of a general idea we have already encountered. Constitutional norms are legal conditions for the valid exercise of authority on the part of the legislature and the government, in much the same way in which other legal norms lower down the legal hierarchy are authorizing conditions for judges and administrators. However, as long as the legislature or the executive themselves have the final say on whether some alleged enactment of a norm on their part is to be considered as conforming with the authorizing constitutional norms, the principle of constitutional legality will remain ineffective. Or, to be more precise, it will remain ineffective as soon as the decisions of the legislature and the executive pass the threshold of absolute nullity. Citizens as well as subordinate organs of government will then be faced with the alternative of either having to treat a law or an executive decision that is suspected of unconstitutionality as null at their own risk or of having to defer to the legislature's or the executive's interpretation of the constitution.

The first alternative is normatively unattractive and impracticable, while the second potentially turns material constitutional law into a series of non-binding exhortations and reduces formal constitutional law to the barest procedural standards sufficient to lift a decision over the threshold of absolute nullity. A constitution not solidified by guarantees of legality would be acceptable, then, only if there were some convincing general legal-theoretical reason to think that acts of organs whose powers are immediately conferred by the constitution cannot be subjected

[3] Kelsen, *Allgemeine Staatslehre* (n 2 above) 254–5. The Austrian constitution of 1919, drafted in part by Kelsen himself, was a noteworthy exception.

[4] See for Kelsen's conception of the powers of a constitutional court Kelsen, 'Wesen und Entwicklung der Staatsgerichtsbarkeit' (n 2 above) 1836–48; Kelsen, 'Wer soll der Hüter der Verfassung sein?' (n 2 above) 1873–4. The focus of Kelsen's argument is on the legality of legislation. But he explicitly includes review of the acts of all highest organs of government, ie of all organs that immediately execute the constitution, in the powers of the constitutional court.

[5] See Kelsen, 'Wesen und Entwicklung der Staatsgerichtsbarkeit' (n 2 above) 1819–20; Kelsen, 'Die Lehre von den drei Gewalten oder Funktionen des Staates' in *Die Wiener rechtstheoretische Schule* (n 2 above) vol III, 1625–60, at 1654–7.

[6] See Kelsen, 'Wesen und Entwicklung der Staatsgerichtsbarkeit' (n 2 above) 1826–34 and the illuminating discussion in Horacio Spector, 'Judicial Review, Rights, and Democracy' in *Law and Philosophy* 22 (2003) 285–334, at 305–14.

to legal control. However, there is no convincing reason, Kelsen argues, to claim that the acts of the highest organs of government cannot be subjected to the same standards of legality that we apply to all other exercises of public power. Hence, 'guarantees of legality' in the form of a possibility of independent judicial review ought to be extended to the constitutional level.[7]

Kelsen's argument for the creation of a constitutional court appears to be afflicted, however, by a number of problems concerning its status as well as its consistency.[8] The problem of status arises because Kelsen's argument allows for a modest as well as for an ambitious interpretation. At times, Kelsen admits that there may be sound 'political' (as opposed to 'jurisprudential' or 'legal scientific') reasons to reject the creation of a constitutional court in a particular polity[9] and he appears to stop short of denying that a constitution not protected by a special constitutional court wholly lacks the force of law.[10] What he is concerned to point out, according to the modest interpretation, is only that one standard argument often used against the creation of a constitutional court (or to advocate a very restricted understanding of the powers of such a court) is based on indefensible reasoning, reasoning that mixes political advocacy with jurisprudential analysis. According to this standard argument, the most important of the decisions that would have to be taken by a constitutional court would inevitably be 'political' and not 'legal'. Since courts cannot legitimately take political decisions, the power to take these decisions should not be assigned to a court.[11]

As we have seen, Kelsen rejects a conception of the role of courts that rests on a qualitative distinction between legal and political decisions. The pure theory, in undermining such a distinction, shows, according to Kelsen, that there are no jurisprudential reasons, reasons relating to the nature of adjudication, to believe that actions of the highest organs of state cannot meaningfully be subjected to judicial enforcement of the principle of constitutional legality. Since judicial decisions

---

[7] See Kelsen, 'Wesen und Entwicklung der Staatsgerichtsbarkeit' (n 2 above) 1862 and Kelsen, *Allgemeine Staatslehre* (n 2 above) 254 for clear expressions of the view that a constitution remains defective unless it is enforced by a constitutional court.

[8] My way of setting up the problem is inspired by the discussion in Dyzenhaus, *Legality and Legitimacy. Carl Schmitt, Hans Kelsen, and Hermann Heller in Weimar* (Oxford, 1997) 102–60. See also Michel Troper, 'Kelsen et le contrôle de constitutionnalité' in Michel Troper, *La Théorie du Droit, le Droit, l'État* (Paris, 2001) 173–93 and Michel Troper, 'Kelsen, la théorie de l'interprétation et la structure de l'ordre juridique' in Michel Troper, *Pour une théorie juridique de l'état* (Paris, 1994) 85–94.

[9] See Kelsen, 'Wer soll der Hüter der Verfassung sein?' (n 2 above) 1921–2.

[10] Kelsen allows that a guarantee of legality might take the form of a personal criminal liability of the officials whose acts are in question. But he emphasizes that such guarantees are highly inefficient. See Kelsen 'Wesen und Entwicklung der Staatsgerichtsbarkeit' (n 2 above) 1835–6.

[11] Kelsen attacked the view as put forward by Carl Schmitt in *Der Hüter der Verfassung* (Berlin, 1931). Schmitt argued that the president of the Weimar Republic, and not a constitutional court, ought to function as the 'guardian of the constitution'. This claim was partly based on an interpretation of art 48 of the Weimar constitution. See Carl Schmitt, 'Die Diktatur des Reichspräsidenten nach Artikel 48 der Weimarer Verfassung' in Carl Schmitt, *Die Diktatur. Von den Anfängen des modernen Souveränitätsgedankens bis zum proletarischen Klassenkampf* (Berlin, 1928) 211–57. But Schmitt's view was clearly dependent on the general assumption that sovereign power alone is capable of deciding hard cases of constitutional conflict.

are always 'political' there is no reason to think that the political nature of the decisions of a constitutional court poses any special problems of legitimacy. The question whether constitutional conflicts ought to be subjected to the jurisdiction of a
constitutional court, therefore, is an open political question.[12] All Kelsen's argument
claims to show, under the modest reading, is that this political question cannot be
answered negatively on the basis of an account of the nature of adjudication.[13]

Kelsen's modest negative argument, it has been claimed, lets the opponent of
constitutionalism 'off the hook'. It reveals Kelsen as an author who, due to his positivist commitments, cannot offer a real defense of the priority of constitutional
legality over discretionary political choice and hence of the idea of democratic
constitutionalism.[14] To make matters worse, the modest interpretation of Kelsen's
argument apparently leads to a problem of inconsistency. Kelsen, even while claiming that all judicial decisions are political, holds on to the view that the constitutional court, in arbitrating cases of constitutional conflict, will be capable of acting
as a 'guardian of the constitution'.[15] This description clearly raises the expectation
that constitutional review will enforce genuine standards of constitutional legality
against political decision takers, instead of just taking political decisions in their
place. Put more abstractly, the activities of a constitutional court, Kelsen seems to
suggest, are premised on the possibility of distinguishing between the subjective
and the objective legal meaning of the actions of the organs of state—legislature
and executive—that are to be controlled. The court is to enforce against these
organs the principle that their actions can have a binding effect only if they objectively comply with constitutional law. But it is unclear whether Kelsen's modest
negative argument leaves us with the conceptual space to describe the activities of
a constitutional court as the enforcement of a principle of legality. How can the
court be enforcing constitutional legality if its decisions are inevitably political?
The modest argument, it seems, does not simply fail to show why a system with a
constitutional court is preferable to one without. It seems altogether to undercut
the ideal of constitutional legality.

If it were possible, on the other hand, to make sense of the idea that a Kelsenian
constitutional court would be acting as a guardian of the constitution and if a constitution unguarded is indeed a defective form of law, the question whether there
ought to be a constitutional court could not really be open, from Kelsen's jurisprudential point of view, in the way suggested by the modest negative argument. The
outlines of a more ambitious argument are implicit in Kelsen's general theory of

---

[12] See for this reading of Kelsen: Richard Posner, *Law, Pragmatism, and Democracy* (Cambridge/
Mass, 2003) 250–92. A similarly restricted account of Kelsen's theory of adjudication is to be found in
Neil MacCormick, 'The Interest of the State and the Rule of Law' in Neil MacCormick, *Questioning
Sovereignty. Law, State, and Nation in the European Commonwealth* (Oxford, 1999) 27–48, at 40–4.
[13] See for the clearest example of the modest argument Kelsen, 'Wer soll der Hüter der Verfassung
sein?' (n 2 above) 1921–2.
[14] See for this criticism Dyzenhaus, *Legality and Legitimacy* (n 8 above) 108–23.
[15] See Kelsen, 'Wer soll der Hüter der Verfassung sein?' (n 2 above) 1873. The emphasis on the court
as a 'guarantee of legality' is equally evident in Kelsen, 'Wesen und Entwicklung der Staatsgerichtsbarkeit'
(n 2 above) 1839.

democracy and the rule of law. An argument against the institution of a constitutional court would have to show, it seems, that there are sufficient reasons to *override* the impairment of the ideal of the rule of law inevitably entailed by the absence of a constitutional court. But such an argument cannot be successful in a constitutional context that obviously does aim to put procedural and substantive legal constraints on exercises of legislative and executive power. One can reject the institution of a constitutional court only if one is also willing to reject the principle of constitutional legality as a principle of political legitimacy. However, such a position would be incompatible with a commitment to democracy if democracy is essentially a system of power-sharing between competing social groups that is constituted by legitimating legal constraints on unilateral exercises of legislative power and that is protected by constitutional entrenchment of those constraints.[16]

The ambitious argument, of course, is subject to the charge of being too ambitious, at least if it is presented as a consequence of a positivist and 'scientific' legal theory. The pure theory, it would seem, is either forced to retreat too far in the face of the opponent of constitutionalism or to make claims that it cannot defend without importing unacknowledged normative baggage that has no place in a positivist theory of law.

In what follows, I will try to show that Kelsen's theory of constitutional review can be defended against the criticisms just outlined. Relying on my previous interpretation of Kelsen's principles of legality and of his theory of democracy, I will argue that the negative or modest argument can be read as an integral part of the positive ambitious argument and the charge of inconsistency be dispelled. To show that Kelsen's views on constitutional adjudication are consistent, I will try to demonstrate that they can sustain an account of judicial role rich enough to allow us to explain how judges on a constitutional court can be understood to enforce principles of constitutional legality in all cases they might be called upon to decide. I will argue, moreover, that Kelsen's conception of judicial role remains compatible with the ideal of a utopia of legality, including the idea that a democratic community's constitutional law is not committed to a particular substantive understanding of the common good.

Kelsen's conception of adjudication: Implications for a theory of review

The Schmittian argument against a constitutional court that Kelsen wants to refute claims, to repeat, that a constitutional court, if it were given the power to arbitrate constitutional conflicts, would have to take highly political decisions, decisions not determined by already existing constitutional law. Courts, however, cannot legitimately take such decisions. In particular, they cannot legitimately do so in a democracy where the popular sovereign (or those who represent him) must have

---

[16] See Kelsen, 'Wer soll der Hüter der Verfassung sein?' (n 2 above) 1918–21.

the final power to interpret the constitution. The settlement of deep constitutional conflicts, therefore, cannot reasonably be assigned to a court.[17]

Some of the tools we need to develop a Kelsenian reply to this charge were assembled in Chapter 3. We have seen that when Kelsen claims that there is no qualitative distinction between legal and political decisions he does not want to say, as some commentators have suggested, that judges can simply decide cases on the basis of pure discretion because they have been empowered by jurisdictional norms to do so.[18] Kelsen's emphasis, rather, is on the idea that all official decisions, though partly discretionary, are valid exercises of authority only if they fully comply with all relevant higher order legal norms.

Kelsen's analysis of adjudication assumes that judicial decisions are typically a composite exercise of two different powers. A judicial decision based on a general norm is a) an authoritative interpretation of that norm, and not just the declaration of a cognitive insight into its meaning. At the same time, b) any general norm inevitably authorizes the judge who applies it to exercise a limited amount of genuine discretion in applying a general law to a particular case. These two powers must not be confused, even while ordinary judicial decisions—judicial decisions that apply a general norm to a particular case by enacting a particular norm within the framework set by the general norm—exercise them both. A judge taking an ordinary judicial decision, moreover, must be distinguished from a judge who is acting in the role of a reviewing judge. Kelsen's argument for a constitutional court claims that a judge who exercises a power of review, as do the judges on a constitutional court, is working with the first of these two powers only. A reviewing judge only voids but does not himself enact legal norms. And insofar as he is restricted to the use of the first power, we can say that he is not replacing or usurping the discretionary powers of the reviewed organ. He is merely making a judgment of attribution, though an authoritative one, on behalf of the citizen whose primary powers of review have been internalized by the legal system.[19]

The view that this distinction is implicit in Kelsen's general theory of adjudication finds support in passages like the following:

The judicial decision, the act in which the judicial power expresses itself, is called jurisdiction, as if it only declared a legal state of affairs that already exists in virtue of the general legal

---

[17] See Schmitt, *Der Hüter der Verfassung* (n 11 above) 12–70, and Schmitt, *Verfassungslehre* (Berlin, 1928) 112–21, 129–38, and 363–79. For detailed discussions of the debate between Kelsen and Schmitt see Dyzenhaus, *Legality and Legitimacy* (n 8 above) and Peter C Caldwell, *Popular Sovereignty and the Crisis of German Constitutional Law. The Theory and Practice of Weimar Constitutionalism* (Durham/NC, 1997) 85–119.

[18] See Posner, *Law, Pragmatism, and Democracy* (n 12 above) 268–70. Posner makes the important observation that 'Kelsen would never say, with Hart, that when a judge decides a case in which "no decision either way is dictated by the law" he is stepping outside of the law' (ibid, 269). But he thinks that the reason for this is that Kelsen's concept of law is 'content-free' and 'purely jurisdictional' (ibid, 270). Posner thinks it follows from this that judges will be deciding cases on a legal basis unless they are 'exceeding their jurisdiction, broadly defined, as they would be if they decided a case that was not justiciable or if they decided on the basis of a financial, familial or partisan political interest in the outcome' (ibid, 269).

[19] See Kelsen, 'Wesen und Entwicklung der Staatsgerichtsbarkeit' (n 2 above) 1838–9.

norm. But this is a terminology which clouds—perhaps not without deliberate intent—the full significance of jurisdiction. That there is a concrete matter of fact that is to be connected with a sanction and that it is connected with a concrete sanction, this whole relation is created by the judge's decision. The general law says: whenever someone steals he is to be punished by a prison sentence between six months and two years. The court's decision says: person A stole here and now and is to be punished with a prison sentence of a year, starting today. Without the judge's decision, the general law could not take on concrete form. The judgment that declares the state of affairs determined in general terms by the law to be present in a particular situation and that expresses the concrete sanction, a sanction that the law describes only in a less determinate way, is therefore the individualization or concretization of the general legal norm.[20]

The court's judgment, according to Kelsen, is clearly doing two things here. First, it declares someone a thief. Secondly, it states the precise punishment to be applied to that person. Both decisions are taken on the basis of the general law sanctioning theft. So whatever discretion the judge may have, it is not a power to decide without subsuming the case under any general law. What it means, exactly, to say that the general law needs to be concretized by a judge's decision is not explained all that clearly. But it is possible to venture the following minimal interpretation.

With respect to the first decision, Kelsen seems to claim no more than that someone cannot be considered a thief, that he cannot be considered to have broken the law against theft and be subjected to a punishment, unless he is found guilty by a court of law that orders him to be punished. An exercise of authority, and not just an exercise of cognitive judgment, is involved whenever a court finds someone guilty of theft. But this claim does not commit one to a denial of the truism that there are legal criteria applicable to the question whether someone is a thief, criteria that a judge's decision can and ought to be guided by. Neither does it entail, therefore, that judges have the power to declare people thieves for reasons that are obviously irrelevant to the question whether someone is a thief or not.

Kelsen's point is that there might be room for reasonable disagreement as to whether some particular person's actions fall under the provisions of the general law forbidding theft or not. The evidence may be unclear; the criteria provided by the law on the basis of which the decision is taken may be—deliberately or inadvertently—unspecific or vague or it may be in doubt how to apply them to situations not anticipated by the legislator. In fact, Kelsen believes that this is to some extent always the case, and not just in exceptional cases that are penumbral in the Hartian sense. Kelsen, therefore, argues that an exercise of judgment on the part of the court, backed up by the court's public authority, characterizes *all* applications of general laws to particular cases. This is why the decision of any particular case is an enactment of a particular legal norm.[21]

---

[20] Kelsen, 'Die Lehre von den drei Gewalten' (n 5 above) 1632–3 [my translation]. Similarly Kelsen, *Allgemeine Staatslehre* (n 2 above) 233. For an analysis of Kelsen's views on interpretation in general see Stanley L Paulson, 'Kelsen on Legal Interpretation' in *Legal Studies* 10 (1990) 136–52.

[21] This position resembles that of Hobbes who claimed that 'all laws, written and unwritten, have need of interpretation' and who argued that judges can give authentic interpretations in virtue of the

It is important, however, not to interpret this power of authentic interpretation in the light of a sharp distinction between formal and material authority. Kelsen, as we have seen, does not distinguish between a legal decision's material correctness and its formal validity. Both the norms that formally authorize the judge as well as the material norm ordering punishment for theft are equally part of the authorizing conditions of the judge's decision. The judge's power of authentic interpretation subjects us to his understanding of those authorizing conditions, not to an arbitrary authority to decide either in accordance with the law or in some other way. However, in order for a decision to have a legal basis, it is not necessary for the judge's decision to be demonstrably correct. Rather, a judicial decision has a legal basis insofar as it invokes the relevant formal and material authorizing norms, norms that would be sufficient to justify the decision taken, in a reasonable, informed, and responsible fashion. If these conditions are fulfilled, Kelsen believes, we ought to accept the decision as a valid enactment of a particular legal norm, even if we believe another decision should have been taken. That laws do not apply themselves, after all, is precisely why judges are needed in the first place.[22]

Let us now turn to the second decision the judge is taking in Kelsen's example, the determination of the exact length of the prison sentence. This decision, in contrast to the first, is a genuinely discretionary decision. In allowing for a limited range of punishments of different severity, the law in Kelsen's example explicitly authorizes the judge freely to decide on the basis of his assessment of the merits of the case. This latter power more closely resembles legislative power, the term taken in our ordinary understanding of the term, than the judicial power of authentic interpretation. But it is clearly limited and it is perfectly obvious that its extent will, to a large degree, depend on the content of the positive law. Good legislative craftsmanship,

---

fact that they participate in sovereign authority. Thomas Hobbes, *Leviathan. Revised Student Edition*, edited by Richard Tuck (Cambridge, 1996) 190–2. It should be noted that both Kelsen and Hobbes argue insistently against what they see as the confusion of legal science with judicial authority: 'The Authority of Writers, without the Authority of the Common-wealth, maketh not their opinions Law, be they never so true.' Hobbes goes on to say that the interpretations of the law offered by a judge are 'Authentique; not because it is his private Sentence; but rather because he giveth it by Authority of the Soveraign.' (ibid) Hobbes also signs on to the view that judicial decisions are enactments of particular norms within a framework set by general law: 'For all Lawes are generall Judgements, or Sentences of the Legislator; as also every particular Judgement, is a Law to him, whose case is Judged' (ibid, 197).

[22] This view entails that judges who buy into a view of adjudication that is based on a strong notion of legal determinacy, coupled with a demand for judicial subjection to the law as a decision already taken, are laboring under a form of false consciousness. Legislators and executive, however, may have an interest in maintaining this false consciousness insofar as it increases their power. This is why Kelsen says that the terminology of jurisdiction '*clouds—perhaps not without deliberate intent—the full significance of jurisdiction*'. See Kelsen, *Die Lehre von den drei Gewalten* (n 5 above) 1633. Both Hobbes and Kelsen stress, against the common conception of the division of powers, that judges participate in the creative exercise of public power. In Hobbes's view, the criteria for the legitimate exercise of that participation are ultimately the same criteria that govern the legitimacy of legislative acts. (See Hobbes, *Leviathan* [n 21 above] 194.) A Kelsenian solution to the question of how judges can responsibly exercise their participation in public power should equally be based on the idea of an essential continuity between legislation and adjudication.

Kelsen believes, may well contain the purely discretionary power of judges within very narrow boundaries if such restriction were thought appropriate.[23]

The important thing to note about the picture of ordinary adjudication just painted is that Kelsen's conception of legal hierarchy entails that it applies to *all* organs of state, not just to judges, that enact norms under the authorization of higher order legal norms. It includes legislators working under constitutional constraints as well as the executive and administrative agencies. Any organ of state taking a decision under legal authorization has to work with a conception of the limits of its own authority before it can go on to decide on the basis of its political judgment within the frame set by the authorizing law or set of laws. Some organs of state, especially the legislature, will of course enjoy a much larger degree of political discretion than judges or administrators. But the difference, as Kelsen repeatedly points out, is quantitative, not qualitative. The ordinary judicial decision is the enactment of a particular norm, and this enactment differs from legislative enactments only in its relatively higher specificity and in its relatively higher degree of determination by already existing law.

Nevertheless, Kelsen draws an important qualitative distinction between judges and other decision-takers. Judges, by contrast to other decision takers, do not just participate in the top-down process of law-creation that forms the legal hierarchy by enacting particular norms on the basis of general laws created by the legislator. They also review enactments of legal norms by other judges as well as by political and administrative organs of state that actively participate in the top-down process of enactment of law.[24] The norms that form the basis of review are, of course, the norms that authorize the decisions of the organ under review. The material and formal constitutional norms that give the conditions of valid legislation, for example, authorize a legislator to enact any law he sees fit within the conditions of validity set by the constitution. As we have seen, an ordinary judge is authorized, in much the same way, to apply a punishment for theft by the general legal norm against punishment. A reviewing court, by contrast, is not itself authorized to enact laws by the norms that form the basis of review. The constitutional norms that form the basis of constitutional review, for example, do not authorize the constitutional court to enact general legal norms. When acting as reviewing organs, judges do not exercise free discretion or review how discretion is exercised by the reviewed organs as long as the actions of these organs remain properly authorized. They merely ascertain whether some creative decision taken by another organ remained within its proper boundaries and they void it should they deem it legally defective.[25]

---

[23] See Kelsen, 'Wesen und Entwicklung der Staatsgerichtsbarkeit' (n 2 above) 1851–4.

[24] This distinction is missing from Hobbes. For Hobbes, judges participate insofar as they concretize laws, if necessary by supplying them with the Law of Nature. But they do not exercise a power of review vis-à-vis higher organs of government and they are clearly not institutionally independent. See Thomas Hobbes, *A Dialogue between a Philosopher and a Student of the Common Laws of England*, edited by Joseph Cropsey (Chicago, 1971) 88–9.

[25] See Kelsen, 'Wesen und Entwicklung der Staatsgerichtsbarkeit' (n 2 above) 1839.

Kelsen can give a general reply, hence, to the objection that there is a tension in his argument for constitutional review since his general theory of adjudication assumes that judges inevitably enact law whenever they are applying a law. The charge that a Kelsenian constitutional court could not credibly act as an enforcer of legality since its decisions would inevitably be legislative can be answered by pointing out that a court that is acting in a reviewing capacity does not itself take discretionary decisions or interfere with the discretion exercised by the legislative organ reviewed. It only acts passively, by repealing decisions of other organs should they turn out to have been legally defective. The fact that a court exercises a power of authentic interpretation in determining whether an exercise of discretion is properly authorized (and that its decisions are, in that sense, 'political') must not blind us to the difference between exercises of discretion and the activity of review.

This general reply to the critic of constitutional adjudication, of course, does not suffice to solve our problem. It only seems to shift our attention to Kelsen's conception of a frame of authority set by higher order legal norms. A reviewing court, Kelsen claims, authoritatively determines the scope of the frame of authority within which some other organ of state operates, but it does not usurp that organ's discretionary powers within that scope. Opponents of constitutional adjudication are likely to point out in reply that disputes over the validity of a piece of legislation, understood as disagreements about the scope of the legislator's authority, are the real problem. This will be especially so under Kelsen's conception of legality since that conception claims that the scope of legal authority is determined by an ideal of full conformity of the decisions taken with all applicable higher order legal norms. Kelsen's theory of constitutional adjudication, then, faces a series of additional questions.

Whose understanding of full constitutional legality, the legislator's or the court's, is to be determinative and why? Should a constitutional court only review whether a legislative decision taken by a parliamentary majority is based on an understanding of what the constitution allows for that falls within a range of reasonable disagreement? Or does the court's understanding of what the constitution requires have to replace the legislator's? If Kelsen is committed to the latter option, if the court applies a strict standard of review, in what sense can its use of that strict standard be said to have a legal basis, given that reasonable disagreement about the limits of authority is possible?

In order to answer the first two of these questions, we need to recall some of our earlier discussion in Chapter 3. This discussion showed that Kelsen starts out from the assumption that the question whether a decision remains within its proper frame of authority, in contrast to the question how authority is to be exercised within the frame, is a question for legal science since its answer rests on a judgment of attribution to be taken, in the first instance, by the law-abiding citizen. The law-abiding citizen accepts, to recall, a duty to defer to the law and thus to the discretionary decisions taken by organs of state that objectively comply with their legal conditions of authorization. But the law abiding-citizen does not recognize a duty to defer to the subjective claim of the organ of state to have acted in conformity with the authorizing legal conditions. The review exercised by the law-abiding citizen, hence, clearly is a form of strict review, based on the assumption that we can always distinguish, with sufficient clarity, between the objective and the subjective legal meaning of any act.

The stance of the reviewing judge must be closely analogous to that of the law-abiding citizen since the reviewing judge, in Kelsen's view, internalizes the primary power of review of the law-abiding citizen. The reviewing judge *represents* the law-abiding citizen against the state in its active, top-down, decision-taking capacity. Hence, the reviewing judge must likewise exercise strict review, and only if he does will the state, the legal order as a whole, be able to claim a presumption of legality for its final decisions. Our analysis of Kelsen's conception of democracy allows us to add a further consideration supporting the view that the constitutional court's and not the legislator's or the legislative majority's understanding of what the constitution allows for must be determinative. For Kelsen, as we have seen, the democratic legislator is never more than a temporary majority whose views and interests have to be subjected to a compromise-enforcing legal framework in order for the democratic ideal of an identity or ruler and ruled to have any meaning. The opposite idea that the legislator, since he somehow represents the unity or the general will of the people, must have the power to be the judge of the limits of his own legal authority confuses democracy with the legislative autocracy of one party over another.

Now clearly, these considerations assume that limits of authority are objectively determinable. However, Kelsen admits, as we have seen, that the question whether some alleged exercise of legal power respected the limits set by the norms authorizing norms is subject to reasonable disagreement.[26] It was for this reason that Kelsen claimed that the only viable institutional form the assumption of legal objectivity can take is that of a sovereign legal order that fully internalizes primary review. Internalization of review, to recall, transforms the simple contrast between validity and nullity into the difference between absolute nullity, voidability, and finality. As a result, the assumption of objective determinability of limits of authority is split into two. From a judge's perspective, the assumption of legal objectivity continues to function as a regulative assumption of the activity of review. In front of the reviewing judge, a legal norm enacted by some other organ of state cannot claim a presumption of legality. From the perspective of the citizen, however, the assumption of objective limits of authority is cashed out in terms of an institutional division of powers of decision and powers of review. This division ensures that the law no longer authorizes any active organ of state to be the final judge over the limits of its authority, but it also subjects the citizen to a presumption of legality that covers both voidable norms as well as norms that have acquired finality.

The judgments on substantive legality made by reviewing judges, in other words, exclude those of the law-abiding citizen. But in order for this exclusion to

---

[26] See Kelsen, 'Über Staatsunrecht' in *Die Wiener rechtstheoretische Schule* (n 2 above) vol I, 1037–8.

be acceptable, both judges and citizens will at the very least have to be able to hold on to the view that the assumption of legal objectivity is meaningful as a regulative assumption guiding judicial review. What is more, citizens will have to be able, in order reasonably to accept the exclusionary force of the decisions of reviewing judges, to assess whether the regulative assumption of objectivity indeed guides reviewing judges whose judgments they disagree with.

As a regulative assumption, the idea of legal objectivity provides an outline of the role judges have to play in review. This role can roughly be described as follows. On the one hand, the reviewing judge cannot simply equate the 'subjective meaning' of the act under review with its 'objective meaning'. He cannot simply take the claim of the deciding organ to have acted in a manner consistent with its terms of authorization at face value. In cases where the conditions of authorization include material norms, a judgment of review will therefore inevitably have to rest on an assessment of the question whether the decision under review fully conforms to the material norms it invokes as a ground of authority. Moreover, a reviewing judge must insist that procedural shortcuts are not permissible, for example on the basis of the claim that the state is faced with an exceptional situation. The judge, after all, represents the law-abiding citizen, not a citizen who is willing to defer to the personal authority of his country's leaders.

On the other hand, however, judicial review into the limits of the authority of active, power-exercising organs must remain properly deferential. A decision that fully complies with the conditions of authorization is to be regarded as valid, even if the judge happens not to think of it as the best decision that could have been taken on the basis of the law. The element of genuine discretion involved in every top-down exercise of power is to remain with the primary decision taker. Its exercise, after all, is that which is to acquire legitimacy by being subjected to constraints of legality. The deference required of the judge, once again, has the same structure as the deference required of the law-abiding citizen. The latter agrees to accept as legitimate exercises of discretion that do conform to all authorizing conditions, regardless of what he thinks about their further merit or demerit. Without this element of content-independence, the legality of a decision could not exclude normative disagreement concerning matters of substantive justice. As a result, we could not arrive at a notion of legal legitimacy which allows for the peaceful cooperation under law of citizens deeply divided in their views of the good.

It is doubtful, needless to say, whether this abstract description of judicial role gets us very far. One might complain that the task of review, of trying to hold a balance between abdication of judicial responsibility and usurpation of discretionary power, must be meaningless unless there is a bright, determinate, and uncontroversial line dividing mere review of the limits of authority from second-guessing of merits. No such bright line, however, exists, as Kelsen himself seems to admit in making the claim that assessments of constitutionality are subject to reasonable disagreement. The critic will go on to argue that a constitutional court claiming the power to take final decisions in all cases of constitutional conflict cannot possibly be a mere guardian of constitutional legality. It cannot itself be subject to the law but will turn out to be an Ersatz-sovereign with dubious legitimacy. And this is so especially because Kelsen's general picture of judicial role has not, so far, supplied us with an informative legal standard to be applied in strict review.

In order to meet this challenge, the Kelsenian must bring into play the political context of Kelsen's argument for a constitutional court. The stance of the law-abiding citizen, as we have seen, makes full sense only in a Kelsenian democracy. The same must be true, in virtue of the relation between the law-abiding citizen and the reviewing judge, of the institution of a constitutional court. The distinction between the objective and the subjective meaning of an act of legislation, clearly, could not be particularly relevant in a legislative autocracy whose constitutional norms merely serve to identify but not to constrain, and thereby to legitimize, the directives of a legislator. It therefore seems reasonable to assume that a standard that can justifiably guide strict review into the limits of authority must be developed from the idea that the main function of a constitutional court is to facilitate and protect the proper functioning of a Kelsenian democracy.

My talk of a guiding standard should not be taken to suggest that the defender of a Kelsenian constitutional court will claim that the constitution, if interpreted correctly, always provides one and only one obviously correct answer to any constitutional dispute. Decisions taken by the constitutional court remain political in the sense of being authentic interpretations of the constitution. But this is not necessarily a problem. The function of the standard we seek is not only that of providing guidance to judges, and it is decidedly not to allow them to claim that they do not bear any political responsibility. Rather, it is to allow subjects of the law reasonably to adopt the stance of a law-abiding citizen with respect to all decisions that have been or that can be subjected to review by the court. Since questions of full constitutionality are and will always remain subject to reasonable disagreement amongst democratic citizens, we cannot pay proper deference to each other as democratic citizens without paying deference to a constitutional court. But we will not be able to pay proper deference to each other, by paying deference to the court, and to know and be reciprocally assured that we are doing so, unless the court is deciding constitutional conflicts in an appropriate manner, on the basis of an adequate understanding of its constitutional function. This understanding must draw its content from Kelsen's theory of democracy. Before I go on to draw out the implications of this claim, I want to show that it finds support in Kelsen's concept of constitution as well as in his description of the powers and the operation of a constitutional court.

Kelsen on the concept of constitution

Kelsen's constitutional theory is somewhat confusing because it employs the term 'constitution' in several different senses.[27] First, Kelsen talks about 'a constitution

---

[27] See Kelsen, 'Wesen und Entwicklung der Staatsgerichtsbarkeit' (n 2 above) 1818–26; Kelsen, *Allgemeine Staatslehre* (n 2 above) 248–55, Kelsen, 'Die Lehre von den drei Gewalten' (n 5 above)

in the legal-logical sense'.[28] The constitution in the legal-logical sense is the basic norm. A legal system's basic norm, as we have seen, is not an enacted norm. It simply expresses the assumption that the norms belonging to some positive legal system are objectively valid. The link between the normativity of the basic norm and the normativity of the norms belonging to some positive legal system is forged by the fact that the basic norm authorizes a set of rules governing the creation of all other norms of a legal system. These rules Kelsen calls the *material* constitution.[29]

This terminology is somewhat counterintuitive. In Kelsen's usage, the term 'material constitution' is not to be equated with 'substantive constitution', ie it is not opposed to 'procedural'. A material constitution may well be fully procedural. What makes the material constitution material, according to Kelsen, is its function. It determines the conditions of validity of general legal rules. In other words, it governs the process of legislation. The material constitution plays an indispensable role in any legal order since the rules governing the creation of general legal rules indirectly authorize all more particular legal norms. What is more, these rules define the identity of a legal system since they set out the limits of change that preserves legal continuity. Every legal system therefore necessarily has to contain a material constitution. This material constitution, in contrast to the basic norm, is a set of positive (though not necessarily of written) rules with specific, even if perhaps only procedural, content.

Kelsen goes on to claim that the constitution in the material sense can, but does not have to, take the form of a constitution in the *formal* sense.[30] A constitution in the formal sense exists wherever the basic rules governing legislation have been given special constitutional form. This is done by putting the rules of the material constitution under the protection of a special rule for constitutional amendment that creates a clear distinction between ordinary and constitutional laws and between ordinary and constitutional legislation. The constitution in the formal sense is the beginning of 'constitutionalism'. Note that the formal constitution, according to this conception, may still be purely procedural. But its existence does entail that the constitution in the material sense turns into a higher law that in some way or other restricts the powers of the ordinary legislator. It makes sure, at the least, that the procedural rules governing legislation are no longer subject to his tampering. Very commonly, the formal constitution brings about and protects a distribution of legislative power to several organs of state that need to cooperate in order to enact valid law. Typical forms of formal constitutionalism, in this sense, are constitutions

---

1650–60. The discussions in Carl Schmitt, *Der Hüter der Verfassung* (n 11 above) 38–40, as well as in Dyzenhaus, *Legality and Legitimacy* (n 8 above) 149–57 contain serious misunderstandings. A valuable analysis of Kelsen's concept of constitution is offered in Robert Alexy, 'Hans Kelsens Begriff der Verfassung' in Stanley L Paulson and Michael Stolleis (eds), *Hans Kelsen. Staatsrechtslehrer und Rechtstheoretiker des 20. Jahrhunderts* (Tübingen, 2005) 333–52.

[28] See Kelsen, 'Die Lehre von den drei Gewalten' (n 5 above) 1650–2.
[29] See Kelsen, 'Wesen und Entwicklung der Staatsgerichtsbarkeit' (n 2 above) 1819.
[30] See ibid, 1819–21; Kelsen, 'Die Lehre von den drei Gewalten' (n 5 above) 1654–7.

that divide legislative power between a parliament and a head of state or between several levels of government. Of course, democratic constitutional rules that put rights of participation in the political process under special protection against disenfranchisement also fall into this category since they express the idea of a sharing of power between a majority and a minority.

In addition, the constitution in the formal sense, according to Kelsen, may contain more than just procedural rules governing the legislative process. Once constitutional form is available, it becomes possible to put material limits on ordinary legislation by incorporating a bill of rights into constitutional law. As a result, ordinary laws can be unconstitutional not just in virtue of being procedurally flawed, but also in virtue of having a content that violates a substantive normative principle, privilege, or guideline protected by the form of constitutional law.[31]

Kelsen notes that the creation of a formal constitution containing a bill of rights restricting the permissible content of ordinary legislation is often described as introducing a distinction between 'formal' and 'material' unconstitutionality. A 'formally' unconstitutional law, according to this usage, is a law that is procedurally flawed, whereas a 'materially' unconstitutional law is a law whose content contradicts a normative principle or violates an interest explicitly protected by the constitution. But Kelsen thinks this usage—a usage that, of course, does not sit well with his own understanding of the difference between a material and a formal constitution—is redundant. What it means for a law to be 'materially' (or, for that matter, 'formally') unconstitutional in a system with a formal constitution containing a bill of rights is that the law in question failed to be enacted in the right way, namely as a constitutional amendment.[32]

Kelsen's dismissal of the ordinary understanding of the formal/material distinction need not be read as an attempt to reduce material to formal or procedural illegality, the terms understood in their ordinary sense. Rather, it is motivated by the idea that both the procedural as well as the material elements of a formal constitution serve the same normative purpose as well as by the claim that questions of procedural constitutionality need not be less controversial or important than issues of material or substantive constitutionality. Any constitution in the formal sense introduces a plurality of political voices into the process of legislation and thus constrains unilateral exercises of political power, and this function is equally served by procedural as well as material constitutional provisions.

Once a formal constitution has come into existence, the question of the constitutionality of legislation will acquire a significance it could not have possessed in its absence. The existence of a formal constitution is likely to give rise to situations in which the decisions of an organ or set of organs that are commonly recognized to have legislative power can make a prima facie claim to be valid while their full procedural or substantive conformity with all constitutional rules conditioning the

---

[31] See Kelsen, 'Wesen und Entwicklung der Staatsgerichtsbarkeit' (n 2 above) 1820.
[32] Ibid, 1820–1.

valid exercise of legislative power is open to doubt. Of course, attempted acts of legislation can fail to amount to acts of valid legislation even in a system without a formal constitution. But since any purely material constitution is merely procedural and likely to be of a lesser procedural complexity than any formal constitution, questions of constitutionality, in a system without a formal constitution, will tend to boil down to simple questions of 'pedigree' that are unlikely to give rise to deep disagreement. What is more, since such a constitution, in any case, will tend to put relatively unrestricted power into the hands of a single person or institution, there is less incentive for decision-takers not to observe the constitution and hence little point to introducing explicit safeguards of the legality of acts of legislation.

The institution of a constitutional court, then, is meaningful only in a system with a formal constitution. But the reverse holds as well: formal constitutionalism, insofar as it is likely to give rise to controversies over constitutional legality, is meaningful only if protected by a constitutional court. The formal constitution's function is pre-eminently to constrain exercises of legislative and executive power, not just to constitute a facilitating legal form for such exercises. Formal constitutionalism, thus, is meaningful only as an acknowledgement of the fact of reasonable pluralism, as a template for an ongoing practice of lawful mediation of conflict between social groups divided over conceptions of the good. But this, as we know by now, is just another description of the ambition of democracy.[33]

Further evidence of the close connection between formal constitutionalism and democracy is provided by Kelsen's analysis of the mode of operation of courts engaged in review. The power exercised by a court engaged in constitutional review is the power to void unconstitutional acts of organs of state charged with the immediate execution of the constitution. To void a norm enacted by an organ of state is to 'remove it together with its legal effects'.[34] If the act is an act of legislation, we have to distinguish between the voiding of the act with respect to a particular case and the general voiding of the act for all cases. The first takes place if an ordinary court refuses to apply a law to a particular case because it considers that law unconstitutional. Clearly, there are convincing reasons to centralize this form of judicial review and to empower a special constitutional court altogether to repeal unconstitutional pieces of legislation. Only a constitutional court endowed with the generalized and centralized power authoritatively to repeal constitutionally defective acts of legislation—as well as other unconstitutional acts taken by organs of government in immediate execution of the constitution—will, in Kelsen's view, be a fully effective safeguard of constitutional legality.[35]

However, Kelsen argues that any court in a system with a formal constitution is by default entitled to refuse to apply laws it considers unconstitutional to the cases it has to decide.[36] This view comes out quite explicitly in Kelsen's analysis of a

[33] See ibid, 1862–8; Kelsen, 'Wer soll der Hüter der Verfassung sein?' (n 2 above) 1897–921.
[34] Kelsen, 'Wesen und Entwicklung der Staatsgerichtsbarkeit' (n 2 above) 1830.
[35] See ibid, 1835–40.
[36] Kelsen hints at this argument in 'Die Lehre von den drei Gewalten' (n 5 above) 1658–9.

'technical imperfection' that was a common characteristic of the constitutions of constitutional monarchies. The question here is the following: Can a constitution validly issue a general prohibition against strict judicial scrutiny of acts of legislation that have an appearance of legality, for example by conforming to formal rules for promulgation? Kelsen does not flatly deny that it is possible for a legal order to simply declare that what is duly promulgated as law is to be considered as such by judges, and hence not reviewable under a strict standard of scrutiny. But he suggests that such a provision would be incompatible with a democratic constitution as well as with the principle of legality in general.[37]

Given our analysis of Kelsen's understanding of democracy, this view should not occasion surprise. A constitutional clause of this kind cannot be understood as a mere signal to judges. It is unavoidably also a signal to the citizens, whom the judges represent in exercising review, that they will at least potentially not be treated as subjects of the law but rather as objects of a unilateral exercise of power. Under a constitutional clause blocking review of the constitutionality of acts of the highest organs of state, constitutionally defective acts set by these organs would neither be null—assuming the state could successfully enforce conformity—nor voidable, since there would be no way for subjects of the law to challenge a legally defective act of state in court. But this means that all constitutional provisions exceeding the rules of due promulgation are potentially only so much rhetorical flourish. And this, according to Kelsen, is the predicament in which the so-called 'constitutional' monarchies tended to end up.[38]

According to the pure theory one would be making a mockery not just of the ideal of the rule of law but also of democracy by claiming that the principle of popular sovereignty can be invoked to continue a practice of freezing the judiciary out of the business of review in a democratic republic. Courts, in a democratic constitution, thus ought to be entitled to review the constitutionality of ordinary laws at least in the minimal sense of being entitled to refuse to apply them if they deem such laws unconstitutional. Any attempt to restrict or bypass this review would, in the absence of a centralized mechanism for voiding unconstitutional laws, turn the democratic republic into absolutism by another name since it could not be anything other than an act by which a temporary majority unilaterally rejects its subjection to principles of constitutional legality. The generalized power of constitutional review to be exercised by a special constitutional court is merely a centralization of the diffuse power of judicial review that by default pertains to any court in a formally constitutional system.

This claim provides a clue as to how to understand Kelsen's claim that the autocratic constitutional picture advocated by Schmitt can only be justified on political but not on 'scientific' jurisprudential grounds. Was Kelsen really letting Schmitt

---

[37] See ibid, 1658–9; Kelsen, *Allgemeine Staatslehre* (n 2 above) 254.
[38] For a similar argument in a common law context see David Dyzenhaus, 'Intimations of Legality amid the Clash of Arms' in *International Journal of Constitutional Law* 2 (2004) 244–71.

'off the hook'? Is it true that Kelsen's argument for constitutional adjudication was ultimately incapable of offering a substantive defense against Schmitt's view that constitutional guardianship is a sovereign prerogative?[39]

Kelsen claims that his argument for a constitutional court is not meant to criticize Schmitt's rejection of a constitutional court insofar as that rejection is based on Schmitt's political ambitions.[40] This disclaimer is based on the assumption that Schmitt's arguments against the constitutional court as well as his arguments for a presidential dictatorship are advocating the introduction of an autocracy that is to replace the democratic system of the Weimar Republic. Kelsen, in other words, makes the limited admission that it is possible to defend autocracy coherently on political grounds, though not, we must add, on the basis of a notion of legal legitimacy and not on the basis of an argument that claims that dictatorial powers of the state can be justified on democratic grounds. One cannot, according to Kelsen, read autocracy into a constitution like the Weimar constitution because any such reading would have to deny, on arbitrary grounds, that the Weimar constitution, as a piece of positive law, contains a positive acknowledgment of pluralist democracy. Put differently, Kelsen denies that Schmitt's views, in particular his views on the powers of the president under art 48 of the Weimar constitution, are defensible as interpretations of the Weimar constitution since that constitution is undeniably democratic.

The claim that Kelsen let Schmitt off the hook, I conclude, is not warranted.[41] When Kelsen says that there can be no jurisprudential but only political reasons against introducing constitutional adjudication into a legal system that already has a formal constitution he is saying that a principled rejection of constitutional adjudication can only be based on a rejection of formal constitutionalism itself. Kelsen's disclaimer admits that a political movement could reject the aim to create a utopia of legality, to bring to convergence the perspectives of the law-abiding citizen and the reasonable individual. Such a rejection entails a refusal to accept the idea that legality is an independent source of legitimacy. A movement committed to such a refusal, Kelsen thinks, could therefore have no reason to take any principled interest in formal constitutionalism, in the democratic identity of ruler

[39] See Dyzenhaus, *Legality and Legitimacy* (n 8 above) 157–60.
[40] See Kelsen, 'Wer soll der Hüter der Verfassung sein?' (n 2 above) 1921–2.
[41] Dyzenhaus, *Legality and Legitimacy* (n 8 above) 120 defends the claim that Kelsen let Schmitt off the hook by claiming that Kelsen's 'conclusion [...] was not that Schmitt's argument is wrong, but that it should have been presented as a political argument, not couched in the language of legal science'. This seems to me to be confused. One can reject an argument as wrong even while not committing oneself to the claim that its conclusion is false. Moreover, it is far from clear that Kelsen refused to deny the conclusion of Schmitt's arguments. The issue here concerns the question how Schmitt's views are to be described. Schmitt argued that the president was the 'guardian of the constitution', endowed with the power to take a decision on the exception under the Weimar constitution. Kelsen clearly and explicitly denies this claim. Kelsen's claim is that what Schmitt presents as an interpretation of the Weimar constitution is really a political plea for an anti-constitutional autocratic coup d'état. The admission, then, is that the pure theory as legal science does not rule out that there may be political or moral reasons which speak for such an autocratic coup.

and ruled, or in the idea of legality itself. Schmitt's arguments are abusing legal science, and in so doing they are abusing the normative commitments that alone make it meaningful.

Kelsen's way of describing the conflict between the pure theory and a constitutional dualist like Schmitt, to be sure, carries normative commitments. It is based on a certain view of the function of law (as well as on a certain understanding of democracy), namely on the idea that law aims to put legitimating constraints on exercises of political power in order to allow for peaceful cohabitation in a pluralist society. The normative commitments that animate this view of law, as Kelsen acknowledges, are not themselves justified by the pure theory. The pure theory, rather, presupposes acceptance of the ideal of a utopia of legality. What the pure theory does is to show how the normative commitments that give rise to the hope for a utopia of legality can be coherently implemented in a scheme of legitimate legality. In showing how these commitments can be coherently implemented, the pure theory justifies the hope that the normative commitments that would have to underpin a well-functioning pluralist society are practically viable. It shows that the aim to create such a society is therefore a reasonable aspiration for those who would not think of politics as being based on a friend-enemy distinction. This seems to me to be no small service.

Constitutional values and judicial role

Let me now take up the task of drawing out the implications of Kelsen's understanding of democracy for an adequate account of judicial role. This account, as we have seen, must provide meaning to the regulative assumption of the objective determinability of limits of authority if Kelsen's argument is not to collapse into a crude assertion of judicial supremacy that undercuts the utopia of legality. Put differently, it must allow Kelsen to claim that a court can act as a guardian of the constitution even while its decisions, since they do not trivially follow from determinate law, inevitably amount to exercises of interpretive authority.

Kelsen himself, unfortunately, does not provide us with a very detailed analysis of the way in which a constitutional court would have to act in order to be able to claim the role of constitutional guardianship. He does offer an argument for the claim that a constitutional court would be in a position to decide all conflicts about the meaning of the constitution on a legal basis. But this argument is deceptively simple and seems to merely gloss over the real difficulties. Kelsen argues that a court engaged in review of legislation has to decide whether the law in question was enacted in the constitutionally prescribed way or not. What it means for a court to judge that a law was not brought about in the constitutionally prescribed manner is to judge that it ought to have been enacted as a constitutional amendment. Kelsen claims that all questions of constitutionality are justiciable on the basis of this formal test since the constitutional court will always be able to subsume any apparent legislative act (or other decision) under the constitutional norms that determine the conditions of full legality. If the decision under review is judged to fail to meet any of these conditions, the court will authoritatively invalidate the norm depending on that decision.[42]

This description of the court's activity, needless to say, only makes the question of what guides the court's subsumptive activity all the more pressing. While Kelsen raises the issue of the permissible standards of review, he treats it in a somewhat cursory fashion and what he says does not really add anything to the general picture already outlined.[43] A reviewing court has to check alleged exercises of legal power for full conformity with the norms on higher levels of the legal hierarchy. This review, Kelsen reaffirms, has to include a strict scrutiny of both procedural as well as material conditions of legality.

Kelsen asserts, in a more positivistic vein, that it would be inappropriate for a constitutional court to decide on the basis of meta-positive moral principles. The preambles of many constitutions, he observes, contain general declarations of purpose that invoke 'the ideals of justice, freedom, equality, equity, decency, and so on, without providing any further determination of the meaning of these terms'.[44] Such invocations, Kelsen argues, do not empower a reviewing court to strike down an otherwise valid law on the basis of the claim that it is substantively unjust. All valid constitutional provisions have constitutional status because they have constitutional form. Their validity rests on the fact that they happen to enjoy the protection of the rule for constitutional amendment. Any judicial invalidation of a piece of ordinary legislation, in other words, must be justified by the claim that the law in question violates some enumerated provision actually contained in the body of the positive constitution.

But this demand tells us little about how judges are to determine whether some law violates a constitutional provision, whether it can be struck down on the ground that it ought to have been enacted as a constitutional amendment. In particular, the demand does not entail, as Kelsen clearly acknowledges, that judges will be able to subsume the enactment of a law under a constitutional provision that functions as a condition of its invalidation only if such subsumption is uncontroversial. Kelsen argues, rather, that judges on a constitutional court will inevitably have the power to interpret authentically constitutional provisions that may serve as conditions of the invalidation of laws. If a constitution contains a bill of rights it will therefore be advisable, from a democratic point of view, to formulate the constitutional restraints on legislation as precisely as possible.[45] But if a constitution's provisions are vague and unspecific, judges cannot be blamed for having to be creative in reviewing legislative and executive acts for constitutionality.

The situation, then, is this. The constitutional court is needed to bring about final judgment on the full legality or illegality of acts that have an appearance of

[42] See Kelsen, 'Wer soll der Hüter der Verfassung sein?' (n 2 above) 1886–8.
[43] See Kelsen, 'Wesen und Entwicklung der Staatsgerichtsbarkeit' (n 2 above) 1848–54.
[44] Ibid, 1852.   [45] Ibid, 1853.

legality. But it seems clear, notwithstanding the fact that the court's decision must always be presented as the result of a subsumption, that the court will not always be able to arrive at an answer to the question whether a law that has the appearance of legality was indeed enacted in the right way without relying on political or moral judgment. A formal constitution that contains a bill of rights will force judges on a constitutional court to decide whether some ordinary law is materially violating the bill of rights before they can arrive at the conclusion that the law in question is invalid since it was not enacted in the right way, namely as a constitutional amendment. Moreover, Kelsen does not believe that the inclusion of a bill of rights is the only aspect of a formal constitution that may make it impossible for constitutional judges to arrive at their decisions on the basis of uncontroversial criteria of legality. Disputes about the meaning of power-conferring constitutional provisions, as Kelsen was well aware, may well be as intractable, especially in times of political crisis, as disputes about the meaning of material constitutional norms.

We therefore need a more substantive account of what makes it possible for Kelsen to maintain his ambitious view of the scope of justiciability in the face of these difficulties than is offered by Kelsen himself. Such an account, I have already suggested, must be based on the relation between formal constitutionalism and democracy.

Kelsen's conceptions of democracy and constitutionalism, to start with, clearly have a number of negative consequences with respect to an adequate understanding of judicial role. For reasons already explained, Kelsen has to reject any constitutional theory that rests on a notion of constituent power, on a variant of the idea that the constitution or some constitutional provision is to be interpreted as the result of an enactment attributable to a higher will of the people whose real or assumed intentions are determinative of constitutional meaning.[46]

If we deny the possibility of a theory of constituent power, we must accept a limited continuity of ordinary politics with constitutional politics. Recall that the constitution itself, the list of rights and principles enjoying the protection of constitutional form is supposed to be open to democratic change, in order to allow, for example, for lawful transition from capitalism to socialism and vice versa. A non-essential constitutional norm can be nothing more than the temporarily sedimented outcome of an earlier conflict of interest that has been settled by way of compromise and that was never meant to be a permanent expression of the community's moral identity.

But if a constitutional provision is itself open to change in a democratic society, there can be no sufficient justification for judges to pretend that a determinate

---

[46] This rejection applies not just to 'originalist' theories that attempt to read the constitution in terms of an actual exercise of constituent power but also to theories that work with a hypothetical idea of constituent power which takes the constitution to be expressive of a normative conception of public reason. Kelsen would therefore reject John Rawls, *Political Liberalism* (2nd ed, New York, 1996) 231–40 who sees the supreme court as the 'exemplar of public reason' protecting the 'higher law of the people from the ordinary law of legislative bodies' (ibid, 233).

solution to some bona fide dispute between a democratic majority and a democratic minority over its implications for some present situation is already contained
in the past compromise. If they engaged in such pretense, judges would inevitably
deny to one of the parties to the present dispute, and to its legal challenge, the standing it deserves in a democratic constitution.[47] Generally speaking, constitutional
provisions that can be changed without destroying the democratic nature of the
constitution may not legitimately be regarded as expressing the moral purpose of
the constitution.

The idea that the constitution is to provide an open framework for the ongoing
renegotiation of the identity of the community does not just force a rejection of
theories of constituent power. Kelsen would have been equally skeptical of a
Dworkinian understanding of constitutional adjudication.

Undoubtedly, there appear to be some broad similarities, at least at first glance,
between Kelsen's project, as interpreted here, and Dworkin's conception of jurisprudence. What I have said so far would appear to suggest that there is rough agreement
between Kelsen and Dworkin on 'the most abstract and fundamental point of legal
practice', namely to 'guide and constrain the power of government' so as to make
sure that 'force not be used or withheld, no matter how useful that would be to ends
in view [. . .] except as licensed or required by individual rights and responsibilities
flowing from past political decisions about when collective force is justified'.[48] This
appearance of agreement, however, does not fully withstand close scrutiny.

Kelsen, I suspect, would have taken issue with Dworkin's understanding of the
idea that law is an interpretive concept.[49] Dworkin introduces his understanding
of interpretive concepts by the use of an example. He imagines a society whose
members, in their interactions, abide by certain rules of courtesy. If that practice is
a reflective practice, members of the society will not simply habitually follow a
number of agreed upon rules of courteous behavior. For a reflective practice to
persist, there will have to be some general agreement, if only in the broadest terms,
about the point of courtesy, for example agreement on the idea that courtesy is a
matter of showing due respect. Such agreement, in Dworkin's terminology, constitutes a *concept* of courtesy. There will also have to be agreement on a number of
paradigms of courtesy. People have to agree that some things are required by courtesy if anything is.

But people who agree on the general point that courtesy is linked to showing
proper respect may disagree about the *conception* of courtesy, about the precise
reasons for showing respect and consequently about the question to whom respect
is owed and why. Such disagreements, of course, will sometimes lead to disagreement about what courtesy requires in particular situations. Given these conditions,

---

[47] Kelsen's argument here overlaps to some extent with Waldron's attack on the idea of entrenchment
as pre-commitment. See Waldron, *Law and Disagreement* (n 1 above) 266–70 and Stephen Holmes,
'Precommitment and the Paradox of Democracy' in Stephen Holmes, *Passions and Constraint. On the
Theory of Liberal Democracy* (Chicago, 1995) 134–77.

[48] Ronald Dworkin, *Law's Empire* (London, 1986) 93.

[49] See for Dworkin's analysis of interpretive concepts ibid, 45–86.

Dworkin claims, an individual will have to rely on his or her own view as to which conception of respect shows the practice in its morally most attractive light in order to make a bona fide attempt to do what courtesy requires. Disagreements about what courtesy requires in any particular instance, in other words, cannot be separated from disagreements about what set of moral principles best explains the overall point of showing respect to others in a way that honors the paradigms of courtesy. The concept of courtesy, hence, is interpretive, insofar as no reflective attempt to follow established rules of courtesy will be able to avoid the question of the best conception of proper respect.

In Dworkin's view, this basic picture can serve as a guide to understanding legal practice.[50] The concept of law is given, Dworkin claims, by the general purpose of legal practice to constrain the power of government in accordance with the best political theory that can be made to fit with the sum of past political decisions as to when the use of collective force is justified. Judges, at least on the assumption that legal practice is a reflective practice, are in the same position as citizens of courtesy. In order to decide any particular legal case in a way adequate to the general concept of law, they will have to commit to and decide on the basis of one or another conception of law. In other words, a judge, while giving due attention to constraints of fit that play a role analogous to that of paradigms of courtesy, must attempt to make sure that his decisions are based on the morally most satisfactory conception of law.[51]

This account of how law justifies exercises of power is at odds with the ideal of a utopia of legality. Recall that the utopia of legality claims to be able to accommodate both socialists and liberal capitalists, on the condition that both are willing to acknowledge that any attempt to realize their respective conceptions of a perfectly just social order must remain within the normative boundaries set by respect for democratic law. This accommodation, as we have seen, can work only if the conception of democratic legality that is to legitimize whatever *temporary* and *revisable* solution to the conflict society has settled on is not itself committed to any particular side in the dispute. If a conception of democratic legality were so committed the decisions to which it leads, as well the conception itself, would have to be defended on the basis of the claim that one of the two disputed views of a fully just society is morally superior to the other. But in this case, democratic legality could not mediate disputes over the moral superiority of socialism or capitalism.

The reason for the incompatibility of Dworkin's approach with Kelsen's utopia, then, should be obvious. All Dworkinian conceptions of law, even while laboring under a constraint of fit with the legal past, will interpret the constitution in the light of a comprehensive ideal of just social order. Any such ideal will surely include a

---

[50] See ibid, 87–113.
[51] This general description applies to all three interpretive conceptions of law Dworkin introduces in *Law's Empire*. The position he calls 'pragmatism' gives no weight at all to constraints of fit. But this stance, Dworkin claims, is to be understood as an answer to his interpretive question that is given on the basis of an acceptance of Dworkin's general concept of law.

stance on issues that Kelsen wants to see excluded from and subjected to the legit-imating force of a conception of democratic legality. But this entails that Dworkinian interpretivism is incompatible with Kelsen's argument about the justificatory force of democratic legality. It is likely to turn into standards of legality a set of substantive values that must be excluded by a conception of democratic legality if the latter is to serve its purpose of mediation in a pluralist society divided over the common good.

This incompatibility between Kelsen's and Dworkin's views can also be brought out by reflecting once again on the perspective of the law-abiding citizen. The law-abiding citizen, as we have seen, accepts a duty to defer to political decisions that have proper legal authorization, even if he does not believe that they optimally reflect the best theory of justice that could be read into the sum content of all past legal decisions. As we have also seen, the deference that we pay to the state as law-abiding citizens in a utopia of legality is really a deference that we, in Kelsen's view, owe to each other as democratic citizens. Kelsenian courts represent the law-abiding citizen against organs of state that actively exercise political power. But if courts are to represent the law-abiding citizen, a notion of proper judicial role must include a notion of proper deference to democratic law. It must give expression to the duties of respect that democratic citizens owe to each other by restricting itself to the enforcement of limits of authority.

Dworkin rejects such restrictions on courts, and this rejection is a symptom of the fact that he rejects the picture of community on which these restrictions are based. Dworkin does not start out from the idea of the law-abiding citizen. His starting point, rather, is the view that citizens are entitled to be treated in accordance with the morally optimal interpretation of his concept of law. And this entitlement, from the point of view of the Dworkinian moral agent represented by a Dworkinian judge, is considered to be non-negotiable. None of the normative disputes amongst members of a community that might lead to disagreements about the content of the best conception of law can justifiably be subjected to a democratic process of legal arbitration whose outcomes claim content-independent legitimacy. Rather, one or another comprehensive answer to such disputes, an answer that is needed, inevitably, to form of any conception of law, must govern that process. This, in turn, implies that it must be up to judges to decide, in the process of arriving at adju-dicative decisions, what that answer is.

Dworkin's argument leaves it unclear why a citizen who disagrees, perhaps quite reasonably, with the interpretive conception of law that the judges employ should hold himself to be obliged to defer to their decisions or to consider them legitimate. This question becomes especially pressing once it is admitted that judges them-selves are likely to disagree over the best conception of law. Dworkin cannot invoke a Kelsenian notion of the identity of rulers and ruled that would allow dissenters to identify with legal decisions that are animated by political views they happen to dis-agree with. The judge, after all, must, in taking a controversial decision, claim that a dissenter who relies on a conception of law different from his own is morally mis-taken. He must, in other words, officially repudiate the dissenter's view on account of giving a wrong picture of the moral identity of the community: much like the Rousseauian must hold that the outvoted misunderstood the authentic content of the general will. Dworkin thinks that courts are entitled to take such a stance since they are obviously better equipped to judge on issues of principle than legislators or ordinary members of a democratic community. But the observation that judges are more likely to 'get it right' than other decision-takers, even if true, cannot provide judicial decisions with legitimacy in the eyes of those who find themselves in disagreement with the legal conceptions preferred by the courts.[52] Dworkin's argument appears to assume, implausibly, that legitimacy can be dispensed with in a modern pluralist society.

Note that the conflict between Kelsen and Dworkin cannot be portrayed as a dispute about the best conception of law in the Dworkinian sense, as a dispute taking place on the turf of Dworkinian interpretivism. Kelsen is committed to the view, to be sure, that the utopia of legality is the morally most defensible overall regulation of the use of coercive force. If this is true, then Dworkin must be wrong to claim that a legal order committed to his preferred conception of law, law as integrity, offers the morally optimal overall regulation of the use of coercive force by a society against its members. But it would nevertheless be wrong to say that Kelsen is simply offering a different specification of Dworkin's concept of law. The utopia stops short of committing itself to any Dworkinian conception, as it must if it is to express the mutual respect its citizens acknowledge they owe to each other.

Kelsen, despite appearances, is working with a *concept* of law that differs from Dworkin's. The difference between Kelsen's and Dworkin's concepts of law is due to a difference in the objects of interpretation, in the objects to which the two theories attribute a moral purpose. Dworkin claims, to recall, that concepts and conceptions of law are outgrowths of *legal practice*. The pure theory of law, however, is not a theory of legal practice, if that term is understood in Dworkin's sense. It is a theory, and thus an interpretation of, *legal order*. Put rather crudely, a theory of legal practice is a theory concerned with the activities of judges and lawyers whereas a theory of legal order is a theory of the state and its relationship to the law. Theories of legal practice and theories of legal order are, of course, related. A theory of legal order like Kelsen's, as we have seen, is likely to have implications for a theory of judicial role and thus for legal practice. But a theory of legal practice, on the other hand, will also be committed, implicitly or explicitly, to some view of legal order or of the law-state relationship.

Dworkin's concept of law is from the start committed to a dualist account of legal order. Dworkin opposes government and the state, to legal practice. The law, as doctrinally purified and imbued with moral content by legal practice, is a bridle to be imposed from the outside upon government and the legislature, both of which are viewed with habitual distrust. The function of the enforcement of this moral

---

[52] See Ronald Dworkin, 'The Forum of Principle' in Ronald Dworkin, *A Matter of Principle* (Cambridge/Mass, 1985) 33–71, at 70.

bridle on political decision takers is to make sure that the outcomes of the political decision taking process do not take anything away from the morally optimal scheme of individual rights that can somehow be imposed on past legal content. Legal practice, in other words, is a bulwark against governmental trespass of individual moral rights. In order to be an effective bulwark against such trespass, courts must be allowed to decide on what they think is the best theory of individual rights attributable to the legal past and be allowed to exploit that theory as a standard of legality to the fullest extent possible.[53]

Kelsen's perspective is altogether different. His concept of law emphasizes that the point or purpose of legal order is to make sure that properly authorized political decisions are legitimate, even if it is possible reasonably to disagree about the substantive moral quality of the content of the norms enacted through these decisions. The notion of proper authorization involved, as we have seen, is not morally neutral. Kelsen thinks that the fact that members of modern societies reasonably disagree over many of the questions that must be answered by any Dworkinian interpretive conception of the law raises fundamental problems of legitimacy, problems that cannot be solved by simply empowering one particular organ or institution unilaterally to decide these questions. Disagreement, from a fallibilist perspective, gives rise to duties of mutual respect for each other's views. Democracy, according to Kelsen, is the best form of government because it is the only form of government that has institutional room for these duties of mutual respect without committing us to epistemic abstinence and curtailment of public debate. Our view of the role of judges, in Kelsen's view must, therefore, be tailored to fit the theory of democracy, and not the other way around.

This, of course, does not entail that Dworkin is morally wrong, at the end of the day, not to accept the normative priority, in adjudication, of democratic legality over more substantive accounts of justice. The problem, rather, is that a view like Kelsen's is simply ruled out by undefended dualist assumptions implicit in Dworkin's concept of law, rather than argued against. This exclusion would be justifiable only if Kelsen's utopia of legality could be shown to be incoherent or self-defeating. But if the utopia of legality is at least a coherent ideal, Dworkin's interpretivism, as it stands, would seem to beg the question against it as a theory of what best justifies exercises of public power. In order to avoid such question begging, theories of legal order ought to be given priority over theories of legal practice. They constitute the more encompassing theoretical perspective and they make visible morally important alternatives that tend to be covered up by Dworkin's concept of law.

So far, our analysis of the implications of Kelsen's constitutionalism for a conception of judicial role adequate to a constitutional court has led to mainly negative results. It has told us what judges on a constitutional court in a Kelsenian democracy

---

[53] These dualist assumptions are implicit in all of Dworkin's conceptions of law, despite the fact that they are most clearly developed in 'law as integrity'. 'Pragmatism' denies that people have rights, but it does so in the course of answering the internal interpretive question what rights legal practice ought to attribute to subjects of the law.

must avoid to do in order to honor their role: namely to attribute to the constitution a full-blown account of the good community, either on the basis of Dworkinian interpretivism or on the basis of a theory of constituent power. Is there something more positive to be said about the conception of judicial role that will allow a democratic constitutional court to act in accordance with the regulative assumption of legal objectivity?

The task of a constitutional court, I claimed above, must be to police the grounds of legal legitimacy, the conditions that make it possible for citizens reasonably to defer to the law. The main conditions of legal legitimacy, as we have seen, are the full realization of the principle of legality implicit in the thesis of the identity of law and state and the realization of democracy, as a means of extending the idea of legal legitimacy to the legislative level. The role of a constitutional court in a utopia of legality, therefore, must be to protect the integrity of these two conditions of legal legitimacy. In particular, the constitutional court must protect the integrity of the democratic political process since this task is clearly one that ordinary courts exercising powers of review are much less well equipped to perform than a centralized institution whose decisions take place in the watchful eye of the public.[54]

The conception of integrity of democracy to be protected by the court is to be understood with reference to the political culture that ought to accompany the institutionalized decision-taking procedures of a well-functioning democracy. This political culture, as we have seen, is guided by a moral ideal of civility and mutual respect in a pluralist society. Formal constitutionalism, for Kelsen, is ultimately an entrenchment of this ideal of civility. Constitutional rights have the function to protect temporary minorities against temporary majorities by making sure that minorities are not frozen out of the political process, that their interests are heard in public and reflected, at least to some extent, in the legislative decisions taken. The constitutional court's main function in scrutinizing the legality of legislation and in voiding what it considers unconstitutional acts of legislation must be to protect the essential rights of access that will allow minorities to make themselves heard: Since a minority is to be recognized as a potential future majority, it must have the right to organize itself politically, freely to advertise its policies, and to have its representatives run for office in fair and open elections, and so on.

Kelsen's understanding of democracy suggests that these essential rights must not be read in a narrow formalistic fashion. Their function, after all, is to give minorities an effective voice. To some extent, constitutional rights not essential to all instantiations of democracy can be interpreted as serving the same basic function. If there is disagreement on the question whether some ordinary law violates any constitutional provision, the court should therefore approach the issue by asking itself whether the law in question violates the freedoms essential to democracy or whether it curtails the effective use of these freedoms. The court, in other words, should be

---

[54] Kelsen's conception, as I interpret it, has strong affinities with John Hart Ely, *Democracy and Distrust. A Theory of Judicial Review* (Cambridge/Mass, 1980).

enforcing the attitude of reciprocal respect that democratic citizens are obliged to exhibit towards each other. Insofar as this attitude has a moral content, the court must enforce that content. But it may not be guided, in its attempt to subsume ordinary laws under constitutional norms, by moral considerations other than those included in the duties of mutual respect democratic citizens owe to each other.

The justification for this approach lies in the fact that the court cannot read the constitution simply as a set of procedural rules if it wants its decisions to be adequate to the constitutional context within which it operates. It must work under the general assumption that the constitution is a democratic constitution and that the protection of rights of access and participation as well as of the conditions of the effective exercise of these rights is necessary if the constitution is to remain a democratic constitution.[55]

It is impossible to accept that a constitutional court is a meaningful institution and to criticize it for operating on this limited normative assumption. A constitutional court is a meaningful institution only in a democracy characterized by some degree of formal constitutionalism and not in a legislative autocracy the constitution of which boils down to a set of simple procedural rules that mainly serve to identify, but not to restrict, the actions of a unified agency. Those committed to the normative superiority of democracy over autocracy cannot reasonably deny the justifiability of a constitutional court aiming to protect the rights essential to democracy and their effective exercise. A rejection of a constitutional court operating on this normative basis would have to go hand in hand with a rejection of democracy itself.

One might suspect that the approach outlined here must ultimately collapse, despite my earlier protestations, into Dworkinian interpretivism. The reasons for thinking that Kelsenian judges will inevitably end up having to act in accordance with a Dworkinian conception of judicial role are readily apparent. Kelsenian judges, if engaged in the activity of review, will have to enforce the substantive legality of political decisions, the full conformity of these decisions with all relevant formal and material authorizing norms. What is more, Kelsen admits that questions of full legality will typically give rise to reasonable disagreement, even while reviewing judges must labor under the regulative assumption that limits of authority are objectively determinable. Judges on a constitutional court, it appears, will therefore still have to take what they think of as the best decision, if faced with a hard case,

---

[55] The idea that the constitutional court functions mainly as a protector of the integrity of the democratic process guides is evident in Kelsen's positive conclusions as to how its procedures ought to be organized. Just as litigants in the international sphere the parties to a constitutional conflict need to be treated, by the court acting in the role of an arbitrator, as having equal standing. Kelsen emphasizes that the right to appeal to the court ought to be as unrestricted as practically possible. He thinks that the court must operate publicly and claims that the trial in court ought to be organized in an adversarial fashion. Kelsen stresses, moreover, that the court is itself a public forum for the exchange of reasons and the articulation of interests involved in a social conflict of interest that will allow a minority to make its case heard if ordinary parliamentary proceedings fail to allow for sufficient articulation of minority interests. See Kelsen, 'Wesen und Entwicklung der Staatsgerichtsbarkeit' (n 2 above) 1857–62.

and they will have to do so in the light of some conception of the normative purpose of the constitution. How, then, can Kelsenian judges avoid playing on Dworkinian turf, offering an interpretive conception of the law in Dworkin's sense?[56]

The answer to this query is that the Dworkinian is right to point out that Kelsenian judges on a constitutional court do take the decisions they think best. But 'best', in a Kelsenian context, does not mean what it would mean in any of Dworkin's conceptions of law. First, Kelsenian constitutional judges are guided, in their interpretive efforts, by the aim to decide conflicts about the scope of constitutional rights in the way that best protects the well-functioning of democracy. In so doing, second, they of course take the decisions they believe are best, all things considered. But a judge may well come to believe that a decision is best, all things considered, even if it does not express the conception of political justice or the substantive understanding of equal concern and respect to which he adheres. What makes the decision best, rather, is the fact that these decisions sustain a form of legal order that is considered superior to a form of legal order in which judges tried to directly optimize the moral content of law, through their own decisions and in accordance with their own comprehensive standards of political morality.

This stance may seem paradoxical. But it is not any more paradoxical than the idea that I may have a duty, as a citizen, to obey a law that I think is not as morally good as it could be, but only under the condition that the law was enacted democratically. If there is nothing incoherent about this view as a view taken by a citizen, there would seem to be no reason to believe that there must be anything incoherent about the related conception of judicial role. A citizen who is obeying the law, given such circumstances, is doing what he thinks is morally required, all things considered, even though he believes that the decisions he must accept as legitimate are not as good as they would be if they were taken with the aim to express, to the extent possible, his comprehensive ideal of justice. The reviewing judge, in turn, does not make an attempt to mend the perceived moral imperfections that may befall even laws enacted in accordance with the moral principles underlying democratic procedure. What he does is to settle disagreements over whether a law was enacted in a way that respected the principles of democracy.

Kelsen's position, in order to be at least intelligible and coherent, does not require anything more than that we can meaningfully distinguish between a form of review that settles disputes over the full constitutional legality of a law by relying on the conception of democracy outlined in the previous chapter and a form of review that goes for a more ambitious form of moral optimization. I see no good general reason to believe that the possibility of drawing such a distinction is meaningless. Neither do I see any good reason to suppose that the possibility would exist only if the questions to be addressed within the first kind of review were trivial or had perfectly

---

[56] See Dworkin's criticism of John Hart Ely in 'The Forum of Principle' (n 52 above) 57–69 as well as Ronald Dworkin, *Freedom's Law. The Moral Reading of the American Constitution* (Cambridge/Mass, 1996) 1–43.

obvious answers. Kelsen admits, as we have seen, that there may well be no perfectly obvious or trivial answers to the question whether some enactment respected
the values constitutive of democracy. But why should it follow from this that that
the answer must be sought in a full blown theory of justice rather than on the basis of
a suitably restricted set of moral reasons? And why should we, as citizens, necessarily
be at a loss to assess whether a constitutional court's activities tend to conform to
these restrictions?

In order to arrive at this stronger conclusion, Dworkin relies on the observation
that conceptions of democracy, and hence distinctions between rights essential and
rights not-essential to democracy, are contested and that any choice between conceptions of democracy will have to come to rest on issues of value.[57] This observation is undoubtedly true. But it seems that all we can safely infer from it is that
judges engaged in review cannot avoid relying on a value-laden conception of
democracy. This conclusion, however, is considerably weaker than the one needed
by Dworkin, namely that the choice between different conceptions of democracy,
once there is a constitutional court, can only be internal to legal practice and that
judges therefore must have the legitimate power to decide, in the course of developing interpretive conceptions of the law, what understanding of democracy is to
be adopted by a community. If Kelsen's understanding of democracy, though contested and value-dependent, enjoys sufficient acceptance in some society, or if it is
at least not altogether unrealistic to hope that it might come to enjoy such acceptance, we will not have to draw Dworkin's stronger conclusion. What is more, we
may well think that there are good normative reasons not to draw it.

Let us turn to a final criticism of the Kelsenian perspective offered here. One might,
of course, argue that the conception of judicial role just outlined is too weak to give
meaning to the claim that a constitutional court acting on that conception will be
in a position to decide deep constitutional conflicts on a legal basis. This complaint
draws its force from the assumption that a decision has a genuine legal basis—
as opposed to being valid in virtue of a mere formal authorization—only if the
law which it applies determines a unique answer to the disputed question at hand.
Kelsen's theory of legal order, as we have seen, is based on a general rejection of the
view that a decision can have a genuine legal basis only if such a standard is met.
Any authoritative interpretation of a legal norm, Kelsen claims, can lead to several
equally valid results. The standard for constitutional review I have introduced does
nothing to change this point with respect to constitutional law. It does not narrow
down the interpretive possibilities in any constitutional dispute to one obvious
solution.

But to criticize the standard for this reason would be to misunderstand its function. Its function, on the one hand, is to provide judges with a picture of the kind
of considerations they must invoke or refuse to invoke, if their task is to protect the
utopia of legality. Moreover, the standard has a second and perhaps more important

function, as I pointed out above. Democratic citizens need to be in a position to know whether they are, in deferring to the decisions of a constitutional court, and hence in attributing a presumption of legality to the democratic state as a whole, successfully discharging their duties of deference to each other or merely submitting to a partial will to power. In describing the kinds of reasons that reviewing judges may rely on in taking their decisions, the standard will allow citizens to arrive at a reasonable answer to the question whether the law they are subjected to, given that it either has been or can be reviewed by an independent court, can rightfully claim to be legitimate.

To assess the plausibility of the view of constitutional adjudication just offered, one has to be mindful of the context in which the problem to which it answers arises. A constitutional court, in Kelsen's view, is an essential requirement for the realization of democratic constitutionalism. But a constitutional court cannot function properly unless the political culture within which it operates is by and large committed to interpreting the democratic constitution in Kelsenian terms.[58] The role I attributed to constitutional judges will only be sustainable if citizens themselves are willing to be law-abiding members of a democratic commonwealth and if they have some shared understanding, however rough, of the meaning of the distinction between the conditions of legal legitimacy and matters of substantive justice. The courts will be able to enforce the substantive constitutional legality of legislation, while exhibiting proper deference to the legislator, only in a community whose members are themselves committed to finding such balance.[59] But the utopia of legality could not be completed without the cooperation of judges. In cooperating judges vicariously exhibit the virtues that would otherwise be required of every citizen. By accepting the regulative ideal of legal objectivity as their guidepost, reviewing judges allow the rest of us to be partisans.

[58] This may explain why Kelsen was reluctant to blame the Reichsgericht in the 'Preussenschlag'-affair. See Hans Kelsen, 'Das Urteil des Staatsgerichtshofs vom 25. Oktober 1932' in *Die Justiz* 8 (1932–33) 65–91 and the analysis in Dyzenhaus, *Legality and Legitimacy* (n 8 above) 123–32. This issue needs more discussion than I have been able to give it here. In general, Kelsen argues that Germany faces a choice between autocracy and democracy and that the court is fudging that choice. The inconsistencies in the court's decision are the inevitable result of its reliance on a mistaken conception of adjudicative activity. However, the court's paralysis in the face of this choice is to some extent part and parcel of a paralysis of German political culture in general.

[59] The role played by a constitutional court in a democracy, Kelsen believes, is closely analogous to that of a court that adjudicates in international conflicts between states. See Kelsen, 'Wesen und Entwicklung der Staatsgerichtsbarkeit' (n 2 above) 1868; Kelsen, 'Wer soll der Hüter der Verfassung sein?' (n 2 above) 1883–4.

6

Kelsen's Legal Cosmopolitanism

Throughout this book, I have argued that the pure theory of law must be understood in the light of a normative ambition; the aim to develop a theory of law adequate to the project of realizing an ideal of the rule of law. That the pure theory is indeed committed to such an ambition is nowhere more obvious than in Kelsen's theory of international law.[1] Kelsen himself described his theory of international law as 'one of the most substantial achievements of the pure theory of law'.[2] He credited the pure theory with the dissolution of the dogma of sovereignty, which, in Kelsen's view, constitutes a major hindrance to the development of a *civitas maxima*, of a binding international legal order that includes all national legal orders as dependent parts and that brings about a lawful condition on a global scale.

Kelsen's main line of argument against sovereigntism follows a by now familiar pattern. The dogma of sovereignty is a hindrance to the development of international legal order insofar as it mistakenly claims that the independence of states is necessarily incompatible with the existence of an international legal order that binds states even against their will. In order to remove this hindrance, Kelsen argues, we do not have to commit to the view that the development of a *civitas maxima* is morally desirable. Morally uncommitted legal-scientific argument alone suffices to establish that a binding global legal order compatible with independent statehood is perfectly conceivable from a jurisprudential point of view. Opposition to the realization of the *civitas maxima*, therefore, cannot be defended on the basis of uncontroversial insights into the essential features of statehood. Rather, it will express an unwillingness to accept the subjection of one's own state to international law that can only be justified politically.[3]

However, there are good reasons to doubt whether Kelsen's careful attempt to distinguish between legal-scientific and political elements in perspectives on international law is stable. Kelsen's legal-theoretical arguments about the nature of

---

[1] For a comprehensive account of Kelsen's theory of international law see Jochen von Bernstorff, *Der Glaube an das universale Recht. Zur Völkerrechtstheorie Hans Kelsens und seiner Schüler* (Baden-Baden, 2001).

[2] See Hans Kelsen, *Introduction to the Problems of Legal Theory. A Translation of the First Edition of the Reine Rechtslehre or Pure Theory of Law*, translated and edited by Bonnie Litschewski-Paulson and Stanley Paulson (Oxford, 1992) 124.

[3] Kelsen's most detailed treatment of this theme is to be found in Hans Kelsen, *Das Problem der Souveränität und die Theorie des Völkerrechts. Beitrag zu einer reinen Rechtslehre* (Tübingen, 1920).

international law, it has often been claimed, are themselves informed by his undeniable sympathy for the project of legal cosmopolitanism, of realizing a *civitas maxima*.[4] They appear to draw on an implicit normative basis that is not made explicit (and not explicitly defended by) Kelsen.[5] My aim in this chapter, as in earlier chapters, is to offer a defense of a Kelsenian perspective that concedes this point and that tries, instead of defending the legal-scientific standing of the pure theory's account of international law, to explicate the normative basis of Kelsen's views as well as to show that it grounds an attractive ideal of international legality.

Kelsen and the dogma of sovereignty

According to the classical theory of sovereignty, exemplified by authors such as Hobbes or Austin, law is a system of coercive rules that bindingly regulate all possible conflicts amongst the law's subjects.[6] Legal rules, however, cannot bindingly adjudicate the conflicts of two subjects of the law unless both are subordinated to a higher authority that functions as the sole legislator, the final interpreter and the effective enforcer of legal rules. But independent states as the subjects of international law, the theorist of sovereignty argues, are not subordinated to each other and neither are they subject to some third higher authority with the features of a Hobbesian or Austinian sovereign. It follows that, properly speaking, there is no international law.[7]

Note that the sovereigntist argument can be understood to establish more than that there is, at present, no international law (or that it is at present still very different from municipal law).[8] International law is, by definition, a law amongst independent states. But only sovereign states, according to the sovereigntist, are truly independent and a state's sovereignty is incompatible with genuine subjection to an externally imposed law. There are only two options, then, according to the sovereigntist argument, for organizing the international sphere. Either we have to create a world state whose subordinate parts would lack political independence and whose law would be nothing but a domestic legal system writ large. This prospect,

---

[4] See ibid, 204: 'According to the generally recognized view, it belongs to the nature and concept of the law of peoples that it constitutes a society of states equal in their rights. The conception of the coexistence of a plurality of commonwealths that, despite their factual difference in their territorial extension, the size of their people, and in the effective means of their power, are bound together into some form of higher community is an eminently ethical conception. It is one of the few genuinely valuable and incontestable elements of modern cultural consciousness.' [my translation]

[5] See for example Danilo Zolo, 'Hans Kelsen: International Peace Through International Law' in *European Journal of International Law* 9 (1998) 306–24; Hedley Bull, 'Hans Kelsen and International Law' in William Twining and Richard Tur (eds), *Essays on Kelsen* (Oxford, 1986) 321–36.

[6] See Thomas Hobbes, *Leviathan. Revised Student Edition*, edited by Richard Tuck (Cambridge, 1996) 111; John Austin, *The Province of Jurisprudence Determined*, edited by Wilfrid E Rumble (Cambridge, 1995) 18–37.

[7] Austin famously claimed that international law is just positive morality. See Austin, ibid, 112, 124.

[8] See for the latter view H L A Hart, *The Concept of Law*, edited by Penelope Bulloch and Joseph Raz (2nd ed, Oxford, 1994) 208–31.

needless to say, appears both unrealistic and unattractive. Alternatively, we can accept that the international sphere is characterized by the coexistence of a plurality of sovereign states coordinated by a system of standards that, while they are embedded in a mostly concordant practice and while they are observed by most states most of the time, inevitably lack some of the key features of genuine legal norms.[9]

In the case of a domestic legal system, we assume that the authority of the law over the subject is, at least potentially, all-encompassing. Domestic legal systems claim a monopoly of force. The liberty of subjects to act as they please depends on the silence of the law. All conduct of subjects, therefore, is in principle regulated by law since it is either legally prohibited or legally permitted. All possible conflicts amongst subjects of the law, by implication, are amenable to solution on a legal basis and thus subject to the jurisdiction of the courts.

The international legal order, by contrast, is essentially limited in regulatory scope, the sovereigntist claims. The agents whose conduct is subject to international law, namely states, are presumptively free to act in whatever way they deem necessary, prudent, or morally required unless they have chosen to undertake obligations with respect to some particular subject matter. There remains a wide area of state action, in the international sphere, that is not subject to any legal regulation, where states can legitimately choose to employ force at their own discretion. What is more, even where states subject themselves to rules of international law, they may reserve the power to act on their own interpretation of these rules, including the power to act on their own understanding of whether any conflict they run into is covered by a legal regulation to which they have previously subjected themselves. As a result, there can be no compulsory adjudication of all possible international disputes.[10]

Both aspects of this contrast, according to the sovereigntist, are necessary consequences of the sovereignty of states. Just as the sovereignty of the state grounds its potentially unlimited authority over its domestic subjects, it ensures that states are presumptively free of international legal obligations. In Kelsen's view, this sovereigntist view mistakenly interprets contingent differences in the actual degree of the development of national and international legal order with essential differences grounded in the very nature of the state. As a result it understates the developmental capacities of international legal order.[11] Contrary to the sovereigntist, we are not faced with an exclusive choice between an imperfectly domesticated state of nature and a world sovereign.

In his first major publication on international law *Das Problem der Souveränität und die Theorie des Völkerrechts* Kelsen proclaimed, for these reasons, that the concept

---

[9] Martti Koskenniemi interprets the doctrinal history of international law as a series of unsuccessful attempts to finesse this choice. See Koskenniemi, *From Apology to Utopia. The Structure of International Legal Argument* (Cambridge, 2005). Koskenniemi's analysis is obviously inspired by Kelsen's own reading of the doctrinal development of international law in *Das Problem der Souveränität* (n 3 above).

[10] For an influential Kelsenian criticism of such doctrines inspired by Kelsen see Hersch Lauterpacht, *The Function of Law in the International Community* (Oxford, 1933).

[11] This motivation for attacking sovereigntism is rightly emphasized by von Bernstorff, *Der Glaube an das universale Recht* (n 1 above) 49–53.

of sovereignty ought to be 'radically eliminated' from the vocabulary of international law.[12] This rhetoric, however, needs to be taken with a grain of salt. It is important to realize that Kelsen did not reject the dogma of sovereignty outright. Rather, he emphasized that it contained an important kernel of jurisprudential truth which he tried to adapt to his own purposes. Rightly understood, sovereignty, Kelsen argued in *Das Problem der Souveränität*, turns out to be a property of legal systems, not of states.[13]

Kelsen's argument to this conclusion is simple. Sovereignty is usually described as a highest power or authority that is not dependent on or derived from any other power or authority. Clearly, the term cannot reasonably be taken to refer to a power in the order of causality, because that order does not contain any power that is not itself dependent on causal antecedents. In particular, the state's power to motivate its subjects to comply with its demands is clearly not a causally unconditioned power. The idea of sovereignty will be meaningful, then, only if sovereignty is understood as a property of a normative order. We can say that a normative order is an 'absolutely independent' or 'highest' order if and only if all norms that belong to it depend on a basic norm that is not itself derived from any other norm. The state, by implication, can be sovereign only insofar as it is itself identical with a legal order that possesses absolute normative independence. The theory of sovereignty is thus transformed into the theory of the identity of legal system.[14]

However, Kelsen claims that the dogma of sovereignty contains an important kernel of truth. In Kelsen's view, absolute normative independence is a necessary attribute of any independent legal system. An independent legal system, just like a classical sovereign, is not subject to any external normative constraints, however much it may limit the powers of the particular persons or institutions which it authorizes to perform certain acts; the law regulates its own creation and application. What is more, Kelsen argues that any legal system, just like a state in the sovereigntist view, must claim a monopoly of the legitimate use of force,[15] a view that, as we will see, carries the implication that the law's regulatory scope is unlimited. Finally, Kelsen holds on to a variant of the claim that sovereignty is indivisible in arguing that, from a jurisprudential point of view, there can only be one legal system to which all other legal orders must be subject as parts.[16] Kelsen's transformation of the theory of sovereignty into a theory of legal system, then, preserves at least some of the traditional attributes of sovereignty as essential attributes of legal order. Kelsen's attacks on skepticism about international law crucially rely on these residual sovereigntist elements in his own conception.

Kelsen observes that few sovereigntists are willing flatly to deny the existence of international law. Most adopt the 'dualist' view according to which there is a

---

[12] Kelsen, *Das Problem der Souveränität* (n 3 above) 320.   [13] See ibid, 1–101.

[14] See ibid, 4–21 and Hans Kelsen, *Principles of International Law* (New York, 1952) 438–44.

[15] See ibid, 13–15; Hans Kelsen, *Peace Through Law* (Chapel Hill, 1944) 3; Hans Kelsen, *Law and Peace in International Relations. The Oliver Wendell Holmes Lectures, 1940–1941* (Cambridge/Mass, 1942) 11–14.   [16] See Kelsen, *Das Problem der Souveränität* (n 3 above) 102–20.

normatively independent system of international law that exists alongside national legal orders, but one that qualitatively differs from national legal systems in the respects outlined above. But this mediating view, Kelsen believes, is indefensible. Kelsen argues that it is logically impossible to conceive of two equally valid but conflicting legal norms. If two potentially conflicting groups of norms, such as national and international law, are to be considered as jointly valid, it must therefore be possible to solve any apparent conflict between members of the two groups by relying on some principle of precedence. But any such principle, Kelsen claims, will inevitably make both groups of norms members of the same legal system by normatively coordinating them. To conceive of all valid law as a systemic unity is therefore an inevitable methodological postulate of legal thought.[17]

In Kelsen's view, there are only two available forms of normative coordination of legal systems. Either one of the two systems is subordinate to the other as its ground of validity or both, while being independent of each other, are subordinate to a third system that provides a ground of validity to both.[18] Any coherent jurisprudential conception of the relation between international and national legal norms, Kelsen concludes, will therefore either have to adopt the point of view of a particular national legal order or the point of view of international law. In the first case, the legal theorist will take the basic norm of some national legal order to be the basic norm of all law and acknowledge the validity of international legal norms only insofar as they have been transferred into the national legal system, through procedures of recognition dependent on the national legal system's basic norm.[19] In the second case, he will claim that the basic norm of international law authorizes all national legal systems and makes them dependent parts of the global legal order.[20]

In both cases, however, jurisprudence will be forced to adopt a *monist* perspective. For both the jurisprudent who starts out from a nationalist perspective as well as for the jurisprudent who adopts the perspective of international law, there is only one legal system which contains both the norms that we commonly consider as international norms and those that we commonly consider to be national legal norms. Kelsen argues that a third option for portraying the relationship between national and international legal norms, where norms of both groups are considered to be valid, does not exist. All dualist positions, Kelsen claims, must therefore collapse into either nationalist or cosmopolitan monism once their implications are thought through.

All sovereigntist positions, Kelsen concludes, are therefore committed to a radical denial of the existence of international law, despite their attempts to pay lip

[17] See ibid, 107–14; Kelsen, *Introduction to the Problems of Legal Theory* (n 2 above) 111–12, 117–19; Hans Kelsen, 'The Pure Theory of Law and Analytical Jurisprudence' in Hans Kelsen, *What is Justice? Justice, Law, and Politics in the Mirror of Science* (Berkeley, 1957) 266–87, at 284.

[18] See Kelsen, *Introduction to the Problems of Legal Theory* (n 2 above) 112–13.

[19] See Kelsen, *Das Problem der Souveränität* (n 3 above) 151–204.   [20] See ibid, 204–41.

service to the idea that there is international law.[21] If we adopt the nationalist interpretation of the relation between domestic and international law, we are committed to holding that there is no law between national legal orders that could bindingly regulate conflicts between them. From each particular national perspective, norms of international law will have standing only insofar as such standing is recognized in the national legal system, and there is no necessity, from a nationalist perspective, for such recognition to be contained in any national legal system. Sovereigntism therefore fails to secure the value it purportedly aims to protect, namely to make room for a society of politically independent states equal in their sovereignty. The only way out of this solipsism, Kelsen argues, is to take the view that there are objectively valid norms of international law that oblige a state to recognize other systems and their laws on certain conditions to be specified by international law. But to admit this, Kelsen claims, is to adopt a cosmopolitan stance and to assume that all national legal systems form dependent parts of one single global legal order because they all derive their standing from international norms of recognition.

Kelsen claims that the pure theory's dissolution of the traditional dogma of sovereignty (or rather its transfer of attributes of sovereignty from the state to the legal system) does not commit a jurisprudent to adopt a legal cosmopolitan perspective. Whether he ought to adopt this perspective, Kelsen claims, is a political question, dependent on considerations of value external to the pure theory as a legal science. What the pure theory establishes, according to Kelsen, is nothing more than that nationalist solipsism and legal cosmopolitanism are the only two available jurisprudential options for conceiving of the relationship between national and international law, assuming that both are to be jointly valid.

Nevertheless, Kelsen's description of the options jurisprudence faces in conceiving of the relation between national and international law clearly has important normative implications, as Kelsen himself is willing to admit.[22] If it is indeed the case that any coherent sovereigntist conception of international law will make

---

[21] This might seem a problematic interpretation. Kelsen himself at times affirms that nationalist monism amounts to a denial of international law. (See Kelsen, *Introduction to the Problems of Legal Theory* [n 2 above] 116–17 and Kelsen, *Das Problem der Souveränität* [n 3 above] 317.) But he also frequently makes the claim that both approaches are indifferent in the sense that they will both lead one to attribute the same legal obligations to states. (See Kelsen, *Principles of International Law* [n 14 above] 445–446.) I doubt that there is an inconsistency here. The nationalist monist denies international law in the straightforward sense that, for him, norms of international law have validity only as parts of a national legal order, ie as national legal norms. But, insofar as international norms are incorporated into a national legal order, a Kelsenian would of course want to maintain, they are just as binding on the organs of the state as any (other) national norm. And, of course, nationalist and internationalist perspectives might well lead to perfectly content-equivalent descriptions of the legal duties of a state if a state follows a policy to incorporate norms of international law routinely and fully. However, there can be no guarantee that content-equivalence will obtain as incorporation does not have to be complete. A potential practical difference between the two perspectives therefore remains.

[22] See Kelsen, *Introduction to the Problems of Legal Theory* (n 2 above) 124: 'Although it [Kelsen's theory of international law, LV] was certainly not arrived at by political design, it is an achievement that may nevertheless have political import.'

it impossible to conceive of the coexistence of states as legally ordered, and if the existence of legal order among states is, other things being equal, morally desirable, it will follow that those who are inclined to embrace the anti-cosmopolitan conception of the relation between national and international law will naturally have to bear very heavy burdens of moral justification.

But is a legal-theoretical argument about the structure of legal system really competent to saddle critics of cosmopolitanism with such a heavy burden of moral proof? There are good reasons to think that the answer to this question should be negative. Kelsen, as we have seen, argues that if both international and national norms are to be considered as valid, jurisprudence is forced into some variant of monism. This view has been convincingly criticized by H L A Hart and Joseph Raz.[23] Kelsen's thesis of the unity of international and national law is said to involve an untenable conception of the identity of legal system (as grounded in a basic norm) that leads to obviously absurd consequences. The membership of a norm in a legal system can only be determined, Hart and Raz argue, with reference to the practices of identification that in fact characterize the activity of the primary law-applying institutions of some legal system.

The second of the two criticisms I will discuss is a normative criticism. But it is intimately related to the point made by Hart and Raz. Kelsen's claim that his theory of international law is not based on a political evaluation of the developmental prospects of international law but rather on a necessary presupposition of coherent jurisprudential thought must surely be unfounded if Hart's and Raz's criticism is successful. It seems, then, as if Kelsen were the one guilty of trying to defend or at least to favor a substantive view on how the relationship between national and international law ought to be organized, from some normative point of view, under the false guise of a legal-theoretical argument.[24]

One of the most influential criticisms along these lines was made by Carl Schmitt. Kelsenian legal cosmopolitan—in virtue of the claim that international law, like any other legal order, necessarily claims a monopoly of force—is committed to a principle Kelsen himself calls 'the bellum justum principle': All legally unauthorized use of force on the part of a state, ie all use of force that is not itself the application of a sanction for previous breaches of international law on the part of some other state, is to be regarded as criminal.[25] Schmitt doubted that we should welcome the shift to the 'discriminatory concept of war' implied by this principle and

---

[23] H L A Hart, 'Kelsen's Doctrine of the Unity of Law' in H L A Hart, *Essays in Jurisprudence and Philosophy* (Oxford, 1983) 309–42; Joseph Raz, *The Concept of Legal System. An Introduction to the Theory of Legal System* (Oxford, 1970) 95–109; Joseph Raz, 'Kelsen's Theory of the Basic Norm' in Joseph Raz, *The Authority of Law. Essays on Law and Morality* (Oxford, 1979) 122–45, at 127–9.

[24] Versions of this criticism are to be found in Zolo, 'Hans Kelsen: International Peace through International Law' (n 5 above); Martti Koskenniemi, *The Gentle Civilizer of Nations: The Rise and Fall of International Law, 1870–1960* (Cambridge, 2001) 238–49 and Anthony Carty, 'The Continuing Influence of Kelsen on the General Perception of the Discipline of International Law' in *European Journal of International Law* 9 (1998) 344–54.

[25] See Kelsen, *Principles of International Law* (n 14 above) 33–8; Kelsen, *Law and Peace in International Relations* (n 15 above) 36–48.

tried to defend the traditional idea that international law allows for warfare between two equally legitimate belligerents.[26]

According to Schmitt, Kelsen's cosmopolitanism denies that states have a *jus ad bellum* only in order to criminalize those who resist the international legal status quo, a status quo that may well be grievously unjust. The *bellum justum* principle has the undesirable effect of making it impossible to revise an unjust legal status quo through the use of force. What is more, the principle, Schmitt claims, favors a totalization of war, as those who take themselves to be fighting a criminal enemy will tend to reject the restrictions imposed by the traditional standards of the *jus in bello*. Only a 'concrete' order of sovereign political communities that recognize each other as sovereign, and that accept that resort to force will at times be unavoidable to adapt international legal order to changing circumstances, will be capable of preventing this totalization of war, of channeling violent conflict into a form that is at least regulated by a *jus in bello*, and of providing an effective remedy for injustices in the international status quo.[27]

One need not agree with Schmitt's reasons for wanting a revision of the inter-war international system in order to concede that the *bellum justum* principle indeed requires moral justification. This demand will only be more pressing once we have reason to believe that the necessary unity of national and international law cannot be defended on logical grounds. Kelsen's insistence on the purely scientific character of the pure theory, one might suspect, merely conceals his inability or unwillingness to defend his own preference for the cosmopolitan option on the basis of an explicit moral argument, even while his claim that there is an exclusive choice between nationalist and internationalist monism clearly tried to stack the deck against the nationalist, by forcing the latter into a denial of international law.

In what follows, I will address these two criticisms of Kelsen's theory of international law in turn. I will first argue that Hart's and Raz's attack on the pure theory's conception of the identity of legal system is only partly successful and that it consequently need not undermine the Kelsenian argument for legal monism. I will not try to defend Kelsen's claim that his description of jurisprudential alternatives in the theory of international law follows from an impossibility to conceive of the joint validity of two norms that do not form part of the same legal system. What I will claim, rather, is that Kelsen's description of the alternatives we face in thinking about the relation between international and domestic law makes sense once we read his theory of international law as an integral part of the project of developing a conception of law adequate to the ideal of an international utopia of legality.

---

[26] See Carl Schmitt, 'Die Wendung zum diskriminierenden Kriegsbegriff' in Carl Schmitt, *Frieden oder Pazifismus? Arbeiten zum Völkerrecht und zur internationalen Politik 1924–1978*, edited by Günter Maschke (Berlin, 2005) 518–97. The same concern is evident in Hedley Bull, 'Kelsen and International Law' in William Twining and Richard Tur (eds), *Essays on Kelsen* (Oxford, 1986) 321–36, at 329–30.

[27] Carl Schmitt, *Der Nomos der Erde im Völkerrecht des Ius Publicum Europaeum* (Berlin, 1997) 285–99; Carl Schmitt, *Der Begriff des Politischen. Text von 1932 mit einem Vorwort und drei Corollarien* (Berlin, 1963) 45–54.

The debate with Hart and Raz, I will conclude, therefore ultimately turns on the wider question whether the project to develop a theory of law suitable to the hope for an international utopia of legality can be shown to have an adequate moral motivation.

It there is such a motivation, the Schmittian criticism will likewise turn out to be misguided. Kelsen's works on international law, I will argue, do contain a plausible account of the values that will be served by an internationalization of the utopia of legality and of the conditions of the ideal's viability on a global scale. Kelsen's hesitation to adopt an unqualified cosmopolitan stance does not have to be read as a sign of incoherence or covert dishonesty. Kelsen is right, rather, to insist that a jurisprudent or statesman who acknowledges the attraction of the ideal of an international utopia of legality and who adopts a concept of law adequate to that ideal will still face a political choice between nationalism and cosmopolitanism that is not dictated by legal theory. The benefit of Kelsen's portrayal of the relation between domestic and international law, I will conclude, is to be seen in the help that it provides in taking such choices as responsibly as possible.

Kelsen's doctrine of the unity of law—a defense

In this section, I want to discuss the claim that Kelsen's thesis of the necessary unity of national and international law depends on an untenable conception of the identity of legal system. Raz offers a reconstruction of the basic structure of Kelsen's theory of legal system that will be helpful for understanding the point of the criticism.[28] According to Raz, Kelsen's theory of legal system rests on two axioms:

1. *Two laws, one of which directly or indirectly authorizes the creation of the other, belong to the same legal system.*
2. *All the laws of a legal system are authorized directly or indirectly by one law.*

Raz goes on to make explicit two important theorems that derive from these axioms.

3. *If one law authorizes the creation of another or if both are authorized by a third law then both belong to the same legal system.*
4. *Two laws, neither of which authorizes the creation of the other, do not belong to the same system unless there is a law authorizing the creation of both.*

The first axiom introduces the idea of chains of validity (in Raz's terminology). Legal norms exist, in Kelsen's view, because they have been enacted in accordance with the procedural and substantive standards provided by higher order legal norms. Hence, we can construct chains of validity linking legal norms with the higher-order legal norms that directly or indirectly authorized their enactment. The second axiom claims that all chains of validity belonging to one legal system must stem from one single non-positive legal norm, the basic norm, that functions as a common ancestor of all norms belonging to the same legal system and that provides them all

---

[28] See Raz, 'Kelsen's Theory of the Basic Norm' (n 23 above) 122–7.

with normative force. Taken together, the two axioms provide a full criterion of the identity of a legal system. They allow us to determine whether any law belongs to a legal system or not.

Raz argues that Kelsen's framework fails as a theory of the identity/unity of legal system since it contains two separate flaws, relating to the first and second axiom respectively.[29] The first axiom entails theorem 3. But theorem 3 is false since the fact that two norms are linked by a chain of validity is insufficient to ensure that they form part of the same legal system. If theorem 3 is false, then so must be axiom 1. The second axiom entails theorem 4. However, theorem 4 is equally false, in Raz's view, since it is possible for two laws to belong to the same legal system even if there is no law authorizing the creation of both. If theorem 4 is false, so must be axiom 2 from which it derives. In what follows, I will look at the criticisms of both axioms in turn.

Chains of validity

Kelsen's first axiom claims that all norms belonging to one chain of validity belong to the same legal system. But it seems that there are obvious counterexamples to this view.[30] Suppose country A peacefully grants former colony B independence. In country B, a constitutional assembly, authorized by an act of A, then creates a new constitution, and this constitution, notwithstanding the prior grant of independence from A, is considered to give rise to a new and independent legal system. Members of the constitutional assembly, in the legal profession, and the wider public in B take the view that the validity of the norms of their national legal order no longer depends on the act of A that granted independence since the law granting independence is not considered to be a part of B's legal system.

Kelsen's theory of the identity of legal systems, it seems, cannot accommodate such a scenario. On Kelsen's view, as Hart and Raz interpret it, the legal system that has come into existence in B, since it is linked to the legal order in A by a chain of validity, must still be part of the legal system of A and the normative force of its norms must still depend on the constitution of A. But this result is patently absurd. The existence of a chain of validity linking two sets of legal norms, then, clearly cannot be sufficient for making them part of the same legal system.

The problems raised by the example are, of course, perfectly analogous to problems raised by the relation between national legal orders and international law. Let us assume that international law contains norms that purport to authorize national legal orders, such as norms governing the recognition of states and determining their spheres of authority.[31] Would this fact be sufficient to establish that all national legal

[29] See ibid, 127–9. A fuller statement of these points is given in Raz, *The Concept of a Legal System* (n 23 above) 95–108. Both criticisms are anticipated in Hart, 'Kelsen's Doctrine of the Unity of Law' (n 23 above).

[30] See Joseph Raz, 'Kelsen's Theory of the Basic Norm' (n 23 above) 127–8; Hart, 'Kelsen's Doctrine of the Unity of Law' (n 23 above) 319.

[31] See Kelsen, *Principles of International Law* (n 14 above) 212–16 on the principle of effectiveness in international law.

orders form dependent parts of one single international legal system and that the validity of all national law depends on international law? Hart assumes that Kelsen is indeed committed to such a view.[32] But it would surely seem that an affirmative answer to this question is as untenable as the conclusion that B's legal system is still part of A's legal system. What we need to ask, therefore, is whether a proponent of the pure theory of law is really committed to the view that all national legal systems form dependent parts of international law merely because there are norms of international law purporting to regulate the recognition of states.

Oddly enough, Hart failed to take account of the fact that Kelsen's discussion of the relation between national and international law explicitly denies this view. Kelsen argues, to recall, that it is possible for a proponent of the pure theory to adopt either of two jurisprudential perspectives in conceiving of that relationship. He can, on the one hand assume the sovereignty or absolute normative independence of his own state's legal system and treat the most fundamental laws of the legal system of his own state as the content of a basic, non-derivative norm. It follows from adopting this perspective that norms of international law lack validity unless one's state has decided to adopt them into its own legal order. Alternatively, the legal theorist can take the view that international law grounds the validity of national law. Adopting this perspective means to postulate the existence of a basic norm of international law and to assume that the most general norms of the legal order of one's own state are valid only insofar as they are authorized by that norm.

Of course, the pure theory does not claim that legal theorists can bring a legal system into existence simply by deciding to postulate some basic norm or other. Kelsen argues that there are constraints of effectiveness that restrict the choice of basic norms available to the legal theorist.[33] Any justifiable choice of perspective will have to fit the pattern of interaction that is to be interpreted as the subject matter of legal regulation as well as possible; it ought to interpret as much behavior as possible as exhibiting conformity to law. Kelsen appears to assume, however, that this principle has no straightforward application when it comes to the relationship between national and international law. The reason for this is not hard to make out. The relations between states are stuck in a transitory stage between an international state of nature that would clearly fail to support the internationalist hypothesis on the one hand and a state of undeniable subjection of states to a binding international legal regulation (that would make nationalist monism unavailable) on the other. Constraints of efficiency, as a result, do not fully determine the jurisprudential perspective on international law.

This analysis is clearly pertinent to the situation Raz describes in his example. Constraints of efficiency are unlikely to force a legal theorist in B to afford any legal significance to the historical fact that the parliament of A presumed to authorize

[32] See Hart, 'Kelsen's Doctrine of the Unity of Law' (n 23 above) 318.
[33] See Kelsen, *Introduction to the Problems of Legal Theory* (n 2 above) 59–61; Kelsen, *Law and Peace in International Relations* (n 15 above) 14–16; Kelsen, 'Value Judgments in the Science of Law' in Kelsen, *What is Justice?* (n 17 above) 209–30, at 224–7.

the constitutional assembly in B, just as they are unable to force a nationalist to accept the view that the legal order of his own state is valid only because his state is recognized under international law. And once a jurisprudent in B adopts the perspective of absolute normative independence, the historical fact that the legislator in A enacted a law that granted B independence will be jurisprudentially irrelevant, in Kelsen's view, for describing the law of B from that perspective.

Kelsen is not committed, I conclude, to the claim that the fact that a law enacted by the legislator in A purports to authorize the constitutional legislator in B establishes that there is a chain of validity linking the legal systems of A and B. Purported chains of validity, in Kelsen's view, possess legal significance only on the basis of a prior choice for one or another particular legal perspective. And it may well turn out that a number of different choices will live up to threshold requirements of effectiveness, and thus be jurisprudentially viable, even while they deny, from their point of view, the existence of chains of validity that would be taken to exist from some other point of view. Hence, citizens and officials in B are free to embrace the pure theory of law and to choose to adopt the perspective of absolute independence. And if they do, that choice will deny legal relevance to what Hart called the 'relationship of validating purport' linking B's legal system to A's.[34]

This reply to the first criticism, however, seems to be open to a decisive challenge. One might argue that the Kelsenian in B will be able to avoid the conclusion that B's legal system is part of A's legal system only if he chooses to affirm the absolute normative independence of B's legal system. But this affirmation inevitably comes at the price of a denial of the supremacy of international law. The reply I have given, one might therefore suspect, in effect concedes Hart's point that legal norms of whatever kind can have validity in B only in virtue of their recognition as valid by B's citizens and, more importantly, its legal officials.

This criticism overlooks that Kelsenians in B need not adopt the perspective of absolute normative independence to avoid the conclusion that B's legal system is part of A's. They have the further option to adopt the cosmopolitan perspective according to which both the legal system of B and the legal system of A are parts of an encompassing international legal system. Such a move makes the assumption of absolute normative independence unavailable since the cosmopolitan perspective claims that the international legal system is in exclusive possession of the attribute of absolute normative independence. But internationalism does not therefore force us into a denial of the *political independence* of B.

It would be perfectly possible for the citizens and officials of B to adopt the view that their legal system is a part of the international legal system—and that it consequently lacks absolute normative independence—without having to accept that it is a part of the legal system of their former colonial power A. Once jurists in B adopt an internationalist perspective, they can rely on the principle of effectiveness

---

[34] The solution is equally applicable to Hart's example of the 'Soviet Laws Validity Act'. See Hart, 'Kelsen's Doctrine of the Unity of Law' (n 23 above) 319.

and make the claim that their political community is to be recognized as independent, as being immediately subject to international law (but not to any other state), since it has achieved effective control of a certain territory. Reliance on this principle would make the relationship of validating purport between the law of A that granted independence and the legal system of B as irrelevant to the validity of the laws of B as would the adoption of the perspective of absolute normative independence. The Kelsenian is therefore not forced to concede Hart's doctrine of recognition under the guise of nationalist monism in order to avoid the conclusion that B's laws take their validity from a law of A's.

The thrust of my argument can be summed up as follows. Raz's example fails to establish that Kelsen's theorem 3 and, by implication, his first axiom should be regarded as false. Kelsenians can reasonably dispute the claim that they have been offered an example of a chain of validity that links two legal systems which are clearly distinct. Both those who would assume the perspective of absolute normative independence as well as those who would embrace Kelsenian internationalism can deny, in different ways, that the authority of the constitution of B rests on a law of A. Kelsen's theory of delegation, then, does not necessarily lead to the counterintuitive conclusions Hart and Raz impute to it.

The principle of common origin

The second criticism against the pure theory's account of the identity of legal system attacks the second of Kelsen's two 'axioms', namely the view that all the laws that belong to one legal system must depend on one and the same basic norm. Let us now turn to an assessment of this second criticism.

Raz imagines 'a legally minded *observer*' coming to a country that has a written constitution but that also acknowledges the validity of customary law not based on the written constitution.[35] The legally minded observer then asks himself whether the customary law and the law based on the written constitution form part of the same legal system or not. Kelsen, Raz observes, will refer such a question to the theory of the basic norm: Since neither set of norms depends on the other, and since there is no further positive law from which both derive, the answer will turn on whether there is one basic norm authorizing both the customary law and the written constitution (as well as the laws that depend on it) or not. But this referral to the basic norm, according to Raz, leads into an empty circle.[36] To identify the content of the basic norm, Kelsen claims, we have to look at 'the facts through which an order is created and applied'.[37] But as Raz points out, this means that we already have to know which norms form part of the legal system to determine the content of the basic norm. The legally minded observer will consequently be at a loss to answer the question whether both the customary and the written law he observes

[35] See Raz, 'Kelsen's Theory of the Basic Norm' (n 23 above) 128–9.
[36] Raz, *The Concept of Legal System* (n 23 above) 102.
[37] Hans Kelsen, *General Theory of Law and State*, translated by Anders Wedberg (New York, 1961) 120.

to be effective in the society he is investigating form part of the same legal system or not by having recourse to the basic norm. The theory of the basic norm, therefore, fails as an account of the identity of legal systems.

In order to answer questions of identity, Raz argues, we must look directly to 'the facts through which an order is created and applied'. In order to determine the identity of legal systems, our legally minded observer must focus on the institutions that authoritatively apply the law, in particular to courts as the primary law-applying institutions. If he can observe that both customary legal norms and enacted laws are applied by the same courts we can conclude that they form part of the same legal system without invoking the principle of common origin.[38]

The relevance of this criticism for the general question at hand should be obvious. According to the institutionalist view of the identity of legal system just outlined, a legal system with a determinate identity can exist only once there is a system of courts such that all and only the norms recognized by these courts form part of the legal system. However, as Kelsen himself recognizes, there seem to be no international law-applying institutions whose practices of recognition could provide a comprehensive standard of this kind for the identification of international law. Hence, the institutionalist concludes, the Kelsenian claim that a cosmopolitan interpretation of international law is already available to jurisprudence must be rejected. Kelsen's position, then, will fail to raise any challenge to the institutionalist view if the principle of common origin is indeed indefensible. The reason is simple. In the absence of an international practice of recognition, the principle of common origin is the only basis for making the claim that an international legal system already exists.

Kelsen, I suspect, might have been tempted to give the following reply to the second criticism. Raz clearly assumes that the legally minded observer is in a position to ascertain that both sets of norms his example talks about are, in one way or another, valid legal norms for the society he observes. According to the pure theory of law, it is an a priori truth that customary law and statute cannot fail to belong to the same legal system if they are both valid law.[39] Whether custom and statute form part of the same legal system or whether there are two legal systems in force in the observed society, therefore, could never be an open question for a Kelsenian legally minded observer once it is admitted that both have legal quality. Accordingly, it makes no sense to criticize Kelsen for not providing a criterion that can serve to answer this question.

I have already expressed my agreement with the view that these claims cannot be defended as necessary conditions of coherent jurisprudential thought. Let me therefore try to provide an alternative account of the possible motivations for a monist conception of law, by relying once more on our fictional protagonist, the Kelsenian law-abiding person. Her primary interest would be to ascertain what

---

[38] See Raz, *The Concept of a Legal System* (n 23 above) 89–97.
[39] See Kelsen, *Introduction to the Problems of Legal Theory* (n 2 above) 111–25.

the law requires, in the community in question, what someone ought to do on the assumption that she aims to be a law-abiding member of that community, either as a citizen or as a judge or some other kind of official. Accordingly, the question of the identity of a legal system can be relevant only insofar as it bears on answering the question of what one ought to do as a law-abiding citizen; it can have no theoretical interest, for the law-abiding person, independent of her normative query.

If the law-abiding person finds, from an empirical point of view, that both customary norms and legislated norms are considered to be valid law by large groups of members of society, she will naturally hypothesize that she ought, as a law-abiding member of society, to comply with both. But this hypothesis commits her to the task of constructing an interpretation of legal order that shows both the customary and the enacted norms to be parts of the same legal system. If both customary and enacted norms are assumed to be valid law in the community in question, law-abidingness requires her to act or to decide in conformity with customary as well as enacted law. But if the aim of law-abidingness is to be meaningful, it must be possible to comply with both. This claim does not rule out the possibility of prima facie conflicts between two norms belonging to the same legal system. However, the legal system must necessarily possess the resources to dissolve any such apparent conflict.

Practically speaking, this is saying that it has to be possible—from the perspective of a citizen who wants to figure out what he is objectively obliged to by the law, or from the perspective of a judge charged with applying general legal norms— to find solutions to whatever conflicts may occur between the customary and the enacted norms by relying on some higher-order rule of precedence, for example on the principle that custom binds only where enacted law is silent or that there are certain fundamental customary laws that cannot be abrogated by legislation. Whoever holds on to the idea that both custom and statute are binding must hold that it is in principle possible to respect both as such in one's behavior. As a consequence, he must be entitled to presume a content of the basic norm that makes joint conformity possible. Any such presumption, however, will make both custom and statute normatively coordinated parts of the same hierarchy of norms. The question whether there is one or whether there are two legal systems, then, can never become a question for the law-abiding person.

Needless to say, this reply to Raz's second criticism gives rise to some serious worries. First, the reply might be accused of simply begging the question against the Razian objection. To claim that there must be a possibility to conform to both the rules of custom and statute because both are valid law is just another way of saying, it seems, that we already know that both custom and statute form part of the same legal system. If they did not, the requirement of the possibility of joint conformity could not be raised. But whether both custom and statutory law indeed form part of the same legal system is precisely what is at issue here. We therefore need an independent criterion to settle the question of identity before we can make any appeal to the demand for the possibility of joint conformity.

Second, the line of argument in the reply of course entails the Kelsenian view that jurisprudence is unable to acknowledge the existence of a plurality of legal systems. The Kelsenian legal theorist asks what we ought to do, on the assumption that we want to be law-abiding. This question, as Kelsen himself emphasizes, is always asked from the perspective of a particular legal system. All law that bears on answering the question, as asked from the perspective of some legal system, must belong to that same legal system. What is more, rules that, for whatever reason, are understood not to bear on the question of what law-abidingness requires are not just taken not to belong to the legal system whose perspective we assume. Rather, they must be denied legal quality altogether since the question of what law exists, in the mode of validity, is a normative question. But this view, one might object, is simply crazy (and also unmotivated). We know that there could be several different legal systems. We also know that there in fact are several different legal systems. What could possibly be more obvious?

Both worries stem from a common source. Clearly, the claim that both custom and statute are law in the observed society is open to a rather different interpretation than I have so far given it. It need not mean more than that both sets of norms enjoy a certain degree of effectiveness and that the attitudes of sufficient numbers of members of society towards both exhibit enough of the features that usually characterize the recognition of some social rule as a rule of law to allow us to classify both customary and statutory rules as legal rules in some descriptive sense. Under this reading, the claim that both custom and statute are valid law need not entail that anyone ought to consider both custom and statute as a binding standard of behavior or that it must be possible to exhibit joint conformity to both.

A variant of Raz's example will help to assess the force of this objection. Let us assume the observed society is divided into two opposed camps, the 'customarians' and the 'statutists'. The customarians do not merely believe that custom takes precedence over statute wherever both conflict. They take it, rather, that the whole system of statutory law is an altogether illegitimate abrogation of the ancient freedom that is their inalienable birthright. Statute, according to the customarians, has no legal force, despite the fact that the statutists mistakenly believe so. The statutists, in turn, do not simply claim that statute abrogates custom wherever both conflict. Rather, they believe that the 'ancient constitution' is nothing but an incoherent and mostly obnoxious hodgepodge of outdated superstitions that lack all legal force since it was superseded by the written constitution and the laws that depend on it. Let us assume, finally, that there is no third group that takes a mediating view between customarians and statutists.

The likely result of this situation will be institutional separation between customarian and statutist legal institutions, both characterized by different practices of recognition. Now clearly, there is a sense in which the question whether our society has one or two legal systems might meaningfully be asked. What is more, an institutional criterion of identity will give us what must indisputably be the right answer to this question, namely that there are indeed two legal systems. Kelsen, however, seems to be committed, by empty definitional fiat, to the view that there is really only one.

Once again, we have to ask whether Kelsen is really forced to accept this unpalatable conclusion. The answer would appear to be negative. As I pointed out above, the law-abiding person would certainly start out from the hypothesis that two sets of laws that are considered to be valid law by large groups of members of society are both valid and therefore parts of the same legal system. But this assumption is defeasible even on Kelsenian grounds. Kelsen claims that any legal system, in order to exist, has to be effective to some degree. It is therefore a necessary condition for attributing validity to both custom and statute that both be effective. What is more, both will have to be effective with respect to the same group of subjects. Hence, the hypothesis that both custom and statute are valid would be defeated, in our example, by considerations of effectiveness, by the total absence of members of society who exhibit fidelity to both custom and statute.

The law-abiding person, then, will unavoidably have to adopt either the customarian or the statutarian point of view. It will of course be possible to claim, from an external point of view, that she is legally entitled to do something according to custom that she does not have a legal right to do according to statute. But such a claim does not tell her what she is legally entitled to do. And from either of the two points of view she might adopt to figure out what she is legally entitled to do, either custom or statute will turn out to lack legal force. Admittedly, none of this disproves an external observer who claims that there are two legal systems, despite the fact that all members of society, once they adopt the perspective of law-abidingnesss, will believe that there is only one. But to insist on this point, it seems to me, involves a change of subject that the Kelsenian is entitled to reject, unless there are independent reasons to establish that a legal theory based on the perspective of law-abidingness cannot be valuable or meaningful. I conclude that the Kelsenian denial of the existence of several legal systems is not as implausible as it might appear at first glance.

This still leaves us with the complaint that Kelsen is begging the question for unity. This complaint can be disarmed in much the same way as the craziness objection. Sociological disunity can be modeled in a Kelsenian framework as non-recognition of custom from the statutarian point of view and of statute from the customarian point of view. In the situation of total opposition between defenders of customary law and defenders of statute, considerations of effectiveness would, as we have seen, quickly force a law-abiding person to embrace either the customarian or the statutist perspective. But this puts us in much the same position, for all practical intents and purposes, we would arrive at if we relied on practice-based criteria to delimit identity of legal systems.

More interesting than our example of total separation, however, are instances of disagreement, amongst members of a society and its legal practitioners, including its judges, about whether there is a normative relation between custom and statute and about the exact form of that relation. It is imaginable, for instance, that some members of a society or of its legal elites will believe, while others will deny, that both statute and custom are binding. It is likewise imaginable that all members in a society agree that both statute and custom are binding while they disagree over the nature of the normative relationship between both. It is here (where practice-based or institutional criteria fail to provide clear-cut answers to the question of the nature of the normative relationship between custom and statute) that the law-abiding person is likely to adopt a position that will differ practically from that taken by defenders of a practice-based or an institutional criterion of identity.

At least as long as considerations of effectiveness do not clearly defeat the hypothesis of unity, the stance of the law-abiding person will inevitably be biased towards interpreting the widest possible set of effective social rules as parts of one legal system. The law-abiding person will be in a position to deny a rule membership in the legal system whose perspective she adopts only by denying its legal quality altogether. But since she is presumably interested in the power-constraining effects of increasing legalization she will avoid that conclusion wherever possible. Inevitably, the law-abiding person will base her judgments about the structure of legal order on hypotheses that cannot be cashed out fully in terms of sociological observation. But it is not all that clear, once we adopt the perspective of law-abidingness, whether it is fair to say that this stance begs the question for unity. The charge presupposes agreement on the point that a satisfactory account of the identity of legal system must be one that appeals to purely descriptive criteria (and implicitly to a restrictive understanding of the scope of legal order). The pure theory, however, rejects this assumption rather more consciously, it seems to me, than its critics realize. The question must be, then, whether it has good reasons to do so.

The situation described in Raz's example is analogous to the situation that obtains in the choice between a nationalist and an internationalist perspective on the relation between domestic and international law. In both cases, an identification of the law, as Kelsen himself admits, will require a choice of perspective that is not itself determined by considerations of effectiveness or by the positive content of the law and that will express normative ideals or ideological predispositions. In one sense, admittedly, this is just another way of saying that Raz's second criticism is well-justified. The choice for any perspective will be a choice for assuming one basic norm and not another, which means, of course, that appeal to a basic norm cannot guide the choice of perspective. Raz is right, therefore, to observe that the theory of the basic norm is a failure on the assumption that its aim is to provide us with a descriptive criterion of the identity of legal system.

What I have been concerned to argue is that this observation does not suffice to settle the fate of a Kelsenian theory of legal system. The pure theory's account of the identity of legal system, even while incompatible with standard positivist assumptions about the nature and function of such an account, is not obviously incoherent or implausible and it does not lead to the absurd conclusions that critics have imputed to it. The criticism of Kelsen's monism therefore leads us back to a wider disagreement between Kelsenians and positivists about the nature of jurisprudence: namely to the claim that Kelsen has no good reason to privilege the perspective of normative questions about the law, and hence of the construction of the widest possible unity, over a purely descriptive stance.

I will return to the question whether Kelsen has a good reason to privilege the perspective of normative questions about the law, in the context of a theory of international law, when I address the second of the two criticisms I outlined in the introduction to this chapter. Before we turn to this issue, I must say a few things about Kelsen's conception of the purpose and structure of legal order in general and of international legal order in particular. The adoption of a normative perspective that forces us into a monist conception of the relation between national and international legal order will have a point only if an effective global legal order forms a morally meaningful ideal and if its realization is practically feasible without endangering the political independence of the states subject to it.

On the viability of legal cosmopolitanism

Kelsen's clearest statements about the normative purpose of legal order are to be found in some of his works on international law and international legal reform that were written in the 1940s. The 1940–41 Oliver Wendell Holmes Lectures *Law and Peace in International Relations* are a case in point:

Law is, essentially, an order for the promotion of peace. Its purpose is to assure the peaceful living together of a group of individuals in such a manner that they may settle their conflicts in a peaceful manner; that is, without the use of force, in conformity with an order valid for all.[40]

This ringing proclamation would surprise any reader of Kelsen's key legal-theoretical works. But it nevertheless fits in well with his general account of legal order. The claim that a legal order is essentially a regulation of the use of force is implicit in Kelsen's account of the structure of legal norms. As we have seen, what characterizes a norm as a legal norm, according to Kelsen, is the fact that it lays down the conditions under which coercive force ought to be applied against a member of society.[41] As I pointed out in Chapter 2.I, a basic norm does not just require that coercive force ought to be applied in accordance with the norms validated by it. It also determines that it is impermissible to apply coercive force on any other basis. Wherever a legal order exists, all use of force is therefore *automatically* either a delict or an authorized sanction. No legal order could fail to claim a monopoly of force and to sanction all unauthorized violence since its essential purpose is to secure

---

[40] Hans Kelsen, *Law and Peace in International Relations* (n 15 above) 1. See also Kelsen, *Peace Through Law* (n 15 above) 3 and Kelsen, *Principles of International Law* (n 14 above) 17–18. It should be mentioned that, in the second edition of the *Pure Theory of Law*, Kelsen retracted the claim. See Hans Kelsen, *Reine Rechtslehre. Zweite, vollständig neu bearbeitete und erweiterte Auflage* (Wien, 1960) 38–41.

[41] See Kelsen, *Introduction to the Problems of Legal Theory* (n 2 above) 26.

peace.[42] The prohibition of unauthorized uses of force implicit in any basic norm, in turn, grounds the law's completeness. Once a legal system exists—however rudimentary its body of positive norms—all social disputes are therefore amenable to legal decision.[43]

The question whether cosmopolitan monism is a viable or meaningful interpretation of the practices we call 'international law' depends on whether Kelsen's general conception of legal order is applicable to these practices. In particular, it depends on the question whether it is possible to attribute a monopoly of force to the system of rules that go by the name of 'international law'.

A positive answer would require us to interpret all use of force between states as being either criminal or as being an instance of law-enforcement, of the application of sanctions for a prior breach of law. At first glance, this claim hardly appears to be convincing. As Hedley Bull pointed out, Kelsen's attempt to hold on to the Hobbesian idea that the law is necessarily claiming a monopoly of force appears to put him in a particularly bad position to establish the legal quality of international law. The view that international law claims a monopoly of force, Bull claims, 'strains against the facts'. There is no general agreement among states to treat all use of force either as a crime or as a sanction. Kelsen's defense of international law, as a result, amounts to little more than 'wishful thinking'.[44]

The claim that 'there is no general agreement in treating acts of force as either a delict or a sanction', however, is hardly uncontroversial. The Kelsenian can point out that the idea appears to have found a firm foothold in positive international law, through the UN Charter which issues a clear prohibition of the use of force or the threat of the use of force as a means of politics.[45] It is true enough that the principle is at times honored only in the breach. But this is true, the Kelsenian might reply, even of legal orders that undoubtedly do claim a monopoly of legitimate force and whose claims are universally recognized as successful.

On a more principled level, Kelsen claims that international law can be interpreted as a primitive legal order.[46] A primitive legal order is a legal order that possesses no specialized institutions of adjudication and of law-enforcement but whose subjects nevertheless accept the principle that they are entitled to use force against others

---

[42] Kelsen, *Law and Peace in International Relations* (n 15 above) 12: 'Law is an organization of force: the law attaches certain conditions to the use of force in relations among men. It authorizes the employment of force, acts of coercion, only by certain individuals and only under certain circumstances. The law allows, under certain circumstances, conduct which under all other circumstances is "forbidden", or, in other words, is the very condition for similar conduct on the part of another as a sanction. The individual who, authorized by the legal order, applies the coercive measure—the sanction—acts as the organ of this order or of the community constituted thereby. Only this individual, only the organ of the community, is authorized to employ force. Hence, one may say that the law makes the use of force a monopoly of the community. And precisely by so doing, law insures peace to the community.'

[43] See the discussion of Kelsen's conception of legal order in Chapter 2.I below, at 42–3.

[44] Bull, 'Hans Kelsen and International Law' (n 5 above) 329.

[45] See Kelsen, *Principles of International Law* (n 14 above) 44–64.

[46] See Kelsen, *Introduction to the Problems of Legal Theory* (n 2 above) 108–9; Kelsen, *Law and Peace in International Relations* (n 15 above) 48–55.

only in reaction to prior breaches of the law on the part of others. The ascertainment of a breach of law, under such conditions, falls to each individual subject of the law and the enforcement of the law takes place by way of self-help. A primitive legal order, needless to say, is deficient with respect to the purpose of securing peace, as it lacks a centralized adjudicative power and a centralized mechanism of enforcement. However, a primitive legal order, Kelsen argues, is a genuine legal system to which his formal notion of completeness would be applicable.[47]

In support of Kelsen's interpretation of international law as primitive law, one could point to the undeniable fact that states rarely engage in the use of force without offering some kind of justification that looks suspiciously like the kind of justification we ought to expect them to offer if Kelsen's claims held true. One of the main planks of the tradition of just war theorizing, after all, consists in the idea that a war is justifiable only as a reaction to a violation of a state's rights. So it may not be altogether implausible to claim, even apart from pointing to positive international law, that states tend to recognize the principle that use of force is legitimate only if it takes the form of the application of a sanction against the breach of a rule of international law.

Once we have reached this point, it is not too difficult to take the argument a step further. Once states recognize the principle that use of force is legitimate only if it takes the form of the application of a sanction against the breach of a rule of international law, Kelsen argues, they can no longer reasonably object to the institution of a compulsory system of impartial international adjudication empowered to decide all disputes among states.[48] After all, they would already have given up the power to use force according to their own discretion in accepting the law's monopoly of force. The introduction of a binding system of international adjudication that remedies the deficiencies of a primitive legal order will not introduce anything new into the subjection to the law itself. Since the law is formally complete all disputes among states are decidable on a legal basis, so there can be no reasonable objection against treating all conflicts among states as legal disputes amenable to adjudicative solutions.

On the other hand, the undeniable deficiencies of a primitive legal order entail that a refusal to submit to international adjudication would carry the risk of frustrating

---

[47] The claim that international law is a primitive legal order also informs Kelsen's treatment of normative consistency between international and national law. Kelsen refrains from arguing that national law that violates international law is null if it is not voidable (as it usually is not). The primary guarantee of legality on the international level, rather, is the collective punishment by means of war and reprisal that states inflict on each other in reaction to perceived violations of international law. (See Kelsen, *Introduction to the Problems of Legal Theory* [n 2 above] 117–19.) However, Kelsen emphasizes that this situation is nothing but a contingent defect of legality and that there is no legal-theoretical reason to think that international law could not apply directly to individuals and offer guarantees of legality that do away with collective punishment. The realization of an international legal order directly applying to individuals can be interpreted as a second step in the creation of a global utopia of legality that should follow the establishment of international peace between states.

[48] See Kelsen, *Law and Peace in International Relations* (n 15 above) 145–70 and Kelsen, *Peace through Law* (n 15 above) 13–34.

the purposes of the initial commitment to the rule of law in international affairs we can already attribute to states. Hence, a state cannot permanently refuse to submit to a compulsory scheme of international adjudication without casting doubt on its commitment to the rule of law and to the value of peace. If Kelsen's interpretation of international law as a primitive legal system possesses at least some degree of plausibility, Bull's observation that there is no universal recognition of a monopoly of force of international law is no longer easily distinguishable from an active act of non-recognition of this monopoly. But such an act of non-recognition can no longer be justified by an appeal to the idea that international law isn't real or proper law once we find ourselves in a situation where the willingness to give recognition would suffice to motivate institutional reforms that would heal the deficiencies resulting from international law's primitive nature.

We need to take into account one further complication, though. The argument for a compulsory scheme of international adjudication presented so far does not sit well with Kelsen's general account of adjudication. Kelsen, as we have seen, explicitly rejects the claim that a system of general positive legal norms could fully and precisely determine the legal meaning of all particular acts in advance of judicial proceedings. A judge who decides a particular case is legislating for a particular case. Such judicial legislation takes place within procedural and substantive boundary conditions set by higher-order norms, but these conditions always leave the judge with a sphere of discretion within which he has to *decide* the case.

This anti-formalist picture of adjudication would seem to imply that a primitive or non-institutionalized legal system must lack the essential property of completeness. Absent a judge empowered to take authoritative applicative decisions, every individual member of a primitive society would have to take on the office of enacting particular norms. But there would be no guarantee for the norms so enacted to be consistent with each other. Neither would we be in a position, in cases of disagreement, to say that someone must have made a mistake. The distinction between being authorized by the law to use force and authorizing oneself to use force, and hence the basis for the claim that all uses of force on the part of state must either be crimes or sanctions, would inevitably collapse. The existence of a complete legal order, it seems, presupposes the existence of a unified hierarchy of courts empowered to determine authoritatively the legal meaning of any particular act.

This reading of completeness, of course, threatens Kelsen's argument for a binding and obligatory scheme of international adjudication. If general legal norms do not determine their applicative instances, subjection to the authority of courts *will* add something new to the subjection to the law as a system of general rules identified by a consensus on the sources of law. Courts will inevitably take 'political' decisions that are not fully contained in already recognized law and only in their doing so will the law's claim to completeness be realized. Hence, subjects of the law would seem to be in a position coherently to claim that they are committed to observance of a set of recognized rules while rejecting unconditional submission to binding adjudication.

I do not believe that this challenge need undercut the cosmopolitan project. If a state accepts the view that the fundamental purpose of legal order, dependent on the law's monopoly of force, is to secure peace, and if it agrees that legal peace is an attractive ideal the realization of which should take precedence, at least to some extent, over other aims of policy, there would seem to be no reason for that state not to allow for some indifference in legal content from the beginning. Since the state in question is committed to the overriding value of peace, it will have a prima facie reason to submit to any legal system that brings about peace, even if it is not perfectly happy with that system's substantive provisions. But if the commitment to the value of peace makes it reasonable to live with a system whose substantive provisions one does not consider perfectly reasonable, one should have no additional problem with accepting a certain amount of discretionary authority of courts that authoritatively apply the law and thus secure the law's completeness; at least not as long as one can be reasonably assured of the independence and impartiality of those courts.[49]

Once we accept this perspective, Kelsen's argument for the introduction of obligatory and binding adjudication can be salvaged in a modified form. It is true that the claim to completeness can be sustained only through partly discretionary exercises of authority on the part of courts. But this is not a special defect of international law; rather, it is a general truth about any kind of legal order. It is therefore quite appropriate to claim that if a primitive legal system fails to create solutions to all particular disputes, this failure is due exclusively to the lack of acceptance for authoritative adjudicative institutions, and not to a lack of clarity or comprehensiveness in the law's substantive content or to an unusual degree of disagreement about its meaning.[50] A refusal to accept authoritative adjudicative institutions, in turn, is likely to be a based on a refusal to recognize the importance of the value that motivates the law's claim to completeness. An unwillingness to submit to a binding scheme of international arbitration, at least as long as that scheme is not catastrophically unjust, cannot credibly be combined with a professed commitment to legal peace.

This line of argument underpins Kelsen's view that the *civitas maxima* requires an international court endowed with the power of compulsory arbitration in all disputes amongst states.[51] Kelsen emphasizes that such a court is to be preferred to a political institution staffed by representatives of states, as a guardian of international legality, as it could be organized in a way that would ensure its independence from any of the parties to a dispute. In fact, throughout the first half of the

---

[49] This line of argument is inspired by Kelsen, 'Wer soll der Hüter der Verfassung sein?' in Hans Klecatsky, René Marcić, and Herbert Schambeck (eds), *Die Wiener rechtstheoretische Schule. Ausgewählte Schriften von Hans Kelsen, Adolf Merkl, Alfred Verdross* (Wien, 1968), vol II, 1873–922, at 1883.

[50] One cannot, then, dismiss Kelsen's theory of international law as 'wishful thinking' merely by pointing out that 'it is not the case that there is normally agreement in international society as to which side in an international armed conflict represents the law-breaker and which the law-enforcer'. See Hedley Bull, 'Hans Kelsen and International Law' (n 5 above) 329.

[51] See Kelsen, *Peace Through Law* (n 15 above).

1940s Kelsen made institutional proposals for the post-war establishment of an international court that aimed to secure a maximal distance of judges from any political power, in particular from their own states of origin.[52] Kelsen's reasons to favor the institution of an international court echo his defense of constitutional adjudication. Judicial independence will allow the court to act more impartially, in conflicts between states, than we could expect a political institution to act.[53] Kelsen's talk about judicial impartiality, of course, is not to be understood as an affirmation of the view that the court would never have to take 'political' decisions that are not fully determined by already existing law. Rather, the idea is clearly that judicial independence will maximize the prospects of equitable decision-making. The objectivity of international law, just like the objectivity of constitutional law, ultimately turns out to rest on the availability of judicial guarantees of legality.

Can Kelsen make room for a plausible notion of political independence compatible with the form of subjection to international law that the ideal of legal peace requires of states? I believe the answer has to be 'yes'. Kelsen's argument, as presented here, makes the claim that a prohibition of the legally unauthorized use of force is a necessary element of any legal order. International law could not fail to contain this rule and still be 'real law'. Kelsen's legal cosmopolitanism further requires that all possible conflicts amongst states be subjected to compulsory international adjudication in an independent international court. But this is all, Kelsen believes, that is needed to speak of the existence of a *civitas maxima*. Legal cosmopolitanism, so understood, certainly need not conflict with the equal enjoyment of political independence by states.

The rule against legally unauthorized coercive acts is by now so widely recognized in positive international law that the claim of its necessary incompatibility with the independence of states has lost any shred of plausibility.[54] The requirement of compulsory international adjudication of all possible disputes amongst states might seem more problematic. Independence is often associated with a highly voluntarist understanding of international law according to which states cannot be legally bound against their own will. Kelsen makes two critical observations about such an understanding of international law.[55]

First, the idea that states cannot be legally bound against their own will amounts to a denial of the very existence of a legal order if it is understood in a radically sovereigntist sense, as implying that states have a legitimate power to decide whether or not to honor their obligations under international law. If we understand the idea in a weaker sense, as claiming that states can acquire obligations only with their consent, states will, at the very least, be bound to their own earlier declarations of will, even if they would prefer not to be so bound, through the rule *pacta sunt*

---

[52] See ibid, 127–40.   [53] See ibid, 48.

[54] Note that I am not claiming here that the rule is morally justifiable or that there couldn't be any reasons for advocating its abandonment. My claim here is only that it does not conflict with political independence.   [55] See Kelsen, *Peace Through Law* (n 15 above) 38–45.

servanda. That states are bound only by their own consent entails that they have a greater power to prevent changes in the legal status quo than they would enjoy in a politically more centralized legal order. But this fact does not make their obligations any less binding than the obligations of subjects of a less consensual legal order.

Second, Kelsen emphasizes that we cannot consider the relatively voluntarist character of international law, as expressed in the idea that states can acquire obligations only through their consent, as a necessary consequence of essential and inalienable attributes of sovereignty or statehood. Rather, the rules that make for the relatively voluntarist character of international law are to be considered as rules of positive international law open to change. The legal power of states to enter into binding agreements includes the legal power to subject themselves to a system of compulsory adjudication and permanently to abdicate the power to act on their own understanding of the requirements of international law.

The claim that, in doing so, states would alienate their political independence seems to have little going for it once it is stripped of its support from sovereigntist rhetoric. States that subject themselves to compulsory international adjudication exercised by an independent court do not thereby submit to the authority of any other political community. And since the court is primarily a law-applying institution, states that subject themselves to its authority, Kelsen suggests, will thereby acquire only such obligations as they should previously have been prepared to recognize. While the concretization of the law through the decisions of the court will inevitably be a partly creative process, the independence of the court will provide reasonable assurance of the impartiality and equitability of its decisions. The scheme as a whole, then, is likely to be the best protection of the formal equality of states, especially since it neutralizes the use of force or the threat thereof as an instrument of policy.

This thumbnail sketch of Kelsen's conception of international legal order should suffice to establish that Kelsenian legal cosmopolitanism is a meaningful ideal. If an international legal order that successfully claims a monopoly of legitimate force will directly serve the value of peace, the moral attractiveness of legal cosmopolitanism should be obvious. This moral attractiveness, what is more, would seem to provide a rationale for the view that a rejection of legal cosmopolitanism will have to bear a special burden of justification. Let us now see, on this basis, how well legal cosmopolitanism can withstand direct normative criticism.

The moral relevance of Kelsen's legal cosmopolitanism

I now return to the second of the general criticisms of Kelsen's theory of international law I outlined in the introductory section to this chapter. According to that criticism, Kelsen wrongly claims that we must choose between a wholesale denial of international law and an affirmation of legal cosmopolitanism because monism is the only way to conceive of national as well as international law as coexisting forms of law. The choice Kelsen wants to force puts the burden of argument on those who would reject the legal cosmopolitan project. But Kelsen's own admission that nationalist monism is a viable jurisprudential option, and his claim that the choice between nationalism and cosmopolitanism is a political and not a jurisprudential matter, betrays an inability or unwillingness to offer a substantive defense of his implicit preference for cosmopolitanism. Such a defense, however, is clearly needed if Kelsen's conception of legal system cannot be defended on purely scientific grounds.

I believe we are now in a position to rebut this charge, by relying on our analysis of the ideal of legal cosmopolitanism in the previous section. On the assumption that a global legal order successfully claiming a monopoly of force would serve the value of peace, Kelsen's attempt to force a choice between nationalist and cosmopolitan monism makes good moral sense. That a global legal order would serve the value of peace (and do so in a way that protects rather than eliminates the independence of and equality among states) will entail that states, other things being equal, ought to be held to a duty to support the growth of such an order. The relation between legal order and non-hegemonic peace explains why jurisprudence has good reason to put the burden of proof on those who intend to embrace nationalist monism. Legal cosmopolitanism is a choice that is explicable, or justifiable, on the basis of a value internal to legal order while the choice for nationalist monism will have to be defended on the basis of values external to the ideal of legality.

However, the acknowledgment that legal cosmopolitanism is an attractive ideal does not entail that there can never be any good reasons not to commit to legal cosmopolitanism. Such reasons might arise, for example, from severe formal imperfections of international legal order that threaten the viability of the ideal of legal cosmopolitanism. A state committed to peace through law may find that a large majority of other states are not so committed, in which case the state in question could not reasonably hope to further the cause of international legality by acting on its commitment to legal peace. A state may also judge that there are overriding moral reasons against respecting international legality that arise from extreme moral imperfections in the content of the law. It seems reasonable, then, for Kelsen to claim that jurisprudence itself, even one that is trying to develop an understanding of law internally related to the value of peace, cannot conclusively bind a state to conceive of international legal order in cosmopolitan terms and consistently to act on that basis.

Reasons for unilateralism of the kind just outlined, however, are compatible with respect for the value of peace. They do not entail a rejection of the view that there ought to be a global legal order with a monopoly of force, if we can be assured that it will be reasonably effective and reasonably just in content. What is more, they do not involve the assumption that an international legal order possessing a monopoly of force is incompatible with independent statehood or the nature of international law. By contrast, genuine sovereigntist positions like Schmitt's will either make the incompatibility claim or else embrace an open rejection of the ideal of legal cosmopolitanism.

Kelsen claims that radical sovereigntists simply do not *want* to pay respect to international law and that they disguise this preference by claiming that international law necessarily differs in quality from municipal law.[56] In the light of the preceding analysis, we can reframe this charge as follows. If the incompatibility claim is unsound, the sovereigntist position, to have any meaning at all, must be taken to imply a rejection of the view that the ideal of legal peace is a morally attractive ideal. However, sovereigntists typically fail to offer a clear rationale for this rejection. Instead, they continue to argue that international law has a special nature that follows from the nature of the state or from the nature of sovereignty. In so doing, they both veil the fact that a legal cosmopolitan understanding of the relation between domestic and international law is perfectly available as well as the fact that their own position amounts to a form of active opposition to the realization of a global legal order. Kelsen's attempt to establish an exclusive alternative between nationalist monism and legal cosmopolitanism can be seen as an attempt to force sovereigntist deniers of international law to provide us with a substantive moral argument for their position.

It is difficult, indeed, to see where such an argument could come from. The early modern originators of sovereigntist thought agreed with the idea that the essential purpose of legal order is to secure peace, and they also agreed that the aim to create an order securing peace was an independently attractive and weighty goal that should preempt most other practical concerns. In contrast to Kelsen, they argued that a sovereign above the law, capable of legally unauthorized action, was necessary for the existence of legal order. This claim, of course, was meant to be perfectly general, to apply in the domestic sphere as much as internationally. However, there are very good reasons to reject the requirement of a legally unfettered sovereign in the domestic sphere. As we have seen, it is perfectly possible to apply strict principles of legality to a state without threatening the integrity of its legal order. Hence, sovereigntism in international law cannot be defended on the basis of a general thesis about the necessary requirements of legality. And if the ideal of legal cosmopolitanism is theoretically and practically viable, it cannot be defended on the basis of special claims about international legality either.

The latter day sovereigntist is left, then, with the task of explaining why legal peace on the international level would be undesirable. The only promising line of argument to such a conclusion seems to be the attempt to defend the claim that a legal cosmopolitan order is necessarily incompatible with political independence as an openly moral claim (and not as a claim about the nature of the state or the law). In order to make such an argument one will have to conceive of political independence in demanding enough a way to make it incompatible with subjection to a legal order claiming a monopoly of force. But any conception that is demanding enough is likely to be morally much more controversial than a view based on a theory about the indispensable requirements of peace and order.

---

[56] See Kelsen, *Introduction to the Problems of Legal Theory* (n 2 above) 124; Kelsen, *Principles of International Law* (n 14 above) 439.

Schmitt's view, as developed in *The Concept of the Political*, is a case in point. Schmitt argues that no political community could possibly be truly independent unless it possessed an unrestricted *ius ad bellum*.[57] An international order compatible with political independence of its member states would therefore have to be based on the recognition that states have a legitimate power to use coercive force as they see fit, and an order built on the *bellum justum* principle, of course, fails that test. I cannot enter into an extended discussion of this view here. Suffice it to say that we are certainly entitled to ask what moral ideas might plausibly motivate an understanding of political independence that declares an unrestricted *ius ad bellum* to be essential to independence.

One answer to this question that is prominent in Schmitt is based on the claim that the distinction between the rule of law and a rule of men is wholly illusory. Schmitt argues that legal norms fail to determine their applicative instances, at least unless the relation between legal rule and applicative instance is implicitly fixed by a homogeneous background culture such that the law expresses a shared cultural identity. However, once such a shared background culture is unavailable, as in the international sphere, an appeal to the ideal of the rule of law will be powerless to remedy the problem since it will fail to reconstitute a determinate relationship between legal rules and their applicative instances. Schmitt concludes that the authoritative application of conclusively binding international law will inevitably have to boil down to a form of discretionary governance exercised by those who have managed to identify their own interests with the cause of international law.[58] The idea of subjection to the law, according to this picture, is altogether empty. A state will either be self-determining—it will take the final decision whether to respect any norm of international law—or it will be subject, directly or indirectly, to the will of another state or group of states. It follows that any appeal to the distinction between a state of nature that is a state of war and a state of peace secured by law can be nothing more than a trick to bolster the indirect rule of those who benefit from the legal status quo.

Schmitt's claim that the contrast between a rule of law and a rule of men is meaningless is intended as a perfectly general claim. Hence, it is open to a Kelsenian reply that was developed earlier. It is wrong to assume that the ideal of the rule of law is dependent on a strong notion of legal determinacy. Rather, the ideal promises to ensure that disputes about the meaning of general rules and normative commitments, however political, are capable of being arbitrated in a way that is acceptable from the perspective of law-abidingness. To claim that this promise is meaningless is to claim that it is unreasonable to assume that there are values internal to legal order that could be brought to bear on political decisions through the right kind of institutional framework and the proper attitudes of citizens and officials. But Schmitt presents no argument for rejecting these assumptions. His claim that a

[57] See Schmitt, *Der Begriff des Politischen* (n 27 above) 45–54.
[58] See Carl Schmitt, 'Völkerrechtliche Formen des modernen Imperialismus' in Carl Schmitt, *Positionen und Begriffe im Kampf mit Weimar—Genf—Versailles, 1923–1939* (Berlin, 1994) 184–203.

system of international law endowed with a monopoly of force and with compulsory mechanisms for the arbitration of disputes amongst states could be nothing more than a vehicle of veiled hegemonic power is not the least bit more convincing, therefore, than his analogous domestic claim that there could be no legitimate constitutional adjudication.

In some moods, Schmitt declares any questioning of the normative basis of his conception of political independence to be flatly illegitimate. Political communities, we are informed, exist only insofar as they successfully claim the power to take the friend-enemy decision. To deny that political communities may legitimately draw this distinction as they see fit, therefore, amounts to a form of politicide.[59] This line of reasoning patently fails to explain why the existence of communities that have a power to take a friend-enemy decision as they see fit ought to be considered as something valuable. It is one thing to claim that individuals are ends in themselves, quite another to say that the same is true of political communities. And Schmitt provides no reasons, as far as I can see, for the rejection of the view that the value of a political community is instrumental, that it is to be judged in accordance with the ways in which it serves individual needs. So what value does complete normative independence, including an unrestricted *ius ad bellum*, have for individual members of a political community? Schmitt's answer consists in the rather controversial claim that a life not sweetened by the prospect of dying for the fatherland would be shallow and uninteresting.[60]

I conclude that the second major criticism of Kelsen's cosmopolitanism, the claim that the pure theory's account of international law expresses a disguised preference for cosmopolitanism that Kelsen is unwilling or unable to defend on moral ground, is unconvincing: at least in its Schmittian variant. Kelsen is right to argue that, given the viability of the ideal of legal cosmopolitanism, radical sovereigntists bear the burden of moral proof, since their position makes sense only once we take it to include a denial of the value of legal peace. Such denials are hard to defend convincingly. Kelsen's diagnosis that sovereigntists have a tendency to retreat instead to an unsustainable metaphysics of sovereignty is well taken.

However, Kelsen's conception of legal cosmopolitanism is subject to a more interesting and important normative criticism, discussion of which will take us back to the dispute between Hartian and Kelsenian understandings of legal system. The upshot of our earlier discussion of that dispute was that Kelsen's legal monism cannot be dismissed on the grounds that it leads to an obviously inadequate understanding of the identity of legal systems. But this result will hardly suffice to settle the dispute between a Hartian and a Kelsenian understanding of international law.

Hart, of course, goes along with Kelsen's attack on the dogma of sovereignty. He agrees that sovereigntists are wrong to claim that an international legal order could never come into existence since it would be incompatible with necessary attributes

---

[59] See Carl Schmitt, *Verfassungslehre* (Berlin, 1928) 22–3; Schmitt, *Der Begriff des Politischen* (n 27 above) 49–52.   [60] See ibid, 35–6.

of statehood or political independence. Hart also agrees with Kelsen that we must reject a radically voluntarist understanding of international law. If there is to be international law, there must be at least some international legal norms whose existence does not depend on voluntary agreement, most notably the rules that confer upon states the power to create voluntary obligations.[61] However, Hart shies away from any stronger claim about the necessary structure of international legal order or about its essential purposes.

Hart rejects Kelsen's attribution to international legal order of the essential purpose to secure peace. To build such an assumption into our concept of legal system, Hart argues, will neither aid understanding nor moral deliberation.[62] Experience suggests that legal systems can be made to serve many purposes. If it is arbitrary to claim that the essential purpose of any legal system is to secure peace, it will be equally arbitrary to hold that an international legal system would necessarily have to claim completeness and a monopoly of force. It is an open question of political morality whether an international legal system ought to be endowed with a monopoly of force. It will be a question of positive law, once an international legal system has come into existence, whether it has been so endowed. It will, finally, once again be a question of political morality whether a monopoly of force, should it have come into existence, ought to be respected under all circumstances.

Someone who adopted this line of argument would not necessarily be committed to a denial of the ideal of peace. He could agree that peace is an attractive value. He might even conclude that we have reason, other things being equal, to support the creation of a global legal system capable of securing peace. But he would deny that the incipient growth of international legal practices has somehow already committed states to the acceptance of an international monopoly of force and he would be apprehensive about the implicit suggestion that states, in order to honor that commitment, must always abstain from the uses of force that do not have a clear legal warrant, even in cases where such uses might reasonably be expected to lead to morally beneficial results. The Kelsenian interpretation of international law, one might fear, will give a concern with mere legality a prominence which it does not deserve and that clouds our moral reasoning.

The Kelsenian framework attempts to put the burden of moral proof on those who would disregard international law or act without legal warrant to help in a particular moral crisis and even more so on those who would choose a path of illegality to structurally reform an international legal system morally imperfect in content.[63] The latter option, in particular, would force a state or coalition of states explicitly to

---

[61] See Hart, *The Concept of Law* (n 8 above) 219–20.

[62] Hart agrees that a municipal legal order, for empirical reasons, will typically have to claim a monopoly of force to be a useful institution. But he denies that we can treat this observation as a necessary truth about all legal systems and he doubts that it applies to international law. See ibid, 213–15.

[63] See Allen Buchanan, 'Reforming the International Law of Humanitarian Intervention' in J L Holzgrefe and Robert O Keohane (eds), *Humanitarian Intervention. Ethical, Legal, and Political Dilemmas* (Cambridge, 2003) 130–73. For Kelsen's opposition to the idea of illegal acts of reform see Kelsen, *Principles of International Law* (n 14 above) 36–8.

adopt a unilateralist policy and hence, according to Kelsen, to bear the stigma of the denier of international law and the disturber of peace. But one might argue that there are no good moral reasons to impose this stigma. After all, those who judge that it might be their duty to act unilaterally, even if illegally, to achieve supremely important moral goals are not likely to claim that any injustice justifies a breach of the peace. Rather, they are likely to try to give the interest in peace what weight it deserves in an overall judgment that takes other values into account.

It does not appear unreasonable to suppose that Kelsen's approach will lead to an undue conservatism, an unjustified discomfort with illegality even where it could be expected to bring about morally beneficial results. Statesmen are more likely to take morally defensible decisions, then, if we let go of Kelsen's distribution of the burden of proof by adopting a Hartian view of the relation between legality and moral purpose. Instead of saying that the existence (or near existence) of international law implies that states are under an obligation to support it, such that illegality would be justifiable, at best, in particular and exceptional circumstances, we should say that there is international law, but that its existence does not as such ground a presumptive obligation on the part of states to support it, neither in its present nor in any future state of development. Insofar as compliance with international law on the part of states, or a known disposition for such compliance, is conducive to peace, that fact ought to be reflected in a responsible overall judgment of policy that takes the value of peace duly into account. But it cannot and should not prejudge its outcome.

To conclude my defense of Kelsen's theory of international law, I will suggest a reason for rejecting this pragmatic challenge to Kelsen's interpretation of international law. The concern with peace that drives Kelsen's attempt to force a decision between nationalist and cosmopolitan monism, I suspect, cannot adequately be taken into account by an interpretation of international law that is based on a Hartian denial of an essential moral purpose of international legal order. It may well be the Hartian approach, then, that unduly limits our moral reasoning.

Kelsen's understanding of legal peace is committed to the understanding of peace that we find in both Hobbes and Kant. According to both Hobbes and Kant, peace cannot be characterized as the absence of actual conflict.[64] Rather, there is war for as long as states claim the right to use force as they see fit in order to protect what they perceive as their legitimate interests or as important moral goals. Legal peace, by contrast, is a condition in which states can be assured that they will not be subjected to some other state's coercive acts on the basis of that other state's judgments of justice or self-interest. A shared commitment of respect for legality, rather, is taken, with the possible exception of truly unusual circumstances, to preempt such judgments. The attack on the Kelsenian framework I have just outlined, however,

---

[64] See Hobbes, *Leviathan* (n 6 above) 88–9; Immanuel Kant, 'Toward Perpetual Peace. A Philosophical Project' in Immanuel Kant, *Practical Philosophy*, translated and edited by Mary J Gregor (Cambridge, 1996) 311–51, at 322.

must surely be committed to the view that it is up to each subject of the law, and in the case of international law up to individual states, directly to weigh the value of peace against other values that might support the claim that some use of coercive force is morally required or justified. In other words, the view cannot be implemented on the level of practical politics without eroding the shared commitment to respect for legality that would make international legal peace possible.

Clearly, a situation in which states acted on a declared policy to give some weight to the value of peace in their judgments of policy but not to accord a significant degree of exclusionary force to international legal norms could not be a situation of *legal* peace, even if it were characterized by an absence of actual fighting. This is not to deny that, if they found themselves in such a situation through no fault of their own, states can do no better than to give what moral weight they honestly believe should be put on the avoidance of open fighting and of the harms it will inevitably bring about. But a state that deliberately terminates legal peace or that deliberately thwarts an opportunity to realize it, by declaring that it will give weight to the value of peace only insofar as it figures in its own comprehensive judgments of justice, will deprive not just itself but all other states (and, more importantly, their citizens) of the assurance against unilateral coercion. It is therefore wrong to claim that the concern with legal peace that underpins the Kelsenian framework can easily be taken into account in the alternative framework for thinking about the authority of international law that I have put into the mouth of the Hartian critic.

Needless to say, this observation can only form a starting point of further debate between proponents of a Kelsenian and a Hartian framework for thinking about the moral status of international law. Whether we will be able to achieve better moral results by embracing a Kelsenian or a Hartian perspective is a complex question that I do not pretend to have settled definitively. My conclusion is much more modest. It is that taking a choice between the Kelsenian and the Hartian conception of legal order already requires an answer to a moral question that is, as far as I can see, very much an open one. To determine the duties of states towards international legality in a responsible fashion will require, therefore, that we take the Kelsenian approach seriously, instead of assuming that a theory of the normative foundations of international law should start out from Hartian ground.[65] This assumption fails to take seriously the hope for the realization of a distinctive and attractive ideal of international order: the non-hegemonic peace brought about by the *civitas maxima* as an international utopia of legality.

---

[65] For a theory of the moral foundations of international law that appears to start from Hartian premises see Allen Buchanan, *Justice, Legitimacy, and Self-Determination. Moral Foundations of International Law* (Oxford, 2004) 20–2.

7

Conclusions—The Pure Theory of Law and Contemporary Positivism

In the introduction to this book I claimed that an analysis of the relation between Kelsen's legal and his political theory would be of more than merely exegetical significance. As I pointed out, contemporary legal positivists disagree about the nature of their project. I suggested that understanding the relation of legal science and political theory in Kelsen might help us understand and evaluate the problem of the relation of legal theory and political theory in contemporary debates about the nature of positivism. In what way, then, does the analysis of the relation between Kelsen's legal and his political theory offered here contribute to a deepened understanding of the legal positivist project?

In order to provide a basis for answering this question, let me pull together the major threads of the argument I attribute to Kelsen. Kelsen's attempt to develop a pure theory of law, I have claimed, must be understood as a part of the larger project of developing a theory of the state that outlines the institutional conditions under which the positive legality of political decisions can exercise a legitimizing force over the content of those decisions, a force strong enough to motivate the adoption of the point of view of the law-abiding citizen.

The main pillar of this project is Kelsen's thesis of the identity of law and state. It claims that the state is identical to its legal order since illegal acts cannot be attributed to the state. Kelsen argues that this thesis can form the backbone of a theory of law adequate to the idea of the rule of law. This claim, however, is open to the criticism that the identity thesis, the claim that the state cannot act illegally, can hold true only if we adopt a trivial and undemanding interpretation of the standards of legality that need to be satisfied in order for an act to be attributable to the state. According to this trivial interpretation, all final decisions taken by persons who are formally authorized to act as public officials are automatically legally valid, regardless of whether they fully conform with all applicable legal standards.

As we have seen, Kelsen circumvents this criticism by refusing to draw a sharp dividing line between jurisdictional norms that provide for the formal authorization of public officials and material norms these decision takers are bound to apply or execute. According to Kelsen, official acts must be in full compliance with all positive legal norms, including all relevant material norms, before they can be attributed to the state. This strong reading of the identity thesis, even while preserving the claim that the state can do no wrong, accommodates the possibility that acts performed by persons or institutions who are designated bearers of public authority may turn out to lack validity. Usually, such acts will at least claim to be exercises of public authority, and they will tend to meet some, though not all, of the legal standards that make an act an exercise of public authority. But according to the identity thesis, they should not therefore be granted a presumption of validity. If an official takes a decision that is not in full conformity with all applicable legal standards, his actions will not suffice to enact a valid norm.

The point of the identity thesis, then, is to undercut any attempt to restrict the requirement of full legality of all acts of state, to block the dualist idea that the state must have the power to appeal to some form of formal authority in order to remedy any lack of full legality. Such attempts can take different forms differing in their extremism, ranging from a Schmittian conception of sovereign decision that ultimately reduces formal authority to the capacity to successfully lead a group into a friend-enemy decision to the idea that judicial decisions are binding, even if materially mistaken, in virtue of the judge's formal authority. To say that *all* legal norms applicable to some decision are conditions of the authorization of the decision-taker, and not merely standards of the legal correctness of his decision, is a way of emphasizing the point that the material legal norms the positive law makes available to deal with some situation are *legally binding* on a decision-taker claiming to apply them. He cannot disregard them and still make a valid claim to be acting as a public official.

In its primary form, the identity thesis applies to the relationship between the state and the individual law-abiding citizen. A law-abiding citizen, since he is committed to obeying the law but not the persons who exercise powers conferred by law, is entitled to regard a decision that is not fully legal as nothing more than an expression of a subjective intention of the decision-taker which is lacking in legal force. As we have seen, Kelsen acknowledges that it would not be practicable for a legal system to leave the question whether a decision is attributable to the state or not up to any individual's private judgment. Hence the replacement of the individual's logical authority to make judgments of attribution with the mechanism of system-internal review: Only if a state provides adequate guarantees of legality, if it makes it possible for the citizen to initiate a review of the substantive legality of any power-exercising decision in an independent court, can it justifiably lay claim to a presumption of legality. This presumption, however, is no longer raised on behalf of any particular organ of state endowed with decision-taking powers. The internalization of review, rather, amounts to a separation of powers that replaces the sovereignty of the legislator or the government with the sovereignty of the law.

Undoubtedly, Kelsen's doctrine of finality ultimately does replace the demand for substantive legality with an appeal to formal authority, at least as far as the relationship of the individual subject with the legal order as a whole is concerned. All legal systems, according to Kelsen, take final decisions and enforce them against dissent as long as they exist. A legal system's final decisions, in order to constitute a genuine social order, must be taken to exclude all interpretations of the law, of the limits of authority on any level of legal hierarchy, that conflict with those provided by the system. More generally speaking, they must be taken to exclude all practical reasons that may, from some individual point of view, speak against action in conformity with the law, as understood by the system itself. The legal system, to recall, claims to be able to settle finally all social disputes. It should be clear that it can do so only if its final decisions are identifiable by its subjects without any reliance on their own judgments of full legality.

But while the claim to be able to take finally binding decisions and to be entitled to enforce them is raised by any legally organized political system, there is a clear difference, for Kelsen, between two different ways of raising this claim: one that allows subjects of the law to continue to define themselves as law-abiding citizens and another that forces them to define their own position as that of subjects of the particular persons who are taken to be empowered, by a small set of relatively unconstraining identificatory rules, to enact binding decisions.

The first understanding of the state's power to take finally binding decisions, the understanding compatible with the idea that citizens obey the law and not those who make or apply it, portrays the state as defending its claim to obedience by an appeal to legality. In order for this appeal to carry significant weight, there have to be legal standards that go beyond bare and uncontroversial formal means of identifying authoritative directives. There have to be laws, ideally constitutional laws, that, to some extent, guide or constrain exercises of power. Once there are such standards, the identity thesis in its strong reading will entail that these standards function as enforceable conditions of proper authorization. As a result, it will start to make sense to take the view that the legality of a decision has a nontrivial normative significance, that it exercises some degree of legitimating force over the content of the decision. This, in turn, implies that the stance of the law-abiding citizen, based as it is on the distinction between objective and subjective legal meaning, will have become meaningful to some extent, and with it the claim made by the authorities that their final decisions merit to be respected because they constitute applications of legal standards.

Internalization of review assumes agreement in principle, between the state and the citizen, on the point that decisions taken by officials are valid only if they substantially conform with all applicable standards of legality. Internalization, therefore, does not replace material with formal authority or grant the power to disregard the law. Rather, it reacts to the problem of possible disagreement between affected citizens and public officials about the objective meaning of the authorizing legal standards. Internalization is a solution to this problem of disagreement which allows a subject to defer to the legal system's claim to be able to determine finally the normative meaning of all acts falling within its sphere of authority and to remain a law-abiding citizen in paying such deference. The internalization of primary review ensures that all disputes about legality, as a reciprocally accepted source of legitimacy, that arise between citizens and public officials are open to arbitration in an

independent reviewing court. Internalization thus gives expression to the fundamental normative intuition guiding Kelsen's strong reading of the identity thesis.
The identity thesis, as we have seen, is compatible with the possibility that the standards of legality which govern attribution of acts to the state are exceedingly thin.
But it entails, in all cases, that no organ of state can unilaterally suspend, choose to
disregard, or decide to exempt from judicial enforcement any positive legal provision that bears on its authority.

A political system's claim to be entitled to take finally binding decisions, and to
enforce them need not be based on an appeal to legality. It would be pointless to
emphasize the distinction between the subjective and the objective legal meaning
of an alleged exercise of public authority if we thought of the criteria of legal validity primarily as means to identify the determinate directives issued by some agent,
group, or institution perceived as possessing or as representing a legitimacy of
meta-legal origin. Such conceptions of legitimacy, according to Kelsen, are typical of
autocracy. The autocratic state, even though it can be interpreted as a legal order,
does not defend its claim to obedience on the basis of a claim to legality. What it
demands of its subjects is obedience to absolute authority grounded in myth, not
law-abidingness. The autocratic state, consequently, rejects the necessity of independent arbitration in disputes about legality between the power-exercising organs
of state and affected citizens. What is more, it may not even commit to the principle
that its decisions, in order to be legitimate, at least ought to aim for full legality.

Kelsen does not deny, as we have seen, that autocracies can be described as rudimentary legal systems. The identity thesis applies to an autocratic state as much as
it applies to a state that bases its demands on claims to legality. But in the context of
an autocracy, the identity thesis forces us to deny the legal quality of all those norms
whose constraining powers the rulers can disregard if they so choose. A power-
conferring and power-conditioning legal norm that does not constitute a ground for
the invalidation of an official decision conflicting with, or at least a ground for punishing officials who fail to comply with it, cannot have the full force of law because
it does not bind those it purports to authorize. But this means, according to Kelsen,
that those who are purportedly authorized by such an unenforceable norm cannot
appeal to it to defend their claim to authority. This thesis has considerable critical
force. Open autocracies, after all, are few and far between. Most actually existing
legal systems mix appeals to legality with a measure of residual autocracy, usually by
relying on variants of Schmitt's norm/exception dialectic.

What the pure theory aims to accomplish is to demonstrate the incoherence of
such mixture. In order to describe a legal system coherently, Kelsen claims, the legal
scientist is forced to choose between either denying the legal quality of law that is
not enforceable against the powerful, thus branding the system an autocracy, or
denying the validity of all acts violating a purported standard of legality. This necessity to choose between autocracy and the rule of law is not explicable, as Kelsen's
official understanding of legal science suggests, on the basis of the logical idea that
a legal system cannot contain two norms, on different levels of legal hierarchy, that

contradict each other. If a logical demand for unity had been Kelsen's whole point against law-state dualism, he ought to have admitted that law-state dualists can save their position simply by invoking the doctrine of normative alternatives. But Kelsen clearly did not think that the doctrine of normative alternatives could, for example, be applied to an autocracy whose rulers enact a formal constitution containing a long list of constraints while tacitly reserving to themselves the power to disregard it at will. The doctrine of normative alternatives, as we have seen, can become operative only through guarantees of legality. The incoherence of the mixture of elements of the rule of law with residues of autocracy, then, must be a justificatory incoherence. An autocracy, Kelsen believes, should at least be forced, by legal science, to defend its claims to legally unfettered authority openly. The process of constitutionalization, on the other hand, must not be undercut by attempts to accommodate residues of autocracy within constitutional frameworks officially committed to the rule of law.

Kelsen's description of law is not neutral with respect to the choice just outlined. His understanding of legal normativity is from the beginning committed to a model of law according to which law plays an essentially power-constraining and mediating role. The pure theory, in keeping with this understanding of the function of law, is adequate to the rule of law insofar as it facilitates transitions from autocracy to the rule of law. This approach, needless to say, leads to a tension between Kelsen's aim to give a descriptively adequate general theory of law and the normative implications of his idea of legal objectivity. As a general theory of law, the pure theory must allow us to treat autocratic legal systems as instances of legal order and thus to make general attributions of justified normativity to these systems, even if they realize the function of constraint only very imperfectly. Kelsen tries to bridge this tension between the pure theory's claim to generality and its normative ambition by attempting to read autocratic legal systems as anticipations of a legal order that more fully realizes the ideal of the rule of law.

Kelsen believes, as we have seen, that autocratic states will always have to refer to ideological sources of legitimacy external to the law in order to fully justify their claims to obedience. This will be true even in some systems that accept the general implications of the strong reading of the identity thesis, ie in systems that accept the idea that only properly authorized acts are instances of public power and that disputes about proper authorization, insofar as the positive law is rich enough to give rise to interesting disagreements about such matters, must be referred to independent courts. The obvious example would be a legislative autocracy that operates on the basis of Kelsen's general principle of legality but that leaves an unrestricted power to enact general norms in the hands of a monarch, a small elite, or a majority that claims that its partial interests can be identified with those of the people as a whole and that takes itself to be entitled, as a result, to disregard the claims of minorities.

But the combination of legislative autocracy and a commitment to the identity thesis in its strong reading is precarious. This precariousness results from the legitimating ideology of the legislative autocracy. The reason why legality has legitimizing force, according to this ideology, is to be sought in some meta-legal justification for the authorization of the legislative autocrat: in the idea that he is God's representative or in the idea that the democratic legislator's decisions, the decisions of a majority, are the unadulterated expression of a higher will of the people that exists independently of its expression in a positive procedure for taking political decisions.

The pure theory as a critique of ideology forces the legal scientist to abstract from all sources of legitimacy external to the law. Legal science, in its attempt to make sense of the content-independent normativity it attributes to the law, has to make do with the resources of legitimacy actually or potentially provided by positive legal order itself. The pure theory as a critique of ideology, as a result, will diagnose a mismatch between the claims to obedience made by autocratic or partly autocratic political systems and the weakness of the justificatory force of their underdeveloped constraints of legality. The move to Kelsenian democracy, and preferably to Kelsenian constitutional democracy, is required to eliminate this mismatch. As we have seen, Kelsenian constitutional democracy helps eliminate the mismatch insofar as it strengthens the power-constraining implications of the strong reading of the identity thesis. It strengthens these implications by providing enforceable substantive standards of legality for exercises of legislative power that are based on a conception of the essential rights of democratic citizens. The normative ambition expressed by the identity thesis remains partly unfulfilled in any state that has not yet taken the step to constitutional democracy.

The precariousness of a combination of the strong reading of the identity thesis with a legislative autocracy built on a legitimating ideology is equally evident if we reverse the direction of argument. The legitimating ideology of a legislative autocracy does not sit well with the view that the state should have to make an unconditional commitment to Kelsen's principle of legality. It fails sufficiently to explain, put differently, why it should matter that disputes about legality are decided by independent courts which represent the primary perspective of the law-abiding citizen. The idea of a distinction between subjection to the law and subjection to the persons legally authorized to take binding decisions will inevitably be put under pressure by any imaginable justification of legislative autocracy. Any good reasons to accept legislative autocracy, to avoid any unnecessary restriction of the autocrat's legislative powers, will automatically be reasons to accept his interpretation of the laws.

Judges in a legislative autocracy tasked with reviewing the substantive legality of acts of state that have an appearance of legality, on behalf of the law-abiding citizen, would not really be in a position successfully to discharge their task. In order to exercise a genuine function of control, such judges would have to be willing to apply objective standards of substantive legality to the state's acts, even if doing so goes against the autocratic legislator's avowed intentions. But such action of reviewing judges, it seems, would inevitably appear alien to the constitutional context of

a legislative autocracy that enjoys de facto legitimacy. The function of laws that
bear on the legality of exercises of legislative power, according to any of the autocratic ideologies, is to allow subjects to identify the content of the legislator's will,
not to constrain it. It is highly unlikely, in other words, that a practice of strict
judicial control of exercises of authority could survive in any other constitutional
context than that of a constitutional democracy.

These observations imply that Kelsen's principles of legality, his understanding
of democracy, and his constitutionalism are ultimately viable only in conjunction
with each other. The law-abiding citizen is subject only to the objective law and not
to the subjective will of those who make it. But his subjection to the law entails that
he is subject to the decisions of those who make law, irrespective of the content of
those decisions, as long as they are properly authorized by the law. In order for the
stance of the law-abiding citizen to be reasonable, then, fulfillment of the conditions
of proper authorization itself must provide a sufficient motivation for drawing the
basic distinction in the first place. But such a motivation can only be provided by
a Kelsenian constitutional democracy, not by a legislative autocracy. The ambition
implicit in Kelsen's basic ideal of the rule of law can only be realized fully in a utopia
of legality. But since the basic ideal already governs the description of all legal systems, the pure theory is committed to a developmental perspective that interprets
autocracies as defective instances of legal order.

Finally, the critical force of the identity thesis is not exhausted by a domestic
utopia of legality. The idea that the state is, in any case, nothing but a legal order
opens up the possibility of conceiving of states as parts of an encompassing global
legal order. The first step into a global utopia of legality, as we have seen, has a rather
limited (though crucially important) ambition, namely to provide a legal regulation of the use of force amongst states. What is more the identity thesis entails that
the fact that domestic laws will retain their validity, after this first step into a global
utopia of legality has been taken, even if they conflict with international law (as
well as the fact that the human beings making up a state are held responsible for
such violations only collectively) is a contingent fact that indicates the relatively
primitive nature of international law. It does not express necessary limitations on
international law's developmental possibility. Hence, the international application
of the identity thesis at least establishes the conceivability of a much more interesting international utopia of legality, of an international legal order in which a state's
compliance with international legal norms would be enforceable, by those who
are affected by its actions, through international guarantees of legality.

According to the interpretation of the pure theory I have offered Kelsen's position is, in some important respects, not positivist.[1] It affirms, rather than denies,

---

[1] According to some authors, positivism as it is nowadays understood is a relatively recent philosophical invention, to be credited to Hart and Kelsen. See David Dyzenhaus, 'The Genealogy of Positivism'
in *Oxford Journal of Legal Studies* 24 (2004) 39–67. From such a perspective, the interpretation offered
here might be taken to show that the positivist tradition should be understood in a less narrow fashion
than is common in post-Hartian jurisprudence.

a necessary connection between legality and legitimacy. It claims, moreover, that this connection is at least potentially interesting enough to ground general duties of obedience to law. It argues, finally, that legality is not just a distinctive but rather the only source of de jure legitimacy of exercises of public power. At least the second and third of these claims put Kelsen at odds with Razian positivism.[2] Moreover, since all three claims are dependent on the availability and on an endorsement of the ideal of a utopia of legality, Kelsen's pure theory of law cannot be classified as a descriptive-explanatory theory on the methodological level. It forms part of a political philosophy.

Kelsen's theory nevertheless puts heavy emphasis on the positivity of law. This emphasis is evident in the view that a legal system's final decisions must be identifiable by its *subjects*, those called upon to obey some final decision produced by the system, without any reliance on their own moral judgments or even their own judgments of full legality.

Things are somewhat more complicated if we adopt the perspective of the reviewing courts representing the law-abiding citizen. The reviewing judge accepts the principle that a legal norm can be valid, that it can exist, only as a result of an actual act of properly authorized enactment. All legal decisions, moreover, in order to have proper authorization, must be subsumable under some higher enacted norm. There are no natural law principles, then, that can have legal validity independent of enactment and that may justify open *contra legem* decisions. As we have seen, this attack on the idea that non-enacted moral rules form part of the law is motivated by an interest in the power-constraining effect of positive rules that authorize and guide official action.

However, Kelsen's theory of legal hierarchy departs in significant respects from the perspective of political positivists who are hostile to the idea of judicial review of legislation. Since the reviewing judge, representing the law-abiding citizen, must treat the demand for full legality, including the demand for full material constitutionality, as a condition of proper authorization, he will often not be able to assess a decision's pedigree by relying exclusively on source-based tests of validity. He must operate, nevertheless, on the assumption that all disputes about full legality are decidable on legal grounds; at least if we are to be able to characterize the stance of the law-abiding citizen as one of fidelity to law. The reviewing judge will therefore, as we have seen, have to be entitled to give expression, in his decisions, to the normative aspirations that underpin Kelsen's utopia of legality: even while he must respect the distinction between a thin morality of democratic citizenship and substantive ideals of just social order.

The pure theory attempts to purify our understanding of legal normativity from all elements that make it unsuitable to a utopia of legality. It is an autonomous science of law insofar as it exploits the positive law itself as a justificatory resource

---

[2] See Joseph Raz, 'About Morality and the Nature of Law' in *American Journal of Jurisprudence* 48 (2003) 1–15.

instead of trying to derive its legitimacy from moral, mythical, or personal sources external to the law. This project of purification must be defended on two fronts, as Kelsen intuitively realized. On the one hand, it has to be defended against those who—like Hartian positivists or theoretical anarchists—claim that any legal theory based on a general attribution of justified normativity to the law must be ideological. On the other hand, it has to be defended against natural law theorists who claim that a conception of justified normativity must be directly related to a substantive theory of political justice. Kelsen's two methodological claims to purity—the separation of legal from social science and the separation of legal theory from theories of justice—try to offer this double defense. Both claims to purity rest on the assumption that a positive legal system can come to realize values internal to positive legality, by protecting social peace in a way compatible with a reasonable person's claim to freedom. To show how these values can be protected by a utopia of legality is to show how the law's claim to autonomous normativity can be sustained.

The success of Kelsen's project, as I have interpreted it, depends on the *viability* of the ideal of a utopia of legality. Recall the mismatch or dissonance I mentioned a moment ago. To make the claim that autocracies are defective instances of legal order, and not merely morally bad states, requires a prior attachment to the ideal of a utopia of legality. There will, of course, be no mismatch between a system's claim to legitimacy and the underdeveloped nature of the legal constraints it puts on political power unless one already assumes that legal order can and ought to develop into a utopia of legality and that one's concept of law should reflect this ambition. But if we have to make this assumption in order to get the theory going, one might ask, what does Kelsen's argument actually show? An argument that successfully establishes the viability of the ideal of the utopia of legality would, I believe, exonerate Kelsen from this charge of circularity.

The viability of the utopia of legality has two aspects. It has to be shown, first, that the utopia is a meaningful ideal, that the values it aims to protect are genuine moral values that have independent standing. Secondly, it has to be the case that the combination of the rule of law, democracy, and constitutionalism, as understood by Kelsen, is internally related to these values, both in the sense that it will necessarily further their realization and in the sense that no other constitutional arrangement would. The Kelsenian jurisprudent will be in a position to claim that autocratic legal systems are not just morally bad, but that they are defective instances of legal order and that the attempt to realize the utopia of legality is a possible remedy for their defects, only if both of these requirements of viability are met.

Even if the viability of the utopia of legality could be established, an opponent of Kelsen's concept of legality would, of course, still be free to reject it on the ground that the utopia of legality has morally troubling aspects or that there is some better ideal of a well-ordered society to which our conception of law should be adequate. But if one rejected the pure theory's conception of legality on such grounds, while admitting that the utopia of legality is at least a viable ideal, one's own conception of legality would necessarily have to be defended in terms of a competing account of the role we expect a legal theory to play in the overall attempt to create a reasonable society. A successful argument for the viability of the utopia would, then, force positivisms opposed to Kelsen's ambitious conception of legal normativity to defend themselves on political grounds, at least if they are unwilling to adopt a methodological-positivist approach.

To illustrate the point, it is instructive to once again compare Kelsen's view with Hart's and Raz's. For both Hart and Raz, there could be no systematic or structural dissonance between the way in which a political system justifies its normative claims and a legal-theoretical description of that system. A legal system's laws may, of course, turn out to be unjust and hence undeserving of obedience for Hart. A legal system may turn out to lack the authority it claims to possess from a Razian point of view and it may be impossible for subjects reasonably to act in accordance with its demands on the basis of other reasons. But such failures will never be considered as defects of legality since they can have no more interesting cause than the fact that some legislator happened to take a morally mistaken decision or the fact that some person or institution endowed with legal power happened to abuse institutional power. For both Hart and Raz, legality itself possesses no or only relatively little potential for morally meaningful development.

This observation points to a kernel of truth in Lon Fuller's famous claim that analytical legal positivists conceive of the law as one-way projection of authority.[3] What justifies Fuller's charge, at least in part, is the fact that a distinction like Kelsen's between democracy and autocracy could not be of fundamental jurisprudential relevance for Hart or Raz. This does not necessarily entail that Fuller's charge is fully justified. After all, Hart's and Raz's positions are perfectly compatible with the idea that those who exercise political power ought to use such power in ways that benefit their subjects as well as with the idea that the decisions of those who hold political power merit obedience only if these decisions succeed in benefiting subjects. What is more, there may of course be moral reasons to prefer democracy to autocracy even for someone who does not believe that democratic procedures enhance the law's claim to authority or legitimacy.

But the point remains that standard forms of contemporary positivism are committed to the view that the idea of *legitimacy* does not constitute an independent dimension of the moral evaluation of exercises of public power. The only dimension of moral evaluation of exercises of public power is constituted by the question whether such exercises are (or can be expected to be) substantively just and good. And this dimension of moral evaluation has no institutional implications. As we have seen, Kelsen argues that even autocratic governments at least claim to be governments *for* the people even if they are not governments *by* the people.[4] Raz echoes this view by saying that all legal systems necessarily claim authority, in the

---

[3] See Lon L Fuller, 'A Reply to Critics' in Lon L Fuller, *The Morality of Law. Revised Edition* (New Haven, 1964) 187–242, at 191–7.

[4] See Kelsen, 'Foundations of Democracy' in *Ethics* 66 (1955) 1–101, at 2–3.

sense that they claim to serve their subjects by providing guidance in the light of reasons for action independently applicable to the subjects. However, this is where the jurisprudential story must end, Raz believes, for an analytical positivist who aims to give a morally non-committed description of the law as an actual social institution. There is no further constitutional step from government that claims to be for the people to government by the people that would necessarily bring us closer to a general validation of the law's claim to authority. Whether the law has at least some of the authority it claims to possess depends solely on whether those who are in authority do a good job or not. And whether they succeed or fail in doing a good job does not depend on whether the constitutional system is democratic.

This restriction of the jurisprudential relevance of constitutional form is clearly related to a restriction of the moral relevance of the rule of law, as expressed by the identity thesis. Once we adopt the view that the authority of law depends on the authority of the persons or institutions who make it and subscribe to Raz's limited account of the possible scope of justified authority, we will not only be committed to the view that the problem of the rule of law, and of its traditional opposition to the rule of men, however wise and benevolent, is not that interesting or important in its own right. We will have a hard time explaining why the philosophical tradition used to put such heavy emphasis on it.

These observations suggest, it seems to me, that the adoption of a legal-theoretical approach that does not commit the concept of law to a political or constitutional ideal will nevertheless have to depend on some understanding of good social order. If the utopia of legality is at least a viable and unique ideal, the defense of conceptions of positivism that refuse to commit to the idea of legal legitimacy must constitute a denial of that ideal. And such a denial would itself appear to be in need of moral justification.

Defenders of a descriptive-explanatory positivist project are sure to complain that Kelsen's decision to read substantively autocratic legal systems as anticipations of a utopia of legality carries the danger of descriptive inadequacy. Does the Kelsenian not arbitrarily replace the sober task of analyzing the general nature of law as it actually exists with the attempt to develop an account of ideal law, an account that engages in the kind of utopian scheming that Julie Dickson thinks is best left to novelists?[5]

The fact that Kelsen's conception of law is informed by an ideal that some positivists do not share is not sufficient, I believe, to sustain the accusation that the pure theory is guilty of wishful thinking. Kelsen exhibits an unwavering commitment to the project of giving a general theory of positive law. I see no good reason why the developmental perspective introduced by the utopia of legality should force us to question this commitment. The pure theory does not compel us to exclude wicked legal systems from our view or to deny their moral shortcomings. It is perfectly compatible with the claim that some legal systems may be substantially

---

[5] Julie Dickson, *Evaluation and the Law* (Oxford, 2001) 90.

unjust to the extent that whatever internal value they possess will be incapable of justifying the normative demands of the law to any significant extent. What the theory claims, and what descriptive-explanatory positivists deny, is that such injustice can be interpreted as a defect of legality and that the utopia of legality constitutes a proper remedy for this defect.

This claim can be accused of being an instance of wishful thinking only if the ideal of a utopia of legality is not viable. But if the ideal is viable, the initial choice for the model of law as legitimating constraint cannot be brushed off as a mere exercise in utopian scheming. If we can reasonably keep faith in law's tendency to evolve in what many would see as a morally significant way, as a result of our adoption of the model of law as constraint, we face a choice whether to describe law in a way that is adequate to this tendency or to describe it in some other way.[6] This choice, as we have seen, will make a genuine practical difference. It bears on the question whether certain kinds of conflicts can be portrayed as legal conflicts and hence as justiciable. It bears as well on our conception of democracy, of the meaning of constitutional rights, our view of legitimate adjudicative practices, and our understanding of the separation of powers. A concept of law indifferent to the ideal will, in this case, inevitably amount to taking an evaluative stance towards the developmental potentialities of positive legal order: particularly if that conception is itself concerned to elucidate the potential role of legal normativity in helping us to act as reasonably as possible.

A defense of the personal conception of authority, then, cannot be given on normatively uncommitted descriptive grounds. It is not enough to claim that the personal conception adequately expresses our pre-theoretical understanding of legal normativity. People's pre-theoretical attitudes towards the law's normativity are not philosophically fine-grained enough to allow us to decide whether our actual legal practices are more deeply committed to a personal conception of authority, as well as to the limitations on justification which it imposes, or to something like Kelsen's conception of legal legitimacy and to the idea of community for which it makes room. The explanatory aim to clear up our pre-theoretical thought about the law's normativity does not provide a sufficient reason to accept the personal conception of authority.

This is not an argument against Raz's conception as much as it is an argument for the claim that its defense must come to rest on an argument for the idea that superior expertise or power to coordinate, the sources of justified authority recognized by the personal conception of authority, are the only possible, as well as the only needed sources of justified legal normativity. But such an argument will itself have to appeal to some social ideal. Whether Kelsen's conception of law is guilty of objectionable utopian scheming is thus a substantive question of social philosophy and not a methodological issue.

---

[6] See Frederick Schauer, 'The Social Construction of the Concept of Law' in *Oxford Journal of Legal Studies* 25 (2005) 493–501.

The fact that the pure theory rests on a general attribution of legitimacy to the law can, of course, also be criticized from the point of view of Hart's normative argument for positivism. Kelsen's idea of legal legitimacy, a Hartian political positivist might suspect, will inevitably lead us uncritically to attribute normative force even to morally bad positive law.

I hope that my analysis has shown that it would be wrong to think of this as a danger implicit in the view I attribute to Kelsen. The legitimacy of law varies in strength, as we have seen, depending on how closely a legal system approximates the utopia of legality. The question whether a subject of a legal system faced with an unjust law ought to obey, all things considered, is thus not automatically answerable on the basis of the internal relation between legality and legitimacy postulated by the pure theory. The Kelsenian will deny, admittedly, that we can routinely end up in a position to make the claim that something is law but that it is too unjust to be obeyed if we live in a utopia of legality. In a utopia of legality, one's moral duty, barring exceptional circumstances, is to obey the law, regardless of its content.

However, the citizens of a utopia of legality will never (and will never have to) accept a law as substantively just only because it is legally valid. They will not make the mistake of treating the legality of a norm as evidence for its substantive moral correctness and neither does the system expect them to. Rather, they will adopt a general critical attitude towards the content of the law, with the aim of constantly improving its moral quality. The fact that it is possible for all citizens reasonably to treat the utopia's laws as legitimate preserves the integrity of the content-related dimension of evaluation of law that is grounded in citizen's ideals of a perfectly just society.

A Hartian should therefore have no trouble in admitting that egregiously unjust laws are not likely to be a frequent occurrence in the utopia of legality. But if the utopia's laws are merely experienced as falling somewhat short of one's ideals, this experience will be based on an ideal of justice or on an interpretation of an ideal of justice that fellow democratic citizens can reasonably dispute. The fact that the citizens of the utopia attribute general legitimacy to the system, hence, is unlikely to be a cause of intolerable injustice, unless we consider the mild torment of heteronomy to which the system will subject some of us for some time as altogether unbearable and take the view that the respect that citizens pay to each other in paying respect to the utopia's laws is of no redeeming value.

Hart thinks that our practical attitude towards the law should be that of an external critic who assesses the normativity of law exclusively from his individual moral point of view and he appears to believe that adoption of this posture on the part of all the members of a society will not endanger social stability but rather have liberating effects. Kelsen, by contrast, claims that criticism of the law's moral quality offered from an external point of view will be most uninhibited and be able to express the widest possible range of opinion in a society in which the law's internal resources of legitimacy have been most fully developed. The aim to foster unrestricted criticism of the content of the law, according to Kelsen, presupposes a reasonable habit of deference to the law's legitimacy. Free censure is possible only in a society in which reasonable respect for legality can make up for the lack of substantive moral agreement, or for some mythical source of legitimacy, as a source of social stability.

If Kelsen is correct, Hart's critical project can deliver us from the torment of heteronomy only if the existence of sufficient moral agreement as a background requirement of social stability can be taken for granted. But in this case, the critical attitude Hart advocates can only be of limited importance to the overall project of creating a reasonable society under social conditions that are characterized by the absence of moral agreement. Kelsen's pure theory, I conclude, offers a more ambitious and at the same time more nuanced variant of social criticism than the one that is prominent in Hart's early works.

The fact that the ambition comes at the price of a departure from what is nowadays considered a positivist perspective, I hope to have argued, should not worry us too much. The pure theory cannot meaningfully be dissociated from Kelsen's overall conception of good social order. As a result, it cannot be meaningfully evaluated unless we understand it in the light of such a conception. But the same will have to be true of competing positivist legal theories, unless they are willing to embrace a narrow form of methodological positivism that is explicitly unconcerned with the practical role of the law in our lives.

What the pure theory illustrates, it seems to me, is that a legal theory which does not restrict itself in this way, which is responsive to our practical needs as subjects of the law, must be an integral part of political theory. The classical exponents of modern political philosophy, Hobbes, Locke, Kant, did indeed treat legal theory as part of a broader political-theoretical perspective. Perhaps not coincidentally, they tended to emphasize the idea that political community is possible only as lawful order. Kelsen's pure theory differs from contemporary legal theories insofar as it can be read as a late exponent of this tradition. If this observation is correct, the pure theory can form a link to this earlier tradition that will allow contemporary legal theory to reconnect with the full breadth of classical jurisprudential thought.

Bibliography

WORKS OF HANS KELSEN

KELSEN, HANS, 'Rechtsstaat und Staatsrecht' (first published 1913), in Hans Klecatsky, René Marcić, and Herbert Schambeck (eds), *Die Wiener Rechtstheoretische Schule. Ausgewählte Schriften von Hans Kelsen, Adolf Julius Merkl und Alfred Verdross*, 2 vols (Wien, 1968) vol II, 1525–32 (Henceforth '*WRT*').

—— 'Über Staatsunrecht' (first published 1914) in *WRT* I, 957–1057.

—— *Das Problem der Souveränität und die Theorie des Völkerrechts. Beitrag zu einer reinen Rechtslehre* (Tübingen, 1920).

—— 'Die Lehre von den drei Gewalten oder Funktionen des Staates' (first published 1924) in *WRT* II, 1625–60.

—— *Allgemeine Staatslehre* (Berlin, 1925).

—— 'Die Idee des Naturrechts' (first published 1927) in *WRT* I, 245–80.

—— 'Naturrecht und positives Recht' (first published 1927) in *WRT* I, 215–44.

—— *Der soziologische und der juristische Staatsbegriff. Kritische Untersuchung des Verhältnisses von Staat und Recht* (Tübingen, 1928).

—— 'Die philosophischen Grundlagen der Naturrechtslehre und des Rechtspositivismus' (first published 1928) in *WRT* I, 281–350.

—— *Vom Wesen und Wert der Demokratie* (Tübingen, 1929).

—— 'Wesen und Entwicklung der Staatsgerichtsbarkeit' (first published 1929) in *WRT* II, 1813–72.

—— 'Wer soll der Hüter der Verfassung sein?' (first published 1931) in *WRT* II, 1873–912.

—— 'Verteidigung der Demokratie' (first published 1932) in Hans Kelsen, *Demokratie und Sozialismus. Ausgewählte Aufsätze*, edited by Norbert Leser (Wien, 1967) 60–8.

—— 'Das Urteil des Staatsgerichtshofs vom 25. Oktober 1932' in *Die Justiz* 8 (1932–33) 65–91.

—— 'Staatsform und Weltanschauung' (first published 1933) in Hans Kelsen, *Demokratie und Sozialismus. Ausgewählte Aufsätze*, edited by Norbert Leser (Wien, 1967) 40–59.

—— 'On the Theory of Interpretation' (first published 1934), translated by Bonnie Litschewski-Paulson and Stanley L Paulson, in *Legal Studies* 10 (1990) 127–35.

—— *Introduction to the Problems of Legal Theory. A Translation of the First Edition of the Reine Rechtslehre or Pure Theory of Law* (first published 1934), translated and edited by Bonnie Litschewski-Paulson and Stanley L Paulson (Oxford, 1992).

—— *Law and Peace in International Relations. The Oliver Wendell Holmes Lectures, 1940–1941* (Cambridge/Mass, 1942).

—— *Peace Through Law* (Chapel Hill, 1944).

—— *Principles of International Law* (New York, 1952).

—— 'Foundations of Democracy' in *Ethics* 66 (1955) 1–101.

—— 'Value Judgments in the Science of Law' in Hans Kelsen, *What is Justice? Justice, Law, and Politics in the Mirror of Science* (Berkeley, 1957) 209–30.

—— 'What is Justice?' in Kelsen, *What is Justice?*, 1–24.

—— 'Absolutism and Relativism in Philosophy and Politics' in Kelsen, *What is Justice?*, 198–208.

—— 'The Pure Theory of Law and Analytical Jurisprudence' in Kelsen, *What is Justice?*, 266–87.

—— *Reine Rechtslehre. Zweite vollständig neu bearbeitete und erweiterte Auflage* (Wien, 1960).

—— 'Vom Wesen der Gerechtigkeit' in Kelsen, *Reine Rechtslehre* (Wien, 1960) 357–444.

—— *General Theory of Law and State*, translated by Anders Wedberg (New York, 1961).

—— *The Pure Theory of Law. Translation from the Second German Edition*, translated by Max Knight (Berkeley, 1970).

LITERATURE

ACKERMAN, BRUCE, *We the People: Foundations* (Cambridge/Mass, 1991).

ALEXY, ROBERT, *Begriff und Geltung des Rechts* (Freiburg, 1994).

—— 'Hans Kelsens Begriff der Verfassung' in Stanley L Paulson and Michael Stolleis (eds), *Hans Kelsen. Staatsrechtslehrer und Rechtstheoretiker des 20. Jahrhunderts* (Tübingen, 2005) 333–52.

AUSTIN, JOHN, *The Province of Jurisprudence Determined*, edited by Wilfrid E Rumble (Cambridge, 1995).

BENTHAM, JEREMY, *A Fragment on Government* (Cambridge, 1988).

VON BERNSTORFF, JOCHEN, *Der Glaube an das universale Recht. Zur Völkerrechtstheorie Hans Kelsens und seiner Schüler* (Baden-Baden, 2001).

BEYLEVELD, DERECK and BROWNSWORD, ROGER, 'Methodological Sycretism in Kelsen's Pure Theory of Law' in Stanley L Paulson and Bonnie Litschewski-Paulson (eds), *Normativity and Norms. Critical Perspectives on Kelsenian Themes* (Oxford, 1998) 113–45.

BINDREITER, UTA, 'Presupposing the Basic Norm' in *Ratio Juris* 14 (2001) 143–75.

BJARUP, JES, 'Kelsen's Theory of Law and Philosophy of Justice' in William Twining and Richard Tur (eds), *Essays on Kelsen* (Oxford, 1986) 273–303.

BOBBIO, NORBERTO, 'Kelsen e il problema del potere' in Norberto Bobbio, *Diritto e potere. Saggi su Kelsen* (Napoli, 1992) 103–22.

BUCHANAN, ALLEN, 'Reforming the International Law of Humanitarian Intervention' in J L Holzgrefe and Robert O Keohane (eds), *Humanitarian Intervention. Ethical, Legal, and Political Dilemmas* (Cambridge, 2003) 130–73.

—— *Justice, Legitimacy, and Self-Determination. Moral Foundations of International Law* (Oxford, 2004).

BULL, HEDLEY, 'Hans Kelsen and International Law' in Twining and Tur (eds), *Essays on Kelsen*, 321–36.

BULYGIN, EUGENIO, 'An Antinomy in Kelsen's Pure Theory of Law' in Paulson and Litschewski (eds), *Normativity and Norms* 297–315.

CALDWELL, PETER, *Popular Sovereignty and the Crisis of German Constitutional Law. The Theory and Practice of Weimar Constitutionalism* (Durham/NC, 1997).

CARTY, ANTHONY, 'The Continuing Influence of Kelsen on the General Perception of the Discipline of International Law' in *European Journal of International Law* 9 (1998) 344–54.

CHRISTIANO, THOMAS, 'The Authority of Democracy' in *The Journal of Political Philosophy* 13 (2004) 266–90.

COLEMAN, JULES, *The Practice of Principle. In Defense of a Pragmatist Approach to Legal Theory* (Oxford, 2001).

CUNNINGHAM, FRANK, *Theories of Democracy* (London, 2002).

DICKSON, JULIE, *Evaluation and Legal Theory* (Oxford, 2001).

DREIER, HORST, *Rechtslehre, Staatssoziologie und Demokratietheorie bei Hans Kelsen* (Baden-Baden, 1986).

DWORKIN, RONALD, *Law's Empire* (London, 1986).

—— 'The Forum of Principle' in Ronald Dworkin, *A Matter of Principle* (Cambridge/Mass, 1985) 33–71.

—— *Freedom's Law. The Moral Reading of the American Constitution* (Cambridge/Mass, 1996).

DYZENHAUS, DAVID, *Legality and Legitimacy. Carl Schmitt, Hans Kelsen and Hermann Heller in Weimar* (Oxford, 1997).

—— 'Hobbes and the Legitimacy of Law' in *Law and Philosophy* 20 (2001) 461–98.

—— 'Intimations of Legality amid the Clash of Arms' in *International Journal of Constitutional Law* 2 (2004) 244–71.

—— 'The Genealogy of Legal Positivism' in *Oxford Journal of Legal Studies* 24 (2004) 39–67.

—— *The Constitution of Law. Legality in a Time of Emergency* (Cambridge, 2006).

ELY, JOHN HART, *Democracy and Distrust. A Theory of Judicial Review* (Harvard/Mass, 1980).

ENDICOTT, TIMOTHY, 'The Reason of the Law' in *American Journal of Jurisprudence* 48 (2003) 83–106.

FINNIS, JOHN, *Natural Law and Natural Rights* (Oxford, 1980).

FULLER, LON L, *The Morality of Law. Revised Edition* (New Haven, 1964).

HARRIS, J W, 'Kelsen's Concept of Authority' in *Cambridge Law Journal* 36 (1977) 353–63.

—— 'Kelsen and Normative Consistency' in Tur and Twining, *Essays on Kelsen*, 201–28.

HART, H L A, *The Concept of Law*, 2nd ed, edited by Penelope Bulloch and Joseph Raz (Oxford, 1994).

—— 'Positivism and the Separation of Law and Morality' in H L A Hart, *Essays in Jurisprudence and Philosophy* (Oxford, 1983) 49–87.

—— 'Kelsen's Doctrine of the Unity of Law', in Hart, *Essays in Jurisprudence and Philosophy*, 309–48.

—— 'Kelsen Visited', in Hart, *Essays in Jurisprudence and Philosophy*, 286–308.

HERSHOVITZ, SCOTT, 'Legitimacy, Democracy, and Razian Authority' in *Legal Theory* 9 (2003) 201–20.

HOBBES, THOMAS, *Leviathan. Revised Student Edition*, edited by Richard Tuck (Cambridge, 1996).

—— *A Dialogue between a Philosopher and a Student of the Common Laws of England*, edited by Joseph Cropsey (Chicago, 1971).

HOLMES, STEPHEN, 'Precommitment and the Paradox of Democracy' in Stephen Holmes, *Passions and Constraint. On the Theory of Liberal Democracy* (Chicago, 1995) 134–77.

JELLINEK, GEORG, *Allgemeine Staatslehre* (Darmstadt, 1960, first published 1900).

KALYVAS, ANDREAS, 'The Basic Norm and Democracy in Hans Kelsen's Legal and Political Theory' in *Philosophy and Social Criticism* 32 (2006) 573–99.

KANT, IMMANUEL, 'Toward Perpetual Peace. A Philosophical Project' in Immanuel Kant, *Practical Philosophy*, translated and edited by Mary J Gregor (Cambridge, 1996) 311–51.

KOSKENNIEMI, MARTTI, *The Gentle Civilizer of Nations: The Rise and Fall of International Law, 1870–1960* (Cambridge, 2001).

—— *From Apology to Utopia. The Structure of International Legal Argument* (Cambridge, 2005).

KRAMER, MATTHEW, *In Defense of Legal Positivism. Law without Trimmings* (Oxford, 1999).

LAUTERPACHT, HERSH, *The Function of Law in the International Community* (Oxford, 1933).

LOCKE, JOHN, *Two Treatises of Government*, edited by Peter Laslett (Cambridge, 1988).

LÜBBE, WEYMA, *Legitimität kraft Legalität. Sinnverstehen und Institutionenanalyse bei Max Weber und seinen Kritikern* (Tübingen, 1991).

MACCORMICK, NEIL, 'A Moralistic Case for A-Moralistic Law?' in *Valparaiso University Law Review* 20 (1985) 1–41.

—— 'The Interest of the State and the Rule of Law' in Neil MacCormick, *Questioning Sovereignty* (Oxford, 1999) 27–48.

MARMOR, ANDREI, 'Authority and Authorship' in Andrei Marmor, *Positive Law and Objective Values* (Oxford, 2001) 89–111.

MÉTALL, RUDOLF ALADÁR, *Hans Kelsen. Leben und Werk* (Wien, 1969).

MURPHY, LIAM, 'The Political Question of the Concept of Law' in Jules Coleman (ed), *Hart's Postscript. Essays on the Postscript to 'The Concept of Law'* (Oxford, 2001) 371–409.

NINO, CARLOS SANTIAGO, 'Some Confusions Surrounding Kelsen's Concept of Validity', in Paulson and Litschewski-Paulson (eds), *Normativity and Norms*, 253–61.

PAULSON, STANLEY L, 'Material and Formal Authorization in Kelsen's Pure Theory' in *Cambridge Law Journal* 39 (1980) 172–93.

—— 'Kelsen on Legal Interpretation' in *Legal Studies* 10 (1990) 136–52.

—— 'Introduction' in Hans Kelsen, *Introduction to the Problems of Legal Theory*, edited by Paulson and Litschewski-Paulson, xvii-xlii.

—— 'The Neo-Kantian Dimension in Kelsen's Pure Theory of Law' in *Oxford Journal of Legal Studies* 12 (1992) 311–32.

—— and LITSCHEWSKI-PAULSON, BONNIE (eds), *Normativity and Norms. Critical Perspectives on Kelsenian Themes* (Oxford, 1998).

—— 'Four Phases in Hans Kelsen's Legal Theory? Reflections on a Periodization' in *Oxford Journal of Legal Studies* 18 (1998) 153–66.

—— 'The Weak Reading of Authority in Hans Kelsen's Pure Theory of Law' in *Law and Philosophy* 19 (2000) 131–71.

—— 'Constitutional Review in America and Austria. Notes on the Beginnings' in *Ratio Juris* 16 (2003) 223–39.

PERRY, STEPHEN, 'Hart's Methodological Positivism' in Coleman (ed), *Hart's Postscript*, 311–54.

—— 'The Varieties of Legal Positivism' in *Canadian Journal of Law and Jurisprudence* 9 (1996) 361–81.

PETTIT, PHILIP, 'Kelsen on Justice: A Charitable Reading' in Tur and Twining (eds), *Essays on Kelsen*, 305–18.

POSNER, RICHARD, *Law, Pragmatism, and Democracy* (Cambridge/Mass, 2003).

POSTEMA, GERALD, *Bentham and the Common Law Tradition* (Oxford, 1986).

RADBRUCH, GUSTAV, 'Gesetzliches Unrecht und übergesetzliches Recht' in Gustav Radbruch, *Rechtsphilosophie*, edited by Ralf Dreier and Stanley L Paulson (Heidelberg, 1999) 211–19.

RAWLS, JOHN, *Political Liberalism* (2nd ed, New York, 1996).

—— 'Reply to Habermas' in John Rawls, *Political Liberalism* (2nd ed, New York, 1996) 372–434.

—— 'The Idea of Public Reason Revisited' in John Rawls, *The Law of Peoples* (Cambridge/Mass, 2001) 129–80.

RAZ, JOSEPH, *The Concept of Legal System. An Introduction to the Theory of Legal System* (Oxford, 1970).
—— 'Legitimate Authority' in Joseph Raz, *The Authority of Law. Essays on Law and Morality* (Oxford, 1979) 3–27.
—— 'The Claims of Law' in Raz, *The Authority of Law*, 28–33.
—— 'Kelsen's Theory of the Basic Norm' in Raz, *The Authority of Law*, 122–45.
—— 'The Rule of Law and its Virtue' in Raz, *The Authority of Law*, 210–29.
—— 'The Identity of Legal Systems' in Raz, *The Authority of Law*, 78–102.
—— 'The Obligation to Obey the Law' in Raz, *The Authority of Law*, 233–49.
—— *The Morality of Freedom* (Oxford, 1986).
—— *Practical Reason and Norms* (Princeton, 1990).
—— 'The Purity of the Pure Theory' in Tur and Twining, *Essays on Kelsen*, 79–97.
—— 'The Problem about the Nature of Law' in Joseph Raz, *Ethics in the Public Domain. Essays in the Morality of Law and Politics* (Oxford, 1995) 195–209.
—— 'Authority, Law, and Morality' in Raz, *Ethics in the Public Domain*, 210–37.
—— 'The Inner Logic of the Law' in Raz, *Ethics in the Public Domain*, 238–53.
—— 'About Morality and the Nature of Law' in *American Journal of Jurisprudence* 48 (2003) 1–15.
—— 'Can There be a Theory of Law' in Martin Golding and William Edmundson (eds), *Blackwell Guide to the Philosophy of Law and Legal Theory* (Oxford, 2005) 324–42.
ROSS, ALF, 'Validity and the Conflict between Positivism and Natural Law' in Paulson and Litschewski (eds), *Normativity and Norms*, 147–64.
ROUSSEAU, J J, 'On the Social Contract' in Michael Morgan (ed), *Classics of Moral and Political Theory* (Indianapolis, 1992) 771–830.
SCALIA, ANTONIN, *A Matter of Interpretation. Federal Courts and the Law*, edited by Amy Gutmann (Princeton, 1997).
SCHAUER, FREDERICK, *Playing by the Rules. A Philosophical Examination of Rule-Based Decision-Making in Law and Life* (Oxford, 1991).
—— 'Positivism as Pariah' in Robert P George (ed), *The Autonomy of Law. Essays on Legal Positivism* (Oxford, 1996) 31–55.
—— 'The Social Construction of the Concept of Law. A Reply to Julie Dickson' in *Oxford Journal of Legal Studies* 25 (2005) 493–501.
SCHEUERMAN, WILLIAM, 'Legal Indeterminacy and the Origins of Nazi Legal Thought: The Case of Carl Schmitt' in *History of Political Thought* 17 (1996) 1–20.
SCHLUCHTER, WOLFGANG, *Entscheidung für den sozialen Rechtsstaat. Hermann Heller und die staatstheoretische Diskussion in der Weimarer Republik* (Köln/Berlin, 1968).
SCHMITT, CARL, *Politische Theologie. Vier Kapitel zur Lehre von der Souveränität* (Berlin, 1922).
—— *Die geistesgeschichtliche Lage des heutigen Parlamentarismus* (2nd ed, Berlin, 1926).
—— *Verfassungslehre* (Berlin, 1928).
—— *Die Diktatur. Von den Anfängen des modernen Souveränitätsgedankens bis zum proletarischen Klassenkampf* (2nd ed, Berlin, 1928).
—— 'Die Diktatur des Reichspräsidenten nach Artikel 48 der Weimarer Reichsverfassung' in Carl Schmitt, *Die Diktatur. Von den Anfängen des modernen Souveränitätsgedankens bis zum proletarischen Klassenkampf* (2nd ed, Berlin, 1928) 211–57.
—— *Der Hüter der Verfassung* (Berlin, 1931).

—— *Legalität und Legitimität* (Berlin, 1932).

—— *Der Begriff des Politischen. Text von 1932 mit einem Vorwort und drei Corrolarien* (Berlin, 1963).

—— 'Völkerrechtliche Formen des modernen Imperialismus' in Carl Schmitt, *Positionen und Begriffe im Kampf mit Weimar—Genf—Versailles, 1923–1939* (Berlin, 1994) 184–203.

—— 'Die Wendung zum diskriminierenden Kriegsbegriff' in Carl Schmitt, *Frieden oder Pazifismus? Arbeiten zum Völkerrecht und zur internationalen Politik 1924–1978*, edited by Günter Maschke (Berlin, 2005) 518–97.

—— *Der Nomos der Erde im Völkerrecht des Ius Publicum Europaeum* (4th ed, Berlin, 1997).

SHAPIRO, IAN, *The State of Democratic Theory* (Princeton, 2003).

SHAPIRO, SCOTT, 'On Hart's Way Out' in Coleman (ed), *Hart's Postscript*, 149–91.

SOMEK, ALEXANDER, 'Stateless Law: Kelsen's Conception and its Limits' in *Oxford Journal of Legal Studies* 26 (2006) 753–74.

SOPER, PHILIP, *The Ethics of Deference. Learning from Law's Morals* (Cambridge, 2002).

SPECTOR, HORACIO, 'Judicial Review, Rights, and Democracy' in *Law and Philosophy* 22 (2003) 285–334.

SREENIVASAN, GOPAL, 'Does today's International Trade Agreement bind tomorrow's Citizens?' in *Chicago Kent Law Review* 81 (2006) 119–49.

STOLLEIS, MICHAEL, *Geschichte des öffentlichen Rechts in Deutschland, vol. 2: Staatsrechtslehre und Verwaltungswissenschaft 1800–1914* (München, 1992).

TROPER, MICHEL, 'Kelsen et le contrôle de constitutionnalité' in Michel Troper, *La Théorie du Droit, le Droit, l'État* (Paris, 2001) 173–93.

—— 'Réflexions autour de la théorie kelsenienne de l'état' in Michel Troper, *Pour une théorie juridique de l'état* (Paris, 1994) 143–60.

—— 'Kelsen, la théorie de l'interprétation et la structure de l'ordre juridique' in Michel Troper, *Pour une théorie juridique de l'état* (Paris, 1994) 85–94.

TUR, RICHARD and TWINING, WILLIAM, *Essays on Kelsen* (Oxford, 1986).

VAN ROERMUND, BERT, 'Authority and Authorisation' in *Law and Philosophy* 19 (2000) 201–22.

WALDRON, JEREMY, *Law and Disagreement* (Oxford, 1999).

WALUCHOW, WILFRID J, *Inclusive Legal Positivism* (Oxford, 1994).

WEBER, MAX, *Wirtschaft und Gesellschaft. Grundriß der verstehenden Soziologie*, edited by Johannes Winckelmann (Tübingen, 1980).

WILLIAMS, BERNARD, *Truth and Truthfulness. An Essay in Genealogy* (Princeton, 2002).

—— 'Relativism, History, and the Existence of Values' in Joseph Raz, *The Practice of Value. The Berkeley Tanner Lectures 2001* (Oxford, 2003) 106–18.

WOOTTON, DAVID, *Divine Right and Democracy. An Anthology of Political Writing in Stuart England* (London, 1986).

ZOLO, DANILO, 'Hans Kelsen: International Peace Through International Law' in *European Journal of International Law* 9 (1998) 306–24.

Index

legal cosmopolitanism
  legal peace, and 194–5, 206–7
  moral criticism of 182–3, 202–6
  viability of 194–200
legal hierarchy 43–4, 80–5
legality
  formal vs material 82–4, 152
  guarantees of 80, 89–94, 144–7, 209
  principle of 21, 25–6, 83, 86–7, 93–4, 209
  as source of legitimacy 61–7, 208–11
  utopia of 25, 73–5, 98–100, 216–221
legal norms
  Kelsen's view of 39–40
  legal duties, and 42
  nullity of 86–9
  use of force, and 42
  voidability of 89–94
legal objectivity
  legal meaning, and 32–9
  as limiting claims to authority 84–5, 88–9
  normative elements in Kelsen's
    understanding of 36–9, 45–50
  as regulative assumption in judicial review
    154–7
legal point of view 12–14, 87 n 25
legal positivism
  methodological 4–5, 215
  as mirror image of natural law 23
  political 5–6, 215
  the pure theory, and 214–21
  Razian 7–10, 215
legal systems
  identity of 39–41, 179, 184–5
  moral systems, and 39–41
  normative coordination of 180
legitimacy
  explained 59–61
  legality, and 61–7, 208–11
  vs Razian authority 67 n 91
  the utopia of legality, and 72–6, 208–14
Locke, John 23 n 77

majority rule
  constitutional entrenchment, and 124–34
  defense of 119–24
monopoly of force
  bellum justum, and 182–3
  legal peace, and 194–5, 206–8
  as necessary element of legal order 42–3,
    194–5

normative alternatives 78–80, 94–8

Paulson Stanley L 24 n 78, 49 n 68, 80 n 5, 96
  n 53
Perry, Stephen 4 n 13, 6–7
Posner, Richard 150 n 18

pure theory of law
  its conception of legal order 39–44
  as critique of ideology 14–15, 50–6, 213
  legal politics, and 15–24
  legal validity, and 11–12, 13–14, 39–41,
    48–50
  as normative science 10–15, 32–50
  theories of justice, and 70–2, 134–42
  as theory of authorization 43–4
  as theory of legal legitimacy 61–7
  the unity of law, and 179–80, 184–94

Radbruch, Gustav 5 n 17
Rawls, John 142–4, 165 n 46
Raz, Joseph 7–10, 12–13, 21–2, 41, 46–7, 49,
  57, 67 n 91, 74 n 105, 87 n 25, 182,
  184–94, 217–19
reasonable person 76
relativism
  democracy, and 141
  different senses of 68–9, 134–41
  liberal neutrality, and 141–4
rule of law
  autocracy, and 211–14
  democracy, and 98–100, 101–2, 124–32
  pure theory as adequate to 16–17, 22–4,
    212
  utopia of legality, and 80, 98–100
Ross, Alf 12
Rousseau, J J 113–15

Schauer, Frederick 6, 74 n 105
Schmitt, Carl 19, 103 n 2, 103, 131 n 71,
  133–4, 147 n 11, 149–50, 161–3,
  182–3, 203–4
Shapiro, Scott 70 n 100
Soper, Philip 74 n 105
sovereignty
  Kelsen's critique of 177–82
  of law 94–8
  popular 161
Sreenivasan, Gopal 131 n 71

Troper, Michel 147 n 8

validity
  absolute vs relative 68–9
  chains of 185–8
  effectiveness, and 60 n 86, 106, 186
  intrinsic 39–40
  justification, and 11–12, 35–6, 41–2,
    48–50
  principle of common origin, and 188–94

Waldron, Jeremy 6, 60, 97 n 55, 129–30
Weber, Max 11 n 47, 62 n 87
Williams, Bernard 15, 51 n 73